The Structure of Business

Niamh Geraghty
WLBS1

The structure of business

Martin W Buckley

SECOND EDITION

 Pitman

PITMAN PUBLISHING
128 Long Acre, London WC2E 9AN

A Division of Longman Group UK Limited

© Longman Group UK Limited 1990

First edition published in Great Britain 1985
Second edition 1990
Reprinted 1991, 1992

British Library Cataloguing in Publication Data
Buckley, Martin W. (Martin Wilfred), *1943–*
  The structure of business. – 2nd ed.
  1. Business studies – Bibliographies
  I. Title
  658

  ISBN 0-273-03204-6

Printed and bound in Singapore

Contents

Contents

Preface

In the first edition the aim was to provide a text for those studying 'Structure of Business' as part of the series of examinations leading to the London Chamber of Commerce Private Secretary's Certificate. That aim remains unchanged. However, since then there has been a growing recognition of the importance of 'business studies' in both schools and colleges and it has become a popular subject at 'A' level. Many science and engineering courses incorporate a broad ranging business component. This edition has been expanded to take account of these trends.

A word of warning: no textbook can ever tell the students all they need to know. Furthermore, textbooks rapidly become dated. The good student will draw upon a variety of other sources – not least their own experiences – but also the comments of their teachers and publications such as *The Times, Financial Times, The Guardian* and *The Economist*. The author has also found HM Treasury Economic Progress Reports, Lloyds Bank Economic Bulletins, and the various bank reviews a valuable source of additional information.

In writing this book I have drawn upon many years of teaching business subjects. I owe a debt of gratitude to many of my colleagues at Huddersfield Polytechnic who, often unwittingly, have influenced my thoughts and ideas. Thanks must also go to June Collinson who so carefully deciphered and typed my notes. Examination questions at the end of each chapter have been reproduced by permission of the University of Cambridge Local Examinations Syndicate, the Associated Examining Board and the London Chamber of Commerce Examinations Board. Finally, I wish to thank my wife and family for the support they have given me throughout the revision of this text.

Martin W Buckley
July 1989

Part 1
Setting the scene

Chapter 1

The mixed economy

All economies, regardless of the stage of their development, or their political complexion, have to answer three fundamental questions:

- What commodities should be *produced*? Remember the resources available within any economy are limited and therefore the decision to produce one commodity means that others will not be produced.

- How will these goods and services be *provided*? We have to decide who will produce these goods, and what methods of production should be used.

- How will we *distribute* these goods among the population? Various groups within the community will all make competing claims for consideration. How much should we give to consumers, business or government?

Economic systems

These questions can be answered in different ways. One way is to allow the community, through the State, to make these decisions. Such systems are often termed *planned* or *command* economies. The USSR is often used as an example of this system. Alternatively, we can create a system where decisions are taken by the individual rather than the State. The State plays a passive role, interfering with private decisions as little as possible. Community interest is best served, it is said, by individuals following their own interests. The United States is cited as the economy nearest to this system. Such systems are variously referred to as capitalist, *laissez-faire* or free enterprise.

Free enterprise system

- Private ownership
- Freedom of choice

- Competition
- Free market

The first distinguishing feature of this system is the private owner-ship of capital. Any of us can purchase whatever tools of production, equipment, buildings or stock are needed to carry on business or for other private purposes. We can buy and sell these assets just as we like.

Secondly, free enterprise emphasises freedom of choice or 'entrepreneurship'. By freedom of choice we mean you are free to choose your own job and to decide what goods and services you should buy. Businesses or enterprises have a similar freedom. They may buy whatever resources they wish, use them however they want to, enter those markets which they believe to be the most profitable, and generally organise their affairs as they think best.

Thirdly, competition: firms compete with one another for our business; moreover, having obtained it they cannot even then be sure of it for the future. Firms have to ensure that they provide goods and services that the consumer likes at prices that are com-petitive, and if they do not they will very quickly go out of business!

Last, capitalism's controlling mechanism is the 'market', and as traditionally the Government plays a passive role – not interfering – we can say the 'free market'. It is in the free market – in which businesses and individuals buy and sell goods and services – that prices are determined.

The price system

The price system is the means by which the three basic questions we asked at the beginning of this chapter are answered under free enterprise. The price system works by allocating a value to all goods and services available within that society. In essence we are asking ourselves how much are we willing to pay for land, labour, capital, raw materials or the goods and services produced with them. If more of product X is wanted, the price of this commodity tends to rise – a 'green light' for business people indicating that they can earn high profits. Similarly, when the demand for product X falls, prices fall – a 'red light' for business people. They will quickly seek other pro-duction possibilities which will yield a better return on their investment. By this means the decisions of business are brought into line with the decisions of consumers.

Let us look at how the price system answers our three basic questions.

1. *What goods and services this society will produce* is determined by the importance consumers attach to individual products. The higher they value the product, the more they are willing to pay, and

as we have seen, producers will move in accordance with these wishes.

2. *How will these goods and services be produced?* Remember we are looking at a competitive market, where efficiency is rewarded by sales and profits, and inefficiency by losses and eventual bankruptcy. Firms seek to produce at the least cost possible; they will seek out the best available combination of raw materials, technology and labour. It may be possible to vary the raw material input – in many cases a wooden spoon may be just as useful as a plastic spoon. Moreover, labour and technology may be interchangeable. Consider the position of the typist and the word processor. The higher the cost of an input the more sparingly it will be used and the greater the search for a substitute.

3. *How these goods should be distributed* among the population is determined by the income the individual has available. The greater his income the more the consumer is able to buy. But that income is dependent upon what resources he owns and how effectively he uses them. The resources may be physical – ownership of land or plant and equipment will yield an income. Others will obtain an income by selling their labour to someone else. The amount they will receive will depend on intelligence, training, work effort, and often just a bit of luck.

Advantages of free enterprise

- Individuals have the right to choose how to use their resources.

- Only those goods for which there is a (profitable) demand will be produced.

- There is minimum government interference in the affairs of business or consumers.

- Market forces may stimulate competition and act as a spur to efficiency.

- It is the consumers, not business or the State, who are sovereign and determine what should be produced.

Disadvantages of free enterprise

- Inequalities of power between groups or individuals may be used to the detriment of the consumer or employee, e.g. shoddy goods or unsafe working conditions.

- Free market forces may result in the production of goods and services which may be against the best interests of society, e.g. drugs or pornographic material.

- Socially desirable goods, e.g. health, education may not be produced in the right quantity.

- Anti-social practices, e.g. pollution, anti-competitive agreements need to be controlled.

- It is impossible to guarantee full employment, stable prices or economic growth.

Central planning

Central planning was a concept developed and extended by Marx. Horrified by social injustice and the degradation of the worker caused by the nineteenth-century British factory system, he argued that the only remedy was control by the state. Such a system was called a command economy, because there was a lack of choice. The State owned the country's resources, it owned and operated industry. The individual was subservient to the State which took decisions in what it perceived to be the best interest of the whole community. The State rather than the consumer was sovereign, and decided what and how to produce the goods and services, and moreover, who should receive these goods and services.

Advantages of central planning

- The system aims to maximise community rather than individual interests.

- Inequalities of power between individuals (and groups) do not exist. All decisions are taken by the State.

- There is a more equitable distribution of goods and services.

- State planning may limit the impact of inflation, unemployment and recessions.

Disadvantages of central planning

- There is no consumer choice.

- Freedom of the individual, e.g. where to work, is limited in the interests of the State.

- There is no way of knowing whether State decisions are in the best interest of society.

- The State is incapable of planning on a country-wide basis. There are problems of communication, co-ordination and control.

The mixed economy

We have discussed two extreme economic systems, but no country fits nicely into the patterns described so far. In the United States, most often used as the example of free enterprise, the Government has intervened in the economy to protect the employee and the consumer, to control business and regulate the level of economic activity. Conversely, in the USSR features of the market system exist. Farmers are allowed to sell a part of their produce for profit in local markets. People are free to choose their own occupation. Consumers are given freedom of choice as to what goods and services to buy from those which are available.

All economies are, in fact, a mixture of both the free enterprise and the planned systems. Yet, as we have seen the mixture can vary, moreover, it may vary within an individual economy over a period of time. Thus in the United Kingdom (UK) central planning assumes more importance when a Socialist rather than a Conservative Government is in power. Again the UK was, during the Second World War, one of the most highly planned economies ever seen.

The UK and France are often cited as examples of the mixed economy. While many of the decisions relating to what goods and services should be produced, how they should be produced and who should receive them are decentralised (i.e. left to the market), the State does intervene in many ways.

Public goods and services – the price mechanism is unable to supply certain goods and services satisfactorily. Examples include defence, the fire service, law courts, and prisons, though the list is much longer. These services provide benefits which are indivisible and are shared by everyone. Thus the State takes over the provision of these services and finances them out of taxation.

Merit goods – the State goes further and may well finance services out of taxation which could be, and are, provided by the market system. For example, in the United States the health service is financed and run by private organisations. In the UK the National Health Service is State-run. Education is provided by the State in the UK and many other countries, yet it is possible to provide education through the market system. Consider the British public school system (which actually consists of private schools financed by the parents of the pupils attending those schools). In South-East Asia much post-school education and training is financed in the same way.

What is not certain is that if left to the market, sufficient of these services will be provided. Moreover, there is a benefit to society from having a healthy, well-educated workforce or a good system of roads and motorways.

7

Transfer payments – not only does the Government raise money through taxes but it redistributes some of this to different groups of people. Money raised through taxes on income or expenditure may be used to help people who are unemployed, pensioners, or those with large families. Other possibilities would be to give grants encouraging firms to invest, or helping a firm in financial difficulties. To the extent that rich people will buy different goods and services from poor people, and that individual companies will make different investment decisions, transfers of this kind distort the market.

Subsidised goods – nationalised industries sell their services on the open market. Some are successful and make a profit while others are not so fortunate and incur losses – which of course the taxpayer has to make good. These amounts paid by the taxpayer are really a subsidy to the industry allowing it to sell its product at a price less than cost. The reasons why this should be allowed are so complex and so important that the next section is devoted entirely to a consideration of State enterprise.

State enterprise

When talking of State enterprise it is simple to think just of the large nationalised industries (or public corporations as they are called in the UK). There are over 25 State-owned firms in the UK. Most West European countries have nationalised industries in the past. A list of nationalised industries in these countries would reveal distinct similarities. For different reasons and in a variety of ways many countries have taken over large parts of the energy, transport, and communication industries.

The debate over public ownership occurs for both economic and political reasons. In the UK nationalisation is associated with the Labour Party's desire to create a more socialist society. Conservative politicians, conversely, would seek to avoid further nationalisation or even roll back the frontiers of state intervention.

The reasons for nationalisation

1. We have already noted that there may be goods and services which would not be produced if the decision was left to the forces of the market. The cost of providing electricity for people in remote districts is such that it could not, and would not, be provided commercially. Many of the commuter services around London are uneconomic. Social justice may be the reason why governments are anxious to provide the service. Alternatively, practical considerations such as the consequent reduction in road congestion, road accidents, and even pollution may decide the issue.

2. Many nationalised industries are capital intensive, accounting for approximately 20 per cent of the total investment in Britain during 1975. It was considered doubtful whether these industries, if in private hands, could raise the necessary finance for development. Moreover, the profitability of these industries may be insufficient to attract the necessary investment.

3. Similar arguments are used where the Government steps in to bail out firms in financial difficulties. In recent years the Government has taken major shareholdings in both British Leyland and British Petroleum in return for providing much-needed financial assistance.

4. Strategic arguments may also lead to nationalisation. Energy, transport, and communications are needed to fight a war successfully, or merely to ensure unimpeded economic growth. Doubts about the ability of the private sector, especially if controlled from abroad, to guarantee these services will result in, at a minimum, state interference if not outright nationalisation.

5. In later chapters we will see that governments have a number of economic objectives, such as maintaining stable prices or high and stable levels of economic activity. The attainment of these objectives may be found more easy by a government which has increased its control over large sectors of the economy as a result of nationalisation. Thus when the State finds that private business people are not investing sufficient funds to maintain high levels of employment and economic activity they may try to make good the deficiency by increasing their own investment expenditure in the nationalised industries. Or perhaps the Government wishes to reduce the current level of pay settlements – how better to do it than by ensuring the public sector workers receive only what the Government believes to be desirable? Yet again poorer regions and isolated communities may be helped by the Government deciding to maintain the uneconomic operations of nationalised industries in those areas.

6. Nationalisation can also permit *economies of scale*. Competition between private gas companies would result in a multiplicity of distribution systems. A unified system for gas or electricity supply throughout the whole country would require just one distribution system resulting in lower prices to the consumer. The integration of the steel industry's activities so that they are all carried out on the same site will again result in savings – savings in terms of heat and transport. Nationalisation also permits the use of larger, more efficient production units, or perhaps even administration units. Of course it is not necessary to nationalise the gas or electricity industry to obtain these advantages of size, they could be achieved just as effectively by a private organisation. The argument against leaving the industry in private hands would be that it was a monopoly – capable of holding the consumer to ransom, and charging high prices so as to make large profits.

9

Nationalisation may be defended on other grounds as well as those listed above. It allows the Government to lead by example, to encourage research and development and better labour relations, it can ease the problems of a declining industry. Again, foreign control of basic industries may be unacceptable to developing countries because decisions relating to those industries are taken outside the country and not necessarily in that country's best interests.

Yet public enterprise is not without drawbacks. Nationalisation is seen as resulting in a restriction of consumer choice. This arises out of its monopoly position in the industry. However, this need not necessarily be so. In Britain private and public airlines, steel-makers and bus companies have existed alongside one another.

The existence of a private sector alongside a public sector goes some way towards damping the criticism that nationalised industries are not faced with competition – remember competition is admired because it provides an incentive to operate efficiently and make the best use of the available resources. Competition also exists between industries, gas competes with coal, electricity and oil, as does rail with road transport.

However, the incentive to compete may not be so great as in private industry. A firm that fails to make a profit will ultimately be dissolved. The nationalised industry is under no such threat. It is able to rely on handouts from the taxpayer to subsidise its loss-making operations.

Inefficiency is also sometimes thought to creep into state enterprise for other reasons. Many are very large-scale organisations serving millions of consumers spread over a wide area. There are obvious problems in administering such units. Communication may be slow or inefficient; co-ordination of activities takes time and money, while public accountability often results in excessive control mechanisms.

The relationship with government may also cause inefficiency. Government objectives may conflict with those of the industry, important investment decisions may be deferred, or uneconomic operations in an area of high unemployment be retained. Perhaps the real criticism here should be levelled, not at the industry, but at the Government.

Privatisation and deregulation

Since May 1979 a major aim of the Conservative Government has been the exposure of the public sector to competition. Behind this policy is the belief that competition will result in a more flexible and enterprise-based economy.

By privatisation we mean the return of State-owned activities and assets to the private sector. This has been achieved by sales of shares on the Stock Exchange (e.g. British Telecom or British Gas), or the sale of the business to management and employees (e.g. National Freight Corporation).

Deregulation is the range of alternative ways in which the public sector is exposed to market forces. Thus services commonly operated by the local authority (e.g. refuse collection/disposal) or by the National Health Service (e.g. catering and laundry services) may be put out to tender. Alternatively, legislation may be introduced to allow competition in areas which were previously statutory monopolies. Thus the private generation of electricity is now permitted, and the British Gas monopoly relating to the sale of gas appliances has been broken.

Many other countries are following the British example. In Europe most governments are committed to some form of privatisation programme. In Japan the State-owned Nippon Telegraph Telephone has been turned into a company with the shares being sold to the public. In America, where the scope for privatisation is less, deregulation of air services has resulted in lower prices and more competition.

Summary

We are unlikely to reach any firm conclusion about the superiority of one system over another. While the argument is conducted in the language of the economist, at heart the dispute is political. It is about the role of the State within an economy and the freedom of the individual. If you believe that a high degree of equality is required within society you should be willing to sacrifice some of the economic advantages of free enterprise to this ideal. Equally, advocates of free enterprise have to suffer the problems and limitations of the market.

In the UK it is generally believed that the mixed economy with its particular blend of private and public enterprise is right for us. A large measure of individual freedom exists, but within a framework of checks and balances instituted by the State. However, this blend has not always been right for us, nor would it be correct to assume that it is best for others. In particular, developing countries may benefit from a higher degree of central planning than exists in the UK, for they may have neither the political processes nor the economic framework (adequate communication and transportation) necessary for free enterprise to be successful.

Setting the scene

Examination questions

1 Explain how economic wants are satisfied and scarce resources allocated under:
   (a) a system of free enterprise;
   (b) a command (centrally planned) economy.
2 What do you understand by the term 'free enterprise' or 'capitalism'? What is the role of the price mechanism in a free enterprise economy?
3 In what ways does the State intervene in a mixed economy and for what reasons?
4 Using examples drawn from your own country explain why state ownership has occurred.
5 What do you understand by 'the economic problem'? How do different countries/economic systems attempt to resolve it?
6 (a) Explain the term 'mixed economy'.
   (b) What is the role of the Government and public enterprise within a mixed economy?
7 Under the headings of 'What', 'How' and 'For Whom', show how the fundamental economic problems are solved in:
   (a) a free market economy;
   (b) planned economy.

Chapter 2
The structure of business: I

The private sector

Within a mixed economy there are numerous organisations that have been created to satisfy our demands for goods and services. In this chapter we will be looking at the objectives and structures of these organisations.

Figure 2.1 shows that such organisations exist in both the public and private sector. Within the private sector, the organisation may take one of several forms, for example, sole trader, partnership, or company. The public sector's commercial activities, e.g. (gas, electricity, coal, rail) are normally undertaken by 'public corporations'. Other State activities – the provision of education, defence, aid to industry, or local services, to name but a few, are provided by central or local government administrative units. These administrative units are the subject of separate chapters.

Firms in the private sector are owned by individuals or groups of individuals. Often these individuals work for, and rely on, the firm for their living. Yet even if the owners do not work for that firm the profits generated by its activities may still make up a substantial

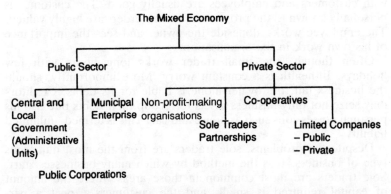

2.1 Public and Private Sector Organisations

part of their income. Thus we can say that the most fundamental objective of the firm in the private sector is to produce a profit for its owners. An economist would go further – he would argue that the firm will try to maximise profits. For many firms, especially those in a competitive industry, this would undoubtedly be true, but for some, other objectives will rank as high as (perhaps even higher than) profitability. Examples could include being a market leader, sales maximisation, or ensuring the stability of the firm.

Let us now consider each of these business units in turn.

The sole trader (sole proprietorship)

The simplest form of business unit is the sole trader. Sole traders set up their own businesses. They are the sole owners or proprietors. Characteristically they:

- provides the capital to run the business (though they may borrow from banks or relatives);

- work in the business by themselves, though they may have other paid assistance;

- make their own decisions – though they would be wise to seek advice from the numerous organisations set up to help small businesses.

- bears the risks of loss or receives the profits of the business.

The formal procedures required to set up as a sole trader are few. Having obtained premises if necessary and purchased whatever equipment is necessary, trading may begin. Being their own boss, upon making a decision, they are able to implement that decision immediately – far more quickly than any other organisation, and thus adjust to change in market conditions rapidly. Relationships with customers and employees are usually good. The customer is personally known to the proprietor, and his orders are highly valued. The employee works alongside the owner and sees the importance of his own work in the organisation.

Often though, the small trader works long hours with few holidays. Ill-health is a constant worry. More importantly, should the business fail, the owner alone is liable for its debts. Creditors may seize not only business assets to recoup their debts but also his personal possessions such as house and car. This is termed 'unlimited liability'.

Despite the problems, sole traders are from the most numerous type of business. It is the method by which many businesses start. Sole traders are most common in those areas where the amount of capital required is small, and the customers expect a per-sonal service.

Profits

In a mixed economy 'profit' has a number of important functions.
1 It is a reward for risk taking. A business brings together people, materials, machines and money to produce those goods and services demanded by society. Yet the business can never be completely certain of this demand. People have freedom of choice and their demand for a particular item will depend on factors such as:

- their disposable income
- prices of other goods
- personal tastes and fashion
- government policy (e.g. taxes/subsidies)
- future price or output expectations

Thus there is always a risk that our business will not sell what it has produced and will make a loss. A reward – in the form of profit – is therefore necessary to persuade people to accept the risk arising out of uncertainty. The level of profit required will, or course, vary with the degree of risk involved. Such people, who risk their money in business ventures, are sometimes termed entrepreneurs.
2 It is a spur to efficiency. Profits are the means by which the investor assesses the success of his investment. Business therefore seeks to reduce its costs by managing its resources in the most efficient way possible, and developing new and improved methods of production. Moreover, in the longer term only the efficient firm will survive as less efficient firms will find that they are unable to compete with the former on price or quality.
3 It is a guide to resource allocation. Profits indicate society demand pattern for goods and services. When an industry is expanding and the demand for its products is high, profits likewise will be high. This acts as an inducement for entrepreneurs to invest and undertake extra production. Conversely where profits are low entrepreneurs will seek other opportunities which yield a greater return on their investment. In this way resources move to meet the wishes of the consumer.
4 It provides the resources for expansion. Profits have always been an important source of finance for business. Roughly 60 per cent of the funds required by business to finance their new capital needs is provided by retained profits.

Setting the scene

Partnership

Should our sole trader wish to expand finance may need to be raised outside his immediate family. Permanent, or long-term finance is often difficult to obtain. The most usual source of finance for a sole trader – the commercial bank – is only willing to lend for shorter periods of time. The answer for most sole traders is to take a partner. The business thereupon is known as a partnership. This is defined by the Partnership Act 1890 as 'the relationship which subsists between persons carrying on a business in common with a view to profit'. Normally the membership of a partnership is restricted to twenty, though accountants and solicitors are not bound by this.

The business now has the advantage of extra capital available which can be used to expand. Additional help is now available, releasing our sole trader from the problem of long hours, no holidays, and illness. With the extra help there is the possibility of specialisation, one partner buying, the other selling, so that the sole trader is no longer a jack of all trades, but can become more proficient at one part of the business. In other ways the partnership is the same as the sole trader – the partners provide the finance, make the decisions, and normally work in the business. Good personal relationships still exist with customers and employees. Legal formalities are few and the degree of privacy high.

Limited partnership

A variation upon an ordinary partnership as described above is the limited partnership. In this organisation there is a partner whose liability is limited to the amount of money that he has invested in the firm. Should the firm go bankrupt the creditors cannot touch his personal (as opposed to business) assets. In return for this privilege the limited partner undertakes not to take part in the management of business. He may inspect the firm's financial records and tender advice to the partners involved in the day-to-day running of the business, but should he at any time involve himself in its management or administration he will lose his 'limited' status and become an ordinary partner. The Partnership Act 1907 requires at least one ordinary partner in any partnership business. Thus there is always at least one partner who is fully liable for the debts of the business.

The major drawback of the partnership, like that of the sole trader, is unlimited liability. In fact, in some ways, the situation is worse. Partners are not only responsible for their own actions, they are responsible for the actions of their partners. Thus the foolish or untimely act of your partner may not only ruin the business but also deprive you of your personal possessions. Other potential difficulties may arise in obtaining the agreement of your partners on some issue. If this is not forthcoming it may well result in the dissolution of the partnership. If fact, death, insanity, and bankruptcy, as well as disagreement, will result in the termination of the partnership agreement. To maintain the business as a going concern the continuing partner has the difficult task of finding money to buy out the other partners at short notice. Often, to avoid these financial difficulties upon the death of a partner, each partner will insure the life of the other partner. In the event of this partner's death the partnership then receives a capital sum from the life assurance company which is used to pay off the family of the deceased partner. The surviving partner then becomes the sole owner of the firm.

The Partnership Agreement

The written or oral terms agreed to by the partners are known as the partnership agreement or articles of partnership. In law it is not necessary for the partnership agreement to be written. In many cases the precise terms of the agreement have to be inferred from the actions of the partners in running the business. Of course, such a situation is not ideal and may easily lead to disagreements between the partners. For this reason the Partnership Act 1890 lays down specific rules which will bind the partners where the partnership agreement is silent. This might include for example, a clause saying that all profits and losses should be shared equally.

A written partnership agreement will commonly cover the following points:

- Partnership name and business address
- Names and addresses of partners
- Duration of partnership
- Nature of business
- Capital contributions of partners
- Duties of partners
- Provisions for salaries or drawings
- Distribution of profits or losses
- Methods of resolving conflict
- Procedure for dissolution.

The limited liability company

One major problem of both sole traders and partnerships as forms of business organisations was the lack of capital to finance expansion. Yet there are many people who have small amounts of money which they may be willing to invest in industry. The overriding consideration of these people is the safety of their personal fortunes. During the industrial revolution in nineteenth-century Britain many were the stories of once-rich families being reduced to poverty by the partnership principle of unlimited liability. It is not surprising there was an unwillingness to invest in industry or commerce.

The answer was provided by the 'joint-stock' company which allowed people to invest their money without unlimited liability or involvement in the management of business. The earliest examples were the East India or the Hudson's Bay Company created by Royal Charter. Parliament later granted limited liability to companies concerned with transport – canals and railways. But the procedure was cumbersome and costly, and eventually in 1855 Parliament enacted the first Companies Act. This gave general protection for shareholders who invested in a company which was registered as having limited liability.

The business person who wishes to convert their firm into a company does so by submitting certain documents to the Registrar of Companies. (The advantages and disadvantages of partnerships and limited companies as forms of business organisation are shown in Table 2.2). The documents are examined, and if they comply with the requirements of the Companies Act the formation of the company will be registered. The major documents required by the Registrar are listed below.

1. The Memorandum of Association This document gives basic information of interest to shareholders and other people who may deal with the proposed company. It contains six clauses:

The name clause. The name by which the company chooses to be known. If liability is to be limited this must be followed by the word 'Limited' where the company is private and by 'Public Limited Company' (normally abbreviated to PLC) in the case of a public company. As a matter of law, this name must be displayed outside all the company's places of business and used in all its correspondence. It is the name in which the company sues or is sued.

The registered office clause. This indicates whether the company is registered in England, Wales, or Scotland and its address. This is necessary to ensure that important documents do reach the company and its officers.

The limited liability clause. Where the promoters wish the company to have the benefit of limited liability they must state this fact (it is possible to form unlimited companies by the omission of this clause, moreover an ordinary partnership that exceeds twenty partners will automatically become an unlimited company and be judged by company law).

This clause is notice to all who deal with the company that in the event of it failing, it is only the assets of the company that are available for the payment of the creditors' debts.

The capital clause. The amount of share capital which the company can raise must be stated (the nominal capital) together with the value of the shares it is to be divided into, say £1, 50p, or 25p (nominal value). The word 'nominal' is used to indicate that this is the value of the capital quoted in the company's accounts. However, the price people are willing to pay for each share will depend upon the company's profits and prospects. Investors may be prepared to pay £1 for each 10p share in a prosperous company, but only 10p for a £1 share in a badly run, loss-making business.

The 'objects' clause. This clause indicates the purposes for which the company was formed, e.g. machine-tool engineering, retailing bakery, stockbroking, etc. By the *ultra vires* doctrine should a company enter into a contract beyond its powers that contract is of no effect: it is as though it had never been entered into. The justification for this clause is that it protects shareholders from directors and managers changing the scope of the company's future activities. Nowadays though, the protection given is largely illusory because the clause is phrased so widely that companies are only rarely prevented from entering into different kinds of business activity.

Section 9(i) of the European Communities Act of 1972 changes the position for an innocent co-contractor by allowing him to enforce the *ultra vires* agreement against the company. In such a situation the company may require that any loss made by it should be made good by the directors who first entered into that illegal contract.

Table 2.1 The choise of business unit – A comparison between partnerships and limited companies

Partnerships	Limited companies
Formalities	
Formation by agreement, oral or written	Registration of documents as laid down by Companies Act. Procedure complex and often costly
No special formalities – little or no expense	
No public documents to file	Documents available to public, include Memorandum and Articles of Association as well as annual accounts
Financial results not open to public inspection	
Dissolution normally by agreement of partners. Few formalities	Winding up by procedure laid down in Companies Act on agreement of members or creditors

Agreement of co-partners to be obtained before transferring interest to new partner (NB: difficulties in calculating value of share partnership)	Shares freely transferable (private companies may put restrictions on this). No problems over valuation where there is a Stock Exchange quotation

Personality and liability

The partnership is not recognised as a separate legal person – it can only sue or be sued through the partners Property must be vested in names of partners	Recognised as having an existence separate from that of its members. It can sue or be sued, purchase land, or raise money in its own name
Normally partners have unlimited liability (NB: exception of limited partner) All assets, business and personal may be seized to satisfy creditors' claims	Where the company includes the word 'limited' in its name the shareholder's liability is limited to his invested capital. Personal assets are not at risk

Membership

Normally 2–20 (NB: exceptions, e.g. accountants/solicitors may have more, a banking partnership limited to 10)	Any number in excess of 2 (NB: private companies may limit the number of shareholders)

Power to contract

Fixed by Partnership Agreement, but can be altered by agreement (express, or implied from course of dealing)	Laid down in Memorandum and Articles of Association. These can only be altered by procedure in Companies Acts.

Control

General partners have the authority to act as agent of the firm. The contracts entered into bind his co-partners (a limited partner will lose his special status if he acts for the firm)	Shareholders vest power to manage firm in the directors. Directors must act in accordance with Memorandum and Articles – otherwise liable to the company for their actions
The organisation has the ability to react quickly to changed circumstances	Changes in policy are made after consultation between managers, directors, and (sometimes) shareholders
Partners may specialise in different areas of business. But often deficient in financial or marketing skills.	Specialist managers employed. Non-executive director of wide business experience may be appointed to the board

Finance

Normally available from family, friends, and bank. Traditionally, partnerships limited to those areas where little capital is needed, e.g. retailing, building, catering, and the professions	May pool the resources of large numbers of small investors. Has greater ability to borrow from other sources.

Lack of finance often prevents growth and the benefits of increased size are not obtained	Growth not retarded by lack of finance and economies of scale may be realised (NB: there may also be diseconomies of scale!)

Relationships

Close links can be maintained between the firm, its suppliers, and customers. Similarly morale, motivation, and employee/employer relationships often better	Sheer numbers of suppliers, customers, and employees may preclude same relationships developing

Taxation

Partners pay income tax on profits	Company pay corporation tax on all profits (including retained earnings). Shareholders pay income tax on their dividends.

The association clause. This is a declaration made by those signing it that they wish to form a company and will accept the shares allocated to their names.

2. *The Articles of Association* This document refers to the internal constitution of the company. It gives information on such issues as the rights of the shareholders, the powers of directors, and the holding of meetings. While it is possible to draw up your own set of internal regulations, this is not necessary because the Companies Act 1984, Table A, Schedule 1, provides a specimen set of articles. These articles are eminently fair to all interests and will automatically apply should no other Articles of Association be registered.

3. *Statements required by the Registrar* The Registrar of Companies also requires a statement of norminal capital (a tax is payable on this – 0.50 per cent), a list of directors, their addresses, together with a statement indicating their willingness to act as directors and also a declaration that the Companies Acts have been complied with.

Before 1980 the distinction between a public and private company was enshrined in the 1947 Companies Act. This defined a private company as one having a membership of between two and fifty members (excluding past employees), restricting the right to transfer shares, and prohibiting the company from inviting the general public to subscribe for shares. A public company was defined as one having a membership of seven or over, and not having any of the restrictions mentioned above. The Companies Act of 1980 redefined a public company – now more correctly referred to as a public limited company –

as one which has an authorised capital of at least £50,000 and having at least two members.

Private companies were then defined as those companies not conforming to the requirements of a public limited company. Private companies were no longer allowed to invite the general public to subscribe for shares but the restrictions on transfer of shares and membership were lifted. However, for the 762,000 private companies existing at the time of the Act there is no requirement that they change their articles and it is suggested that these restrictions will continue to apply.

Should the Registrar of Companies be satisfied with the documents presented to him, he will issue a certificate of incorporation, making the business a separate legal entity with a life quite separate from that of its shareholders. At this stage a private company may commence business and enter into any contract allowed by its 'objects' clause. There is, however, a further requirement before a public limited company can start business – it must obtain a trading certificate.

The trading certificate is again issued by the Registrar of Companies on receipt of documents indicating that the company has the necessary financial stability to start business. Where the company is raising capital by issuing shares to the public the company must submit a prospectus (i.e. the document inviting the public to buy shares in the business) to the Registrar and statements that the minimum capital necessary to run the business has been subscribed (this is as stated in the prospectus) and that directors have paid for their shares.

Where the promoters and directors can raise sufficient finance without appealing to the public, a statement in lieu of a prospectus (containing much the same information as the prospectus) will be submitted to the Registrar in addition to the statements mentioned above.

Ownership and control

The principle of limited liability has encouraged the development of extremely large firms, experiencing problems entirely different from those experienced by sole traders and partnerships. Ownership of large public limited companies is in the hands of perhaps thousands of shareholders. Obviously all these shareholders cannot be involved in the running of the firm, and, in practice, policy decisions are made by a board of directors and put into effect by salaried managers. There is, it is said, a divorce between ownership and control.

In principle, there should be few problems arising out of the difference between ownership and control of the company. Control of the company lies in the hands of those owning shares in that company. Exercise of that control arises from meetings which the directors have to call for the shareholders to sanction their actions. Thus at the annual general meeting (AGM) which is held after the publication of the company's annual financial results, shareholders will scrutinise the performance of the company and the policy of the directors and vote upon the appointment of directors and the payment of dividends. Extraordinary general meetings and special general meetings will also be held periodically at the request of the shareholders or directors in order to discuss and vote upon urgent issues.

But to control the activities of directors is rather more difficult in practice. We have already noted that it is impossible for all shareholders to take part in the running of the company (even if they wanted to). The very diffused nature of shareholdings also makes it impossible for the shareholders to act together and put pressure on the directors. Company meetings are held during working hours, often far away from where the investors live and work. It is not surprising that these meetings are normally poorly attended. The absence of a majority of shareholders from the meetings means that effective control of the company can be exercised with very much less than 51 per cent of the votes. Indeed, the directors' own shareholdings may be sufficient to secure control of the company.

Perhaps the only group which can successfully challenge the power of directors is the institutional shareholders. Pension funds, insurance companies, unit and investment trusts are big business.

Together these institutions account on average for nearly two-thirds of all purchases of ordinary shares in British industry as a whole. The size of the institutions and the importance of their holdings would in many cases give them the authority to demand a director on the board to represent their interests. Yet traditionally they have indicated their unwillingness to interfere in or become involved with the running of a company. Recently though, the institutional investor has seemed more willing to intervene in company affairs. In particular, where severance payments to ex-directors have been high, the decision of the board has been challenged. Take, for example, the Post Office Pension Fund which challenged in the courts, the 'golden handshake' of £650,000 offered by Associated Communications Corporation to its former Managing Director.

The divorce of ownership from control in a public limited company would not be so worrying if the objectives of shareholders and directors were the same, but often they are not.

The objectives of the investor are threefold. They are to ensure:

- *Safety of capital* – that the value of their investment does not diminish through poor policy decisions or unforeseen changes in the market or technology.

- *A good return on their investment* – many shareholders measure the success of the company by the size of the dividend cheque received annually. A consistently high dividend convinces them of the soundness of their investment. Yet a high dividend payment is not always possible. In Britain 60 per cent of all moneys needed for expansion come from retained profits. (But assuming the expansion is successful, investors will see the return through enhanced values of the shares on the Stock Exchange, and higher profits in later years.)

- *Marketability* – it is no good your capital being safe and earning a high rate of return if the shares cannot readily be converted into cash.

Yet boards of directors and salaried managers may take a wider view to that of the investor, and although accepting the importance of profit as an objective believe that the following are just as important.

- *Security* – the maximising of profits may bring risks which are unacceptable to the director (or salaried manager). The director's job depends on the continued existence of the company. From this point of view it is far better to under-achieve and to survive.

- *Status and prestige* – directors may wish to be identified with a large company, a household name, or a market leader. One way this might be realised is by greater sales. Yet these extra sales may be unprofitable to the company because it has gone beyond the point of most efficient operation. Directors may also insist on prestigious offices, or investment in projects which have a low profitability but give the company a high public profile.

- *Power* – increased sales not only bring security but they also bring greater power. As directors control larger organisations, more people are responsible to them. Their power in the industry is also increased as competition from competitors becomes more muted.

The degree of incompatibility between the motives of the shareholder and director will obviously vary from company to company. Where directors have substantial shareholdings, the incompatibility is at a minimum, but where the board consists largely of executive directors drawn from the ranks of salaried managers, differences in objectives are likely to exist.

The board of directors

Overall control of the company is vested in the board of directors. Directors are appointed by the shareholders and therefore the shareholders can be said to have ceded control of the company to them. Whereas the function of the shareholders is to provide the finance necessary for the smooth running of the firm and to bear the risk of failure or success of the company, directors are responsible primarily for determining policy. Their function is to survey the environment within which their company works and to identify the threats and opportunities available to the company in future years. On this analysis is based the company's future strategy. Whatever the strategy it cannot be implemented without people, and consequently directors are vitally interested in (and responsible for) ensuring that the essential positions within the company, the senior staff, are filled by people of the highest calibre, and that the morale of the workforce generally is as high as possible. Finally, while the success of the directors' strategy or policy is measured by the financial results of the company, directors will also be concerned to see that the company has adequate reserves of cash (or near-cash items, e.g. finished goods or debtors) and that stringent controls on expenditure are maintained.

In exercising their duties, directors are sometimes likened to trustees because (by law) they owe duties of good faith and care to the company. In particular they must ensure that they use their power properly for the benefit of all shareholders, and that they avoid situ-

---

In 1986 new insolvency laws were introduced. These affect the position of directors in two ways. First directors may be disqualified from taking part in the management of any company, either directly or indirectly where they have been judged to be unfit to act in that capacity. In prosecuting directors the DTI is not looking for any conduct of a criminal nature, but merely at the overall competence of an individual to act as a director – or any other managerial function – within a company. Disqualification may be for between 2–15 years.

Second, where the court believes that directors have 'carried on trading beyond the point where they ought to have concluded that the company was unable to avoid insolvency' they may be personally liable for the company's debts. Directors are liable not because there is a deliberate course of wrongdoing but because they have not taken every step to minimise the loss to the company's creditors. Negligence, ineptitude or incompetence on the part of a director are sufficient to make them personally liable.

---

ations where there is a conflict between the company and their personal interest. Consequently, directors must disclose any financial interest they have in a contract entered into by the company.

Directors are also required to exercise a reasonable standard of care in the course of their duties. What is a reasonable standard of care is variable depending upon the degree of, or particular, expertise of the director. Thus an executive director with accounting qualifications and responsibility for the financial function within a firm would be expected to exercise a far higher degree of skill in money matters than other directors.

Chairperson   The board of directors is headed by a chairperson who is the titular head of the company, responsible for the control of the directors' meetings and representing the company's interests in external affairs. It is often, but not always, a part-time position, given to a person of wide business experience, capable of taking a more detached view of the company's activities than other directors.

Managing director   The managing director is normally a full-time appointment, responsible to the board for the implementation of board policy and the daily running of the firm.

Directors   Directors may be full-time or part-time, executive or non-executive. Full-time directors tend to have executive responsibilities within that company. For example the production director will be head of the production function within the organisation, taking part not only in deciding policy (as a director) but also seeing that it is implemented properly throughout the company. Part-time directors seldom have an executive function and are appointed because of their proven ability with other companies. They meet infrequently at board meetings and often have directorships with other companies at the same time.

The company secretary

All UK companies are required by law to have a company secretary. He or she is the organisation's chief administrative officer and is responsible for:

- **ensuring the company complies with the law.**

- **maintaining statutory registers, e.g. shareholders, mortgages.**

- **convening and recording meetings of the board of directors.**

- **administration of pensions and insurance, patents and licences.**

  In small companies the secretary often also acts as accountant, lawyer or personnel manager.

Large companies also often employ part-time or non-executive directors. Important public figures – Members of Parliament or individuals associated with consumer interests may be appointed to lend respectability or trustworthiness to the company. Equally importantly these individuals may represent the company's interests outside the organisation.

Many more non-executive directors are appointed to the board of directors because of their skills and wide experience in company affairs. Being uninvolved in the day-to-day running of the business such directors are expected to contribute a broader, more independent view of any situation.

Worker directors Some companies have also experimented with worker directors. Quite apart from giving board deliberations wider views and greater breadth of experience the aim has also been to improve employer/employee relationships through

- better communication with the workforce and
- worker involvement in decision making at the highest levels.

Union attitudes to 'worker directors' have varied. The Steel Unions accepted seats on the group boards of British Steel Corporation whilst the Railway Unions rejected a similar offer of seats on the Board of British Rail. Generally, though the union movement's response has been unfavourable, with many of its leaders arguing that acceptance of directorships may be seen by the rank and file as a sell-out to the company. The position of the union official as a worker director certainly involves a conflict of interest in that they have to acquiesce to Board decisions which are against their members' interests.

Co-operatives

Consumer co-operatives The Co-operative Wholesale Society (CWS) and the Co-operative Retail Society (CRS) evolved during the nineteenth century. Their objective was to eradicate the conflict of interest between the supplier (who wished to sell at a high price) and the consumer (wanting to buy at a low price). The members of the co-operatives are the consumers who purchase its goods. They have the right to elect the management committee which runs the business and share the profits made from its operations. The 'shareholders' have only one vote each (regardless of their investment in the society) which prevents sectional interests gaining control and using it to their advantage.

In Britain the CRS consists of members of the CWS. It is from this source that the CRS obtains its stock. The CWS provides the CRS with the benefits of bulk buying which the societies could not hope to achieve

The CRS has experienced increasing competition from super-markets since the Second World War and its share of the market has been decreasing. This can be attributed to lack of business expertise on the part of its management committee and its salaried staff, together with an inability to provide the necessary finance for expansion.

In the UK the Co-operative Bank, the Co-operative Insurance Society, and the Nationwide Building Society are also examples of co-operatives operating in the field of commerce. Abroad, farmers' co-operatives for the purchasing of feed, fertilises, and seed and the marketing of animals and farm produce have also proved popular.

Worker co-operatives Worker co-ownership in industry arose out of earlier attempts at industrial democracy and worker participation. These co-operatives take the form of a company which is limited by shares in which workers have some degree of control over the policy and running of the firm, they bear the risks of failure and reap the benefits of success.

Worker co-operatives, sometimes called producer co-operatives flourish outside the UK. These is, for example, the very successful Mondragon experiment in northern Spain. In the UK worker co-operatives are not so popular. They have failed to find managers of the right calibre, while capital finance has often been beyond the resources of the worker-members. In virtually all cases, successful worker co-operatives have started life as some other form of enterprise.

The means by which co-operatives have developed are various. The initiative of Ernest Bader who gave his own firm to his workforce and founded the Industrial Common Ownership Movement is important. There are now over a dozen firms run on similar lines to Scott Bader Company Limited. Other businesses have been sold to the workforce – Landsman Co-ownership (which produces caravans) and the National Freight Corporation (privatised by Margaret Thatcher's Conservative Government) are examples of this. Within the shoe and textile industry there are still a number of producer co-operatives, throwbacks to those that were first developed in the latter part of the nineteenth century.

Public corporations

The essential feature of a public corporation is that the assets of an industry have been taken over by the State so that the industry is owned, managed, and controlled by the community. Public corporations, also known as nationalised industries, are only part of the public sector; as we have already seen, however, they are an important part. They employ 4 per cent of the working population and account for $5\frac{1}{2}$ per cent of the country's output.

Whereas the main objectives of a private firm are to provide goods and services which are demanded by society and thereby to survive, make a profit, and grow, the objectives of the public corporation are more complex. While public corporations are nationalised so as to ensure that certain goods and services are provided efficiently, it does at the same time have to pursue non-commercial goals.

Consider the case of British Rail. Efficiency may require the closing of several lines or the curtailing of the timetable, but economic and social effects upon that region may be devastating. Both the British Steel Corporation and the National Coal Board have faced similar decisions. Yet again the cost of supplying gas, water, or electricity to outlying districts may be far higher than the consumer could possibly afford to pay. But what would be the effects of depriving the community of these essential services?

On purely commercial grounds none of these services would be provided and yet, of course they are, on the insistence of the Government. The Government sees public corporations as a legitimate means of pursuing its wider economic and social objectives. In the past, Governments have imposed operational constraints on public corporations such as:

- a requirement to sell products/services at a price different from that which would be determined by free market forces. Prices may be forced up as a form of taxation, or reduced to ensure the continued operation of uneconomic activities.

- the retention of inefficient working practices to maintain employment or appease the unions.

- instructions to purchase uncompetitive UK products, e.g. the sale of British Coal to the Central Electricity Generating Board.

- using capital investment plans as a means of increasing or reducing the level of demand in the economy.

- controlling pay awards in an attempt to influence the level of wage settlements.

- control over the range of commercial activities undertaken.

In all the above examples the Government has decided that the commercial gain accruing to the public corporation is outweighed by the public gain from a conflicting course of action. As these are political decisions it is then difficult to evaluate the performance of a public corporation solely in commercial terms. Rather, it should be judged having regard to the degree of government interference.

The structure of public corporations

A public corporation has a distinct legal personality which arises from the Act which nationalised it. It can enter into contracts in its own name and be used on these agreements.

The capital of the public corporation is owned by the Government and traditionally it is to the Government that the public corporations turn for extra finance. This has taken the form of subsidies out of general taxation to finance deficits on operations, borrowing for investment purposes, together with government subsidies and grants.

A public corporation is supervised by a Government minister, who, as we have already seen, is able to give general directions to the industry regarding matters of public interest. The Government minister is also empowered to appoint the members of the corporation's board.

In general terms the board is responsible for the day-to-day running of the corporation business, but the detailed powers of each board can be found in the Act of nationalisation. It is the duty of the board to remain within these powers.

Control of the public corporations lies initially in the hands of a Government minister who is responsible to Parliament. This role is twofold: first to represent and defend the views of the corporation in Parliament, and secondly to explain their own dealings with the board. Any MP may question the minister, but they are only expected to answer questions on policy matters, and certainly not on the day-to-day administration of the board's affairs. Greater accountability to Parliament is achieved through debates upon public corporations which follow the publication of their financial results. Investigations and reports from the All-Party Select Committee on Nationalised Industries are also available to MPs, as are the 'efficiency reports' on nationalised industries commissioned by the Government and prepared by the Monopolies and Mergers Commission.

Acts of nationalisation have recognised the need to make public corporations directly responsible to members of the public by the creation of Consumers' Councils. These councils normally have the right to be advised of any plans affecting customers, they may themselves give advice to the board on these plans, and protest legitimate consumer complaints. Councils also have the right to make representations to the appropriate government minister. In practice the effectiveness of this form of control is doubted. Members of the councils are appointed by the minister, and may not adequately reflect the interests of the consumer. Additionally, lack of finance and staff prevents councils from conducting their work effectively.

Examination questions

1 Three of your friends, Tom, Dick, and Harry, have decided to set up in business as computer consultants. Initially, Tom and Dick will keep their existing jobs and work for the firm on a part-time basis. Harry, however, will work full-time for the new firm from the start. All three are providing the firm with £2,000 in capital. In addition Tom's wife is lending the firm an extra £1,000, but is not going to take part in the running of the business. All three of them have come to you for advice on what type of business organisation to form, and what, if any, other arrangements should be made.

2 What advantages are to be gained by a sole proprietor who decides to convert his enterprise into a partnership? Are there any consequent disadvantages? *(PSC)*

3 Outline the composition and functions of the board of directors within the public joint-stock company. *(PSC)*

4 In what circumstances is State control of private business justified? Suggest briefly what you think the objectives of these publically owned industries should be.

5 Compare and contrast the aims the characteristics of public corporations and private organisations.

6 Describe the major characteristics of a public limited company explaining the particular advantages or disadvantages arising from these characteristics *(PSC)*.

7 In what ways would the financial accountant of a large company be able to do a more effective job if he were made Finance Director? In what ways would his responsibilities change?

8 (a) The Government has decided to privatise public libraries. How might this decision be implemented?
  (b) As the Chief Librarian of a Public Library, write a report to the local Member of Parliament either supporting or condemning this proposal. *(CAMB. 1987)*.

9 You are the Managing Director of a firm producing telephones. The Government had decided to privatise the British telecommunications industry.
  (a) How might the employees of your firm view the decision?
  (b) How might you view the decision, and in what way might your perception of the Government's action be (i) similar to, and (ii) different from, that of your employees?
  (c) What *short* and *long term* financial and organisational issues might the Government's decision present? *(CAMB. 1985)*

10 Compare the role of part time directors with that of full time employees (both management and worker) on the board of a company.

Chapter 3

The structure of business: II

In Chapter 2 we noted a great diversity in the form of business organisation a firm could adopt. This diversity is also reflected in the industry they belong to, the labour and technology they use, or even their size. In this chapter it is this last aspect – size – which we shall consider in some detail. With the development of modern industrial economies we have seen a growth in the size of business units and the development of multinational corporations. Yet the small firm sector still plays an important part in advanced economies (*see* Fig. 3.1). So how important is size to the business person and the economy, and what problems result from increasing the scale of business operations (or for that matter remaining small)?

The small firm sector

The most authoritative definition of the small firm comes from the Bolton Committee's report on firms (*Report of the Committee of Enquiry on Small Firms*, Chairman J. Bolton) which was issued in 1971. A small firm, it said, was generally one which employed less than 200 people as well as having three additional characteristics:
1. A small share of its market.
2. Owners who worked and took a personal interest in the business.
3. Not part of another (larger) organisation.
This was modified for certain sectors, for example construction – twenty-five employees or less, retailing – turnover of £50,000 or less, catering – all establishments except 'chains' or 'multiples'.

By whatever measure is used – number of firms, output or employment small firms play a significant role within the UK economy. The Bolton Committee went further, arguing that their existence was vital to the dynamism of the economy. It pointed to a number of important economic and social functions. These were as follows:
1. They perform tasks for which large-scale industry is ill suited – for example where there is only a small market or where the products do not lend themselves to mass-production techniques.

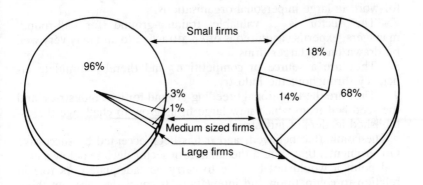

Manufacturing firms by number

Manufacturing output

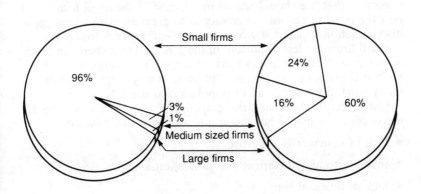

Manufacturing firms by number

Manufacturing employment

Source: Business Monitor 1986

3.1 Three ways of comparing the importance of small medium and large firms within the UK

2. They are often more efficient than large firms, having lower overhead costs.
3. They can adjust to changed market conditions more rapidly than their larger counterparts.
4. Many are selling a combination of product and personal services.

5. They are an important source of innovation in product, processes, and services.

6. They provide jobs for people whose personality ill suits them for work in large impersonal organisations.

7. The sector is a valuable training-ground for 'all-round' managers, expertise acquired is often attractive to and may very well be drawn on by larger firms.

8. They are a source of competition, and thereby stimulate efficiency throughout the industry.

9. They are the traditional breeding-ground for new industries, and the seed-bed from which new large firms grow to challenge the established leaders of industry.

The committee believed, and it has been accepted by successive Governments, that should the small firm sector decline below a critical point it would not be able to carry out adequately its role in relation to competition and innovation. It concluded 'we can think of no substitute for the dynamic influence of new firms in preventing the ossification of the economy' (Bolton Report, para. 19.6), and suggested that 'we should regard the decline of the small firm sector past the point of economic viability as so great an evil that energetic discrimination to avert it would be justified' (para 8.16).

Small firms are less important in the UK than elsewhere. In Japan 66 per cent of all employees work for small firms compared with the United Kingdom's 30 per cent. Put another way, Japan has twice as many small firms per head of population as the UK.

Until recently the small firm sector was declining. The reasons for the decline are many, but the major problems faced include:

- lack of managerial expertise.

- inability to afford clerical and professional help.

- lack of financial support.

- high level of competition.

- inability to survive economic recession.

- Government bureaucracy and the complexity of legislation.

Since 1980 the decline of the small firm sector seems to have been reversed and there is a net increase of approximately 30,000 small firms annually. (Yet such statistics do not give the full picture. There are, on average 160,000 business start-ups each year but there are also 130,000 small businesses which cease trading. The mortality rate amongst small firms is high for the reasons mentioned before).

Paradoxically it was the recession of the early 1980s which caused the renewed interest in the small firm sector. For many people, using their redundancy payments to set themselves up in business was a far better alternative to unemployment. Other groups of workers faced with redundancy have formed worker co-operatives. Both self-employment and worker co-operatives have been aided by the growth of the service sector within the economy – where start-up costs are low and there are few barriers to new firm entry.

The growth of the small firm sector has also been aided by large firms reviewing the extent of their operations. In many cases they have decided to concentrate on key profitable activities. Peripheral activities have been closed down – resulting in the sub-contracting of these operations to small firms. Alternatively these activities may be sold to their employees and management who, recognising the gap in the market, are willing to set up their own business. Such sales are commonly termed management buy-outs.

Aid for small firms

The Government sees small firms playing a vital role in the regeneration of the economy. The focal point for Government aid is a separate division within the Department of Trade and Industry – the Small Firms Service.

In 1988 the DTI launched a new 'Enterprise Initiative' which is designed to provide a comprehensive package of help to small firms. Under the initiative a small firm can obtain help and advice on a whole range of problems ranging from marketing, design, quality to business planning and information systems. It will also provide advice and assistance to firms planning to export and help the firm solve technical problems.

Three other areas have been singled out for special attention. First, the Government has tried to encourage the movement of finance into the small firm sector. For example, the Business Expansion Scheme is designed to encourage outside investors to invest risk capital by allowing the investor tax relief on the investment at his highest rate of tax. Another measure, the Loan Guarantee Scheme is intended to save those worthwhile projects which might fail through lack of bank finance. Government loan guarantees are available to the banker if the borrower pays a $2\frac{1}{2}$ per cent premium to the DTI. Secondly, the Government has created a more favourable tax regime by reducing the higher levels of income tax, creating a reduced rate of corporation tax for small firms, introducing thresholds below which firms do not have to register for VAT, and generally making it easier to pass businesses on to the next generation intact by changes in capital transfer tax.

Finally, steps have been taken to reduce the burden of 'oppressive' legislation in the small firm sector. Legislation has reduced the financial and other statistical information required of small firms. Small firms are now also exempt from much of the employment protection legislation, e.g. that relating to unfair dismissal.

Large-scale industry

Throughout the twentieth century we have seen a continuing trend of firms increasing both in size and complexity. Let us consider size first. In 1910 the largest 100 companies' share of total manufacturing output was 15 per cent, today it is over 40 per cent. Equally, the concentration of sales among the five largest, businesses in each industry has risen dramatically. In some industries the five largest firms account for 90 per cent of all sales; while the average for British industry as a whole is 47 per cent (*see* Figure 3.2). But output or turnover is only one way of measuring size. Size can also be measured by looking at total employees, capital employed or profits earned, and as we can see from Table 3.1 the results can be very different.

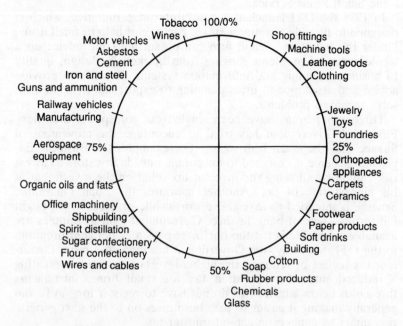

Source: *Business Monitor* P.A. 1002 1986

3.2   Concentration Ratios for selected UK industries

Table 3.1 The top ten European firms measured by employees, capitalisation, profits and turnover.

Employees	Capitalisation	Profits	Turnover
1 Siemens (G) (i)	Shell (N) (iii)	Shell (N) (iii)	Shell (N) (iii)
2 Philips (N) (i)	B Telecom (UK) (vi)	B Petroleum (UK) (iii)	B Petroleum (UK) (iii)
3 Daimler (G) (ii)	B Petroleum (UK) (iii)	B Telecom (UK) (vi)	I R I (I) (viii)
4 Unilever (N) (v)	Fiat (I) (ii)	Daimler (G) (ii)	Daimler (G) (ii)
5 Fiat (I) (ii)	Unilever (N) (v)	B A T (UK) (viii)	Volkswagen (F) (ii)
6 Volkswagen (G) (ii)	Daimler (G) (ii)	Unilever (N) (v)	Fiat (I) (ii)
7 B Telecom (UK) (vi)	General Ascurazioni (I) (ix)	I C I (UK) (iv)	Unilever (N) (v)
8 C G E (F) (vii)	Nestle (SW) (v)	B. Gas (UK) (vii)	Siemens (G) (i)
9 B A T (UK) (vii)	B Gas (UK) (vii)	Nestle (SW) (v)	Deutsche Bundesposte (G) (x)
10 Hoechst (G) (iv)	I C I (UK) (iv)	Hoechst (G) (iv)	Philips (N) (i)

Source: *Financial Times* Top 500 survey 1988
Key: F France, I Italy, SW Switzerland, G Germany, N Netherlands, UK United Kingdom

(i)	Electrical Equipment	(ii)	Automobiles
(iii)	Oil	(iv)	Chemicals
(v)	Food	(vi)	Telecommunications
(vii)	Untilities – Gas, Water, Electricity	(viii)	Conglomerate
(ix)	Insurance	(x)	Consumer

Business has also become increasingly complex. First, many large firms operate numerous establishments – an establishment being a separate plant or factory. The top fifty in the UK operate on average fifty establishments each. Secondly, the establishments operated are not even likely to be in the same industry. More and more firms are becoming multi-product. Thus Hansen plc, which is by no means unique, has establishments operating in tobacco, departmental stores, office equipment, kitchen and domestic appliances, leisure equipment, building products, textiles, confectionary, health products and restaurants.

Management buy-outs

Management buy-outs occur when:

- **large public companies sell to their managers and employees operations which do not fit logically with the main business of the organisation, and are often unprofitable because of the excessive amount of time management has to devote to these operations.**

- **a business goes into liquidation but individual parts of the failed business may still be viable. For example, when Dunbee Combex Marx toys went into liquidation a rescue bid was mounted for Hornby – the model railway company owned by the group.**

  Characteristically, managers (and employees) will have to extend themselves financially to obtain the necessary capital. Even so the amount raised is often as little as 20 per cent of the purchase price. The remainder is put up by City institutions in the form of loans secured on the assets of the company.

Traditional economic theory would have us believe that the reason for this growth in size of business unit was economies of scale. That is, the idea that unit costs of production fall as the scale of operations increases. These economies fall into five broad categories – technical, marketing, financial, managerial, and risk-bearing.

Technical economies

1 Economies of increased dimensions. A doubling of cubic capacity or volume can be achieved with a 59 per cent increase in material, hence its alternative name 'the six and ten rule'. The principle applies to tankers, factory/warehouse space, pipes, etc.

2 Economies of linked processes. If processes are integrated in one plant, savings in production time and transportation costs occur. Similarly, integration of processes in iron-and steel-making may result in a saving of over 20 per cent on fuel costs.

3 Economies of gearing. In large-scale operations there can be full utilisation of all equipment. For example if we have three linked processes with a machine capacity of X–200 units per day, Y–300 units, and Z–400 units, a minimum production level of 1,200 units per day (or some multiple thereof) is required to keep all machines working throughout the day.

4 Economies of long production runs. Where heavy fixed costs are incurred, as in car production, the greater the number of units produced the smaller the fixed cost per unit (it is estimated that in oil refining an 800 per cent increase in throughput from 0.5 million to 4 million tons reduces the unit cost by 56 per cent).

Marketing economies

1. Economies of purchase. The large-scale purchaser of raw materials or components can often obtain benefits (e.g. credit terms, discounts and prompt delivery) that will not be granted to smaller buyers. The greater these costs are as a percentage of total costs the more valuable the saving.

2. Economies of selling and advertising. Better utilisation of the sales force occurs through promoting a whole range of products rather than just one. Moreover, the reputation of one popular product may sell the rest of the range. Costly, but cost effective (because the expense is shared between so many units of production), advertising on television may be used.

Financial economies

The larger organisation is able to find capital more easily – certain sources of capital are not available to smaller firms. It can provide fixed assets as security for the loan and a profit record which can be used to assess risk. These factors may also result in finance being obtained more cheaply by large firms.

Potential diseconomies of large-scale organisations

Most of the diseconomies will occur as a result of the organisation structure becoming exceedingly complex. Co-ordination of activities becomes more difficult as greater numbers of people are involved (especially where, as is often the case, they are employed in different geographical locations). As the command chain lengthens it becomes increasingly difficult to control the various parts of the organisation. This allows under-utilisation of management and waste to creep in. A lengthening of the command chain will also cause delays in communication to occur. This slows the decision-making process and reduces the firm's ability to adapt quickly to changed circumstances. Motivation often suffers in large organisations, they are accused of being impersonal. Employees lose their identity and become alienated from the firm. Moreover, the 'bureaucracy' may prevent employee initiative and innovation.

Factors influencing the size of the firms are shown in Fig. 3.3.

Managerial economies

1. *Size allows specialisation of management* – which in the same way that division of labour encourages greater production, enables managers to become more proficient in their work and deal with a greater volume of work.
2. *Large firms are able to afford highly expensive specialists.* They are also more likely to attract them with good working conditions, prospects of advancement, and fringe benefits.

Risk-bearing economies

1. *Diversification.* Greater security can be achieved by not being reliant upon one product, market, customer, or supplier.
2. *Research.* Today the cost of research and development is so high that only the large and powerful can afford it (or the possibility of loss should the investment fail).

Improvements in efficiency are the most often quoted motive for business expansion. but often such statements hide other motives which may not be so praiseworthy or in the public interest. These alternative motives include:
1. *Market dominance.* This has obvious advantages. It gives the possessor a degree of security. The firm through its monopoly or dominant position can control prices in the industry, often allowing high profits to be an made. Lack of competition means there is no incentive for the firm to improve its product or service, profits are more than adequate and it may decide to opt for a quiet life. For the same reasons there is little reason for such a firm to invest heavily in research and development of future products. This motive is probably far stronger than many business people would have us believe. It could account, equally as well as economies of scale, for the large number of horizontal mergers and take-overs in the UK.
2. *Defensive.* Business may feel vulnerable for many reasons. The growth of other firms in the same sector may reduce its own power, perhaps even threaten its long-term independence or survival. A declining market will encourage growth by merger or take-over activity to reduce competition and the possibility of a price war. Alternatively, the increased size may give the business greater strength to survive a price war.
   Defensive motives may also be paramount where powerful interests exist among the firm's suppliers or customers, and the additional size is needed to bargain with them on equal terms. Yet again, a merger can be used to guarantee sources of raw materials, to secure markets, or to spread risks.

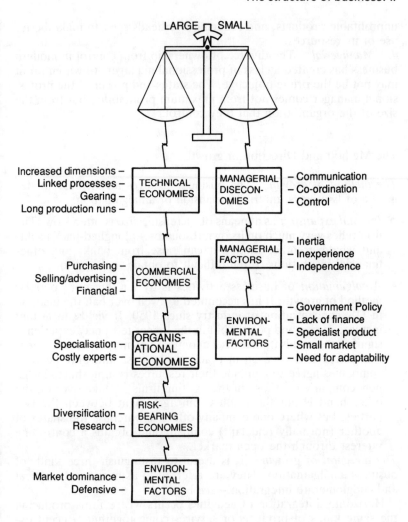

LARGE ⇕ SMALL

Increased dimensions – Linked processes – Gearing – Long production runs –	TECHNICAL ECONOMIES	MANAGERIAL DISECON- OMIES	– Communication – Co-ordination – Control
		MANAGERIAL FACTORS	– Inertia – Inexperience – Independence
Purchasing – Selling/advertising – Financial –	COMMERCIAL ECONOMIES		
		ENVIRON- MENTAL FACTORS	– Government Policy – Lack of finance – Specialist product – Small market – Need for adaptability
Specialisation – Costly experts –	ORGANIS- ATIONAL ECONOMIES		
Diversification – Research –	RISK- BEARING ECONOMIES		
Market dominance – Defensive –	ENVIRON- MENTAL FACTORS		

3.3 Factors influencing the size of a firm

3. Financial. Such motives exist where the existing management of a business is not utilising assets to the best effect (e.g. large un-utilised cash resources) or where the market value of the shares does not reflect the underlying value of the assets (possibly because of recent losses, e.g. Dunlop). In these circumstances conglomerates such as Hanson Trust or Lonrho will take over the 'failing' business and by injecting new management, rationalising production, cutting unprofitable products, and reducing overheads seek to make better use of its resources.

4. *Managerial.* The divorce of ownership from control in modern business has created a class of professional managers to whom profit may not be the prime objective. The status and power of the professional manager comes not from maximum profitability but from the size of the organisation that they control.

The Method and Direction of growth

The method of growth. The business achieves an increase in size in one of two ways, internal expansion or amalgamation.

- *Internal expansion* as a means of increasing size is often slow. The firm relies very much on its own resources – ploughed-back profits and whatever other money it can raise from banks and other financial institutions (often difficult to obtain and costly).

- *Amalgamation* of business activities is by far the more popular method of growth. It has accounted for well over half the increase in UK concentration of industry since 1950. It yields an instant increase in size and power (but in the longer term may experience significant organisational diseconomies). A merger occurs where two (there is no reason in practice why it should only be two) companies agree to combine their resources issuing shares in the new company for those in the existing firms. A take-over on the other hand is not the result of an agreement between the two parties, but where one company offers to purchase the shares of another (normally reluctant) company and obtains a controlling interest through the open market.

The direction of growth. It is useful to distinguish three kinds of business amalgamation. They are referred to as horizontal, vertical and conglomerate integration – *see* Fig. 3.4.

Horizontal integration of activities occurs where firms producing the same kinds of products or services come together. Recent examples include: Habitat – Mothercare; Ratners Jewellers – H Samuel; Guinness – Distillers Company.

Horizontal integration provides considerable scope for economies of scale. It is also used to increase market share, eliminate competition, or fight off a bid from another company. This has been the most common form of amalgamation in the UK.

Vertical integration involves bringing together under common ownership different stages in the production process. It may take the form of a firm acquiring ownership of a supplier of raw materials (termed 'vertical backward integration') or forward integration where a firm secures its production outlets (e.g. Singer Sewing Machine shops). Common aims of vertical integration are to secure supplies of raw materials or output for finished goods and to obtain economies of linked processes. Vertical mergers account for less than five per cent of the values of all merges.

Lateral integration is said to occur when there is little relationship between either products or processes of the separate firms. Firms having such a diversity of interests are often termed 'conglomerates'.

The motives for diversification of interests are many. The reasons most commonly quoted include, the need to:

- get out of a product reaching the end of its life cycle
- get out of a market which is highly competitive
- utilise management skills more efficiently
- make a capital gain on the break-up and sale of the firm's assets
- avoid monopoly and merger legislation by expanding outside traditional markets.

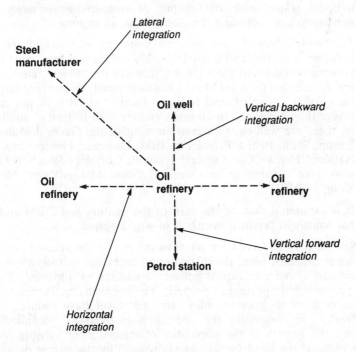

3.4 The direction of growth

Multinational corporations

A multinational corporation is a business which undertakes planning, financing, production, marketing, and research and development upon an international basis. These activities will be performed in many countries, with management, for the most part, being drawn from the host countries. Ownership is not necessarily dominated by the parent country, and the shares may be traded on Stock Exchanges in several countries.

The multinational corporation is not a particularly new form of business enterprise, though its rapid growth is certainly a twentieth-century phenomenon. Examples of multinational corporations date back to the seventeenth century and the establishment of the Hudson's Bay and East India Companies by British trades. Today the majority of multinationals have their origins in the United States, the UK, Japan, and West Germany.

The importance of multinationals can be gauged in a number of ways:

- As early as 1968 international manufacture had overtaken international trade, with the output of overseas subsidiaries of multinationals exceeding the global value of exports

- The world's largest 100 economic units are split roughly 60:40 between countries and companies. No company comes near the very big countries like the United States or the Soviet Union, but few realise that General Motors has sales nearly 70 per cent larger than South Africa's Gross National Product (GNP), 60 per cent bigger than Nigeria's, or 10 times greater than Ireland's! Similarly, there are well over a dozen firms including: General Motors; Exxon; Shell; British Petroleum; IBM; Unilever; Phillips; Mobil; National Iranian Oil; General Electric; Chrysler; Standard Oil; who have a turnover in excess of either Malaysia's or Hong Kong's GNP

- It is estimated that by the turn of the century some 200 multinationals will produce over half of world output.

Several reasons have been put forward for the remarkable growth of multinationals. First, the relaxation of exchange controls allowing more easy transfer of capital between countries has obviously been of paramount importance. Second, improvements in communications such as telephones, telex, and air travel have reduced the difficulties in controlling the operations of overseas' subsidiaries. Third, the growth in the popularity of management by objectives has reduced the need for day-to-day control by the parent organisation. Finally, manufacture in overseas countries is seen as a way of avoiding many of those countries' import tariffs and restrictions.

Reaction to the growth of multinationals has been mixed. While they confer obvious benefits on those countries within which they operate, the relationships between state and company have often been strained. The benefits can be summarised as follows:

Benefits of multinationals

The balance of payments

- The development of new manufacturing capacity by the multinational will cause an inflow of foreign currencies into the host country.

- Imports may be reduced as goods which were not previously produced in the host country are now available to satisfy local demand.

- Exports may be increased by the multinational's overseas sales efforts.

Competition.   Competition within the host country is stimulated, with beneficial effects upon prices, efficiency, and innovation. The import of better management and production techniques by the multinational will force domestic producers to improve their own standards of efficiency in order to survive. In addition their heavy investment into the research and development of new products and processes again forces local firms to reappraise their effort in these areas.

Increased production.   This results in a higher level of employment (often in areas of high unemployment) and a higher GNP and standard of living.

Disadvantages

As we have already noted, the growth of multinationals has been viewed with concern by many host countries – both industrialised and developing. The concern stems from the sheer size and financial strength of many multinationals. This concern is hardly surprising when we remember that the GNP of some host countries, especially among the developing nations, will be considerably less than the turnover of many of the multinationals operating within their territory. The feeling of concern has led to the seizure of multinational assets in several countries and stringent control upon their operations in many others.

Basically, the problem is that host countries believe that decisions taken to further the interests of the multinational (often based in some foreign country) will have significant and detrimental effects upon their economy. Consider the case of Chrysler UK. In 1975 the American parent of Chrysler UK announced the decision to close down its British operation (a decision which was later reversed) and to supply the British market (and a large Iranian contract for cars), from its production units on the Continent. The potential impact upon the balance of payments was thus twofold – a reduction in exports and an increase in imports. Equally worrying was the impact upon employment, especially as many of the jobs at risk were in Scotland where little alternative work was available. Considerable pressure was put upon the British Government and eventually an agreement was hammered out whereby Chrysler UK would be kept open in return for a Government rescue package of £162m. in public money and loan guarantees.

Multinationals are often thought to contribute significantly to international monetary crises. It is logical for them to protect the value of their reserves against currency fluctuations. They will therefore move their (often sizeable) reserves between countries as currencies appreciate and depreciate. Let us take the example of an American multinational with subsidiaries in the UK and Japan. Should the sterling exchange rate depreciate while at the same time the yen is appreciating, our multinational may very well decide to transfer its sterling reserves to Japan. But in doing so it creates an even greater pressure on the sterling exchange rate. Sterling may very well depreciate further, even in situations where there is no underlying imbalance between sterling and other exchange rates.

Finally, multinationals are also able to adjust their affairs so that profits are taken or declared in those countries where the tax system is most advantageous. The UK Monopolies Commission severely criticised the Swiss drug multinational Roche for inflating the prices of raw materials British subsidiaries purchased from its Swiss parent. The effect was to reduce the difference between what was claimed to be the cost price and the selling price, causing low profits to be declared in the UK. The inflated prices of raw materials charged by the Swiss greatly increased the profits made overseas in countries where profits were not so highly taxed.

Competition policy

Competition is admired for its beneficial influence on prices, efficiency, and innovation. The element of competition means that no firm is able to control market prices and thereby increase profits. It is only through a policy of competitive pricing that a firm can expect to gain sufficient orders to survive. Firms in their desire to increase profitability will seek to improve the efficiency with which the product is produced. They will also be searching for those new and improved product designs which will give them a competitive advantage in the longer term.

The role of competition policy is to ensure that viable competition exists in all sectors of industry. In practice there are two very different approaches.

The *automatic rule* approach is that all monopolies, mergers creating a monopoly situation or agreements limiting competition are bad. Hence legislation bans monopolies, mergers and other agreements automatically. Much of United States' legislation is of this type. Critics argue that it is harsh and inflexible.

Conversely, the *discretionary approach* believes that to assume all monopolies, mergers and agreements limiting competition are against the public interest is unfair. Each case must be judged on its merits. The UK has adopted this approach. Legislation exists to investigate monopolies, mergers, etc, with the power to control those situations which are seen as being against the public interest. This pragmatic approach has been criticised as being open to political pressure, inconsistent in its decisions and generally ineffective.

Monopolies and mergers

The Fair Trading Act 1973 gives the Secretary of State for Trade and Industry or the Director General of Fair Trading the power to refer to the Monopolies and Mergers Commission any situation where over 25 per cent of the supply of a product or service is under the control of one person, or two or more people acting together. The legislation extends to local as well as national monopoly situations and also to the investigation of public sector monopolies. Where a monopoly is found to operate against the public interest the commission's recommendations may be enforced through statutory orders or by the Director General obtaining undertakings from the firm(s) concerned to comply with those recommendations.

Where a merger is proposed and will result in the combined parties controlling over 25 per cent of any market, or where the combined assets are in excess of £15m. it may be referred to the Monopolies and Mergers Commission by the Secretary of State. Should the commission find the proposed merger to be against the public interest the Secretary of State can prevent it taking place.

Since 1980, as Table 3.2 indicates, the work of the Commission has been expanded to cover anti-competitive practices and efficiency audits of nationalised industries.

Anti-competitive practices comprise any business practices which could distort or restrict competition in the production, purchase or sale of goods within the UK. Thus in 1982 the London Electricity Board was referred because of its policy of selling domestic electrical appliances through its showrooms in such a way as to give rise to losses. In 1984 Ford Motor Company was referred due to its policy of refusing to grant licences for the manufacture or sale in the UK of certain spare parts for Ford vehicles.

Under the Competition Act 1980 the Director General of Fair Trading may investigate such practices and, where a case is found, refer them to the commission for consideration. In practice, not many references are made as firms will quickly change their business practices rather than face the adverse publicity arising from a reference

Table 3.2 Workload of the Monopolies and Mergers Commission 1981–86

	Total
Merger references	37
Monopoly references	19
Competition references	4
Efficiency audits	19
Total	79

Where the practice is found to be operating against the public interest, the Director General may accept an undertaking to change its practices from the firm concerned, or the Secretary of State may enforce compliance through statutory orders.

The Competition Act 1980 also gave the Secretary of State power to refer to the commission questions relating to the efficiency, costs and services provided by nationalised industries. Such references are intended to replace the incentives to efficiency that the market place provides for private firms.

Competition policy in the European Community

The EC competition law applies to practices which may affect trade between member states. It takes precedence over national law. The commission's powers to regulate anti-competitive behaviour fall broadly into three categories:

1 Under the Treaty of Rome, Articles 92–94, member states are forbidden to give aid to industry or firms which could distort competition. Excluded from this general prohibition are items such as aid to disaster areas, depressed regions, and new economic activity. Member states are required to give (but do not always comply) the

commission details of any aid planned so that its legality can be determined.

2 Article 85 bans restrictive practices which limit output, determine prices, allocate markets, and limit investment.

3 Article 86 bans 'abuse of a dominant position'. A dominant position exists where a large firm is able to use its strength to impose unfair terms on suppliers, retailers, competitors, or consumers. An abuse occurs where the dominant firm does, in fact, act in this way. Large firms found guilty of an infringement of Articles 85 or 86 will be subject to heavy fines. The maximum is 10 per cent of annual sales affected by the abuse.

In 1980 IBM was accused of abusing a dominant position by withholding information on new products from competitors. Eventually IBM gave way in 1984 by agreeing to modify its trading practices in a way which avoided the 'abuse'. Many cases are resolved in this manner.

Restrictive trade practices

These exist where one or more parties accept limitations on their ability to make decisions regarding prices, output, or conditions of sale. By the Restrictive Trade Practices Act 1976 such agreements have to be registered with the Director General of Fair Trading. Non-compliance with these requirements renders the parties liable to prosecution. All agreements registered with the Director General will be referred to the Restrictive Practices Court whose function it is to decide whether the agreement is in the public interest. The onus of proof is placed upon the parties wishing to rely on the agreement who must show that it has one or more of the following beneficial effects:

- the agreement is necessary to protect consumers from physical injury;

- the removal of the agreement would rob consumers of some substantial advantage;

- the agreement was necessary to counter the action of another group restricting competition;

- without the agreement fair terms could not be negotiated with a monopolist;

- without the agreement serious and persistent unemployment would occur;

- the removal of the agreement would cause loss of export earnings;

- the agreement was necessary to maintain other agreements which the court had already declared to be in the public interest.

Cartels

Individual firms may achieve greater control over their market not only through mergers and takeovers. A similar effect may be achieved through agreements with other firms, concerning shares of the market, agreed selling areas, information sharing or price fixing agreements. Firms involved in such arrangements are said to have formed a 'cartel'. The most well known cartel of modern times is undoubtedly Organisation for Petroleum Exporting Countries (OPEC).

The majority of cartel arrangements lay down production or sales quotas for each firm and the prices at which the product or service will be provided. For example, OPEC's charter states, 'members shall study and formulate a system to ensure the stabilisation of prices by, among other means, the regulation of production'. Further agreements on the distribution of profits, methods of preventing newcomers entering the industry, and penalties for non-compliance with the cartel arrangements may also be made. Interlocking directorates, that is the practice of directors in one firm becoming non-executive directors on the Boards of one or more of their rivals may sometimes be used to 'police' the agreement.

For a cartel arrangement to be successful three conditions are necessary. First, the members need to control the supply (or a substantial part of it) of the product. It is the reduction of supply by members which precipitates the price increase. Secondly, cartel members must be able to agree policy and co-ordinate their actions accordingly. Should members avoid their obligations under the agreement the cartel will quickly disintegrate. Finally demand for the product must be fairly insensitive to changes in price. Where substitute products exist cartel members will not be able to raise prices much without loss of demand.

Cartel arrangements allow firms to charge higher prices and make greater profits than when trading independently and competitively with one another. For precisely these reasons legislation now exists in both America and Europe which makes such agreements illegal. In many developing countries though similar legislation has not been passed.

Examples of cartels may still be found in both America and Europe. Until recently the International Air Transport Association (IATA) regulated the prices airlines could charge – this was with the agreement of both European and American Governments. Then in 1982 the United States withdrew from the IATA agreement with the result that today air fares (per mile) in America are one third cheaper than those in Europe. Put another way 'deregulation' as the Americans call it – or competition – meant that in 1984 it cost roughly the same to fly from London to Madrid as it did from London to New York. In Europe

IATA continues to exist because no European Government is prepared to let its flag-flying airline go into liquidation – and most governments doubt the ability of their airline to survive competition!

In addition to proving that beneficial effects do arise from the agreement the court must also satisfy itself that those beneficial effects outweigh any detrimental aspects its implementation might cause. Thus in 1959 the court held that although the Cotton Yarn Spinners Agreement had the effect of mitigating local unemployment, prices would be higher than in a free market and declared the agreement void. In practice the vast majority of agreements have been found to be against the public interest. (One interesting side-effect resulting from the court's almost overwhelming rejection of collusion was the increase in merger activity during the 1960s and 1970s.)

Resale Price Maintenance (RPM)

This was the policy of manufactures to specify prices at which their product should be sold (together with penalties for non-compliance). The procedure for dealing with such agreements is very similar to that for restricitive trade practice, embodying a general prohibition and a number of 'escape' clauses as follows:

* abolition would result in public health being endangered;

* abolition would result in a substantial reduction in retail outlets;

* abolition would result in a general increase in prices;

* abolition would result in a reduction in after-sales service;

* abolition would result in a substantial reduction in quality or variety of goods available.

This legislation which was first introduced in 1956 and was amended by the Resale Prices Act 1964 has been exceptionally successful. Fixed prices for a manufacturer's products have almost entirely disappeared.

Examination questions

1   In view of the benefits of large-scale organisation why do small firms continue to exist?
2   Outline the major difficulties facing small firms. In what ways has the Government helped small firms overcome these difficulties?
3   'The bigger the better.' How far do you agree with this view regarding the size of business units.

4 Explain the motives of the firm which expands its activities by:
   (a) horizontal integration;
   (b) vertical integration;
   (c) lateral integration.

5 Why do governments seek to encourage competition? Give examples of government measures which may be introduced to encourage competition.

6 Is there a case for your government taking more effective measures to limit the activities of multinational corporations with your country?

7 Briefly explained why some firms attempt to control or merge with other firms. What problems are likely to occur from the merger of two large commercial companies?

8 You are to assume you are personal assistant to the managing director of a small manufacturing concern – Mah Ling Ltd. The company is engaged in the manufacture and sale of central heating equipment in Malaysia. The managing director, Cecilia Lim, who has been appointed to the position, has ambitious plans for the next decade. In particular she plans to double or treble existing manufacturing capacity, expand sales into the North European market and set up a subsidiary servicing central heating equipment.
   Several members of the board of directors are unhappy about these proposals, and the managing director has asked you to prepare a paper considering the economic and organisational implications of remaining small or pursuing the policy of growth.

9 The Government praises small firms for their 'dynamic influence' on industry and commerce. Explain the benefits of small firms to the economy and outline their problems.

10 Since mergers lead to an increase in efficiency they should be encouraged. How far do you agree with this statement?

11 (a) What is a 'small' firm and why do such firms exist?
   (b) From a *human* perspective, what problems and opportunities might such firms present?
   (c) What effect might an increase in the proportion of small firms have on the UK economy? *(CAMB. 1985.)*

12 Seven out of ten people who set up businesses on their own fail within five years whereas nine out of ten franchises survive. Examine the reasons for this.

13 Before 1981 management buy-outs were unknown in the UK. In 1986 there were 281 with a total value of £1.2 billion. Analyse the reasons for this growth. *(AEB 1989.)*

14 'Legislation such as that concerned with employee and consumer protection and the regulation of potential monopolies cause the loss of international competitiveness. This is too high a price to pay' To what extent do you agree? *(AEB 1989.)*

Chapter 4

The organisation, its environment and social responsibility

The environment of business

Organisations do not exist in a vacuum. They are part of society – a society which provides the resources and accepts the output of the firm. It is society which provides the opportunities for organisations and yet also places limitations on their freedom of action. This is the environment of business.

Until recently the importance of the environment was not recognised. It was thought that a successful organisation was one which had efficient work practices and organisational structure together with a caring attitude for its workforce. Now, it is undoubtedly true that a firm's chances of survival are enhanced by these factors, but it is wrong to believe that a boundary can be drawn between the firm and its environment. The causes of success and failure may be found within the organisation, but they are just as likely to be found in the firm's environment. Let us take a simple example to illustrate that point.

It is widely believed that there is a connection between smoking and certain respiratory illnesses. A tobacco firm may therefore have difficulty in maintaining sales of its product, even though the firm is efficiently run by a caring management. This was very much the problem faced by Imperial Tobacco (later the Imperial Group) in the 1960s. Public and governmental attitudes to smoking hardened. Taxes were increased and advertising restricted. Imperial's answer was to reduce their dependence on this market by diversifying into other products. But history is replete with examples of firms or industries who have failed to note a change in their environment and take corrective action in time. Consider the case of the British textile or the Swiss watch industry.

Figure 4.1 illustrates the point we have made – the firm is working within its environment. To carry on its business the firm needs certain inputs from society. While raw materials, labour, and capital immediately spring to mind, there are many others. Perhaps the organisation needs licences from central or local government to carry on its business, or maybe it needs Government help to finance ex-

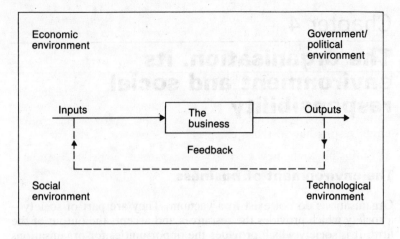

4.1 The organisation and its environment

ports or limit competition – these are as much inputs into the firm as raw materials and labour. Other environmental inputs may place limitations upon the freedom of the firm. Consider the restraints imposed by law to protect employees and consumers, or market forces which prevent firms charging exorbitant prices for their products.

For the business to be successful it has to transform the inputs received form the environment into an output which is acceptable to that environment. How successful it is in obtaining the necessary demand for its product depends on a large number of factors. The price and quality of its products are of prime importance, especially in a high competitive market. Consider the case of the British car manufacturers who have been losing their share of the UK market to products from the rest of Europe and Japan. The judgement of many consumers has been that the foreign car is both cheaper and at the same time more luxurious. Changes in taste may also affect the level of demand. Long hair for men threw many a barber out of business, but rising demand for desk-top computers has created a growth industry.

The success of the business though, does not only depend upon the goods and services it produces but also upon the way in which they are produced. Throughout the twentieth century there has been a trend requiring business to become more socially responsible than before. This is reflected in the growth of pressure groups and their success on such issues as consumer protection, employee welfare, and the environment. Products of certain companies have been unofficially boycotted because of links with South Africa or Israel, or alternatively because of the low wages paid in some of their factories and plantations in Africa and Asia. We shall return to the problem of social responsibility at a later point in this chapter.

All successful companies are aware of their environment. Figure 4.1 shows the successful business monitoring the feedback that it receives from the environment regarding its product and practices. In practice the environment is always changing, creating opportunities to exploit and threats to be avoided. Businesses are constantly responding to these changes. The response is twofold:

(a) adjusting to the new environment – perhaps by producing a new or improved product, by improved labour practices, or reducing pollution; and

(b) changing the environment in favour of the business – falling sales may be reversed by advertising, trade associations may pressure governments for changes in the law, while large multinational companies may even be able to cover losses on trading by negotiating subsidies (e.g. the Chrysler Corporation and the British Government in 1975).

The environment of business is complex – there are many factors which the successful organisation must consider. The more important of these factors are illustrated in Fig. 4.2.

We have now divided the business environment into two parts – the macro-environment and the micro-environment. The distinction between the two is significant – firms have little or no control over their macro-environment yet by their actions may affect, or be affected by, their micro-environment

The macro-environment

1 The economic environment. Pick up any newspaper and turn to the business pages and you will see many references to the impact of the economic environment upon firms. The state of the economy, which is measured by key indicators such as unemployment, inflation, economic growth and the balance of payments forces the Government to act in a particular way. Thus action to reduce the rate of inflation by monetary control or fiscal policy will often result in a firm's sales being reduced. Conversely, attempts to encourage the growth of exports or to reduce the level of unemployment may lead to opportunities to increase sales.

But, of course, there are many other factors apart from these which the organisation may wish to monitor. For example, the state of the international economy may be of great significance to a firm the majority of whose sales are made abroad eg, Jaguar. Or consider

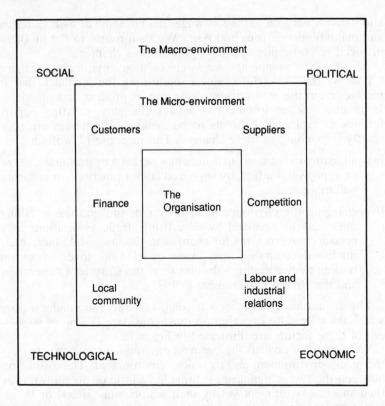

4.2 The environment of business

exchange rates, the value of the dollar in terms of other currencies is of importance to all firms who import oil – oil prices being quoted in dollars.

Other firms may be interested in changes in the population structure – consider how a falling birth rate and an ageing population affect the prospects of different industries.

These economic trends within the environment are studied closely by business managers in an attempt to predict the direction and level of economic activity together with the Government's response.

2. *The political environment.* Attitudes of the Government have a direct impact on the environment of business. In Britain the attitudes towards business have ranged from distrust and antipathy to enthusiastic support. Potential governments' attitudes can be gleaned from the political parties' manifestos – their blueprints for action if elected.

The twentieth century has seen increased involvement by the Government in the affairs of business (*see* Fig. 4.3). The legal framework within which businesses operate has become increasingly complex. The Government has acted to regulate economic organisation by licensing business activity, nationalisation, monopoly and merger legislation, and company law. Both the consumer and the employee are better protected than ever before.

Yet activities of the Government seek not only to constrain business but also to provide it with opportunities. The Government seeks to promote research and development through the Science Research Council, the use of robotics through direct Government grants, the growth and efficiency of small business through subsidised consultancy and the Small Firms Service, a separate division at the Department of Industry. There are many other examples covering the protection of home industry, the encouragement of trade, the finance of industry and the provision of college-based courses providing skilled personnel for industry and commerce. The role of the state in the UK is considered in more detail as a separate section later in this chapter.

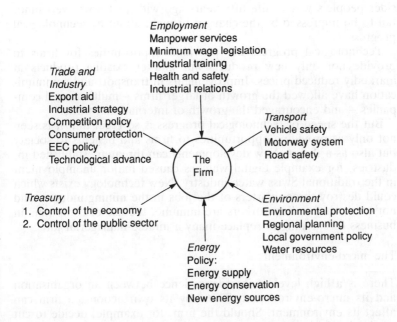

4.3 How the firm is affected by central government activity

3 The social environment. The attitudes of society provide a framework within which an organisation operates. These attitudes can be reflected in law – perhaps relating to the freedom of the individual, competition, or the protection of the consumer. They are equally likely to be found in the unenacted customs of society – the value that is placed upon education, the role of women in society (or the workforce), even our attitudes to work, leisure, and the environment. These attitudes are not constant, they vary over time. Indeed all the attitudes mentioned above (embodied in law and custom) have undergone recent change.

Attitudes also affect the internal workings of the organisation. The Japanese believe that the firm offers the workers a job for life. This results in the Japanese worker having a more positive attitude towards his employer, who in turn involves him in the policy and decision-making more frequently than in other countries. Relationships in France tend to be more formal than in the United States, which again is reflected in the rather more formal structure of French organisations.

4. The technological environment. The past century has seen a rapid growth in the use of technology. The application of scientific principles to industrial problems has resulted in a dramatic increase in the goods and services available for ordinary people. If we consider people's way of life fifty years ago with that now, we cannot fail to be impressed by the changes brought about by technological progress.

Technological progress has provided opportunities for firms to provide not only new products but market existing products at markedly reduced prices. Improvements in transport and communication have allowed the growth of larger firms – multinational companies – and encouraged the growth of international trade.

But the speed of technological progress is so great that it is seen not only as providing opportunities to firms and benefits to society but also as a threat. New developments can threaten established industries, for example digital watches caused major unemployment in the traditional Swiss watch industry. New technology exists which could destroy three-quarters of the jobs in the mining industry and not even white-collar workers are immune, the use of computers in business threatening to replace many a middle-managerial job.

The micro-environment

There is a high level of interdependence between an organisation and its micro-environment. Thus, by its own actions, a firm can affect its environment. Should the firm, for example, decide to cut production because of a reduction in demand this will mean:

- negotiations with trade unions to reduce the work force
- reducing pressure on competitors
- reductions in 'raw material' from suppliers
- less choice for customers
- less demand for finance (and banking facilities)
- less demand for goods and services generally as more people are now unemployed in the area

Equally, the firm will be affected by its micro-environment.

Suppliers. Over each input into the production process two questions have to be answered – where do we get the input from and how much will it cost? The fact that we are able to obtain supplies now and for a reasonable price does not necessarily mean this will always be the case. Many firms have bought up their suppliers of 'raw materials' so as to ensure continuity of supply.

Labour and industrial relations. Changes in relative wages paid in different industries or new technology may mean that labour skills are either not available or become more costly. The attitudes of workers and the action of trade unions must be taken into account when considering changes in organisation and production processes.

Competition. The degree of competition in an industry will also have important implications for the organisation. Markets in Western economies vary from highly competitive through to pure monopoly. In highly competitive markets producers have little control over price and output, and are therefore very concerned with product design, price, quality, and after-sales service. Concern over declining sales may force firms to integrate forwards and take over outlets for their products (eg Singer Sewing machines, Leyland Paints, Ready-Mix Concrete).

Many more markets though are oligopolistic: that is, controlled by a few firms. Here private agreements on price and output (although illegal in many countries) are often made with competition being reduced to claims on quality, after-sales service, and social responsibility. Pure monopoly, that is, a single supplier of a product or service from whom we have to buy, may arise through the development and patenting of a product or process (eg Xerox Copiers) or through nationalisation. Traditionally, such sellers are motivated by self-interest and maximisation of profits, though in practice the watchful eye of the Government prevents too obvious abuse of a monopoly position.

Customers. An economics text book will tell you 'the consumer is king', a store manager will tell his staff 'the customer is always right'. Both are emphasising the central importance of the customer to the business. Without his custom the raison d'être for the firm ceases to exist. In practice this means that the firm must be alive to the requirements of the customer. The successful business will use marketing research to identify these requirements. There will be a regular stream of new products at the right price and quality. The firm will also ensure that there is an efficient after-sales service and quick response to customer complaints.

Well over three quarters of the world's motor cycles were UK made in 1950. Today it produces less than one per cent. In the 1960s the Japanese entered the market with new products and production methods. Consumers liked the cheaper, more advanced bikes and the Japanese scooped the market!

Finance. The average business will borrow money from a wide range of sources. Each of these lenders has to be convinced that lending money to the business is the correct decision. Lenders who believe that a firm is in financial difficulties will quickly withdraw support from that firm. Thus, failure to pay a supplier's account on time, or a dishonoured cheque may result in the firm being refused credit on future transactions.

Directors of large public companies will spend much time explaining their strategy to institutional investors (life assurance companies, pension funds etc) so as to retain their goodwill. Failure to do so will affect the firm's standing in the business community (eg reduced share price, higher cost of borrowing) and make it far more difficult to raise additional funds in the future.

The local community. The term describes people and institutions, including local government, in the area where the firm has set up business. Local government provides much of the infra-structure needed for the economic production of goods and services. In return for these services local taxes are levied on businesses.

As a whole the community expects business to be an integral part of that community and by its actions improve life in that area – an obvious example would be the control of pollution. In many countries local laws are passed because of the unwillingness of businesses to accept their obligations. In the UK planning applications for office/factory extensions may be refused or the firm closed down where firms fail to acknowledge their local or social responsibilities.

The role of the state

The twentieth century has seen a dramatic expansion in the role of the State in Britain. Throughout the nineteenth century the doctrine of *laissez-faire* with its emphasis on individualism and self-help served to limit the extent to which the Government intervened in the workings of the economy. Certainly, the Government provided a stable framework for industry and commerce through the provision of non-commercial services such as law and order, defence, and foreign relations, but little more.

Today the State is involved in almost every aspect of our lives, and the distinction between business and governments has become increasingly blurred. In part this involvement has arisen through the Government's desire to achieve certain macro-economic objectives such as stable prices, a high level of employment, economic growth, and a satisfactory balance of payments. But governments have also come under increasing pressure from the electorate, firstly to develop and expand social services thus providing a 'safety net' for the less fortunate members of society, and secondly to prevent the abuse of power and position by large business units.

This section looks at how the British government, working through its departments, local authorities and agencies affects its citizens and business.

Government departments

Government departments are the primary means by which government policy is affected. These departments vary considerably in the work they undertake. Certain departments, for example Education and Health, are directly responsible for the provision of a specific service throughout the UK, some such as the ministries for Wales, Scotland and Northern Ireland co-ordinate a wide range of activities within their area, while others – the Treasury and Cabinet office are prime examples – act as co-ordinators of government policy.

A summary of the role undertaken by the major government departments is shown in table 4.1

Quasi autonomous non-governmental organisations

One prominent characteristic of central government in the UK is the extent to which it delegates its responsibilities to other bodies. There are of course exceptions to this – defence, taxation, and social security are the most important examples – but the majority of other government departments discharge their duties through non-departmental public bodies. These bodies, which are often

Table 4.1 Major Government Departments

Department	Major responsibilities	Associated Agencies
Treasury	Economic forecasting, control of the economy, supervision of government departments, local authorities and nationalised industries spending, Exchange Rate policy, representation of UK interests on international bodies such as IMF, World Bank and EEC	Board of Inland Revenue, Customs and Excise, Bank of England.
Education and Science	Provision of full-time education for all children up to the age of 16, part-time or full-time further education for 25% of school leavers, higher education for 14% of 18-year-olds, adult education (vocational and non-vocational)	Local authorities (schools, colleges of further education, colleges of technology), Universities, Polytechnics
Transport	Responsible for an efficient system of transport, road safety legislation (eg drink/driving, safety belts), overseas nationalised rail system, regulates other transport industries	Transport and Road Research Laboratory
Environment	Approval of local authorities' structure plans (these form the basis for regional and local plans). Implementation of housing policy (building regulations, slum clearance, property modernisation) through local authorities. Conservation of buildings and national parks. Control of environmental pollution	Local authorities Countryside Commission Royal Commission on Environmental Pollution
Employment	Aid to the unemployed through benefits offices and job centres/clubs. Improving the skills level of the UK workforce, employee protection, minimum wages, conditions of employment, improving industrial relations	Training Agency Health & Safety Executive, Employment Medical Advisory Service, Industrial Tribunals, Wages Councils, Advisory Conciliation and Arbitration Service (ACAS).

Department	Major responsibilities	Associated Agencies
Trade & Industry 1 Trade	Representing UK trade interests to international organisations (eg GATT, EEC). Assistance to exporters (information, advice, finance), Export insurance cover	British Overseas Trade Board, Export Credits Guarantee Department
2 Industry	To provide an environment conducive to industrial expansion, distribution of government aid, to provide a service to small firms	
3 Corporate and Consumer Affairs	To control monopoly, merger, restrictive trade and anti-competitive practices, Consumer safety and protection. Supervision of Patent Office, Insolvency service.	Monopolies and Mergers Commission, Office of Fair Trading.
4 Technological Advance	To promote the rapid assimilation and exploitation of new technology. Finance of scientific research.	British Technology Group, various Research Councils and centres.
Ministry of Agriculture, Fisheries, and Food	Policies for agriculture, horticulture, forestry and fisheries, food quality and supply. Water resources and sewerage (with Dept of the Environment)	Intervention Board for Agricultural Produce (support to farmers under the Common Agricultural Policy), Agricultural Development and Advisory Service, Farm Animal Welfare Council. Forestry Commission Regional Water Authorities
Energy	Policies for energy supply and conservation. The development of new energy sources. Relationships with the nationalised 'energy' industries, International collaboration on energy questions	Advisory Council on Energy Conservation, Energy Technology Support. Atomic Energy Authority, British National Oil Corporation, National Coal Board, International Energy Agency
Foreign and Commonwealth	All aspects of overseas relationships, foreign policy, international negotiations. The protection of British	Embassies and consulates. Overseas Development Administration

Department	Major responsibilities	Associated Agencies
	interests – property and persons abroad. Aid to and co-operation with developing countries	
Health and Social Security	The social security system, the National Health Service, local authority social services, public health and hygiene. Treatment of offenders under 17 (shared with Home Office)	Regional and District Health Authorities, Health Education, local authority social service departments
Home Office	The maintenance of law and order, police service, courts and prisons, Civil Defence, regulation of firearms, dangerous drugs, gaming and lotteries, immigration and nationality questions, race relations, sex discrimination. Broadcasting	Metropolitan and provincial police forces, Probation Office, British Broadcasting Corporation, Independent Broadcasting Authority

collectively described as 'quangos' or quasi autonomous non-governmental organisations, are controlled by people appointed by the minister concerned to whom they are responsible for the discharge of a specific duty such as the running of, the Housing Corporation, the Gaming Board, or the Council for Small Industries in Rural Areas. The Bank of England is probably the most important and powerful quango.

At one time as many as 3,000 quangos were thought to exist. In 1979 a review of these bodies was instituted as a result of which many were abolished. In April 1987, 1,643 quangos aided government departments in the discharge of their duties.

Quangos fall into one of three categories – executive bodies, advisory bodies, or tribunals. Executive bodies such as the National Health Service, British Council, Commission for Racial Equality or the BOTB provide services to the public or industry, employ staff, and spend money on their own account.

Advisory bodies undertake research or collect information, thus giving ministers facts and informed opinion on which to base a decision. For example the Secretary of State for Education and Science discharges its duties in respect of research on the advice of the Advisory Board for the Research Councils, while the Secretary of State for Energy takes advice form the independent Advisory Council on Energy Conservation.

Although ministers may be required to consult an advisory board, the majority are created at the discretion of a departmental minister and arise out of their need for advice. Membership of the body varies according to the work involved, but will normally reflect the diversity of public opinion on the subject concerned. It represents an attempt on the part of the minister to involve key interests in the making (and in some cases the implementation) of government policy.

Where important issues are involved the Government may appoint a Royal Commission which will consider and make recommendations on a specific matter. The members of the commission, who are chosen for their experience and expertise, take written and oral evidence from all interested parties before submitting their recommendations. The Government may implement their proposals wholly, in part, or alternatively they may decide to shelve the report and take no further action.

Administration tribunals, although outside the court system, exercise a judicial function. Many owe their existence to the large amount of social legislation (and its complexity) introduced in the last fifty years. Compared with courts, tribunals have an extremely limited judicial function. This function, their constitution and procedures are detailed in the legislation which created them. Tribunals may determine disputes between private citizens, for example rent or industrial tribunals, or alternatively may arbitrate in disputes between a government department and private citizen, for example social security.

Local government

Local government is a further, and very important, example of the way in which central government delegates the implementation of policy to other bodies. An extremely wide range of public services is provided through the democratically elected councils which represent local communities. The provision of services on a local rather than national basis is beneficial for the following reasons.

1 It would be impossible for any central organisation to deal efficiently with public services distributed to a population of 56 million living in an area of over 94,000 square miles.

2 It is a means by which the public exercises control over local affairs, prevents excessive central power, and, if necessary, expresses its disaffection towards central government policy.

Local Government structure in England and Wales was established in 1972 and reformed in 1986. The reformed system is shown in Fig. 4.4

For most of England and Wales there are two tiers of local government organisation. County authorities are responsible for providing services which either require planning and administration over a

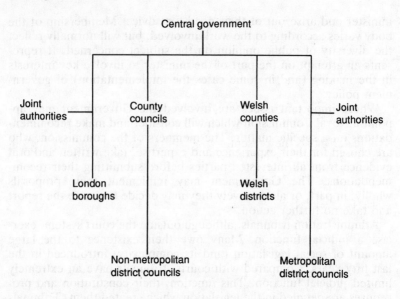

4.4 Local government structure in England and Wales

wide area or need the support of substantial resources. District authorities administer those services best provided on a local basis. A major distinction, however, is drawn between 'normal' county areas and six heavily populated areas – West Midlands, Greater Manchester, Merseyside, South Yorkshire, West Yorkshire and Tyne and Wear which were given the title of Metropolitan Counties. In 1986 the Metropolitan County Councils and the Greater London Council were abolished leaving just one tier of local government – the metropolitan district councils and the London Boroughs. Many of the functions previously undertaken by these councils have now been transferred to the District Councils and London Boroughs. Where efficiency demands that a service, e.g. police, fire services etc, is carried out over a broader area, then that service is run by joint authorities administered by representatives of the authorities using the service.

The range of services provided by local authorities is remarkably wide. These services can be classified by function:

protective: police
                fire
                consumer protection
environmental: building regulations
                pollution

	control of nuisances
	roads and transport
	planning
personal services:	education
	careers
	social services
	housing
	recreational

Table 4.2 shows the present distribution of local authority functions.

Table 4.2 Distribution of local authority functions under the London Government Act 1963, and the Local Government Act 1972

Authority	Responsibility
England	
(1) London	
– Joint Authorities	Fire service
– London boroughs	Housing, strategic planning personal social services, environmental health, education (outside Inner London), leisure services
(2) Metropolitan areas	
– Joint Authorities	Transport, police, fire services
– Districts	Strategic and local planning, housing, personal and social services, environmental health, education, leisure services.
(3) Non-metropolitan areas	
– Counties	Straight planning, education, personal and social services, transport, police, fire services, consumer protection
– Districts	Local planning, housing, environmental health, leisure services
(4) Wales	
– Counties	Strategic planning, education, personal and social services, transport, police, fire services, consumer protection
– Districts	Local planning, housing, environmental health, leisure services

Social responsibility

As we have seen, organisation is not only affected by its environment, it in turn can affect that environment. By advertising it may change people's demand for goods and services, perhaps it may pollute the atmosphere or river, or by bribery secure some advantages it would not otherwise receive. It is the ability of the organisation to alter its environment which has caused increasing concern. If this power is not effectively controlled the unscrupulous firm can appropriate an unfair share of social benefits. Thus large firms may be under little competitive pressure, leaving them free to negotiate beneficial terms with both customers and suppliers. Moreover, its decisions may have an important impact upon the local community and may even determine central government's allocation of resources.

Increasingly, therefore, business has been required to become more socially responsible to the community which has allowed it to engage in business activity. A socially responsible business organisation is one which has an awareness of the 'social' problems which arise out of its relationships with customers, employees, suppliers, the Government, and the community, and is willing to commit resources to solve some of these problems.

Yet even when a business accepts social responsibility as one of its objectives it may still be criticised. Consider a chemical company, a major employer in an area of high unemployment. The company discharges effluent into the river which kills all living organisms in and around the river. It has received an order from a statutory authority requiring it to stop this pollution. The cost of treating the effluent would raise the firm's costs so much as to make it uncompetitive. The firm has a choice, close down, with all the consequences for the local community, or negotiate agreement to continue polluting the river. In which course of action is it being socially responsible?

The point which is being made is that there is no acceptable definition of what constitutes socially responsible action. Social responsibility varies according to your attitudes. However, a majority of people would accept the following as being areas of concern for the socially responsible firm:

Employee relations

- The education and training of staff.
- The working environment.
- Job satisfaction.
- Attitudes to disadvantaged groups.

Consumer protection

- Product safety.
- Misleading advertising.
- Complaints from consumers.

The environment

- Pollution.
- Noise.
- Restoration of land to natural uses.

Financial honesty and openness

- Bribery and corruption.
- Company control and ownership.
- Executive pay and compensation.
- Contributions to political parties.

Most organisations accept that they owe a responsibility to society, but in many cases this has not been translated into action as fully as we would like. There is, after all, a basic conflict between social responsibility and profitability. Money invested in social responsibility comes out of the company's profits, and if the shareholders do not receive what they believe to be a fair return on their investment they are unlikely to contribute to the future capital requirements of the company. Moreover, while managers as individuals may believe in social responsibility, as managers of the business they are evaluated strictly upon economic performance. The rewards go to the managers who keep costs down most successfully – and that includes the cost of social responsibility. The conclusion must be that social responsibility cannot be left to the whims of individual firms and managers but must be enforced by legislation. The growth of consumer and employee protection legislation is part of this process.

Examination questions

1 What do you understand by the term 'the environment of business'? Using an organisation or industry of your choice, show how the environment provides both opportunities for and constraints upon that organisation/industry *(PSC 1985)*.

2 A personnel manager has been invited to give a talk to new employees on the relationship between business and society. What would you expect him to include in his talk when considering
(a) how an organisation is assisted and constrained by the State and
(b) how an organisation may influence and affect central and local government (PSC 1987).

3 Outline the obligations which any business has to its employees and show how they may conflict with its obligations to other groups *(AEB)*.

Setting the scene

4 Consider the statement that for any business enterprise change must be regarded as inevitable *(AEB)*.

5 What do you understand by the term 'economic environment'. Why is it so important in the operation of business? *(PSC)*.

6 A large service organisation holds a dominant position in the local economy. Outline the social responsibilities it may have to the local community and the ways in which it may attempt to discharge these obligations.

7 An increase in the importance of the Government and the public sector proves that society is becoming more socially responsible. Discuss.

Part II
The economic environment

Chapter 5

Economic growth

The measurement of economic activity

Economic activity is the process by which scarce resources are changed into the goods and services demanded by that country's population. The money value of that output (goods and services) is termed the national income. Generally speaking, the more resources there are for this transformation process and the more effectively they are used the larger is that country's national income.

Official estimates of national income for the UK are compiled and published annually by the Central Statistical Office and appear under the title of 'National Accounts', or until recently 'National Income and Expenditure' (the Blue Book).

In practice, the national income of the UK is calculated in three different ways:

- by summing up the output of all firms in the UK

- by calculating the income earned by all the different people in the UK

- by looking at how the money that has been spent is earned.

The output measure

This process is rather more complicated than just adding up the output of all firms because the output of one firm is the input of another. For example, the output of the farmer – the wheat he grows – will be the input of the miller. Equally, the output of the miller – the flour – is the input of the baker. To include in the national income the output of all three would be to double-count the value of the wheat and the flour. The problem of double-counting can be avoided in one of two ways. To understand this, let us look more closely at an example of the production process for bread.

From Figure 5.1 we can see that the farmer produces wheat worth £1. This is the 'value added' or value created by his labours. Now the miller will use this wheat to make flour which is worth £3, but

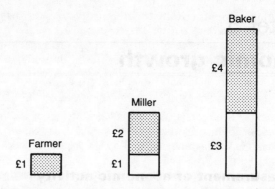

5.1 Illustration of added value

his value added is £2. This is obtained by deducting the cost of inputs (wheat – £1) from the value of his final output (£3). The total inputs of the baker are £3 (this is made up of added value – farmer £1, and added value of the miller £2). To this he adds value of £4 making a final price for his output of £7.

The first method of calculating the value of national output of goods and services is to take the value added (total output less inputs) by each firm in the production process – the shaded area in Figure 5.1. This is £7.

The value added of £7 is the same as the final price of the output. Clearly then, the second method of calculation is to ignore the intermediate stages of production and just add together the final value of goods and services produced. That is output produced for consumption rather than incorporation into any other product.

The income measure

When goods and services are produced the people who help create those products or services are rewarded for their effort. Such payments are known as factor incomes because they are paid to the factors of production – the providers of land, labour and capital. The aggregate of such income is one basis for calculating national income.

It is the gross value of incomes which is included. This is the value of the factors' services. The fact that tax (and for labour National Insurance Contributions) is deducted is immaterial. The value of their contribution to output is the gross income they receive.

Not all incomes are included. State benefits paid out of National Insurance Contributions are excluded. They have not been generated by employment, but are a compulsory transfer from the person earning that income to the person receiving it. To include the transfer payment as income of the person who originally gave value for it and also the State beneficiary would be double-counting.

Gross Domestic Product (GDP), Gross National Product (GNP)

Gross Domestic Product is defined as the value of all goods and services produced in a country over a given period of time. Put another way, it is the incomes earned by UK residents working in this country.

But not all goods and services which are produced within an economy are produced with resources owned by that country. For example, many American firms have subsidiaries in the UK and Western Europe.

Historically, the UK has invested heavily overseas and now receives income from these investments in the form of rent, profits, and interest.

To take account of this fact an adjustment is made to the previous calculation of GDP by deducting all payments made to overseas countries resulting from their investments here, and adding to it payments made to the UK arising from our investments overseas.

Gross National Product as this figure is called, is the value of all final goods and services produced as a result of resources owned by that country wherever they are at work. For the UK this adjustment to GDP is positive, with GNP being larger than GDP. This reflects the investments made by the UK overseas in previous years. For many countries though, especially among the developing nations, the adjustment results in a national product smaller than the domestic product.

The expenditure measure

National income may also be calculated by looking at the expenditure of the people and organisations within the economy. As before we must take care not to double-count. The purchases we wish to include are for final consumption or capital investment. Consumer spending is by far the most important item in the expenditure measure of national income (over 60 per cent). General Government consumption (over 20 per cent) covers expenditure by both central and local government.

So, approximately 80 per cent of the GNP of the UK is used for consumption. The remainder we term investment. Investment is required in order to maintain and enhance the flow of goods and services in the economy in future years. It is required to replace the existing stock of capital equipment which has been depreciated in value by use over the past period. Approximately 10 per cent of GNP, or nearly half of total investment, is used to replace the capital stock used up. The figure which is left after allowing for depreciation of capital stock (ie 90 per cent of GNP) is referred to as Net National Product (NNP).

The national income may be underestimated because much economic activity goes unrecorded. The work of women in the home is considered to be one major omission though all the odd jobs around the home done by different members of the family fall into the same category.

Other economic activity which goes unrecorded is often termed the 'black economy'. The black economy is commonly associated with tax evasion. Traders who fail to declare their full turnover and employees who have an undisclosed (job) source of income are all part of the black economy. By comparing national income calculations of income (which is underestimated because of the black economy) and expenditure the Central Statistical Office estimated its size as 3.5 per cent of GDP for the UK.

Underestimation of national income is not only a problem for advanced economies but also for developing economies where a substantial number of transactions will be on a barter basis.

Net National Product is, technically, the goods and services available in any year to satisfy consumption without sacrificing future for present consumption. Yet many countries seek to invest more than this minimum amount in capital stock because they wish to improve on their present standard of living. This requires extra investment in new techniques and processes. The extra investment required is termed Net Capital Formation (NCF).

Figure 5.2 shows the relationship (for the UK) between GDP and GNP, and how depreciation and NCF reduce the goods and services available for consumption.

The use of national income statistics

The annual Blue Book, *National Accounts*, appears some nine months after the end of the year to which it relates. It is an important source of information which can be used for many purposes.

The Government, in its attempts to control the economy, will use the accounts to determine how the economy has performed over the previous periods, and whether Government objectives (inflation, growth, unemployment, international trade) have been achieved. A

Net investment income from abroad		Depreciation of capital stock
		Net capital formation
Gross Domestic Product at actor cost	Gross National Product	Public and private consumption

5.2 Different ways of looking at GNP

trend established over a number of years may be revealed by the Blue Book, and the Government may adjust its policies to meet these changed conditions. Firms in the private sector will similarly benefit from the use of national income statistics.

If, for example, the National Accounts revealed a change in pattern of consumer spending this would have implications for both business and the Government. Some possible implications are as follows:

- Taxation – effect on VAT – Customs and Excise – corporation tax.

- Impact upon unemployment – regional problem.

- Health and welfare – employee and consumer.

- Effect on imports of raw materials or finished goods.

- Increased need for education and training.

- Private and public investment decisions.

- Protection of home industry.

    Listed below are some of the tables contained in the Blue Book; their relevance to the Government and business does not need explanation. Similar information is published in many other countries.

- Analysis of income (sources).

- Analysis of expenditure.

- GDP by industry – subsidies to industry, investment by industry, profitability of industry, employment by industry.

- Public corporations – profitability, employment, investment.

- Central government – current and capital expenditure, sources of income.

- Local government – cost of services provided, capital expenditure, sources of revenue.

- International trade – imports and exports.

It would be wrong to claim that past trends are a perfect indicator of what is going to happen in the future. They are not, but the information provided in the Blue Book is a sound base upon which to base government policy decisions for the future. Neither must it be thought that the Blue Book is the only source of information available to the Government – it is one of many, but its comprehensive coverage of all aspects of the economy should indicate its importance.

The need for care in using national income statistics

1. Increases in national income from year to year reflect not only the growth in output but also the process of rising prices. Consider the following situation:

Country X	Year 1	Year 2
National income	100	108
Retail Price Index	100	105

The growth of national income in money terms is 8 per cent. However, as inflation during the same period has increased by 5 per cent the real growth in income or output is 3 per cent.

Thus, if we wish to compare national income over a period of time (and perhaps establish a growth rate) we need to find how prices have moved in the same period and use this to discount money national income. For example, measured in money terms the UK national income grew by 136 per cent between 1975 and 1981. In real terms (constant prices) though, the increase was a mere 6 per cent with national income actually declining between 1979 and 1981.

Table 5.1 shows the real growth in gross domestic product between 1981 and 1987 for the UK.

1982	1983	1984	1985	1986	1987
1.6	3.3	2.4	3.7	3.0	4.4

Source: Economic Progress Report June 1988

Average growth in this period has been 3.1 per cent which is significantly higher than the 2.5 per cent per annum averaged since the end of the Second World War.

Just as important though is the fact that this growth has been steady. When an economy moves rapidly from boom to slump business people find it difficult to manage efficiently. Investment (with its impact on future economic growth) is commonly a casualty in such situations.

2. Two countries may have very similar national incomes and yet their populations enjoy considerably different standards of living. This can occur for the following reasons:

(a) The national income statistics do not show the effect of better-quality goods, improved conditions of work, or a shorter working week, yet all these contribute to a higher standard of living.

(b) Where the size of the population is different we can say that normally the economy with the higher population will have the lower standard of living. This point is easily understood if we express national income as a figure per head of population. See the following example.

   Both country A and country B have a national income of £1,200 m. The population in country A is 20 million and in country B 50 million.

		National income per head(£)
Country A	$\dfrac{1,200}{20}$	600
Country B	$\dfrac{1,200}{50}$	240

(c) Not all of the national output is available for consumption. Some is required for the replacement of existing capital stock and some for new investment projects. There is no requirement that countries should invest the same amount of their national output, and in practice it is very unlikely to happen. Japan, for example, invests 28 per cent of her GNP compared with the UK's 14 per cent.

The standard of living of a country depends primarily on the goods and services consumed in that country. As the national income

measures the amount of goods and services produced it is a relatively good indicator of the standard of living. National income per head of population is often used to illustrate living standards.

Economic factors which determine the standard of living include:

- the country's natural resources
- the size and age structure of its population
- the skills of its workforce
- the level of technological knowledge
- the strength of its international trading position eg, how competitive we are in relation to countries producing the same kinds of good as ourselves, and the terms of trade.

But the standard of living is more than a reflection of material possessions; there are other intangible factors which contribute greatly to the quality of life we enjoy. Consider the hours men worked a century ago, compared with today. The pleasure derived from greater leisure contributes as much to our standard of living as does that obtained from a new watch or radio. Other items which are excluded from the calculation of national income yet which contribute to our standard of living would include beneficial working conditions, the beauty of the environment, liberty, and cultural heritage.

(d) The distribution of wealth in an economy is an important factor in determining the standard of living. The calculation 'per capita income' assumes an equal distribution of wealth, yet there are countries where wealth and riches are concentrated in the hands of a few, leaving the majority with an extremely low standard of living.

Economic growth

Is economic growth desirable? Certainly governments believe so, as would many ordinary people. The major argument in favour of pursuing a policy of growth is that if it is successful living standards rise. As we can see from Table 5.2 a sustained annual increase in national income of 3 per cent will result in living standards doubling in less than thirty years.

But often more important than how one country does over a period of time is how it compares against its neighbours. A consistently higher rate of growth by one country can lead to a very dramatic difference in national income and standard of living within a short period of time.

Governments, perhaps naively, believe that higher growth rates will impress other countries and persuade them to adopt a similar

Table 5.2 Effect of varying growth rates – percentage of growth p.a.

Year	% Rate of growth p.a.			
	1%	3%	5%	7%
0	100	100	100	100
10	110	134	163	197
30	135	243	432	761
50	164	438	1,147	2,946

political/economic system. Certain is the fact that higher growth rates allow a country to strengthen its military capability and defence systems, ease the burden of investment for the future, and enable redistribution of income to proceed without anyone experiencing an absolute cut in their standard of living.

Yet there is a cost to economic growth. Growth requires an investment in education, health, and technology. This investment can only be achieved by consuming fewer goods and services today, a reduction in everyone's standard of living. Moreover, this denial of consumption, if it is to make any significant impact on future standards of living, must be continued for many years. Many countries, though, have followed this path – the Chinese under Mao Tse-tung, Stalin's Russia, and Hitler's Germany all adopted five-year plans which moved resources from production of consumption goods to capital investment goods. Today most developing countries have such plans.

There may also be certain social and environmental costs resulting from economic growth which are not adequately reflected in estimates of national income. A rapid rate of growth requires adjustment in terms of technology and human skills. The change to more sophisticated techniques of production leaves obsolete machinery in its wake, means that less jobs are around for unskilled workers, and that even highly trained workers may find their skills redundant. The costs of this increasing degree of structural unemployment may be difficult to quantify, but they are real and include a higher incidence of mental and physical illness, family problems, and crime.

E. G. Mishan (*The Cost of Economic Growth*) also points to increased pollution, traffic congestion, the erosion of the countryside, and rapid depletion of raw materials as problems arising from fast growth rates.

Factors leading to growth

For most people the case for economic growth is compelling, associated as it is with increased consumption of goods and services and increased leisure. Governments have, therefore, sought to pursue those policies which would encourage growth, yet major disagreement exists over exactly what causes economic growth, and as many as twenty-three potential sources of growth have been identified. In the following sections we will look at a few of the major factors which are thought to lead to growth.

Capital accumulation   For many years economists have noted a correlation between those countries with high growth rates and high investment/GDP ratio. For example, since the Second World War, Japan has had exceptionally high growth rates – often in excess of 10 per cent. At the same time observers have noted that Japan has been investing 28 per cent of her national income in renewing and expanding her capital stock. In the UK the corresponding ratio has been 14 per cent (likewise with many of her European counterparts), and the growth rate has averaged a disappointing 2 per cent.

Yet for many economies the sacrifice needed to raise the investment/GDP ratio even to that of the UK would be too much. In a subsistence economy consumption is already low and a transfer of resources from consumption to investment will cause extreme hardship, if not death from starvation. In such circumstances it is not surprising that some commentators believe that the gap between rich and poor countries is growing.

Human capital   Neither capital accumulation nor technical change is worth while unless there is the necessary manpower to work it. Economic growth depends upon having a pool of skilled labour available. To talk of human capital may seem odd, but all societies invest money in their workforce. The investment made would be in general education (the majority of workers are, after all, required to be both literate and numerate), the more specific skills required by industry (e.g. craftsmen, technicians, and managers), and health programmes.

Moreover the investment has increased hand-in-hand with the greater complexity and sophistication of industry. Consider the technology used today with that of a century ago and the wide range of skills and specialisms now required. Activity rates for young males in Britain are lower now than they have ever been – reflecting the need to stay on at school, or technical college, for longer or enter higher education so as to obtain those qualifications by industry.

The level of investment in education and skills training also depends upon the speed of industrial change. The greater the speed of change the greater the level of structural unemployment which occurs. Workers with unusable skills need to be invested with new skills to become valuable members of the workforce once more.

Technological change   The progress of technological change involves: (a) taking an idea – a pure scientific advance – and (b) identifying and developing its commercial applications to the point where (c) a new product or process is brought to the market.

Invention and innovation provides sources of new growth which prevent economic stagnation within a society, and the ability of an economy to absorb these changes quickly may be a major factor in determining a country's rate of growth. Where the process of technological advance is slow the major problems would seem to be in identifying the commercial applications arising from the scientific discovery and in overcoming opposition to change, from both management and union.

Technological transfer

It is not necessary for a country to invent a process or product to benefit from its development. If another country exploits that invention more quickly than the one where the discovery was made the second country will reap most of the benefits. One cause of high economic growth in Japan has been its ability to borrow and exploit Western technology for commercial purposes more quickly than we ourselves could.

Governments can also encourage the process of growth by providing sufficiently high incentives for business to 'write-off' existing machinery and invest in and expand new capital equipment. Although there are difficulties in calculating accurately the rate of technological change, the measure used most widely is labour productivity. Productivity itself is a measure of the quantity of output – goods or services, which can be obtained for a given input – land, labour, capital, or entrepreneurship. In practice, because of the problems of measuring the inputs of capital or raw materials it is the ratio of output to labour which is most often quoted. In official publications you will find two important definitions of labour productivity.

- *Output per head* – the volume of output produced on average by each person employed.

- *Output per man-hour* – the volume of output produced by each person employed in each hour.

Demand The level of demand for goods and services plays an important part in determining the business person's outlook for the future. A high and stable level of demand encourages the business person to believe that they are able to sell all they can produce. Accordingly they will expand production and investment in plant and machinery. Moreover, an expansionist economy encourages the business to search for better and more efficient methods of production, resulting in greater labour productivity. High levels of demand serve to perpetuate economic growth in that the increased investments lead to more employment possibilities and further increases in the general level of demand.

Examination questions

1 What do you understand by the term 'national income'? Selecting a method of your choice, show how it is calculated.

2 Why is it important to measure a country's economic activity?

3 Why do some countries grow much faster than others?

4 What difficulties are there in comparing national income?
(a) In different countries.
(b) Over a period of time.

5 Why do countries seek economic growth? What are the costs of economic growth?

6 What factors determine the incomes of nations and individuals?

7 Why is economic growth important? How may it be encouraged?

8 Explain the terms 'cost' and 'standard of living'. What forces can raise the cost of living or the standard of living?

9 To what extent can a country's labour force influence the rate of economic growth.

10 Explain what is meant by economic growth and how it is measured. Would a high economic growth rate solve the UK's social and economic problems?

11 You have been asked to compare the living standards of a manager in London with one in New York.
What problems would you face in making these comparisons?
What information in addition to national income figures would you find helpful?

12 In the 1980's UK productivity has grown faster than in any other country apart from Japan. Analyse the impact of high productivity growth upon the economy.

Chapter 6

Inflation

Inflation is a rise in the general level of prices. Try to think of any goods or services which you regularly buy which cost less now than they did say three or four years ago. The answer is that there are very few – the prices of most things we buy have risen. Inflation results in a fall in the value of money, or its purchasing power (*see* Fig. 6.1) – we could also say that the cost of living has increased.

But while the process of inflation implies that items which cost £10 now will sooner or later cost £11 or £12, we must distinguish between the movement in the price of an individual product and the general price level. The price of an individual product is determined

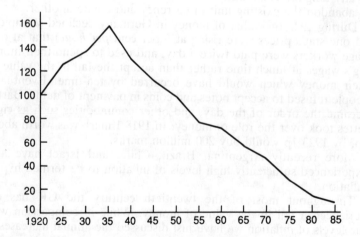

6.1 Purchasing power of the pound 1920–85

Between 1920 and 1935 prices actually fell as a result of deflationary policies. Since 1935 though prices have risen every year.

---

by its costs of production, and what consumers are willing to pay for it. This may move independently of prices generally. For example the prices of home computers are actually falling at the moment while the overall price level is rising. Equally a sudden increase in demand or shortage in the supply of a product may produce a price rise for that product which is in excess of price increases generally.

The reduction in the value of money is not a twentieth-century phenomenon. Throughout history there has been a tendency for prices to rise. It is estimated for example that prices in England doubled during the eighteenth and nineteenth centuries. Where, as in England during the period 1700–1900, inflation was persistent but gradual it is defined as 'mild' or 'creeping' inflation.

The constant worry of governments is that mild or creeping inflation will get out of hand and accelerate to alarming levels. Several countries in Europe experienced this problem (it is called hyperinflation) after the First World War. Hyperinflation exists when public confidence in money drops to such an extent that people are no longer willing to save or hold money. When inflation reaches these levels it is uncontrollable. People expect prices to rise – indeed rise rapidly. In their anxiety to avoid holding notes and coins they actually fuel the inflationary process by bidding up the paper price of any tangible commodity with real value. The normal solution is to abandon the existing unit of currency and create another.

During 1923 the value of money in Germany declined so rapidly (at one stage prices were rising at 5 per cent *per hour*) that at one stage workers were paid twice a day, and used to spend their morning's wages at lunch-time rather than accept the fall in the value of their money which would have occurred by tea-time! Eventually people refused to accept notes and coins in payment of debts. Barter became the order of the day, and other commodities such as cigarettes took over the role of money. In 1918 1 mark was worth about 1p, by 1923 1p would buy 200 million marks.

More recently Argentina, Brazil, Chile, and Israel have also experienced sufficiently high levels of inflation to be termed hyperinflation.

Throughout most of the twentieth century the UK has experienced a fall in the value of money. While in comparison with the levels of inflation we have just discussed the annual increases in this country have been modest, prices rose more rapidly during the decade 1973–83 than we have ever seen before, with annual price rises peaking at 24.2 per cent in 1975 and averaging 13 per cent for the decade as a whole (see Figure 6.2). Put another way, there was a threefold increase in prices during this period. Since 1980 the annual inflation rate has fallen considerably, though in 1988 and 1989 it rose again.

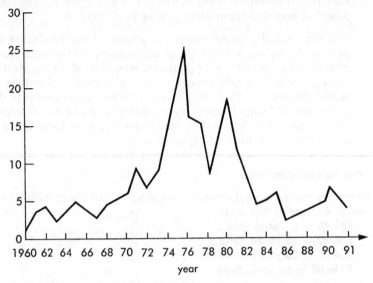

% change in prices

6.2 UK inflation record 1960–91

The effects of inflation

1. Benefits
- Mild inflation encourages businesses to maintain and expand production. Rising prices are associated with a high and buoyant level of demand, often termed 'boom conditions'. Unemployment may be reduced as businesses expand production and the rate of economic growth increased as firms invest for the future.

- Business profits benefit from mild inflation. Buoyant trading conditions result in a high level of demand for most products, while the process of rising prices tends to result in profit margins being larger than anticipated. Efficient producers make large profits. Share prices also reflect the increase in the level of profits. During the upswing of the business or stop-go cycle, share prices rise as investors first anticipate and then receive enlarged dividends.

- As the largest borrower in the country the Government benefits greatly from inflation. Over time the real burden of the National Debt is reduced substantially by inflation. The Government also benefits through increased tax revenue. Wage increases result in poorer sections of society who were previously exempt from tax being dragged into the tax net (even though in real terms they may be no better off than before). For the same reason higher wage-earners find themselves paying more tax.

- For the majority of employees a period of mild inflation is a period of prosperity. Unemployment is low and economic growth provides the worker with a rising standard of living. Not all workers benefit equally though. Those with industrial muscle will secure themselves wages and salary increases far in excess of rises in the cost of living. Employers are willing to grant these increases in the belief that they will be able to pass most of them on to the consumer in the form of higher prices.

The power of inflation

If we assume an annual inflation rate of 5 per cent the textbook which costs £10 today will cost:
   £12.75 in 5 years' time
   £16.30 in 10 years' time
   £34.00 in 25 years' time
   £115.00 in 50 years'time

---

2.   Problems
(a)   External
   Inflation may also adversely affect a country's trading relations with the rest of the world. Where a country experiences inflation at a rate greater than that of its trading partners it will find that:
   - its exports decline as they become uncompetitive when compared with the overseas-produced product;
   - its imports increase as nationals find that foreign goods are relatively cheaper; and
   - overseas investors remove capital from that country in the expectation of a fall in its exchange rate.
(b)   Internal
   - There is a tendency for rates of inflation to increase which may lead to hyper-inflation
   - Rising inflation may damage business confidence. If business people anticipate Government action to reduce inflation they are less willing to invest for the future
   - Inflation may reduce the amount of money available for investment. People are encouraged to spend their money now so as to gain full value from it, or seek non productive investments which will act as a hedge against inflation (eg, objects d'art, precious stones, gold etc). Unfortunately, given the relationship between savings/capital investment and economic growth this must damage our future living standards.

Marianne

- In the long run, rates of interest may be forced up in order to attract savings. When inflation in the UK was at its highest in the 1970s the UK Government was paying in excess of 15 per cent per annum to attract long-term funds – and yet the investor, with inflation running at more than 15 per cent, was still not receiving a real return on their loan. But should the inflation rate and interest rates fall the Government may very well find itself committed to paying unnecessarily high interest payments. (It was for precisely these reasons that in March 1981 the UK Government started issuing index-linked 'gilts' with interest and redemption values linked to inflation – as measured by the RPI.)
- Inflation causes industrial and social unrest as groups compete to maintain or improve their living standards at the expense of others.
- People living upon fixed incomes – incomes which do not rise as the cost of living increases, are hit hardest by inflation. The major groups involved are pensioners. The UK inflation of the 1970s which reduced purchasing power to one-third of what it was at the beginning of the period has prompted many unions to negotiate agreements linking pensions to increases in the Retail Price Index (RPI).
- In a period of inflation the real value of any sum borrowed declines. The man who borrowed £6,000 in 1980 to purchase a house found the real value of the £6,000 he had to repay in 1990 had dropped to a mere £2,000. We can say, as a general rule, that in inflationary times borrowers gain and lenders lose.
- Financial techniques used to plan and control the progress of the firm may be less effective as a result of inflation. For example the balance sheet may not provide a true picture of the affairs of the company. As prices rise the true value of company assets may be under-estimated. Depreciation provisions may be insufficient for the replacement of plant and machinery if based on the original cost of the assets. Profit figures may be equally misleading as it is quite possible for a rise in monetary profits to be more than offset by the reduction in the value of money. (To overcome these problems the UK accountancy profession has been experimenting with various forms of inflation accounting since 1980.)

  Inflation also reduces the effectiveness of budgeting and investment appraisal.
- Rising prices may also cause firms to incur additional costs. For example, the purchasing manager will have to devote more time to ensuring that supplies are purchased at minimum cost. The marketing manager may have to arrange for

catalogues and other business literature (which includes information on prices) to be reprinted. The personnel manager will be involved in the complex process of re-negotiating pay deals, while the accounts department tries to establish what the correct selling price for the product should be having regard for all these changes.

Calculating changes in the value of money

There are many groups who are interested in this information. They include:

- employees and trade unions who claim increased wages because of a rise in the cost of living;

- employers, who wish to limit employee wage claims to the cost of living increase;

- public sector pensioners whose pension increases are based upon the rate of inflation;

- companies who wish to see whether the growth of profits has kept pace with inflation;

- the Government, who is concerned with the impact of inflation upon international trade, the balance of payments, savings, investment, and wage increases.

Changes in the value of money are reflected in the prices of goods and services we see around us every day. The RPI (this is also referred to as the 'cost of living' index) is the most commonly used measure of these changes. The index is calculated as follows:

- By selecting a base year on which to make price comparisons. The RPI in the base year is given the value of 100.

- Approximately 600 goods and services are selected. These represent a typical family's monthly pattern of expenditure. Each item in the index is given a weighting which reflects its importance in the average household budget.

- The list of goods is priced at monthly intervals – approximately 130,000 observations (i.e. prices) for the 600 goods and services are collected each month by the Department of Employment.

- The percentage change in price for each item (since the base date) is then calculated. This, when multiplied by its weighting, provides the figure which is included (along with the calculations made for all other goods and services) in the RPI.

Let us take a simple example and assume that the average family spends its money on just three items – food, shelter, and clothing which have doubled, trebled, and quadrupled respectively in price over the previous period. Let us further assume that food accounts for 50 per cent of the family budget, shelter 30 per cent and clothing 20 per cent. To obtain the new average price level we multiply each price index by its weighting.

	Weight	New Price index (last year = 100)	
Food	0.5 (50%)	200	100
Shelter	0.3 (30%)	300	90
Clothing	0.2 (20%)	400	80
	Average price level		270

The average price level has risen by 170 per cent in the past period. The rise is smaller than that for two of the items in the index – shelter and clothing – because the item with the largest weighting – food – has only increased by a modest amount compared with the other two.

There are obvious drawbacks in the calculation of the RPI.

1 The choice of goods and their weighting is related to what the average family buys. People who do not fall into this group, and there are many of them, must realise that the RPI is only a general indication of how their cost of living has risen. In practice there are many families who find particular price increases very much more significant than the average price level (e.g. house mortgage interest).

2. Our tastes and therefore expenditure, change over time (see Fig. 6.3). For example, as a country's standard of living rises its inhabitants will spend less on food and more on clothing, shelter, transport, and leisure. In the UK the CSO changes the weightings on the cost of living index annually after undertaking a family expenditure survey. Over a long period of time the RPI has very little significance because the goods purchased and their weightings will be fundamentally different.

3. The RPI takes no account of variations in price or quality. There may be significant regional variations in prices with many remote districts paying considerably more for all kinds of goods and services. Improvements in quality may also account, at least partially, for an increase in the price of a product. Cars today, although higher in price than a few years ago, are considerably more fuel efficient, go longer between routine services, and are generally more reliable.

4. The present UK Government has argued that the RPI is not a fair indicator of changes in the cost of living because it does not

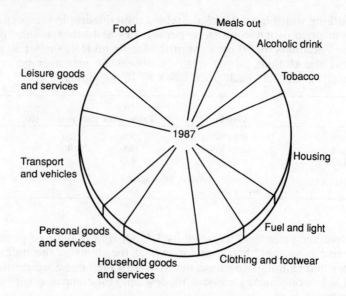

Source: Social Trends 1989

6.3 The weighting of the main categories of expenditure in the RPI

take into account the impact of direct taxes upon consumer purchasing power. When in 1979 the UK Government cut direct taxes but increased indirect taxes, from 8 or 12½ per cent to 15 per cent, the immediate effect was to raise the cost of living by 3½ percentage points. Yet had the RPI been adjusted for the reduction in direct taxes the increase would have been reduced to 1½ percentage points. This is obviously of importance where the index is used for wage-bargaining purposes. To show the impact of direct taxes and social security benefits (for which a similar argument applied) the UK Government introduced a new index termed the Taxes and Price Index (TPI). This showed the increase in pre-tax income which was necessary to maintain living standards, having regard to not only increases in prices but changes in tax allowances and rates. Between 1983 and 1988 the TPI was lower than the RPI. In August 1988 it was approximately two percentage points lower than the RPI.

Causes of inflation

Cost push – imported inflation

The UK is a major trading nation. It is impossible, therefore, for the UK to avoid the effects of rising prices overseas. Increases in the prices of UK imports will be reflected in the costs of production of British industry and eventually (unless the industry absorbs the increased costs through improvements in efficiency) prices in the shops.

Most of the major changes in the RPI this century have been associated with changes in import prices. In 1920/21 import prices nearly halved and retail prices fell by over a quarter. Increases in import prices during the Second World War and the Korean War caused sharp increases in the UK cost of living. Similarly, it was the spectacular increase in oil prices together with the increased cost of raw materials and food in 1973/74 which was largely responsible for the high inflation rates of the 1970s.

But changes in import prices occur not only because of the actions of overseas producers. Changes may also be brought about by fluctuations in exchange rates. Thus a country which experiences balance of payments difficulties may seek to remedy the situation by devaluing the domestic currency against other currencies. The effect is to make that country's exports cheaper, but also – and in this context more importantly – to raise import prices.

Cost push – wage inflation

Many economists see excessive wage demands by strong unions as a major contributor to many inflationary situations. The argument is that powerful trade unions are able to obtain large increases for their members through the threat or use, of industrial action. Firms, too, it is argued, have been guilty in granting these increases in the belief that they could be passed on to the consumer.

The increase in wage costs would not be so worrying if there was a corresponding increase in productivity. An increase in wages would not then necessarily result in an increase in prices. Unfortunately, wage increases have seldom been accompanied by agreements designed to raise productivity. And even when productivity deals were negotiated the effect could be inflationary where other groups sought and obtained similar wage increases without improvements in productivity.

The Wage/Price Spiral

It is often said that inflation is self-perpetuating. The argument goes as follows. Wage increases are conceded by firms, who then pass these extra costs on to the consumers in the form of higher prices. These higher prices then form the basis for further wage claims, and

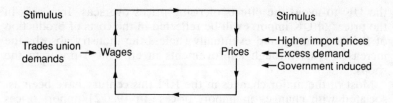

6.4 The wage/price spiral

---

so the process continues. In practice it is not necessarily an increase in wages which starts the process, it is just as likely to be an increase in prices.

Demand pull

Demand pull or excess demand inflation occurs where at a given price level buyers are keen to purchase more than the amount being produced. It is normally associated with near full-employment where the industry finds it difficult to expand production. It is then that the excess demand is absorbed by an increase in the price of goods generally (inflation).

Where there is full employment excess demand may also occur in the labour market. Firms find it difficult to fill current vacancies, and offer wages that are higher than those currently being paid. In this way employees are persuaded to switch employers. The only alternative open to the employer is to use less efficient labour. In either event prices are likely to be increased to cover the increased costs.

Demand-pull inflation can also arise below levels of full employment when it is often termed 'bottleneck inflation'. Inflation is caused by shortages of key workers or materials preventing production of the finished article. For example, since the Second World War a lack of investment in the training of skilled workers by business generally, and the erosion of wage differentials between skilled and unskilled workers (combined with an unwillingness on the part of young men to serve long apprenticeships) has resulted in shortages of skilled employees, especially in the engineering industry. As before, firms are likely to offer more money to obtain the resources they need.

Equally, in wartime as resources are absorbed into the war effort and production of consumption goods declines there is a tendency for prices to rise. It is likely that the Government in such a situation will introduce rationing and maximum prices to control the inflationary pressures. Unfortunately, once the controls are lifted wartime savings compete for the consumer goods available causing prices to rise.

Government induced

Government action may cause or fuel inflation in several ways. A switch from direct to indirect taxation will cause the RPI to rise. Even if increases in taxation do not affect the RPI the effect may be inflationary should employees attempt to offset the reduction in their standard of living by higher wage claims. Equally, the above-average rises in nationalised industry prices, council house rents, and local authority rates of recent years are a result of changes in government policy designed to curb public sector borrowing.

But by far the most telling attack on government policies has come from a group of economists labelled the 'monetarists' who believe the prime cause of inflation is increases in the supply of money. The basis of their argument rests upon the work of an economist, Irving Fisher, who propounded the equation $MV = PT$ otherwise called the quantity theory of money. Briefly M (the quantity of money) when multiplied by V (the velocity or speed at which it changes hands) is equal to P (the general level of prices) $\times$ T (the number of transactions or output). Monetarists argue that V is relatively constant and that therefore increases in the supply of money will result in either an increase in T (output) or at full employment by rising prices (P).

Monetarists believe that Government attempts to maintain full employment through budget deficits have over-stimulated the economy by ignoring the deficit's expansionary effect on money supply (commonly defined as notes and coins together with bank deposits).

A budgetary deficit can be financed in a number of ways. Long-term government stock may be sold to members of the public – a method which merely transfers money from the public to the State and does not involve an increase in money supply. It is all too easy, however, for the Government to avoid this increase in indebtedness by creating new money – that is, printing more pound notes or dollar bills. This was the start of the German hyperinflation of 1923/24. Closer to home, the UK Government expanded notes and coins in circulation with the general public threefold during the 1970s.

An even greater impact on money supply arises when the Government sells Treasury bills to finance the deficit. In the hands of the banking system Treasury bills are almost the same as cash and may be used to increase lending. For each £1 of Treasury bills held the banks can lend up £7 to the public. Monetarists have amassed a large amount of statistical evidence to prove the link between money

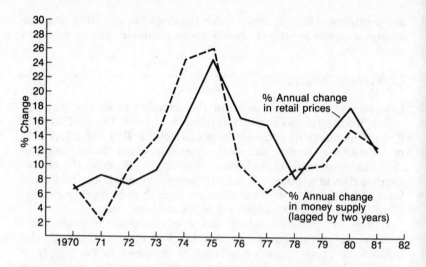

6.5 Comparison of annual changes in retail prices and money supply

supply and inflation. If we accept their argument that the increase in money supply takes approximately two years to work through the system before appearing as higher prices, there does appear to be a remarkable correlation between the two for the UK between 1970 and 1980 (see Fig. 6.5).

Stagflation

In a study of the UK economy between 1862 and 1958, Professor A W Phillips found there was a close correlation between the rate of change in wages and prices and unemployment (see Fig. 6.6). The ability of labour to increase wages depended upon the level of unemployment. When unemployment was high labour bargaining power was reduced, and so were increases in wages. Indeed, at times during the period wages were stable or actually fell. But as unemployment fell annual increases in wages rose. In short, the rate of increase in wages was inversely related to unemployment. Put another way, there was a trade-off between inflation and unemployment. When inflation was low unemployment was high and vice versa. Phillip's work suggested that an unemployment level of between 5 and 6 per cent could be sufficient to guarantee stable prices.

From around 1970 though, the relationship between inflation and unemployment has broken down. Many Western economies have experienced far greater annual increases in wages and prices for a given

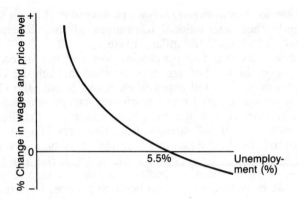

6.6 The Phillips curve

level of unemployment than previously. For this new experience the term 'stagflation' has been coined by putting together STAGnation and inFLATION.

Diagrammatically we can say that the Phillips curve has shifted bodily to the right. While the reasons for the shift are not completely understood the following possibilities have been suggested:
1 By reason of age and skills large numbers of the unemployed may be unemployable. The problems of full employment therefore becomes apparent at higher levels of unemployment.
2 Trade unions have discovered that their bargaining power is not so greatly affected by high levels of unemployment as was once thought.
3 Higher unemployment pay and social security benefits cushion the worker from the effects of unemployment.
4 Workers are now taking into account the movement of prices when negotiating wage rises.

The control of inflation

Government action which is designed to reduce the speed at which prices are rising is termed 'deflation'. Deflationary action may take one of three forms, fiscal policy, monetary policy. or direct controls such as a prices and incomes policy. Commonly, the policies are used in conjunction with one another in what has become known as a 'package deal'. The aim of the package deal was to affect, through a whole series of measures, all parts of the economy simultaneously, and to convince businessmen, financiers, investors, foreign governments, and other international institutions of the Government's determination to reduce the inflation rate.

Fiscal policy acts to reduce purchasing power within the economy. It will act upon the level of aggregate demand through the Government's revenue-raising and expenditure plans. Should the Government wish to siphon off excess purchasing power and reduce inflationary pressures it will plan for a budget surplus – that is, raising more revenue than it will spend during that year. To do this the Chancellor of the Exchequer may decide to reduce government spending but maintain taxation at its current level. But a substantial proportion of government expenditure is planned several years in advance and in consequence is difficult to reduce. It is therefore more likely that the Government will hold its expenditure at present levels (or merely make modest reductions) and increase taxation instead.

Monetary policy aims to curb inflation in two ways. First by announcing monetary targets in advance it acts upon people's expectations regarding future levels of inflation. Should the public expect inflation to fall trade unions may moderate wage claims yet still preserve their members' living standards. Similarly, firms need not increase prices by as much to achieve a predetermined level of profitability. Secondly, by controlling its own borrowing requirement, and the activities of the banking system the Government can achieve a reduction in money-supply growth, reducing demand for both goods and labour.

Direct controls Governments have been reluctant to use monetary and fiscal policy to reduce inflation. To have the economy working at below full capacity is a waste of valuable resources. Deflation also damages business confidence, retards economic growth, and implies a rejection of the commitment to full employment.

Direct controls on prices, or incomes, and at times both, have been the most common alternative. The controls which may be statutory or voluntary seek to restrain price or wage rises, thus breaking the wage – price spiral and moderating the rate of inflation. The British experience of such policies does not hold out much hope for their success. For virtually all of the period 1960–80 some form of control on prices or incomes was in operation. While the policies achieved some short-term success, in the longer term they failed to prevent the UK from having a higher rate of inflation than her major trading partners.

To be successful the policy had to be accepted by both employers and unions. Yet employers disliked having their pricing policy determined by the Government while unions were reluctant to surrender their right to free collective bargaining. Acceptance was often grudging and once the period of restraint was over both parties took steps to make up lost ground. Lastly, policies were seen to be inequitable. Those who had obtained a large pay increase just before the introduction of wage restraint gained against all other groups of workers. Moreover, pay policies often hit workers in the public sector harder than those in private industry – the Government wishing to lead by example.

Examination questions

1 Explain the possible effects of inflation on a manufacturing company including those arising from Government attempts at inflation control. What steps might a company take to counter the problems you have identified? *(AEB)*

2 Identify and discuss the likely effects on a small business of a combination of a high rate of inflation and high interest rates. *(AEB)*

3 (a) Briefly explain how you would measure the rate of inflation.
  (b) Discuss the likely consequences for your company, a UK-based washing machine manufacturer, of a significant increase in the rate of inflation.
  (c) What policy measures might you expect a company retailing your products to adopt in reaction to this change? *(CAMB 1988)*

4 You are given the following information:

Item	1983 price (=100)	1984 price	Price Relative
Fish (can)	40 pence	60 pence	150
Bread (rolls)	12½ pence	12½ pence	100
Lemonade (can)	15 pence	12 pence	80
Wine	400 pence	500 pence	125
			$455 \div 4 = 113.75$

'Prices have increased on average in 1984 by 13.75% in comparison with 1983.'
  (a) Comment on the above index.
  (b) Discuss *critically* possible uses of the Retail Price Index. *(CAMB 1985)*

5 Measures taken to control inflation injure individuals and firms far more than the problem those measure are designed to cure. Discuss.

6 Inflation has been described as the scourge of the twentieth century. How far would you agree with this statement?

Chapter 7

The problem of unemployment

Employment in the UK

The collection of information on the British labour market is the responsibility of the Department of Employment. Such information will be used in both manpower and economic planning. Thus, information on vacancies available, and industries which are expanding employment will have implications for the courses run in government skill centres and further and higher education. Equally, unemployment statistics may be used to make a case for giving help to a particular region or group of employees.

The working population of the UK is approximately 28.3 million – about half the total UK population. From Fig. 7.1 we can see that about 75 per cent of the total workforce are employees in employment. The other two major groups are the self-employed and the unemployed. However, it is not true to say that the working population comprises all men and women between the ages of 16 and 65 (60 in the case of women). 15 per cent of the total workforce between these ages (33.5 million) are termed economically inactive. The reasons why so many people fail to seek work are shown in Table 7.1.

Table 7.1 Causes of Economic Inactivity

	Men %	**Women** %	**Total** %
Long term sick/disabled	8	7	15
Looking after home	0	44	44
Full time student	8	7	15
Retired	4	2	6
Other	7	13	20
Total	27	73	100

Source: *Social Trends 1989*

Nor does the working population comprise solely of people aged 16 to 65. Many self-employed business people, judges and doctors will continue to work after normal retirement age. In 1987 it was

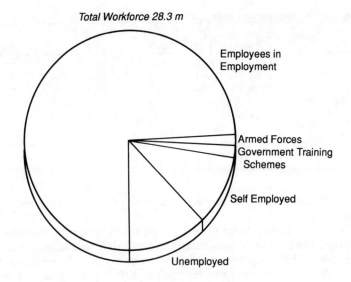

Total Workforce 28.3 m

Employees in
Employment

Armed Forces
Government Training
Schemes

Self Employed

Unemployed

Source: Employment Gazette

7.1 Analysis of the UK working population 1987

estimated that approximately seven per cent of those over retirement age were still economically active.

The proportion of people who are economically active out of the
population of working age is shown in Table 7.2. Two trends stand
out:

- Male activity rates have declined in all age groups. This is not
surprising. The demand for a more highly skilled workforce has
persuaded many young people to study full time for higher
qualifications. Older men are retiring earlier, primarily because
of improved pension schemes.
- Female activity rates have expanded strongly between 1961
and 1986. In 1961 women formed 32 per cent of the working
population. In 1986 the comparable figure was 45 per cent.
Several reasons are advanced for this:
- Women have more control over their lives now due to contra-
ception. The advent of the smaller family has given married
women more spare time. Spare time has also been increased by
the large number of labour-saving gadgets available.

101

Table 7.2 A comparison of male and female activity rates

	Female 1961	1971	1986	Male 1961	1971	1986
15–19	71.2	55.9	71.1	74.9	70.9	73.7
20–24	61.8	60.1	69.2	91.9	89.9	84.5
25–44	40.3	50.6	67.2	98.5	97.9	94.0
45–54 (women)			70.2			
45–59 (men)						88.0
55–59 (women)	41.4	57.4		96.8	94.5	
60–64 (men)			51.7			53.4

Source: *Social trends*

- Social attitudes have moved in favour of the working wife and mother.
- There has been a large growth in the number of jobs available to women since 1961 – particularly in the public and services sector. Between 1983 and 1988 nearly one million new jobs were created – virtually all taken up by female employees – full and part-time.
- Since 1980 all industrial sectors have expanded their use of part-time employees. A survey conducted by the Department of Employment (1980) found that many women welcomed part-time employment as a mean of combining paid work with family responsibilities. If we look at part-time employment by sector (Fig. 7.2) we see that the service industries (remember it is the service sector that is expanding and that women are twice as likely to be employed in a service industry as manufacturing) employing 11 million people offer over 40 per cent of jobs on a part-time basis.

From the employer's view part-time employees give the organisation great flexibility to adjust to changing market conditions. In the UK contracting industries have reduced full time employment more quickly than part-time employment while expanding industries are employing a greater proportion of part-timers. (For other examples of the flexibility that employers are trying to achieve in their workforce see p. 370.)

Let us now turn to look at where these people are employed. Economic development is characterised by changes in the structure of industry, and therefore changes in employment opportunities too. Fig. 7.3 shows the changes which occurred in the UK between 1901 and 1987. First we note the demise of employment in the primary sector, largely due to the decline in agriculture. Today agriculture employs only 1.7 per cent of the working population, in 1901 it was over 10 per cent. Secondly, we can see a small but significant decrease in the secondary sector, and lastly a large increase in tertiary employment. The experience of the UK is not unique. Similar

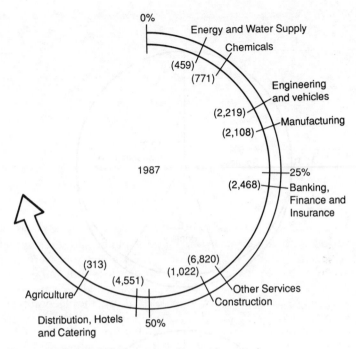

0%
Energy and Water Supply
Chemicals
(459)
(771)
Engineering and vehicles
(2,219)
Manufacturing
(2,108)
1987
25%
(2,468)
Banking, Finance and Insurance
(313)
(6,820)
(1,022)
(4,551)
Agriculture
Other Services
Construction
Distribution, Hotels and Catering
50%

(Figures in brackets indicate total employment by sector)

Source: Social trends in 1989 (adapted)

7.2 Part-time employees as a percentage of all employment by sector

changes have been well documented in other industrialised countries.

Deindustrialisation

Deindustrialisation can be defined in two ways. First it can be seen as the decline of the manufacturing sector in relation to other sectors in the economy – see Fig. 7.3. Second it can be seen as the inability of manufacturing to compete successfully in home or export markets. The UK share of world manufacturing exports has fallen from 25 per cent in 1950 to eight per cent in 1987.

Although most developed economies are experiencing the same movement from manufacturing to service industries it is the speed with which this has happened in the UK that is considered worrying. Even so, most countries are concerned about the potential damage

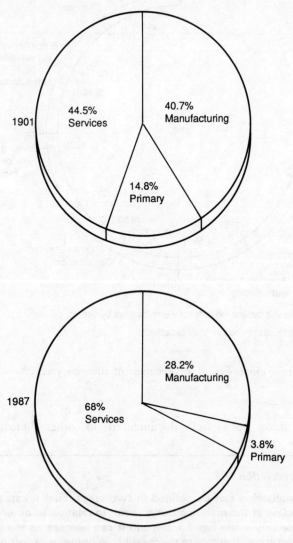

Source: Department of Employment

7.3 Percentage of the total labour force employed by sector 1901–1987

deindustrialisation may inflict on their economy. In the UK we should consider the impact on:

1 The balance of payments. How can a developed country maintain the same level of imports when manufacturing exports are declining?

2 Economic Growth. First, many service industries are dependent upon manufacturing industry for their existence. Second, manufacturing productivity has traditionally been higher than in the service sector, thus a decline in the manufacturing will reduce overall growth rates.

3 Employment. The service sector is unable to absorb the surplus labour redundant to manufacturing. Moreover, many jobs now being created are part-time – and for women. The result is the growth of long term (and particularly male) unemployment.

Many reasons have been advanced for deindustrialisation in the UK. They include:

- The UK is producing the wrong goods, concentrating on traditional (and in many cases declining) industries rather than innovative 'high tech' industries.

- For much of the 1980s the UK has been uncompetitive in world export markets due to the high foreign exchange value of sterling.

- The low level of capital investment and R and D expenditure by UK firms.

- The expansion of the government sector starving manufacturing of the resources it needed for expansion during the 1960s and 1970s.

- The growth of manufacturing capacity in developing countries, and the consequent increase in competition.

- The UK has not paid enough attention to 'non price' competition.

As regards the growing importance of the services sector we may point to the fact that until recently there were fewer opportunities for technical innovation – this sector was labour intensive and productivity low. Between 1961 and 1981 the most important reason for growth in the services sector was the expansion of the Education and National Health Services, each of whom doubled their employees during this period. Indeed, the whole public sector increased in size from employing 23 per cent of the working population to 31 per cent during this period. However, with privatisation and the contracting out of services the size of the public sector is now 25 per cent.

The expansion of the services sector has had important implications for the employment of women. Women are twice as likely to be employed in the service as the manufacturing sector. More significantly the education and health services have traditionally recruited a high proportion of women.

Unemployment

In 1944 the British wartime coalition Government issued a White Paper entitled *Employment Policy*. This committed all post-war Governments to the maintenance of a high and stable level of employment. Full employment was defined as a situation where 97 per cent of those available for work were, in fact, employed.

For nearly thirty years after the Second World War British Governments' attempts to achieve full employment were extremely successful. The mass unemployments of the 1930s (when unemployment in the UK reached a peak of 22 per cent in 1932) seemed to be a thing of the past. Jobs were plentiful, workers could pick and choose between them. In many areas there were more jobs than workers available to fill them. It was not until the end of the 1960s that unemployment as a percentage of the working population rose above two per cent, nor was it until 1975 that unemployment topped one million workers or four per cent.

Indeed, it could be said that post-war government policies were too successful. The use of fiscal policy to iron out the periodic variations in the demand for goods and services often created a situation of over-full employment. This caused several problems. Inflationary trends were exacerbated by workers using their enhanced bargaining power to push for higher wages. Business people were willing to grant these claims in the knowledge that at least part of the extra cost could be passed on to the consumer in the form of higher prices.

Shortages of labour also had their impact on the balance of payments. First, the high prices of UK goods reduced their competitiveness in the international market. All too often the imported product was cheaper than the home-produced equivalent. Second, shortages of labour prevented UK industry from producing the quantity of goods required by the home market – the deficit again being made good by imports.

Economic growth too was hampered by the emphasis on full employment. First the stop-go policy (see p. 167) associated with the maintenance of full employment reduced entreprenurial confidence and therefore the willingness to invest. Secondly, in so far as wages rose faster than prices the profit margins of businesses were squeezed, reducing the money available to invest in new improved machinery or new expanding industries.

Between 1973 and 1986 unemployment grew rapidly from 1.7 per cent to 13.5 per cent. Fig. 7.4 shows that the major surges in un-

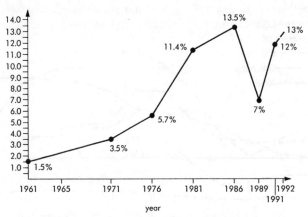

Source: Economic Progress Report October 1987
Annual Abstract of Statistics 1991 (adjusted)

7.4 Unemployment in the UK since 1971

employment coincided with the oil price increases of 1973 and 1979 and the consequent recessions.

Rising unemployment during this period was also experienced by most other developed nations. However, as Fig. 7.5 shows, the growth in unemployment in these economies was slower than in the UK. Several reasons have been put forward to explain the above average rise in UK unemployment post 1979. Chief among them would be:

● *Overmanning*. In 1978 UK manufacturing GDP was 27 per cent – the same as several other OECD countries. Yet, manufacturing employment in the UK was 30 per cent of total employment compared with 25 per cent in the other OECD countries.

● *Exchange Rates*. The discovery and subsequent exploitation of North Sea oil caused an increase in the demand which led to sterling exchange rates appreciating between 1977 and 1982. UK manufacturing exports were in consequence less competitive abroad.

● *UK Government Policy*. The Government's priority was to control inflation by means of high domestic interest rates. This had the effect of reducing demand still further in a recessionary situation.

Since 1986 unemployment in OECD countries has fallen. By 1988 UK unemployment had fallen to eight per cent reflecting the faster productivity growth experienced in Britain than other countries.

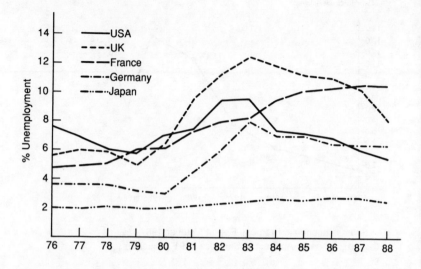

7.5 An international comparison of unemployment

The incidence of unemployment

If all workers were to experience unemployment equally each would become unemployed several times during our working lives. In practice, the incidence of unemployment is very uneven. The following factors are important in determining the likelihood of becoming unemployed.

1. Occupation: Many professional and skilled manual workers never experience unemployment while others, particularly those who are unskilled or provide personal services, experience considerable periods out of work. It is estimated that five per cent of workers in the UK account for 75 per cent of all unemployment.

2. Age: Reductions in unemployment recently have benefited two groups – women and under 25s. There is a hard core of male unemployment (55 per cent of all men unemployed have been out of work between one and three years) which rises with age. Two-thirds of unemployed men over 50 have been unemployed for more than a year.

3. Sex: Male unemployment is consistently higher than female unemployment. In 1987 male unemployment was 11.9 per cent compared with women's 7.3 per cent (this may be explained in part by the unemployment figures being based on the numbers claiming unemployment benefit).

4. *Ethnic group:* Members of the white population are much less likely to be unemployed than other ethnic groups holding similar qualifications. Broadly speaking, 'other ethnic groups' are twice as likely to be unemployed as members of the white population.

5 *Region:* Most countries have regions which are more prosperous than others. In the UK (January 1989) unemployment varied from five per cent in South East England to 16 per cent in Northern Ireland. Rates may also vary significantly within a region. For example the 1981 Census indicated that in the UK's major towns and cities male unemployment was 50 per cent higher in the inner city compared with surrounding areas.

Unemployment and its remedies

There are several categories of unemployment. It is important to distinguish between them as they have different causes and therefore require different treatment.

Transitional unemployment There will always be some people changing their jobs. Some will have been made redundant by their employers. Other people will leave one job, subsequently searching for and finding another one. These workers 'between' jobs may form a substantial proportion of the unemployed workforce in prosperous times and provide a pool of labour from which vacancies are filled. Indeed, it is very necessary for this pool of labour to exist so that industry can adapt to changed circumstances – for example increases in product demand, or labour to work 'new technology'.

This category will also include a number of people, who although classified as unemployed are not really seeking work and those who, through mental or physical disability, are unfit for work.

Government help to the transitionally unemployed has taken two forms:

- *Financial aid* – so that the unemployed person is not forced to accept the first job that comes his way, but may find a position which best fits his skills and aspirations.

- *Search aid* – information on current vacancies and an employment placement service speeds the process by which the unemployed person finds a job.

Seasonal unemployment This arises when the demand for labour varies throughout the year. For example, employment in the building, tourism, and agricultural industries may increase dramatically during the summer months.

The degree of unemployment in these industries can be lessened by having a small core of workers who are willing to work long hours in the peak season and accept short-time working at other times of the year. This core workforce may also be supplemented in busy times by casual workers. Thus students often find holiday jobs in hotels or on farms picking fruit. Such intermittent work may also suit other people who are unable to take up permanent employment. Attempts to reduce unemployment in seasonal trades often concentrate on developing the market for goods and services concerned – tourists may be persuaded to take holidays out of season through low prices, or perhaps advertising may persuade people to buy turkeys at times other than Christmas! Alternatively, it may be possible to combine two seasonal trades whose peak periods do not coincide.

Structural unemployment As with transitional unemployment (sometimes termed frictional unemployment) structural unemployment is caused by changes in the structure of industries. But whereas frictional unemployment is a situation in which the displaced workers will be absorbed into new jobs within a short time, structural unemployment may very well give rise to high levels of long-term unemployment.

A decline in demand has affected many of the industries on which Britain's prosperity was built. Thus the export of Lancashire's textile products were decimated by the growth of the cotton industry in the Far East. The increasing use of oil as a form of power has thrown many Welsh and Scottish miners out of work. Where the change is slow, labour can adjust to the changed circumstance satisfactorily. The workers who retire from the industry concerned are not replaced, those who are unfortunate enough to lose their jobs will find employment in new expanding industries. However, it is where the change is rapid that we have true structural unemployment. New expanding industries are unable to absorb all those made redundant. More importantly, and this is the key to structural unemployment, the jobs which are available may demand skills of a very different nature from those of the displaced worker.

Structural unemployment is often extremely localised. Where an industry is heavily concentrated in an area any downturn in the demand for its products is likely to have a dramatic affect on unemployment. Thus by 1934 the decline in the prosperity of the British coal-mining, shipbuilding, and cotton industries had resulted in unemployment of over 35 per cent in parts of Wales and 30 per cent in parts of northern England and Scotland (when the national average was $16\frac{1}{2}$ per cent). These exceptionally high unemployment rates reflect not only the collapse of work in the industry concerned, but also where these workers spent their wages. Employment in shops, clubs, transport – in virtually every walk of life – was affected as the reduction in purchasing power was felt in these regions.

This unemployment imbalance is still with us today. Regions such as Scotland, Wales, Northern Ireland, and northern England still suffer higher levels of unemployment than the rest of the country

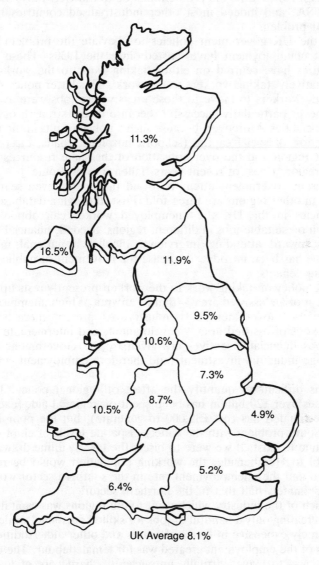

UK Average 8.1%

Source: Department of Employment

7.6 Comparative rates of unemployment in different regions of the UK 1988 (see Fig. 7.6). Nor is the problem unique to the UK. Italy, Sweden, the USA, and indeed most other industrialised countries have a similar problem.

In the UK government policies to alleviate the problem of regional unemployment have existed since the 1930s. These policy measures have centred on either 'taking work to the workers' or alternatively 'taking workers to the work'. This latter policy of persuading workers to move to those areas where jobs were available was never particularly successful, because of the strength of family and social ties. Moreover, because such a policy results in the under-utilisation of social capital (schools, hospitals, roads, etc.) in the donor region and the over-utilisation of the same resources in the host region it has, of recent years, fallen into disrepute.

Present government attempts to aid the unemployed search for work in other regions are three-fold. First, through a database of all vacancies in the UK the unemployed worker can obtain information on suitable jobs in different regions. Second, financial help is given toward attending interviews. Finally, a national mobility scheme has been introduced to ease the movement of public sector housing tenants.

The policy of 'taking work to the worker' presently rests upon the concept of an 'assisted area' – that is, an area of high unemployment where the Government aids industry. At present there are two categories of assisted area – development, and intermediate areas. Various financial incentives are given by the Government to encourage industrial investment (and therefore employment) in these areas.

It is difficult to quantify the affect of regional policy. In two decades over £20 billion has been spent on regional aid, (each job, it is estimated has cost £35,000 to generate), but the poor North, rich South problem with the widely disparate levels of employment continue to exist. If we were to bisect the UK by a line drawn from Bristol to Humberside, the working population would be roughly halved and the unemployment rate in the southern sector would be approximately half that of the northern sector.

Much of the industry which went to the regions was capital intensive, creating only a handful of jobs for skilled personnel while being extremely expensive in terms of grants and other aid. Additionally, much of the employment created was for female labour. The overall effect was to leave, virtually untouched, a hard core of unskilled male labour. Moreover, much of this industry has proved to be highly marginal in the recent recession as parent companies cut back on output. Since 1978 factories in these regions have closed at an alarming rate.

It is argued that regional aid in future should be:

- discretionary and depend upon the amount of employment created

- only available to firms moving into the region, rather than those already set up there.

thus making it considerably more cost effective.

Cyclical unemployment This type of unemployment arises because of variations in the general level of economic activity – the booms and slumps that are often termed the trade or business cycle. The UK has experienced these fluctuations since the Industrial Revolution. The complete cycle may vary in length between four and eight years. A decline in the general level of economic activity – when all businesses suffered a reduction in the demand for their goods and services – was the main cause of the mass unemployment during the 'Great Depression' of the 1930s. It was also a major factor in the recession of the 1980s.

The cost of unemployment

In 1981 the MSC estimated the cost of three million people unemployed to be £13.6 billion in lost output. The State also loses heavily when unemployment rises. Revenue from direct and indirect taxes falls while expenditure on social security payments increases. This was estimated to be £4,500 per unemployed worker in 1981.

It has also been suggested that there is a link between unemployment on the one hand and illness or anti-social behaviour on the other.

It is not only the UK that experiences the trade cycle. All industrialised and developing economies are similarly affected. Indeed, as economies have become more and more linked with one another the trade cycle has taken on an international character. Even in the nineteenth century fluctuations in economic activity among the major trading nations (USA, UK, France, West Germany) followed each other closely. The effects of an increase or decrease in the level of economic activity in one country are quickly transmitted to others.

The impact of a recession, for example, in the USA will rapidly be felt by all countries with whom she trades. Imports of raw materials and finished goods into the USA will be reduced, forcing the exporting nation to cut back on production and therefore employment. Similarly the expansion of economic activity in one country may, through its increased demand for imports, lead to the expansion of output and employment in other countries.

Since the 1930s the severity of the trade cycle has been mitigated by government action on the lines advocated by Lord Keynes. Briefly (this is discussed in more detail in Ch. 9 p. 163), Keynes believed that a government should regulate its spending so as to make up any deficiency in the level of aggregate or total demand needed to maintain full employment. Therefore, during a recession, the Government should expand its spending and conversely during a boom period reduce its spending.

But the traditional remedy is not available to the present UK Government. The Public Sector Borrowing Requirement (PSBR) and public spending are being restricted in order to control inflation. There are also serious doubts as to whether reflationary action by just one government would be successful in raising employment in that country, rather than being dissipated among many others. For these reasons the major thrust of the Government's attack on unemployment has been through a series of special employment measures. These measures are designed to:
- create jobs especially for young people and the long-term unemployed;
- subsidise the cost of employing a young worker thereby increasing their attractiveness to an employer;
- provide all unemployed 16-year-olds with a programme of education, training, and work experience;
- reduce the working population by encouraging early retirement;
- reduce unemployment by means of work-sharing.

Technological unemployment This is a special case of frictional unemployment. Economic growth and a rise in the standard of living are often based upon the introduction of new and improved methods of production. But all too often technological advance is a cause of unemployment – the worker's skills being rendered obsolete by the new technology. So, during the Industrial Revolution the process of mechanisation destroyed many skilled jobs, replacing them with a demand for unskilled labour to operate the machines.

This process continues today, though it is argued that the nature of technological advance has changed. Previously the displaced worker was able to find another job, even though it may not have suited his skills and may have resulted in a drop in wages. Today the introduction of microelectronic circuitry has resulted in many operations becoming highly automated. Many unskilled jobs are lost in the process of automation. A handful of skilled operatives can now control the production process which previously employed scores of semi-skilled or unskilled workers. As the process of computerisation and automation continues it will become increasingly difficult for the unskilled workers to find employment. Technological change will leave in its wake a force of unskilled workers who face the grim prospect of long-term unemployment.

Nor is it just the unskilled who are vulnerable. Automatic cash machines will reduce the demand for bank tellers, while in the office the photocopier and the word processor have already eliminated much of the necessity for routine typing. Moreover, the same machine which is used for word-processing may be used to maintain the book-keeping records, to send and receive electronic mail, or telex messages. In the not too distant future it is anticipated that voice typewriters capable of turning dictation directly into a page of finished text will be operating in many offices.

Many people have voiced concern about the impact of microelectronics on unemployment. Yet the overall effect is uncertain. As we have already seen many jobs will be lost, but others may be created. In particular, the reduction in cost of many goods through using the 'new technology' will increase demand for those goods (and therefore the employment of the people who make them). Extra jobs will be created in the electronics industry to satisfy demand for microelectronic technology. We will see the development of many new products incorporating microelectronic technology. Lastly, increasing wealth and leisure time will enhance demand for many services in the tertiary sector – an area which is labour intensive.

The pessimists who foresee a net job loss arising on the introduction of microelectronic technology may be correct in their prognosis, but the impact of a failure to implement it would be even worse – for it is certain that our competitors will adopt the new technology. A delay or refusal on our part to implement microelectronic technology will mean that British goods rapidly become uncompetitive in world markets, with dire consequences for employment and our standard of living.

Measuring unemployment

Since October 1982 unemployment in the UK has been measured by calculating the number of people who claim benefit as a result of unemployment. Two classifications are produced monthly. Unemployment is first analysed on a *regional* basis – that is, the region in which the unemployed person claims benefit. Secondly, the *industrial* classification indicates the industry in which the unemployed person last worked. A further classification, *occupational*, showing the occupations the unemployed wish to enter, is published quarterly, while unemployment classified by *age* is issued twice a year.

Two major groups are not included in the unemployment statistics. First there are those who although actively seeking work – full or part-time – are for some reason unable to claim benefits. The 1971 Census of Production estimated that nearly a quarter of a million women (the majority married and supported by their husbands) were searching for work but were not included in the unemployment statistics. Secondly, school-leavers – young people seeking their first job – are also excluded.

There are, however, other factors which serve artificially to inflate the statistics. For example the figures include those who fraudently unemployed – that is, claiming benefit but at the same time having some form of undeclared employment. Moreover, there are also those who are unsuited or unwilling to work (though there is little evidence to show that this group is as large as some people would have us believe).

The Department of Employment makes adjustment to the crude figures collected monthly to allow for seasonal factors. For example, in the summer months unemployment will fall with the expansion of tourism and building work. Yet this apparent fall may in fact mask a rising trend in unemployment. Unemployment figures are therefore adjusted to eliminate seasonal variations and reveal the real trend.

The Department of Employment Job Centres and Employment Offices also maintain a register of vacancies based upon information supplied to them by local employers. Each month the *Employment Gazette* publishes statistics on unfilled vacancies, classifying the information by industry and region. An occupational analysis is also published quarterly. The published statistics are, however, not a complete record of all unfilled vacancies in the country – employers do not always recruit through the Employment Offices. They may prefer to use press advertisements or private employment agencies instead.

But taken together the monthly statistics on unemployment and vacancies are a reasonable barometer of the state of the labour market. As business activity falls, for example, we would expect to see a rise in the level of unemployment and a fall in the vacancies notified to Employment Offices. Equally, when the level of economic activity rises the opposite occurs.

By measuring vacancies as a proportion of unemployment, vacancies/unemployment, it is possible to obtain a good indication of the extent of the unemployment problem. Where the result is a figure close to 1.0 unemployment is not so worrying for there are nearly as many vacancies as there are unemployed. As the figure declines though, our concern grows because the supply of labour outstrips the demand. The great advantage of this technique is that it may be used to measure the state of the labour market not only for the whole country but also for a region, industry, or occupation.

Examination questions

1 What do you understand by full employment? Can it be achieved?

2 Many countries have regions in which unemployment is significantly higher than the national average. How has this come about, and what can we do to remedy the situation?

3 How is the level of unemployment measured? How accurate is the measure?

4 While all forms of unemployment cause concern, some give rise to greater concern than others. Discuss.

5 'Large expenditure and uncertain results'. How far do you believe that this is an adequate summary of Government attempts to reduce unemployment by means of fiscal policy?

6 Explain what you understand by the phrase 'the cost of unemployment'? How might policies to combat (a) long term and (b) short term unemployment differ in emphasis?

7 Outline the different forms of unemployment which exist and explain the significance of unemployment for national economic policy.

Chapter 8

International trade

The importance of trade

The principle of specialisation plays an important role both within an economy and internationally. Within an economy we find it more efficient if people specialise and gain expertise in a particular trade of profession. Firms, too, find it profitable to produce only a limited number of products, while even regions may become famous for certain products or services.

The principle of regional specialisation is easily extended to specialisation between countries. International trade then, exists to iron out the deficiencies and surpluses of goods between countries.

A certain amount of trade takes place because of the uneven distribution of raw materials throughout the world. Australia is well endowed with mineral deposits, the UK has North Sea oil, while South Africa has gold.

Variations in climate may also result in trade. It is impossible for the UK to grow those products needing a subtropical climate such as tea or coffee. Equally it is impossible for subtropical countries to grow those crops needing a temperate climate.

Yet the greater part of trade takes place for neither of these reasons. Countries find that they are more efficient at producing some goods than others. This efficiency is reflected in their costs of production and the final prices charged. It is logical for countries to concentrate on making the goods at which they are most efficient, exporting the surplus and using the foreign currency earned to purchase those goods which other countries can produce more cheaply.

Taking the simplified example of two countries producing two products, the theory of comparative advantage shows the benefits of specialisation clearly. Using the same resources, Canada and the UK can produce either of the following:

	Country	
	Canada (units)	UK (units)
Agricultural products	6	4
Machinery	4	8

Now the UK and Canada need both agricultural products and machinery. Without specialisation and presuming both devote half their resources to each product we reach the following situation:

	Canada	UK	Total production
Agricultural products	3	2	5
Machinery	2	4	6

Let us now assume that trade takes place and each country specialises on that product in which they are most efficient and have a comparative advantage. Canada will specialise in the production of agricultural products because she can make six units of agricultural products and Britain only four units. Conversely, the UK, using the same amount of resources, can produce eight units of machinery whereas Canada produces four units. The UK will therefore concentrate on the production of machinery. The effect, as shown below, is that world production of both goods has been increased by specialisation:

	Canada	UK	Total production
Agricultural products	6	–	6
Machinery	–	8	8

Now Canada needs machinery and previously it cost her three units of agricultural products to produce two units of machinery. As long as trade results in her obtaining more than two units of machinery for her three units of agricultural product she has benefited from specialisation and international trade.

The UK has concentrated on the production of machinery because she can produce two units of machinery for each unit of agricultural product, and as long as she obtains more than one unit of agricultural product for two units of machinery she also will have benefited.

If we assume a trading ratio of one unit of agricultural product to one unit of machinery, then both countries are satisfied, and the final position may be something like this:

	Canada	UK	Total production
Agricultural products	3 (6–3)	3	6
Machinery	3	5 (8–3)	8

Even where one country has an absolute advantage – that is, it is better at producing both goods, trade will still be beneficial, as long as there are differences in the relative efficiencies of production. The more efficient country will produce that product at which it is most efficient, leaving the other to produce the good in which it has the least disadvantage.

Even in the unlikely event of two countries having the same cost structure, trade may still be advantageous if specialisation leads to economies of scale and falling prices.

Free trade therefore, is encouraged because it increases real output throughout the world. It provides consumers with a wider choice of goods and a higher standard of living, while the worker has greater employment possibilities. Trade also speeds the introduction of new advanced technology with its potential for even greater efficiency.

Restrictions on trade

Although we have seen a liberalisation of trade in the years since the Second World War all countries still restrict trade in some way. Traditionally, tariffs and quotas have been the most important means of controlling imports. A tariff is a tax imposed on imports. It may be levied on an *ad valorem* basis – that is, a percentage of the value of the import, or alternatively on a specific basis as an amount per unit – £1 per bottle of wine. The tariff has the advantage of producing revenue for the Government though this is not normally the main reason for imposing it.

A quota is a quantitative restriction on imports. The restriction may be in terms of units to be imported (.g. 10,000 cars only) or the value of imports (only £20 m. worth of textiles).

More recently, concern has been growing at the increasing number of non-tariff or administrative barriers on trade. It is impossible to catalogue a complete list, but among the major restrictions are:

- establishment of norms and standards different from those used elsewhere;

- discrimination in public sector purchasing;

- bonds to be deposited with the government of the importing company to cover claims against those goods;

- retesting of products in the importing country;

- tax discrimination in favour of local manufacturer;

- slow customs clearance procedures;

- publicity campaigns, e.g. buy British, or in some cases buy British last!

- foreign exchange controls;
- embargoes.

Reasons for limiting trade

1.   Countries may argue that it is necessary to *protect home industry because it is newly established*. Young industry may very well need protection initially. Neither labour skills nor production systems are fully developed and their costs of production are therefore higher than older-established industries in other countries. Yet the danger of protecting these 'infant' industries is that they come to rely on the high tariff barrier and never become fully efficient (and paradoxically until they compete internationally in a larger market they will never obtain those economies of scale necessary to become more efficient).

2.   A country for *strategic reasons*, may decide to ensure the continuity of supplies for certain products. Thus steel is necessary to the production of so many items that even if other countries (e.g. West Germany) have a comparative advantage we should not allow free trade to put our own steel industry out of business. We are willing to accept and even encourage high-cost domestic production.

3.   *Surplus goods* produced in one country are sometimes *dumped* in another country. By dumping we are referring to the practice of selling goods in a foreign market at a price less than that which is charged in the home market. The aim of dumping is to protect the price of the product in the home market by restricting the amount available there. The danger for the recipient is that the home-based industry may be forced out of business (with a consequent loss of jobs) and that the country is then reliant on imports whatever the price charged.

The price of protection

Although some people in a country will gain from protection, others in the same country will lose far more. The European Community's Common Agricultural Policy (CAP) results in European consumers paying up to four times the world price for certain products. Yet the farmer who produces these products certainly is not four times better off. CAP policy results in inefficient farmers producing products which would be better supplied by farmers in other countries.

It is not only European Community consumers who will lose from these artificially high prices designed to ensure 'agricultural self-sufficiency'. Surpluses – 'wine lakes', 'butter mountains' – often occur. **These surpluses will be disposed of on the world market thus depressing world prices and damaging the livelihoods of far more efficient producers.**

But perhaps the most telling indictment of protectionism came from a UK report into the Multi Fibre Arrangement (MFA) – a set of bilateral agreements limiting trade in textiles and clothing. The conclusion of the report was that, as far as the UK was concerned, the abolition of the MFA would result in a reduction in 'textiles' prices of five per cent, the unemployment of between 10 and 50,000 textile workers, but because consumers were £500 million better off (at 1982 prices), they would spend that money in other ways, and consequently total unemployment would actually fall by 37,000. Yet the MFA still exists!

4. *Unfair competition* also arises from the subsiding of an exports industry by a government. Thus Eastern European countries, anxious for foreign exchange to buy Western technology, often subsidise and sell goods at less than their true cost. Once again the importing country obtains an immediate benefit in the form of cheaper goods, but this may be outweighed by the monopoly position established by the exporter in the longer term.

5. *In times of economic depression*, when unemployment is high and demand for goods and services is low, governments often impose restrictions on trade. The argument is that by restricting imports we are providing jobs for workers in our domestic industry. This tactic may succeed if we can persuade our competitors not to take retaliatory measures. In the more likely event of our competitors taking similar measures against us the demand for our goods and services is once more reduced and unemployment rises. Thus during the Great Depression 'beggar-my-neighbour' policies reduced international trade by 67 per cent between January 1929 and June 1933.

6. Where a country experiences an *adverse balance of payments*, restriction on imports may provide temporary relief. The imposition of a tariff on imported goods will reduce demand for imports while at the same time increasing the demand for home-produced substitutes. As before we have to persuade our trading partners that such measures are both necessary and short term if we wish to avoid those retaliatory measures.

General Agreement on Tariffs and Trade

The General Agreement on Tariffs and Trade (GATT) is a multi-lateral treaty which is recognised by ninety countries accounting for more than 80 per cent of world trade. The basic aim of GATT is to encourage free trade and thereby higher economic growth and rising standards of living. Countries who recognise the treaty accept that:

- Members should not discriminate against trade with another.

- Where protection of home industry is necessary it should be by tariff alone, thereby exposing the true extent of the protection.

- Where changes in the structure of tariffs are contemplated, trading partners should be consulted.

Countertrade

Countertrade is a form of barter between firms (or governments) in different countries. In essence, imports from Country A into Country B are paid for by export from B to A. For example, America sold Saudi Arabia planes and received oil in return.

The resurgence of countertrade in the twentieth century can be traced to the 1950s when communist countries in Eastern Europe found it difficult to pay for Western goods. Their own currency was unacceptable because it was not freely convertible and their reserves of western currencies were very limited. They therefore insisted that firms wishing to do business with them accepted their goods in payment.

Since that time countertrade has increased. The world debt crisis has meant that many firms dealing with (say) a South American country are unwilling to finance that transaction. Indeed, some heavily indebted countries where interest on loans is a major proportion of total exports may be unable to finance imports at all. Hence countertrade is their only means of obtaining foreign products.

From the 'western' companies viewpoint countertrade is a mixed blessing. The company has made a sale but receives other products in payment which, in turn, have to be sold. The lengths to which they have to go are well illustrated by the US tractor company which received iron ore in exchange from Venezuela in return for a shipment of construction vehicles. The iron ore was sold to Rumania who paid with men's suits. These suits were eventually sold in London. The proceeds were then converted into dollars.

It is not surprising therefore that specialist institutions such as export houses have set themselves up as brokers. Because of their contacts round the world they are more capable of disposing of countertraded products. They will purchase such goods, often at a high discount, and, using their expertise, sell at a higher price.

The attitude of GATT and other international trade organisations is

to condemn countertrade. They argue that countertrade (with its bilateral trade deals) is inferior to free multi-lateral trade. It is often a means of selling inferior quality over-priced goods. The producers of such goods, in a freely competitive market, would be displaced by more efficient producers.

- Discussions should take place at regular intervals with a view to further liberalisation of trade.

- Developing countries are not expected fully to reciprocate the reduction in trade values by developed countries but, as their economies grow stronger they should participate more fully in the GATT framework of rights and obligations.

There have been seven rounds of multi-lateral trade negotiations completed since 1947. The seventh – the Tokyo (1979) round took five years and ended with the industrialised nations agreeing to reduce tariffs by one-third. It is difficult to evaluate the effect of the agreement on world trade because of the impact of the early 80s recession and the growth of non-tariff barriers.

The eighth round of negotiations (the Uruguay round) started in 1986 and is scheduled to last four years. The UK is particularly interested in moves to liberalise trade in services.

Members of GATT realise that the process of trade liberalisation is a long-term objective and that customs unions or free-trade areas are a means to this end. Numerous free-trade areas and customs unions have been created since 1948, mainly among the members of GATT, e.g. the EC (Common Market), the Caribbean Economic Community (Caricom), the Association of South East Asian Nations (ASEAN).

The European Community

The EC is a customs union, that is, it has abolished internal customs duties to create a single market for all those countries who are members. Countries outside the customs union are met by a common external tariff whichever member country they are exporting to. The major distinction between a customs union and a free-trade area is the existence of the common external tariff. Thus the European Free Trade Association (EFTA), of which the UK was once a member, although it has abolished tariffs between members allows its members to decide upon their own level of tariffs for imports from outside the association. By this means the UK was able, while a member of EFTA to continue its system of Commonwealth preferences.

Britain joined the EEC in 1973 after two earlier unsuccessful attempts in 1963 and 1966. Attitudes to joining the Common Market have always been divided. Proponents of the Common Market pointed to the advantages of a bigger market – economies of scale and specialisation, the fact that competition was greater would encourage the introduction of new technology, and there would be more possibility of joint products such as Concorde or the European Air Bus. There were also political advantages. The UK's role as an independent world power was coming to an end – joining the Common Market might bring about a resurgence of the UK's political influence, and even if not there were political advantages in belonging to an economic grouping which was as powerful as the superpowers. Yet again there was the hope that economic agreement between the members could reduce political differences and make the likelihood of war a thing of the past.

Many remained unconvinced. On the political front they pointed to the loss of sovereignty and talked of laws made in Brussels being forced upon the UK. They also doubted whether British industry could stand the higher degree of competition, or if economies of scale were to be gained. But by far the greatest criticism was kept for the common external tariff (which would keep cheap imports of foodstuffs from the Commonwealth out) and the Common Agricultural Policy (subsidising inefficient foreign farmers).

In practice, it is very difficult to assess the impact of joining the Common Market. The major reason for entering in 1973 was the projected benefits to trade and industry. These have not manifested themselves, though it is fair to add that the raising of oil prices and later the world recession may have had much to do with this.

British trade with the EC has increased. Moreover, the gap between visible imports and exports has been reduced. Thus while some sectors have suffered from entry it seems that much of British industry has held its own or even benefited from the increased competition. However, there are two points of obvious concern. The UK expected to gain considerably from free trade in services yet there has been little move towards liberalisation of restrictions here. Additionally the recession has caused members of the EC to maintain existing barriers rather than reduce them and also create other non-tariff barriers to trade.

In the decade before joining the EC, the UK's growth rate was persistently lower than that of the Common Market members (approximately 65 per cent of EC members). Since joining the Common Market the UK's rate of growth (along with all other members) has declined. However, the rate of decline has not been as marked as would have been expected if the UK had not joined the Common Market. Between 1973 and 1981 its rate of growth was 71 per cent of that of EC members, while prior to the recession, between 1973 and 1979, the growth rate was actually 84 per cent of

EC members. Thus the claim that higher European growth rates would enable the UK to grow more quickly may have been borne out.

From the UK's point of view, by far the greatest problem since joining has been the community budget. British complaints have centred on the UK contribution to the budget and the inability of the commission to control total – but in particular – farm spending.

The UK objection to the budget centred on the fact that despite being one of the poorest members of the community it contributed 20 per cent of total revenue. The reason for this was two-fold. Traditionally the UK has imported food from the Commonwealth rather than EC States and consequently paid an excessively high amount in import duties. Moreover, Britain, with a relatively small efficient farming sector, was getting far less than its proportion back from the Common Agricultural Policy. In 1984 the problem was solved by the European Council agreeing to give the UK a 66 per cent rebate on the difference between what it gave to, and received from the budget.

Twice in the 1980s the community experienced budgetary crises. The budget, which comprises duties levied on goods imported from outside the community, and (originally one per cent of) VAT receipts, has proved inadequate to meet the demands placed upon it. In 1984, as part of the agreement over the UK budget contribution the VAT receipts ceiling was increased to 1.4 per cent. A similar situation arose in 1988 and member states agreed to contribute 1.2 per cent of GDP to the community budget but also accepted legally binding controls on spending.

Politically the effects of joining the EC are just as confused. The movement to political unity has been slower than anticipated due to the cumulative effects of the oil crisis and the recession. However, concern has been expressed over:
1. The inadequate scrutiny by the British Parliament of an increasing amount of EC legislation.
2. The inability of the UK to take unilateral action (monetary or fiscal) to deal with its industrial or regional problems.

1992 – The Single Market

By 1985 it was apparent that the movement within the EC towards a single market had lost its momentum and the European Council asked the Commission to develop a detailed programme leading to an area without internal frontiers. The result was the 'Single European' Act.

The key to the single market becoming a reality is the abolition of non-tariff barriers within the EC. In particular:
1. *Physical barriers.* Member states have different rules on

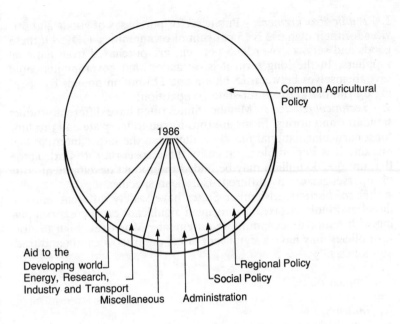

8.1 The EEC budget

product safety, health standards and trade quotas. Customs posts exist to enforce these rules but serve also to raise business costs and limit market opportunities. It is estimated the cost of physical barriers at a minimum is £9,000 million to the community;

Common Agricultural Policy

By far the biggest proportion of the EC budget is spent on the Common Agricultural Policy (see Fig. 8.1). There are two controversial elements:
1 Guaranteed Price System: farmers are guaranteed specific prices for their output, and agricultural pressure groups ensure these are set as high as possible. The result is over production and the build up of tremendous stocks;
2 Export subsidies: where a farmer exports his produce he is guaranteed the difference between the community price and the lower price at which they must sell on the world market.

127

2. *Public Procurement*: Public sector purchases of goods and services for their own use is 15 per cent of communities' GDP. Of these goods and services over 99.5 per cent are purchased from national suppliers. In the long term it is estimated that governments could save themselves between £5 billion and £13 billion pounds by opening up the market to inter-state competition;

3. *Technical barriers*: Member States often have different product standards and norms. Firms are thus forced to innovate and produce for a particular national market rather than the larger international market. It is impossible to quantify these costs (but it is calculated that up to £200 million may be added to product development costs of a passenger car by different European specifications);

4. *Fiscal barriers*: Member States have widely different rates of direct and indirect taxes. Firms incur significant extra costs complying with national accounting requirements. Moreover, high tax/low tax policies may have a significant effect on firms' location and trading policies.

The impact of 1992

1. Industry

- Costs. Many costs borne by the exporter, e.g. administration and customs delays, will be avoided. There are potential economies of scale arising from producing for the single market rather than a series of national markets. However, many firms in order to survive will incur extra costs in restructing their operations

- Competition. There will be greater competition for market share. Firms will not be able to rely on soft home markets for their existence. There will be a greater spur to efficiency and innovation.

- Prices. These may fall due to reduced costs and increased competition.

- Output. Most products will experience an increase in demand, due to lower prices and greater consumer spending power.

- Profits. Profit margins may be squeezed by the competition but increased sales may offset this.

2. The individual

- Standard of living. Price reductions will mean the consumer is better off

- Choice. Competition will provide the consumer with a greater choice of products

- Employment. Re-structuring of industry and commerce will provide both threats and new opportunities for employees. It is estimated that the changes will generate 1.8 million extra jobs.

3. The Government
- Public finance. Government expenditure will fall due to:
  - greater efficiency in public procurement policies, and
  - reductions in social security payments due to extra jobs being created. Revenue will rise as a result of increases in employment, sales and profits

- Loss of sovereignty. There will be greater harmonisation of laws throughout Europe. The ability to use fiscal and monetary policy to control the economy will be more limited.

4. The Economy
- Employment. 1.3–2.3 million more jobs throughout the EC

- Inflation. Overall prices are expected to fall by six per cent due to cost reductions and competition

- Economic Growth. There will be a major impetus to economic activity within the EC adding approximately 4.5 per cent to the GDP

- International Trade. More efficient industry will be able to compete more effectively in overseas markets, thus helping the balance of payments

- Structure of Industry. This will change to reflect 'specialisms' of individual countries. There will be a movement towards the growth of pan-European firms through mergers and takeovers. Many more American and Japanese firms will set up operations within the community rather than be excluded from 'Fortress Europe'.

The balance of payments

The balance of payments is a summary of the transactions which take place between one country and the rest of the world. It records not only the trading transactions discussed previously in this chapter but other commercial and financial transactions entered into by its people, business, and government. Normally the accounts cover a year, but statistics relating to visible and invisible trade are often issued more frequently. Table 8.1 shows the balance of payments for the UK in 1981. These are discussed in more detail below.

Visible trade

The balance of visible trade (issued in the UK as the monthly trade figures) indicates the value of visible or tangible exports and imports. Traditionally the UK has run a deficit on the balance of visible

Table 8.1 United Kingdom Balance of Payments 1987

	£'M	£'M
Visible trade		
Exports	79,622	
Imports	89,784	
Visible balance		(10,162)
Invisible trade		
Shipping and Civil Aviation	(1,618)*	
Travel and Tourism	(1,018)	
Financial and other services	9,882	
Interest profit and dividends	6,568	
Government expenditure	(5,940)	
Transfers	(216)	
Invisible balance		7,658
Current balance		(2,504)
Investment and other capital flows		(1,039)
Balance for Official financing		3,543

* Brackets denote net deficit

trade, imports of raw materials and foodstuffs being greater than manufactured goods exported. During the last decade the following changes have been noted:

1. Manufactured Exports. There has been a decline in importance of manufactured exports which currently account for 50 per cent of total visible exports. They are now worth nearly £10 million less than manufacturing imports. This reflects the increasing competitiveness of the export market. Since 1970 two industries in particular have declined in importance: Textile exports (2.3 per cent of total exports) are now halved in importance. Vehicle exports (six per cent) have almost halved in importance too. The two most important groups of export products in 1987 are, Chemicals – 13.2 per cent and Machinery – 25.3 per cent.

2. Food, beverages and tobacco. Imports of these items have halved since 1971 from 22 per cent to 10 per cent of total imports. This reflects the increasing efficiency of the UK farming sector and the smaller proportion of our incomes devoted to food as we become better off.

3. Semi-manufactured closer imports. Historically the UK would import raw materials and export finished goods. The import of semi-manufactured goods indicates that many developing countries are now carrying out the processing of raw materials to the semi-finished and even in some cases to the finished stage.

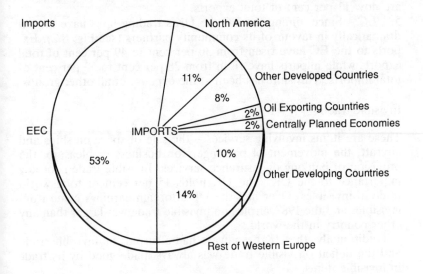

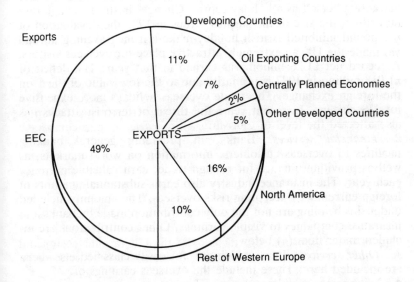

8.2 Geographical distribution of UK trade 1987

The Economic Environment

4 North Sea Oil. This had had two effects. First, oil imports are less than 66 per cent of their 1975 level and, secondly, oil exports are now 11 per cent of total exports.

5. *EC.* Since joining the EC the UK's trading links have moved dramatically in favour of its community partners (see Fig. 8.2). Exports to the EC have risen from 30 per cent to 49 per cent of total exports while imports have risen from 28 per cent to 53 per cent of total imports. This shift has been at the expense of all other groups.

Invisible trade

These are items involving services – the sale of space on ships and aircraft, the movement of passengers on business or pleasure, the provision of banking or insurance services. Invisible trade is of key importance to the UK. The UK holds 15 per cent of total world trade in invisibles. Over half the UK's foreign earnings come from invisibles and the 1987 surplus on invisible trade was larger than any other country in the world.

Traditionally, the UK has always had a surplus on invisible trade and the deficit on visible trade was always made good by its trade in invisible items.

1. *Tourism.* A surplus between 1968 and 1980 reflected the UK marketing herself as a holiday centre. Changes in the exchange rate may affect the size of the surplus – thus in 1977 the devaluation of the pound inhibited British holiday-makers from travelling abroad yet made the UK an extremely attractive place for overseas visitors. A record net £1.26 billion was earned in that year. The deficit of £1,018 million in 1987 is primarily due to the low value of the $ on the foreign exchange. This made overseas holidays more expensive for US citizens. In recent years the threat of terrorist attacks has also affected the level of tourism.

2. *Financial services.* Banks, in providing general banking facilities to overseas customers, information on world markets, as well as providing finance for foreign trade, earn valuable currency each year. The insurance industry also earns substantial amounts of foreign currency by accepting risks overseas. The amounts included under this heading are not the only contribution made by banks and insurance companies to visible earnings. Other contributions are included under item (4) below.

3. *Other services* Items which are not easily classified elsewhere are included here. These include the overseas earnings of:
* Civil engineers and construction firms,
* consultancy firms – architecture, advertising agencies, management consultants, accountants and lawyers;
* the entertainment industry – films and television programmes

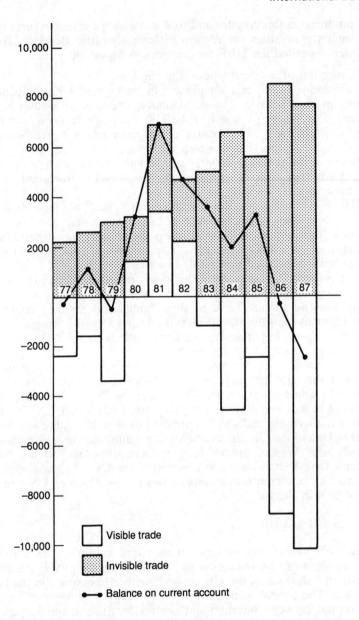

Source: Economic Trends

8.3 The relationship between visible and invisible trade – the balance of payments on current account

produced in this country and sold abroad earn valuable currency, similarly royalties on records. (Remember the Beatles? They were awarded the OBE for 'services to export'!);

● education of overseas students in the UK.

4. Interest, profit, and dividends In past years UK companies have invested heavily abroad. Similarly, overseas companies have found it profitable to invest in the UK – perhaps to overcome the EC tariff barrier – or because of involvement in North Sea oil production. In the year in which the investment occurs the capital amount of the recipient country will benefit, but in future years the repatriation of interest, profit, or dividends will be recorded as an invisible import.

The Government too has lent money (invested) abroad, often to newly developing countries. At times the Government also borrows money from abroad, especially when the country has experienced balance of payments difficulties. Repayments of interest on these loans will be included under this heading.

5. Transfer Private transfers between residents and non-residents may occur for many reasons. For example, immigrant workers may wish to send money back to their families in another country. Government transfers arise from retired Civil Servants living abroad, but also, more importantly, our contributions to the EEC budget and aid to newly developing countries.

6. Government expenditure All governments incur expenditure abroad through the maintenance of diplomatic links and trade missions. Some governments, like that of the UK, also spend large sums of money maintaining a military presence abroad. The British Army in Germany leads to a significant outflow of funds each year, and has led to the UK Governments negotiating various offset agreements with West Germany (e.g. the German Army should buy British tanks). It is also true to say that the UK's balance of payments has benefited considerably from the presence of US armed personnel in Britain.

The capital account

Together, visible and invisible transactions comprise the current balance and are an indication of how well the country is trading. Figure 8.3 shows how the UK current balance has moved in the last decade. The capital account, as its name implies, shows movement of capital between international centres for investment purposes. Thus when British firms, such as Dunlop or Lonhro, decide to extend their operations in Malaysia or Africa, the investment results in a capital outflow being recorded in the UK's balance of payments, but a capital inflow in the accounts of the recipient country. Equally the UK's capital account is the beneficiary when North Americans decide to invest in this country. Traditionally, though, the UK has been a net investor overseas. Thus in every year since 1978 the UK has been a net investor overseas (prior to this date UK firms' investment overseas was strictly controlled. The aim was to see that overseas investment was financed by (profits of overseas operations, or foreign currency borrowing). In 1986 when the overall balance of payments deficit increased from £5.6 billion to £14.6 billion the rise in UK investment overseas almost exactly matched this increase.

Not all investment in an overseas country by firms, or governments for that matter, are for the purposes of producing goods or services there. Both business and governments have temporary surpluses of cash and it is logical to invest this surplus until such time as other investment opportunities can be found. The UK has long been the centre for such investments. For example, large sums of money can be lent for as little as a day on the London Money Market and yet earn interest. It is thought that the sophistication of London's financial infrastructure has been a key feature in maintaining the sterling exchange rate at levels which could not be justified on trading grounds alone (we could also cite the growth of North Sea Oil operations and high interest rates as other important factors). Normally such investments benefit the UK, but a lack of confidence in the sterling exchange rate, or the ability of the Government to control inflation may cause a sudden and massive withdrawal of this money from the UK. Later in this chapter we will see that this action exacerbates any exchange rate problem.

It is extremely unlikely that the current and capital account of any country's balance of payments will offset each other exactly, and therefore a country will either have a surplus or a deficit on its balance of payments (see Fig. 8.4). A balance of payments surplus arises when less has been spent than earned abroad – a deficit is the converse. Figure 8.4 indicates how widely the figures will fluctuate. In 1985 a current account surplus was more than offset by a capital account deficit while in 1987 a current account deficit was compounded by a deficit on capital account. Such deficits and surpluses are settled by currency flows between countries.

In practice the currency flows recorded by the Government rarely agree with the deficit recorded on the current and capital accounts. This arises because it is difficult to record all international transactions and, moreover, payment may be made at a different time to that of exports or imports. The difference between these two figures is termed the 'balancing item' and is inserted in the balance of payments so that, as its name implies, the accounts balance.

No particular concern is shown when a country experiences the occasional deficit on its balance of payments. After all every country

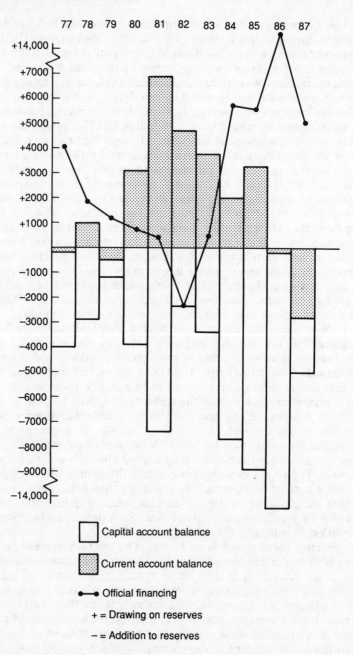

8.4 United Kingdom Balance of Payments 1977–87

cannot be in surplus at the same time. However, where the deficit is large or persists for a number of years the country concerned is expected to remedy the situation.

In the short term a deficit will be financed by running down reserves of gold and foreign currencies or perhaps by borrowing from abroad. But persistent deficits will soon exhaust these resources and the authorities will have to consider measures to halt the net outflow of funds from the country. These will include trading restrictions, deflation, and even possibly devaluation.

We have already considered tariffs, quotas, and other restrictions which have from time to time been placed upon international trade and noted that the most likely consequences are retaliatory measures from those countries which are affected. Governments may also try to make it more difficult for capital to leave the country. For example, France placed restrictions on the amount of currency French tourists could take out of the country and also on investment and other capital flows. As an alternative to restricting imports and other currency outflows, governments have also tried to make their exports more attractive by means of subsidies, or credits facilities.

'Deflation' is the term given to the combination of monetary and fiscal measures which are designed to reduce the level of demand within the economy. By reducing the demand for all goods and services it is hoped that imports of raw materials and finished goods will decline. Monetary measures normally taken will include the restriction of bank and hire-purchase credit, the control of government borrowing, and the raising of interest rates. Higher taxes and lower government spending are examples of fiscal measures. While deflation may secure a reduction in the payments deficit the price paid internally is low economic growth, lower investment, and higher unemployment – results which can be highly embarrassing to a government.

The final alternative open to the Government is that of altering its exchange rate – devaluing the value of the domestic currency against other currencies so that, for example, the pound does not buy as much abroad. Britain, for example, devalued in 1967, reducing the sterling – dollar exchange rate from £1 = \$2.80 to £1 = \$2.40. The effect of this, as with any devaluation, was to make:
– imports more expensive;
– exports cheaper;

The aim of devaluation is thus clear. If exports are cheaper we will sell more, earning greater revenue than before, and with imports being dearer, we are likely to find them less attractive and spend less on them. This will reduce, if not eradicate, the balance of payments deficit.

But a policy of devaluation is not always successful. Exports are cheaper, but to earn more revenue we have to sell far more than previously (readers who have studied economics will realise we are talking about the elasticity of demand for the country's exports). The sterling devaluation of 14 per cent in 1967 effectively meant that we had to sell over 14 per cent more exports to earn the same amount of revenue.

Equally, although imports are more expensive, if the goods purchased abroad are 'essentials', e.g. foodstuffs or raw materials, we are likely to find ourselves buying a similar amount as before from abroad, but this time at a higher price!

Finally, devaluation may also cause inflation. First, because higher import prices for raw materials, foodstuffs, or finished goods will normally be reflected in a higher RPI. Second, if demand for exports increases strongly and cannot be met by exporters, prices of these goods are likely to rise.

The International Monetary Fund

This was set up in 1945, its aims were to:

- bring stability to international exchange rates; and

- help those countries undergoing balance of payment problems.

A subsidiary aim was to encourage the growth of world trade. However, since the movement away from fixed to floating exchange rates the IMF has concerntrated on aiding those countries with balance of payments problems.

Members of the IMF are required to contribute a quota of their gold and foreign currency to the fund. This is based upon their volume of trade. In return they receive special drawing rights which may be used by that country to pay off international indebtness.

Members may also borrow up to 200 per cent of their quota from the fund when they experience balance of payments problems. Loans from the IMF are often accompanied by 'strings' or 'conditions'. For example in 1976 the IMF required the British Government to reduce both the money supply and its own expenditure.

The World Bank

The International Bank for Reconstruction and Development, is also known as the World Bank. Its function was initially to finance post-war reconstruction, but it is now concerned with encouraging international investment in developing countries.

To finance this investment the bank borrows money (quotas) from its members (who must be members of the IMF), and also by issuing its own bonds on the international money market. Interest is charged on the loans to developing countries and the Government is required to guarantee the loans.

The bank also encourages private investment to complete a project. Since its creation the bank has lent many millions of dollars, the majority being to newly developing countries.

Through a subsidiary, the International Development Association, loans are sometimes made to developing countries on advatageous terms – low rates of interest, and lengthy repayment periods.

Stand-by loans may also be granted by the IMF where it believes there is no real balance of payments problem, and that pressure on the currency is caused by speculation. Often the mere fact that the loan has been granted is sufficient to regenerate confidence in the currency.

Exchange rates

International trade is complicated by the fact that each country has its own currency and exporters wish to be paid in that currency. For international trade to be possible then, it is necessary to determine an exchange rate for these currencies. Buyers and sellers of currencies transmit their orders to dealers who, in marrying the two together, create a market in foreign exchange.

Exchange rates determined on the foreign exchange market reflect the supply and demand for currencies. When we import goods or buy services from abroad we offer sterling on the foreign exchange market so as to obtain the local currency required by the exporter. Conversely, when we export goods we will offer the foreign currency received to the foreign exchange market and demand our own currency. In Fig. 8.5 we can see the effect of trade movements upon our rate of exchange.

Should our imports be greater than our exports the supply of sterling will reduce the price of sterling against the dollar. It is the movements of the exchange rate which equate the supply and demand for currencies.

Until 1973, most countries adopted a system of fixed exchange rates. Under this system governments stipulated the rates at which they would exchange currencies. For example, the rate between the dollar and the pound was set at £1 = $2.40. The rate was, however, allowed to fluctuate within narrow bands. But should there be pressure on the sterling exchange rate to move outside the limits determined by the Government, it would step in to buy or sell sterling as the situation demanded (see Fig. 8.6).

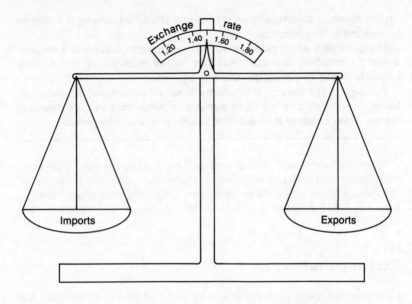

8.5 The impact of imports and exports on the exchange rate

Since 1973 any major nations have experimented with flexible exchange rates – commonly termed 'floating' exchange rates. Under this system it is the free operation of the forces of supply and demand which determines the exchange rate. Yet exchange rates have not been left completely to the mercy of the market forces but rather have been 'managed' by central banks. While central banks would not normally interfere with an exchange rate, if there were unusual circumstances (e.g. speculation against a currency or a

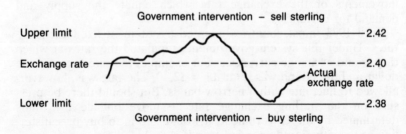

8.6 Stabilisation of exchange rates through government intervention

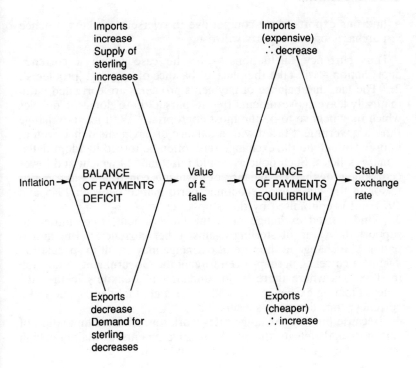

8.7 The process of balance of payments adjustment under floating exchange rates

sudden imbalance in trading) they were prepared to intervene and defend what they perceived as the correct rate.

Benefits and Problems associated with floating exchange rates

Benefits
1. With floating exchange rates a balance of payments problem is corrected automatically. Let us assume, as in Fig. 8.7, that the UK inflation rate is higher than its main competitors and that its goods are less competitive than before. Then, because the UK is importing more than it is exporting, the supply of sterling on the foreign exchange market will be greater than the demand for sterling. To persuade people to hold more sterling the exchange rate of sterling against other currencies will have to fall. At the new lower exchange rate we will:

-   find it more costly to buy imports – hence we will consume less and

- find our exports more competitive in overseas markets – hence purchases of our exports will rise.

Thus currency fluctuations – in the case above a currency depreciation – will take the place of balance of payment 'problems'.
2. The fact that balance of payments problems are corrected automatically leaves governments free to pursue those domestic policies which they believe to be the most appropriate. With fixed exchange rates a government faced with a balance of payments deficit would, in order to defend the exchange rate, often be forced to adopt deflationary policies. Such policies would raise unemployment and lower economic growth. The 'balance of payments constraint' was a major factor in the UK's poor economic performance between 1945 and 1973 and is epitomised by the 'stop-go cycle'.
3. Under fixed exchange rates the Government is committed to support the value of sterling against other currencies. But anticipation of a change in the rate of exchange may result in speculation against a currency perhaps even forcing the Government to devalue in situations where there is no fundamental weakness in the currency. Floating exchange rates allow for a gradual depreciation of a currency, thus deterring speculation.
4 Because floating exchange rates work towards the elimination of surpluses and deficits the need for governments to maintain high levels of foreign currency reserves is reduced.

Problems
1. It is argued that floating exchange rates may restrict the development of international trade. In 1987, when the $ fell from $1.50 to $1.90 to the £, many firms found their profits completely wiped out by changes in the exchange rate. In practice, even a small change can mean the differences between profit and loss.

Avoiding the risk of loss on export contracts.

For firms wanting to avoid loss on export contracts caused by currency fluctuation the two most popular ways are:

Forward Exchange Contracts: The exporter enters into an agreement with his bank stipulating the rate at which foreign currency will be changed into sterling (say, in three months' time) regardless of what happens to exchange rates in the meantime. The exporter can now cost his products so as to make a profit in the normal way.

Option Forward Exchange Contracts: One problem with forward exchange contracts is that the exporter is committed to supplying a specific amount of foreign currency to the bank on the day agreed – even if the export sale falls through. An option forward contract (which again allows the exporter to fix in advance the foreign curren-

cy exchange rate) can be allowed to lapse if the sale does not go through, or more favourable currency terms can be obtained on the market. These contracts also have the added advantage of allowing the exporter to present the currency for exchange between two agreed dates rather than a specific date. Such a deal will cost approximately four per cent of the total finance involved.

Floating exchange rates may also deter overseas investment as a movement in exchange rates between buying and selling an investment (e.g. treasury or commercial bill) could produce substantial capital losses for the investor.

2. Although floating exchange rates allow for a gradual depreciation of a currency over time, there are likely to be short term fluctuations around this trend. Such fluctuations provide opportunities for speculators to buy a currency cheaply and sell later at a better rate. Thus speculation may rise not fall.

3. Fluctuations in exchange rates may not be a result of trading activities. Flows of money into and out of a currency may cause changes in value of the currency that do not reflect underlying trading conditions.

Exchange rate movements

What causes fluctuations in a country's exchange rates? For example why has the sterling/dollar exchange rate dropped form £1 = \$4 to as low as £1 = \$1.10 since 1947. Moreover, why does the same exchange rate oscillate, sometimes quite dramatically over even a short-period of time? The answer is complex; however, the following factors are important.

1 *Inflation* If the rate of inflation is relatively high in Britain compared with other countries the likely result is a depreciation in the value of sterling against other currencies. Inflation has two effects: it makes our exports less attractive as the same goods can be purchased elsewhere more cheaply; imports, because they are lower in price, become more attractive than the home-produced product. Consider the effect in terms of Fig. 8.5: imports are greater than exports, and therefore the supply of sterling on the foreign exchange market is greater than the demand. Currency dealers, to equate supply and demand for sterling, will reduce its value in terms of other currencies. The balance of payments and exchange rate problems experienced by the UK since 1945 have been caused to a considerable extent by it's higher-than-average inflation rate.

2. *Speculation against a currency* A speculator is a person who (in this context) buys or sells currencies in the hope of making a profit by predicting their future prices. Thus if a spectulator believes

sterling is going to depreciate against the dollar he will convert his sterling holdings into dollars. Later, if he is right, he will be able to repurchase sterling at a lower 'price'. For example let us assume an initial exchange rate of £1=$2. Our speculator believes the value of sterling is too high and sells £300 sterling receiving in exchange $600. If the exchange rate subsequently depreciates to £1 = $1.50 he can now buy £400 sterling with his dollars, £100 profit!

The UK's problem has been slightly different. Traditionally, overseas companies and governments have invested surplus funds in the UK. However, should they believe, perhaps quite wrongly, that a sterling devaluation was likely, their immediate reaction is to move their funds elsewhere. Consider the effect on the foreign exchange market. Suddenly a vast quantity of sterling is presented for conversion into foreign currencies. The prediction of exchange rate depreciation is self-fulfiling. The actions of the speculators alone cause foreign exchange dealers to mark the value of sterling down. A recent example occured in the United States where in 1979 speculation against the dollar in favour of gold pushed the price of gold up fourfold to $800 an ounce.

The effective exchange rate

In the UK great attention is paid to the sterling/dollar exchange rate. The inference is that a change in this rate will have a large impact on the value of its exports and imports. Yet, in fact only one-fifth of UK trade is affected by changes in this exchange rate – over 80 per cent of its trade is with countries other than the USA.

The Bank of England therefore issues an 'effective' or trade-weighted exchange rate index based upon the importance of various currencies to British trade. This more accurately reflects the impact on the economy of changes in the exchange rate (see Fig 8.8).

---

3. *Interest rates* Pressure on a currency, for example sterling, which has been caused by a deficit on the balance of payments can be countered by the raising of interest rates. If overseas investors are thereby encouraged to invest more of their funds in the UK the short-term pressure on sterling is reduced. In the longer term, however, the benefits are more doubtful. Should the UK at some stage in the future wish to reduce interest rates or other countries raise their rates, these funds are likely to be transferred from the UK to other more profitable centres. The UK as an international financial centre is particularly vulnerable to such transfer of funds, and the consequent fluctuations in exchange rates.

The pressure of exchange rates mentioned above may be exacerbated if the variations in international interest rates are great. In

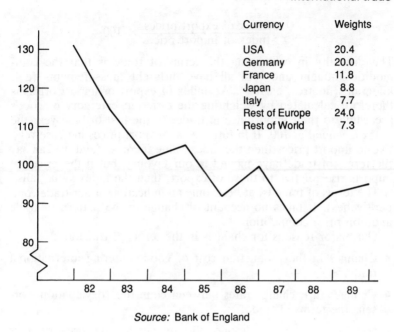

Currency	Weights
USA	20.4
Germany	20.0
France	11.8
Japan	8.8
Italy	7.7
Rest of Europe	24.0
Rest of World	7.3

Source: Bank of England

8.8 UK effective exchange rate 1981–89

April 1983 interest rates varied from 5 per cent in West Germany, 10 per cent in the UK to 16 per cent in Italy. Speculators may very well find it profitable to borrow money in West Germany or the UK, exchange it for lira, and lend the money in Italy!

Terms of trade

The relationship between the prices of imports and exports is known as the 'terms of trade'. The terms of trade tell us how much of another country's products we can obtain by selling a notional unit of our own exports. If export prices increase faster than import prices the terms of trade are said to have moved in our favour because we can now purchase the same amount of imports for less exports.

Conversely, where import prices rise faster than export prices the terms of trade have moved against – we have to sell more abroad to finance the same volume of imports.

The method of calculating the terms of trade is:

$$\frac{\text{Index of export prices}}{\text{Index of import prices}} \times 100$$

The difficulty in calculating the terms of trade is that the commodities bought and sold all have different measurements (e.g. kilograms, metres, barrels). An index of export or import prices is therefore calculated by weighting the different catergory of goods according to their importance in trade. In the first or base year the index is valued at 100. If in future years export prices increase relative to import prices then the index value increase (and we can say the terms of trade have moved in our favour), but if the prices of imports rise relative to those of export, then the index value falls.

The terms of trade is, at best, only an indication of our trade competitiveness. It takes no account of change in the pattern of trade and non price competition.

The major reasons for changes in the terms of trade are:

● Changes in the production cost of goods entering international trade.

● Changes in exchange rates between countries (devaluation worsens the terms of trade).

● Action by a cartel or monopolist to increase the price of their product.

Most countries experience changes in their terms of trade, The UK, for example between 1952 and 1972, experienced favourable changes in the terms of trade with export prices of her finished goods rising more rapidly than import prices of foodstuffs and raw materials. However, 1973/4 saw a fivefold increase in oil prices and the doubling of other important basic materials – the effect was a reduction in her terms of trade from 101.3 in 1972 (1970 = 100) to 75.1 in 1974. Since that time there has been a modest improvement in the UK's terms of trade, but the index is still substantially below that achieved in 1972.

Examination questions

1 What is the value of international trade to a country as a whole and its individual inhabitants? *(PSC)*

2 Why is there a need for countries to engage in foreign trade? What factors prevent the operation of a completely free trade system? *(PSC)*

3 Has the UK benefited from membership of the EEC?

4 Imports of cars into the UK have increased significantly in recent years. Why should this be so? How can it be reversed? *(PSC)*

5 Describe and discuss the problems experienced by a business trading both at home and abroad as the result of a depreciation in the external exchange rate. *(AEB 1985)*

6 The chairman of a large United Kingdom based public company has given the strength of sterling in a particular year as a reason for the company's low level of profits. Other comparable United Kingdom companies attributed their high profit levels to the same cause. Reconcile the apparent contradictions of this statement. *(AEB)*

7 (a) What do you understand by the phrases:
    'market share'; 'import penetration'; 'cross elasticity of demand'?
  (b) How might a UK-based firm attempt to counteract the problems of increasing foreign competition? (If you wish, you may choose to confine your answer to a specific industry.) *(Camb 1988)*

8 'Most bulk chemical products are priced in US dollars'. (*The Financial Times*) Discuss the problems likely to be encountered by a British company involved in the chemical markets at home and abroad. *(Camb 1987)*

9 Explain what you understand by the term 'Balance of Payments'.
  How would the following affect your country's Balance of Payments
  (a) inflation
  (b) a rise in the price of oil? *(PSC)*

10 How far do you agree with the statement that a country will always benefit from free trade? *(PSC)*

11 Discuss the proposition that only those British business organisations involved in foreign trade should pay attention to the fluctuations of the United Kingdom's balance of payments. *(PSC)*

12 What factors determine the external value of a currency on the foreign exchange market?
  Assess the impact of freely floating exchange rates upon
  (a) the economy
  (b) a manufacturing firm.

13 Why is so much importance attached to the process of maintaining a favourable balance of trade?
  Critically assess the ways in which the Government could help achieve this objective.

Chapter 9

Public finance

In a mixed economy the State, although acknowledging the central role of private enterprise in the provision of goods and services does, in some cases, see fit to intervene. Thus the State:

- supplements the market by providing certain services which private enterprise would not supply, e.g. defence, police, prisons, space, and nuclear programmes;
- restricts the market by providing services which can and are provided by private enterprise elsewhere, e.g. roads, medicine, education;
- distorts the market by transferring money between individuals and companies, e.g. grants to the unemployed and pensioners, company investment allowances;
- subsidises the market by providing goods and services at less than their full cost, e.g. losses of nationalised industries, or payment to private firms in financial difficulties;
- uses public revenue and expenditure as a means of controlling the level of economic activity within the economy (this is discussed in detail under the heading 'The budget', below, p. 164.

It is not difficult to see that the State plays an extremely important role in our lives (you might consider your actions on an average day, and how you note state intervention). In this chapter we are interested in how the State raises its income, including the role of the budget and how it spends this revenue.

Government revenue

By far the greatest part of government revenue is raised through taxation. A small sum is obtained from trading activities and past investments but this is virtually eclipsed by the amounts raised from taxes on income, capital, and expenditure (see Fig. 9.1).

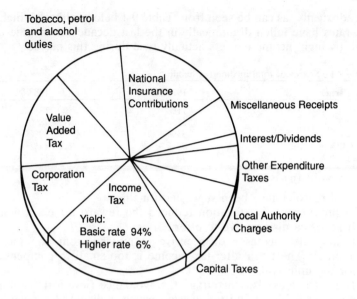

9.1 UK Government planned receipts 1989–90

Taxes on income

Income tax   Taxes on income – that is income tax, corporation tax, petroleum revenue tax and National Insurance contributions yield 51 per cent of total government revenue in the UK. Not all the person's income is liable to tax – a number of allowances are given for wives, dependents, mortgages, pensions, and life assurance. Personal allowances are also given. The aim of the allowances is to raise the threshold for tax above the amount earned or received by the poorer. Those who earn more than the 'average' income will pay tax at a higher rate. In this sense income tax is said to be progressive in that it bears more heavily on those who can afford to pay a greater amount.

Normally, allowances against income are changed each year by the Chancellor of the Exchequer in the budget to keep abreast of inflation. Since 1977 a system of automatic indexation has been used to maintain the value of allowances.

Tax rates in the UK have been reduced considerably since 1978/79. The basic rate has been reduced from 33 per cent to 25 per cent and the higher rates which previously climbed to a maximum of 83 per cent have now been replaced by a single 40 per cent rate.

Paradoxically, as can be seen from Table 9.1 below, although higher tax rates have fallen dramatically in the last decade the income tax paid by high income earners actually rose during this period.

Table 9.1 Shares of total income tax liability

Tax Earners	1976/77	1988/89
Top 1%	11%	13%
Top 5%	25%	28%
Top 10%	35%	39%
Next 40%	45%	44%
Lower 50%	20%	17%

Source: Social Trends 1989

Several reasons have been suggested for this:
- Highly progressive taxation reduced the reward for extra work. It acts as a disincentive to effort.
- It may also act as a disincentive to moving from one job to another. The extra after-tax income is too small to compensate for the upheaval.
- High tax rates also encourage tax avoidance (ie efforts to minimise tax liability) and tax evasion which is illegal. At lower tax rates the amount which can be saved is so much smaller that both tax avoidance and tax evasion are not worth the effort.

In the UK personal taxation accounts for 23 per cent of total revenue. This is broadly in line with that of all industrial countries – 27 per cent (see Fig. 9.2). However, there are wide variations with Norway raising only nine per cent and Australia 56 per cent of revenue from personal income tax.

Fiscal drag

A government does not need to raise taxes to increase tax revenue, this happens automatically thanks to inflation. Each year millions of people receive wage increases to cover the increase in the cost of living. Thus poor people who were previously exempt from paying tax now find themselves dragged into the tax net, while higher wage-earners find themselves paying more tax. This happens even though these people may not, in real terms, be better off than before.

Companies are also affected. Corporation tax is levied on money rather than real profits. So if a company buys machinery worth £100 it is allowed to set off £100 as an expense against profits. Yet five years later when the machinery has to be replaced the company has to pay perhaps £250. Because the tax system ignores the effects of inflation the company pays tax on money which is needed to replace fixed and working capital.

In Britain taxes on personal incomes are deducted by means of the PAYE (pay as you earn) system. Employers pay wages and salaries net of tax (and National Insurance contributions) to the employee, remitting the balance to the Government.

National Insurance Contributions Entitlement to many State benefits eg retirement, pension, sickness, unemployment, widow's benefits and maternity allowances are dependent upon the payment of national insurance contributions. There are two major classes of contributions. Class one covers employed workers and contributions (which are tied to earnings) are paid by both employees and employers. Class 2 flat rate contributions are paid by self-employed people. These do not provide benefits for industrial injuries or unemployment.

Corporation tax This is levied on a company's profits. However, taxable profit is reduced by a system of allowances. The rate of tax is normally 35 per cent, but smaller firms may benefit from a 25 per cent reduced rate of tax. However, allowances mean that the average firms pays only 16 per cent of its profits in corporation tax. The system of corporation tax is designed to encourage investment and expansion of production. Allowances are granted against the purchase of plant and machinery and these may be claimed fully in the year in which the expenditure is incurred. Thus a firm which retains and reinvests its profits will have a lower tax liability than one which distributes its profits.

Reinvestment of profits is also encouraged by treating distributed profits – that is, dividends to shareholders – as being liable for income tax. Those investors paying tax at higher rates may actually seek out companies reinvesting the majority of their profits. Reinvestment and expansion of business activities, if successful, is likely to lead to an increase in the company's share price, and the capital gain made on the sale of the shares will be taxed at a lower rate than their marginal rate of income tax.

Petroleum revenue taxes These are levied under the Oil Taxation Act 1975 and are charged on the profits arising from winning the right to drill oilfields in the UK and the North Sea. The rate of tax is 75 per cent and is designed to ensure that the benefits of North Sea oil production accrue to the UK economy.

Although all countries differ in the way they raise taxes, broad patterns can be seen. Figure 9.2 shows the different ways in which low income and industrialised countries raise revenue. For example, in developing countries personal taxes are far less important than in developed countries. This reflects the difficulties of 'developing' countries collecting taxes from a widely dispersed, poor and agricul-

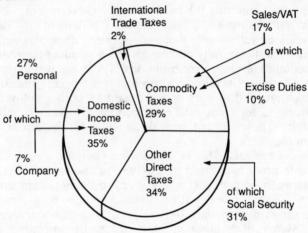

Industrial Countries

International Trade Taxes 2%

Sales/VAT 17% of which

27% Personal

of which

7% Company

Domestic Income Taxes 35%

Commodity Taxes 29%

Excise Duties 10%

Other Direct Taxes 34%

of which **Social Security** 31%

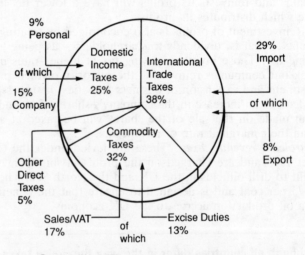

Low Income/Developing Countries

9% Personal

of which

15% Company

Domestic Income Taxes 25%

International Trade Taxes 38%

29% Import of which

8% Export

Other Direct Taxes 5%

Commodity Taxes 32%

Sales/VAT 17%

of which

Excise Duties 13%

Source: World Development Report 1988

9.2 The different ways of raising revenue in industrialised and low income/developing countries

tural community. Similar difficulties prevent developing countries levying social security taxes such as the UK's National Insurance contributions.

Company taxes are a far more important source of revenue to the developing country. Companies are required to keep accounting records and the administrative system needed to collect such taxes is easily created.

Finally, industrialised countries with tariff barriers averaging only five per cent on goods entering international trade raise only two per cent of all tax revenue through such taxes compared with the developing countries' 38 per cent. International trade taxes serve a number of functions for the developing country – they raise revenue, they discourage imports and conserve scarce foreign currencies, as well as encouraging and protecting local industry.

Taxes on capital

Capital gains taxes   These are levied where the owner of assets sells those assets at a price higher than he paid for them. The rate of tax is 30 per cent, but relief is given by (a) exempting certain assets altogether, e.g. your house and car, and (b) allowing exemption from the tax where total net gains do not exceed £5,000 in any year. This tax, introduced in 1962, was designed to catch the large numbers of people who had 'got rich quick' by speculating in land and shares.

Capital transfer tax   This applies where the owner of assets transfers those assets to some other person during his lifetime or on his death. Lifetime transfers are exempt if under £2,000 annually. Transfers on death are exempt if under £110,000. The rate of tax charged on death is 40 per cent. A sliding system of relief covers the situation where a person transfers assets during his lifetime but fails to survive for seven years. Thus, where the transferor dies within three to four years of making the gifts there is relief from 20 per cent of the tax due. This rises to 80 per cent where the transferor dies in the seventh year.

Taxes on expenditure

Value added tax   As its name implies, this is a tax on the value added at each stage of the production process. Consider the following example where we assume the rate of value added tax (VAT) is 10 per cent – in practice, it is 15 per cent at present.

A farmer purchases wheat from a grain merchant costing £550. The grain actually costs £500, but there is the tax of 10 per cent which the grain merchant is responsible for collecting from the purchaser and paying to the Customs and Excise. Now the farmer sows the grain and eventually harvests wheat worth £1550. The value added by the farmer is therefore £1,000 (£1550–£550, the cost of the seed) and the tax to be paid on this is 10 per cent, that is, £100. Thus the bakery which purchases the wheat will pay £1,650 in total. When the bakery has processed the wheat and produced the bread it is worth £2,400. The value added by the baker is £750; the baker will pay tax on this of £75, and consumers will pay the full price of £2,475. The example is summarised below:

	Value added (£)	Tax at 10% (£)	Total (£)
Grain merchant	500	50	550
Farmer	1,000	100	1,100
Bakery	750	75	825
	2,250	225	2,475

In the UK the effect of VAT is limited in a number of ways. First certain basic products and services are zero rated. Examples include food, fuel, buildings, and public transport. Where goods are zero rated vendors do not have to charge VAT on their sales and may also claim a refund of the tax paid by their suppliers and included in the price charged to them. Another group of goods are tax exempted, which means that vendors do not have to charge VAT on their sales but are not allowed to claim a refund of taxes paid at previous stages of 'the production' process. Exemption applies to land, rents, insurance, finance, education, and health services.

Excise duties   These are taxes placed upon goods for revenue-earning purposes and are levied in addition to VAT. As the Government is committed to spending very large sums of money each year it has to be sure that the revenue it plans to raise from taxes on goods does in fact materialise. The Chancellor of the Exchequer does not wish to tax goods only to find that the higher price leads to a significant reduction in the quantity demanded and therefore tax revenue being less than anticipated. In consequence the Government looks for goods which we will buy in roughly the same quantity even though the price has risen. Food, clothing, and shelter are obvious examples, yet as taxes on these goods will bear most harshly on the poor, the Government seeks instead to tax goods which are by convention, rather than nature, necessities. Experience has shown that even though high taxes are placed upon oil, tobacco, alcohol, and cars, people continue to buy these items in large quantities. Figure 9.3 shows the proportion of tax in the final price of selected goods sold in the UK.

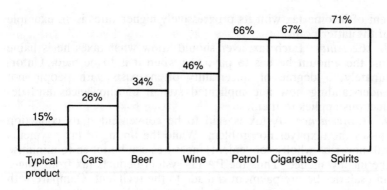

9.3 Tax paid as a percentage of retail price

Protective duties These are levied on commercial and agricultural products entering the EC through the UK. Duties raised by way of the common external tariff are remitted to Brussels and become part of the Community's income.

The principles of taxation

While no tax system is liked, most of us accept that taxes have to be levied and our consideration therefore turns to ensuring that the tax system is just. In practice, that is no easy matter as it involves moral, political, and economic judgements, but its importance is indicated by the fact that the UK lost her American colonies through the imposition of unjust taxes!

Adam Smith argued that there were four basic principles which a government should work to: economy, equality, certainty, and convenience.

1. Economy. Taxes should be collected as efficiently as possible; moreover, we should avoid situations where the tax raised is less than the cost of its collection. In the UK the collection of direct taxes is particularly efficient, costing the State just over 1p for each pound collected.

2. Equality. This can be interpreted in different ways. Obviously, two single secretaries each earning £10,000 should pay the same amount of tax. The tax system should have no favourites! Smith went further though. He suggested that taxes should be proportional to income, and that we should all pay, say, 15 per cent of our income, whatever its level in tax. A more modern argument is that the burden of tax should be similar. The rich man, because of his larger income can afford to pay more than the poor man. The system of income tax with its progressively higher rates is an example of the latter point.

3. *Certainty* Each taxpayer should know what taxes he is liable for, the amount he has to pay, and when it is to be paid. Unfortunately, a degree of uncertainty often exists with people not understanding how a complicated system of allowances and deductions applies to them.

4. *Convenience* A tax is said to be convenient if its collection causes the taxpayer no problem. While the timing of tax payments will never be wholly convenient, measures can be taken to minimise the inconvenience. Thus the PAYE system deducts tax from wages and salaries before payment is made to the recipient. Compare with that local government rates which many people paid as a lump sum in April of each year.

To these four well-established principles of taxation others have been added:

5. Economists suggest that flexibility or the power to vary taxes at short notice is necessary in order to control the level of economic activity within the economy. So, for example, at the present time the Chancellor has the power to 'regulate' or change the VAT rate by 10 per cent in either direction (i.e. VAT may vary between 13.5 and 16.5 per cent)

6. Taxes should not act as a disincentive to effort. While people expect to pay taxes it has been suggested there is a limit to what they are willing to pay; this is sometimes referred to as 'taxable capacity'. Should taxes extend beyond this limit workers are not willing to accept overtime, do not find it worthwhile to move to new jobs, and many will try to evade paying the tax due.

Attempts to prove that high tax rates discourage people from working harder have not been particularly successful. Money is only one of a number of motivators (but see Table 9.1). Power and prestige are two others which are considered to be important.

It is at the other end of the income scale that attempts to prove the disincentive effect have been more successful. In the UK we have a system of benefits which are available to people on low incomes. These benefits are withdrawn as income rises. It has been shown that a person on a low income, who takes on extra work or overtime may find that the means-tested benefits withdrawn and tax deducted are together greater than the income received – a marginal tax rate of over 100 per cent.

Direct and indirect taxation

A direct tax is one where the taxpayer makes payment directly to the tax authorities. Taxes on income and capital are examples of direct taxes. An expenditure tax is cited as an indirect tax because the tax is paid by the bearer of the tax through someone else. As we have already seen, VAT is remitted to the Customs and Excise by each firm in the productive process.

Economists and politicians are divided over whether it is better to use direct or indirect taxes. Readers are advised to consider the points made below and make their own assessment.

Advantages of direct taxes
- Direct taxation is certain in its impact. Income tax or capital transfer tax is levied on the individual, who is unable to pass this liability on to someone else.
- Because such taxes are normally progressive and take account of individual commitments they are deemed to be equitable. Moreover, the tax system can be arranged so as to relieve low earners of any liability.
- It is easier to estimate the yield from direct taxes because people cannot avoid paying the tax.
- Direct taxes are easy and cheap to collect.
- Direct taxes do not affect the cost of living index and will, therefore, not lead to inflationary wage claims. Over a number of years direct taxes may even be deflationary if the Government does not adjust allowances to keep pace with inflation.

Disadvantages of direct taxes
- Direct taxation may be a disincentive to effort and saving.
- Direct taxes do not have the flexibility of indirect taxes – consider the problems the Inland Revenue have faced changing house purchasers' assessments when the mortgage interest rate has changed. As a result of this inflexibility direct taxes cannot easily be used to reflate or deflate the economy.
- The system of allowances creates difficulties of assessment. Professional advice is often required, especially by businesses to ensure that their tax liability is minimised. A less complicated system would release these 'tax experts' for other work.
- Direct taxation may cause inflation. Where employees are concerned with take-home pay (that is income after tax and other deductions) the higher the tax rate, the larger the wage increases they will demand. It has been suggested this was one factor in the accelerating wage demands of the 1970s.

Advantages of indirect taxes
- An individual can avoid paying the tax by not purchasing the goods on which the tax is levied.
- Expenditure taxes do not have a disincentive affect on work and enterprise. The workers or entrepreneurs do not see the fruits of their labour taxed away.

The Economic Environment

- These taxes are concealed in the price charged and consumers often do not realise that they are paying them. Thus the Government can raise its revenue and yet avoid the criticism that it is taxing people heavily – though in fact it may be.
- Indirect taxes may be used for social purposes. Taxes on tobacco and alcohol not only raise revenue but discourage increased consumption of these items.
- They can be used as an economic regulator by the Government quickly to increase or reduce the spending power of the consumer. Alternatively, import duties may be used to regulate trade in specific products or with certain countries.

Disadvantages of indirect taxes
- They are said to be regressive because they do not reflect a person's ability to pay tax. Each of us, whether rich or poor, will be paying the same amount of tax on items purchased.
- It is an inflationary tax. An increase in the tax is likely to affect the final price of the product and therefore the RPI. This has adverse implications for the balance of payments, and those groups with little bargaining power.
- The tax yield is uncertain. No one knows for sure what effect the tax will have on sales of the product. If many people are deterred from buying because of the increase in price the anticipated revenue will not be forthcoming. Even with goods which are conventional necessities the tax revenue is by no means certain. Thus, increases in taxes on cigarettes have led to reductions in tax revenue.

Public expenditure

Public expenditure is defined as all expenditure which has to be financed from taxation, National Insurance contributions, and government borrowing. Such expenditure is controlled by 3 spending authorities. Table 9.2 shows their relative importance.

Table 9.2 Public expenditure by spending authority

Component	% of total spending 1988/89
Central Government	72
Local Government	26
State Industry	2

Source: Economic Progress Report

The control of public expenditure

The twentieth century has seen an explosive growth in the public sector and its spending. At the beginning of this century government

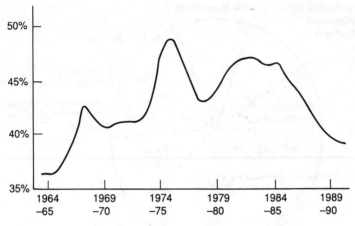

Source: Economic Progress Report (adapted)

9.4 Public spending as a percentage of GDP

expenditure was less than 10 per cent of GDP. Figure 9.4 shows state spending since 1963. We can see that such expenditure reached a peak of 48 per cent of GDP in 1975.

There are many reasons for the growth of state spending in the twentieth century. Perhaps the most important has been the change in people's attitudes towards the role of the State. Today people expect the Government to provide a far greater range of social services – we sometimes refer to this as the growth of the welfare state. Figure 9.5 shows that the broad range of social activities the Government undertakes comprise over 44 per cent, of total expenditure.

From 1979 the aim of the Conservative Government has been to reduce the level of state activity and therefore spending. Initially though the state spending/GDP ratio rose as economic activity declined and greater demands were placed upon the welfare state. Since 1982 public spending has fallen from 47 per cent, and by 1992 is expected to be only 39 per cent of GDP.

Many factors are involved in the fall of this ratio. They include the strength in the growth of the economy (see Table 5.2. p. 81) which has averaged 3.1 per cent between 1982 and 1987, and the constraints placed upon the growth of public spending – forcing the whole sector to look for efficiencies in the way services are provided. The control of public expenditure in the UK revolves around four issues. The first – the right balance between public and private expenditure we have already touched upon. The others are to ensure:
– the best allocation of resources between alternatives

The Economic Environment

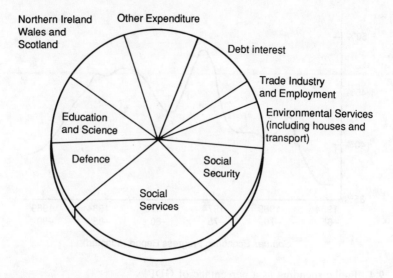

9.5 Public expenditure by function 1989/90

- that money is spent in the way Parliament intended
- that money is spent efficiently without waste.

Both the first and second issues are essentially political. This first revolves around the position of the State in the economy. Some Socialists would argue that the level of state intervention has to be high to remedy the deficiencies of the private sector. Yet Conservatives believe the existence of a large public sector inhibits the growth of private enterprise.

Readers should also be aware that the various political parties would use the resources at their disposal in different ways – what is the best allocation is very much a political question. Figure 9.5 shows how the UK Government utilised its income during 1983–84. However, the Government does undertake a number of policy reviews, the aim being to question the relevance of policies adopted in the past, and often the opinions of the various interest/pressure groups are sought.

On the more technical questions of whether money allocated by Parliament has been spent correctly and efficiently, a number of checks exist. Initially the prime responsibility for ensuring public moneys are spent properly rests with the department concerned. To aid the departments 'expenditure profiles' or budgets are prepared, and deviations from the planned profile have to be explained to the minister in charge. Similar statements are also used in local government and nationalised industries.

With high levels of inflation having caused considerable overruns on government expenditure, especially capital programmes, systems of cash limits, that is, ceilings on expenditure, have been introduced. The Government will review these limits only if circumstances are substantially different from those on which the limits were based. Local authority expenditure is also subject to a cash limit while nationalised industries' borrowing requirements have been subjected to a similar ceiling.

Lastly an audit of central government expenditure is carried out for the Crown by the Comptroller and Auditor General and his staff in the Exchequer and Audit Department. The role of the Exchequer and Audit is not only to verify the accuracy of the records kept by each department by checking a sample of transactions but also that the money has been spent as Parliament intended. Audit reports are presented to the Public Accounts Committee of the House of Commons. Chaired by a senior member of the Opposition the committee vets the reports presented to it and summarises the findings for debate in Parliament.

Similar audit procedures are carried out in local government, where district auditors employed by, but independent of, the Department of the Environment confirm the accuracy of the records. The ensuing report is made to the local authority concerned, but is also available to the public.

The accounts of State-owned industries are audited in the same manner as companies. The audit, together with the annual report and accounts, is presented to Parliament. Additionally, since 1980 the work of the Monopolies and Mergers Commission has been expanded to cover efficiency audits of State-owned industries.

The National Debt

In March 1986 the UK National Debt amounted to £171 bn. The debt arises because, at certain times, the Government, local authorities, and nationalised industries have been unable or unwilling to cover all their expenditure from current revenue. Figure 9.6 shows the history of the debt in the last 125 years. The impact of the two world wars on the debt is dramatically illustrated. Between 1945 and 1951 the National Debt also rose because of government stocks issued to shareholders of firms and utilities nationalised during this period. The decline since 1955 has occurred because the National Debt (i.e. government-sector borrowing) rose less quickly than money GDP – the effect of inflation. Also, since 1979, the

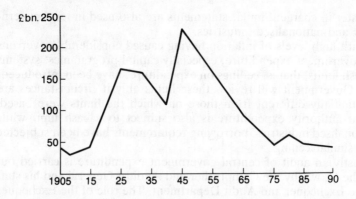

9.6 Ratio of National Debt to GDP 1905–85 (estimated)

Government has successfully limited the growth of State spending.

In Victorian times, the National Debt though small, compared with that of the twentieth century caused considerable worry to Parliament and great efforts were made to reduce its size. In fact they were successful for by 1914 the debt had been reduced from a peak of £840 m. to £650 m. More recently though, people have questioned whether the National Debt is really a burden.

The Public Sector Borrowing Requirement

Government income and expenditure will never balance each other in practice; usually expenditure is greater than income – we often term this a budget deficit. This deficit will be made good by borrowing. It is commonly referred to as the 'Public Sector Borrowing Requirement' (PSBR). Each year in which there is a public sector borrowing requirement the national debt rises – by the amount of the borrowing.

In 1988, for the first time in many years there was an excess of revenue over expenditure in the UK – a budget surplus (see Figure 9.7). Thus rather than adding to the national debt the Government was able to repay some of its borrowing of previous years. This is termed 'Public Sector Debt Repayment (PSDR).

By far the greatest part of the National Dept' is owned by British organisations and individuals. In so far as payments of interest and repayments of capital are from one resident to another there is no burden on society as a whole. The necessary interest payments which amounted to 10.0 per cent of total government expenditure

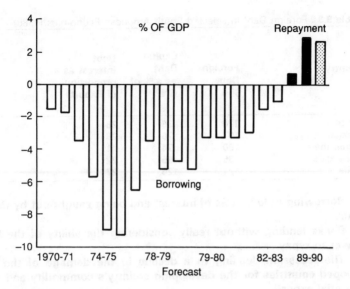

9.7 Public sector debt repayment

are merely transfers, redistributing income from one resident to another. However, a burden may be said to exist within society in that those who make the capital and interest repayments may be a substantially different group from those who receive the payments. Yet another argument which has been put forward is that excessive government borrowing dries up finance (which is badly needed by private enterprise), or at least increases the cost of borrowing. Thus the National Debt may both inhibit growth and increase inflation.

Having regard to the external debt though, payments of interest and capital do represent a real burden to the community. Both the interest and the eventual capital repayment must be met from surpluses in the balance of payments.

National Debt and the developing countries

Under the influence of Keynesian economics most countries have from time to time run budget deficits and financed these by borrowing – and, more importantly, often from abroad. Developing countries trying to raise the rate of economic growth have borrowed heavily from abroad. Figure 9.5 shows the almost impossible difficulties of five developing countries. In some cases interest and capital repayments due to overseas financiers each year are greater than that country's annual export earnings. This is caused by:

Table 9.3 Foreign Debt in selected South American Economies (1988)

Country	Foreign Debt $bn	Capital Debt as a % of GNP	Debt Interest as a proportion of Exports
Brazil	120	39	28
Mexico	107	76	28
Argentina	60	74	41
Venezuala	35	95	22
Chile	21	124	27

1 Borrowing at low rates of interest and being caught out by rising rates.

2 Banks lending without really considering the ability of the borrower to repay.

3 The recession, leading to a decline in the demand of the developed countries for the developing country's commodity and raw material exports.

4 Investment in non-revenue-earning sectors, e.g. hospitals, houses, roads.

The difficulties faced by these five countries are by no means unique. Many African and Asian countries face the same problem, and are quietly re-negotiating the rescheduling of interest and capital payments.

Finally, whatever burden exists is reduced to the extent that government borrowing is backed by revenue-earning assets, for example gas, steel, rail, etc. Not all UK nationalised industries are profitable, yet many do make a contribution to government revenue. Moreover, it is always open for the Government to resell these assets and reduce the overall level of government borrowing.

The budget

Traditionally, the purpose of the budget was to present to Parliament proposals on how:

– revenue was to be raised;

– the revenue was to be spent.

It was very much a 'good housekeeping' exercise in which the objective was to balance income and expenditure. The idea that the budget could and should be used as a tool of economic management would have been rejected out of hand. Conventional wisdom was that the economy, if left to its own devices, would naturally find its equilibrium at full employment.

It was not until after the Great Depression of the 1930s that people came to realise through the writing of Keynes, that conventional wisdom was wrong, and by 'unbalancing' the budget and running a deficit or surplus the level of economic activity could be regulated.

Briefly Keynes's idea was that the Government should, in a recession, expand its own spending to counter the reduction in spending by business and consumers. By extra spending on special projects, or even by giving more money to the unemployed, the Government was going to increase the demand for goods and services, and therefore output and employment.

Keynes's idea is illustrated diagrammatically below. The level of spending needed to ensure full employment is shown by boxes A and B together, yet the current level of demand (box A) is insufficient to ensure full employment of labour. The difference between the current level of demand and that needed for full employment (box B) is termed the 'deflationary gap'. This is the amount of extra spending required from the Government. Now assuming that previously the Government had balanced its budget (i.e. revenue = expenditure) it now needs to budget for a deficit (i.e. expenditure greater than revenue). The budget deficit is financed by government borrowing.

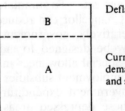

| Planned increase in government spending | | Deflationary gap |
| Level of demand for goods and services to guarantee full employment | | Current level of demand for goods and services |

A budget surplus arises when the Government raises more in revenue that it spends. A budget surplus is deflationary and is used when the Government wishes to reduce the level of economic activity. Let us consider the diagram below. Box X represents the level of demand necessary for full employment.

But total demand (boxes X and Y) is in excess of this. Box Y is termed 'excess demand' because there is no labour available to provide the extra goods and services demanded. The likely outcome is that either the excess demand will be mopped up by rising prices,

Excess demand	Y	Planned reduction in Government spending
Level of demand for goods and services to guarantee full employment	X	Total or aggregate demand

or will be satisfied by imported goods. As neither of these results is particularly appealing to the Government it may decide to reduce its own spending sufficiently to offset the excess demand.

It should be obvious by now that the budget is far more than a statement to Parliament on sources of tax revenue and expenditure. The Chancellor in his budget speech analyses the economy's progress during the past year and its prospects for the future. The measures then announced by the Chancellor on revenue and expenditure are designed to ensure that the prospects for the future accord with the Government's macro-economic objectives. These attempts to control the economy through taxation and expenditure are termed 'budgetary' or 'fiscal' policy.

How fiscal policy may be used

1. Full employment. To stimulate a greater demand for goods and services the (Chancellor can reduce taxes on income or goods and services. Alteratively, government expenditure may be increased. Measures may be designed to aid recovery in areas of high unemployment. Special allowances may be given to firms operating in such areas – employment subsidies or perhaps higher investment allowances. Government expenditure may also be concentrated on projects in these depressed areas. Alternatively, measures introduced can be designed to help specific industries, for example a reduction in car tax or duties on petrol.

2. Stable prices. Should aggregate demand be so high as to cause inflation the Government may reduce the level of demand by increasing taxes – income, capital, or expenditure. Excess demand may also be creamed off by the Government reducing its own expenditure on goods, services, or capital projects.

3. Satisfactory balance of payments. Where a country is suffering a balance of payments deficit, imports may be discouraged by raising customs duties. An increase in income and expenditure taxes generally may reduce demand for all goods and release production for export. Export industries can be helped by larger investment al-

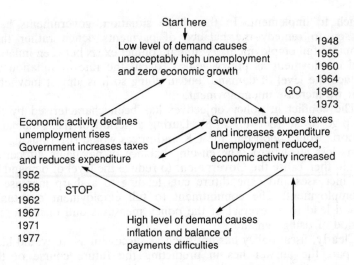

Start here

Low level of demand causes
unacceptably high unemployment
and zero economic growth

1948
1955
1960
1964
GO 1968
1973

Economic activity declines
unemployment rises
Government increases taxes
and reduces expenditure

Government reduces taxes
and increases expenditure
Unemployment reduced,
economic activity increased

1952
1958 STOP
1962
1967
1971
1977

High level of demand causes
inflation and balance of
payments difficulties

9.8 The 'stop-go' cycle

lowances, subsidies, and increasing information to exporters.
Government expenditure on overseas aid and representation may be
reduced.

4. Economic growth. By maintaining a high and stable level of
demand, businesses are encouraged to expand production and also
invest in new plant and machinery. Yet again, new investment may
be made more attractive by raising investment allowances. Additional expenditure on education and training will provide the extra skills
needed by industry.

5. Equality. Fiscal policy is the major means by which inequality
of income can be reduced. Income tax can be graduated so that
high-income earners pay most tax. Necessities, such as food and
clothing, may be zero rated or exempted from VAT while luxury
goods may be taxed more heavily than other goods.

It may have occurred to readers by now that the application of
fiscal policy to a particular macro-economic objective has important
implications for other policy goals. Two examples will illustrate this
point. Since 1944 all UK governments have been committed to maintaining full employment. Often this has meant the Government
expanding its own spending to fill the deflationary gap. Yet for a
majority of the period since the Second World War the UK balance
of payments has been in deficit, and the Government to counter this
problem has needed to reduce the level of demand by raising taxes
and cutting expenditure.

Here then, lies the heart of the problem. Two policy goals may
conflict and the Government has the unenviable task of choosing

which to implement. In the above situation, governments have chosen to remedy the balance of payments deficit rather than promote full employment. A similar conflict exists between inflation and employment as policy goals. To cut the rate of inflation we reduce the level of demand, but in doing so it is almost inevitable that we increase unemployment.

The conflict in policy objectives has been characterised by the 'stop-go' cycle (See Fig. 9.8). During a period of rising demand, imports would flood into the UK and prices would rise (making exports less attractive). The ensuing balance of payments difficulties would then cause the Government to reduce the level of demand by tax increases and expenditure cuts leading to a sharp increase in unemployment. The commitment to full employment eventually would lead to a reversal of the policy measures and once more a period of rising demand.

Clearly, fiscal policy has not been as successful as we would like. In part the answer lies in predicting the future course of the economy. Our understanding of the workings of the economy and our forecasting techniques were such that the information provided for the Government to act upon was generally too little and too late. Thus measures to correct a slump in economic activity were taken when the economy had already turned the corner. Consequently, government action to mitigate fluctuations in economic activity may, in fact, have aggravated it. Moreover, as a consequence of the inability of the Government to control the economic environment, businesses were unable to plan and invest for the future with any degree of confidence.

The making of a budget

Each year the Chancellor has to make decisions on revenue, taxation, and any borrowing for the forthcoming year. These decisions which are announced in the budget are the end of a planning cycle which is, in fact, continuous.

Since 1980 the starting-point for any UK budget has been the Medium Term Financial Strategy (MTFS). The MTFS outlines in broad terms the Government's macro-economic objectives – the position it would like the economy to be in, say, four years from now. It then states again in broad terms the fiscal and monetary policy necessary to achieve that objective. The MTFS therefore provides the underlying theme to budgets for a number of years. For example the Thatcher Government's economic strategy has been to reduce inflation (as a prerequisite to sustainable economic growth) by controlling the money supply. The fiscal policy identified as being consistent with this strategy was reducing the PSBR – in practice, partly by the cutting of government expenditure.

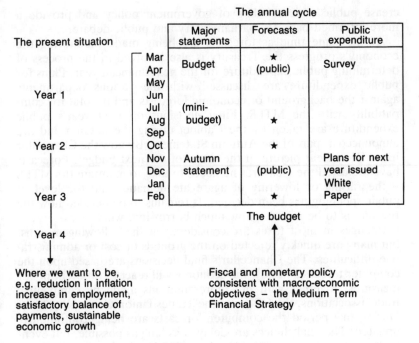

The annual cycle

The present situation		Major statements	Forecasts	Public expenditure
	Mar	Budget	★ (public)	Survey
	Apr			
Year 1	May			
	Jun			
	Jul	(mini-		
	Aug	budget)	★	
	Sep			
Year 2	Oct		★	
	Nov	Autumn		Plans for next
	Dec	statement	(public)	year issued
	Jan			White
Year 3	Feb		★	Paper

The budget

Year 4

Where we want to be, e.g. reduction in inflation increase in employment, satisfactory balance of payments, sustainable economic growth

Fiscal and monetary policy consistent with macro-economic objectives – the Medium Term Financial Strategy

★ = Treasury forecast not available to general public

9.9 The British economy

It must be apparent that as each individual budget has to be consistent with MTFS the range of options open to the Chancellor are more limited than is often assumed. Measures taken in the budget will, first and foremost, be designed to check deviations from the MTFS. The budget will also deal with other issues in so far as measures needed are not inconsistent with the MTFS.

Let us now look at how the decisions taken in the annual budget are arrived at. The decision making process is illustrated diagrammatically in Fig. 9.9. The information upon which decisions are taken is derived from a series of forecasts produced by the Treasury computer. Treasury officials feed into the computer information on the British and world economies together with specified policy measures. The predictions are then appraised for their compatibility with government objectives. Under the Industry Act 1975 the Government is required to make public two forecasts. The first is issued as a supplement to the Chancellor's budget speech, while the second in November/December accompanies the Government's autumn statement. The issue of these forecasts is intended to increase public understanding of government policy and provide a more informed basis for parliamentary and public debate.

At the same time as forecasts are being made monitoring the economy's progress the Treasury is also involved in the process of determining public expenditure for the next financial year. Plans for public expenditure are discussed with the various departments against the background of economic forecasts and in total for compatibility with the MTFS. Final decisions on next year's public expenditure are taken by the Cabinet during the autumn and are announced as part of the Autumn Statement. By now the Chancellor has a fairly clear picture of the shape of the next budget. Forecasts have indicated the measures he needs to take to maintain the MTFS – the raising or lowering of aggregate demand, and the level of public spending has been decided. It remains to be decided how the revenue is to be raised – how much borrowing, what taxes?

Changes in most taxes are considered in the following months, but many are quickly rejected on the grounds of cost or administrative difficulties. The Chancellor's final decisions are based upon the computer forecasts of how the economy will react to different policy measures, together with the representations made by companies, trade associations, the CBI, and the Trades Union Congress (TUC). During this period the computer forecasts are being continuously updated. The final choices are delayed as long as possible, but eventually, a few days before the budget, the decisions are made.

Interest tends to centre on the budget speech itself, but the Chancellor still has to guide the budget proposals through four days of detailed scrutiny by Parliament. Indeed, there have been occasions when it has become clear during the debate that the Chancellor could not rely on a majority of MPs to support specific measures and has amended his proposals accordingly (for example in 1981, the Chancellor halved to 10p his original proposal to increase the duty on diesel oils). The budget resolutions passed by the House of Commons at the end of the debate form the basis of the Finance Bill which normally becomes law in July.

The finance of local government

Many of the public services we take for granted within the UK are provided by the local authorities. A description of these services is part of Chapter 15. Our interest here lies in the financing of these services.

In 1987–88 expenditure by local authorities amounted to £41,000 million – or nearly a quarter of general government expenditure. Broadly speaking this money is raised in three ways:

– Trading Income represents the smallest source of finance. Most local authorities obtain income from services they provide. One important source is council housing. Charges are also made for entrance to sports centres, museums, car parks and evening classes.

- Government grants at present account for nearly half of all local authority revenue. These grants are paid to compensate local authorities for the different amounts that they need to spend to provide a service of a certain level, and to iron out differences they can raise from the community charge.
- The third source of finance – a local tax – has recently been changed.

Until 1989/90 owners of land and property paid 'rates' to help meet the cost of local services. All property – houses, factories, shops and offices – was inspected by the Inland Revenue who placed a value on it. The local authority used this for determining the liability (for rates) of whoever used that property. This was done by declaring the amount of tax which had to be paid on each £ of rateable value.

As a form of taxation, rates had the advantage of providing local authorities with a predictable amount of revenue which was easy to collect. However, rates may be regressive in that there is no necessary correlation between rateable value and ability to pay (eg large houses occupied by pensioners). There were also wide discrepancies in the rates paid by householders/businesses in different areas. Finally, only about one-third of the electorate paid rates in full – a further one-sixth were deemed to be poor and received rate rebates, and the rest lived in the household of someone else who was liable for rates.

In 1990 the system of rates was abolished in England and Wales. It was replaced by a community charge for householders and a national uniform business rate.

The community charge is a flat charge set by the local authority. It is paid by every adult resident in the local authority area unless they are exempt, e.g. people still at school and the armed forces overseas. Alternatively they may be eligible to receive a rebate because they are 'low paid'.

The National uniform business rate (NUBR) retains the old rates system – that is a property tax on business premises, and all such premises will be revalued. However, unlike the old system where local authorities established the tax which had to be paid on each £ of rateable value, it is now the Government which will establish a single uniform rate to be levied throughout the country. This will be collected by the local authority, pooled and re-distributed to local authorities as an equal amount per adult in their area.

It is argued that this will reduce the variability that arose in business rates through some businesses being sited in the areas of high spending authorities, and others in low spending areas. However, the national revaluation of business property has resulted in far higher rateable values in London and Southern England than other areas (in some areas of the north it may actually have declined). Although the Government does not intend to increase revenue raised through NUBR over that raised by rates it is likely that the tax burden will be shifted from the north to the south of England. Thus the Department of the Environment estimates that in the south taxes will rise by 6–27 per cent whilst other regions face reductions of 11–31 per cent.

Examination Questions

1. Economic recession is followed by a deterioration in many economic indicators, e.g. output consumption, investment employment, public revenue trade.
   Explain the impact of an expansionary fiscal policy upon these indicators.

2. Explain why it may be difficult for a government to devise a universally acceptable fiscal policy.

3. What do you understand by the term 'national debt'? Critically examine the view that the national debt is unimportant.

4. What would be the consequences, for industry, of the Chancellor of the Exchequer increasing the rates of expenditure taxes? *(CAMB 1985)*

5. 'We will reduce the level of direct taxation and so increase the incentive to work.'. (Prime Minister: the General Election 1983) Do you think such a policy would achieve its objective? *(CAMB 1985)*

6. How might a change in
   (a) direct taxation
   and
   (b) employers' national insurance contributions, affect the output and after tax profits of a firm? *(CAMB)*

7. Each year every Government raises and spends large amounts of money. How does the way in which a government
   (a) raises the money
   (b) spends the money
   affect the private sector of business? *(PSC)*

8. What are the principles a government will consider when framing an economically desirable tax system? *(PSC 1985)*

Part III
Managers and Management

Chapter 10
Managers and management

Although the term 'management' is commonly associated with business management it is, in fact, used in all forms of organisations and organised activities.

The reasons for this can best be understood by considering the characteristics of an organisation. First, an organisation has a goal or purpose – for a business organisation that would be to provide a product or service to the customer at a profit. Second, for the organisation to provide that service it needs a structure – departments, sections and units and a system of rules and regulations governing their work. Finally, the organisation needs people to undertake all the activities necessary to produce the goods or service. But who makes all these decisions about purpose, structure and people – the answer is management.

```
+-----------------------------------------+
|               MANAGEMENT                |
|   +-----------------+-----------------+ |
|   |                 |                 | |
|   |     People      |    Materials    | |
|   |                 |                 | |
|   +-----------------+-----------------+ |
|   |                 |                 | |
|   |    Machines     |      Money      | |
|   |                 |                 | |
|   +-----------------+-----------------+ |
+-----------------------------------------+
```

10.1 Management – a unifying resource

Management is going to be needed wherever people work together for a common purpose. Thus, management is just as important in the Church, army, football club, rock band or government as in business. Yet not all those people who carry out management functions are called managers. Bishops, headmasters, generals and cabinet ministers are just as much managers as the marketing or production manager of a business organisation.

Management is best seen as a unifying resource (see Fig. 10.1) that brings together all resources used by the organisation so that the objectives of the organisation are achieved efficiently and effectively.

Levels of Management

Within most business organisations three broad levels of management can be identified. These three levels are often termed 'the management pyramid' – see Fig. 10.2.

Senior Management

This is the group of people who have the most authority and power within the organisation. They take the most important decisions –

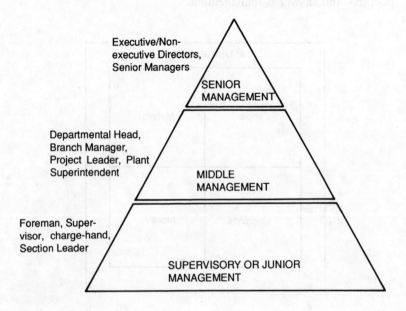

10.2 The Management Pyramid

particularly those relating to the organisation's broad long-term objectives. Their time horizon is often 5–10 years. They are, in a business, responsible to the shareholders for the conduct of the firm. Generally, because of the complexity of their work they will only have a few executives reporting directly to them, though indirectly, through their subordinates, they are responsible for the work of all employees under them.

Middle Management

This group is charged with carrying out the decisions made by senior management. This will often involve developing more detailed short term operational plans to implement the broad objectives decided above them. Their time horizon is commonly one year. Their span of control – the number of subordinates who report directly to them – will vary between 4 and 9. Middle managers are responsible to their superiors for the operations of their 'unit'.

Supervisory Management

These managers are responsible to their superiors for implementing the short range plans which have been devised by middle management. Their time horizon will vary between a week and a month. They are responsible for a group of subordinates – workers – which may be as large as 30.

What managers do

The job of a factory foreman may seem very different from that of a multi-national director yet, in practice, there are common characteristics. Fig. 10.3 shows us three different ways of looking at the work of managers. In each case, whether we analyse the manager's job in terms of roles performed in the organisation, the skills required to carry out the job efficiently, or the functions undertaken, we see similar characteristics required of managers at all levels.

Managerial skills

Technical Skills This is the ability to use the tools and techniques of a particular trade or profession. For the personnel manager this would mean a knowledge of employment law, recruitment procedures, training programmes etc. For the production manager familiarity with plant and equipment, production methods, planned maintenance or stock control would be necessary. Of course, in both

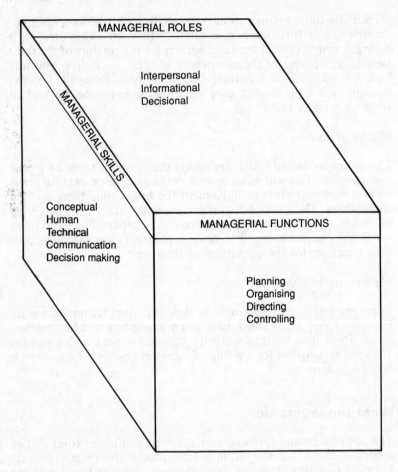

10.3 What managers do

these jobs the actual range of technical skills required would be far greater than we can cover here.

In practice, the amount of time spent using a technical skill decreases as you move further up the management pyramid (see Fig. 10.4). While the production supervisor may spend most of their time dealing with machine breakdowns you are hardly likely to find the financial director of a business drawing up the annual accounts. Yet the knowledge of the process by which the annual accounts are drawn up is vital – in order to control subordinates.

Human Skills Management is often referred to as 'getting things

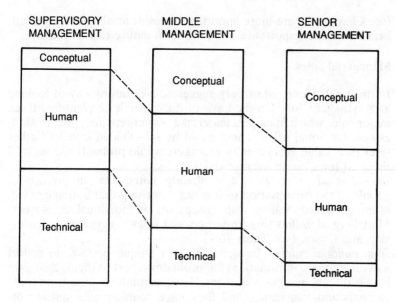

10.4 How managerial skills change at different levels in the organisation

done through people'. While this definition does not reveal the true diversity of the manager's task it does draw our attention to the importance of people in the organisation. Fig. 10.4 shows that high levels of inter-personal skills are needed to lead and motivate staff at all managerial levels within the organisation.

Conceptual Skills This is the intellectual ability to see the whole organisation as a single unit. The manager needs to have sufficient conceptual skills to see how:
– Factors in a situation are inter-related
– A change in one part will affect the 'whole'
in order to solve the problem. This is an ability which is particularly important in senior managers since they plan the activities of the organisation. The good manager will plan to take advantage of (environmental) opportunities and avoid environmental threats rather than merely reacting to changed circumstances.

To these three skills we have just discussed *communication* and *decision-making* are sometimes added. Communication is the subject of a separate chapter (Chapter 15) and all that needs to be said here is that communication skills are equally important at all levels of management within the organisation and that decision-making skills

179

(see Chapter 11) are more important at senior levels of management because of the importance and long term nature of the decisions.

Managerial roles

In the 1960s Henry Mintzberg suggested a different way of looking at a manager's job. On the basis of his research he identified three major roles which managers undertake – interpersonal, informational and decisional roles. These could be sub-divided into 10 further roles (see Table 10.1). Senior managers would probably use most of these 10 roles on an average day.

Interpersonal roles We have already noted the importance of people in the organisation so it is not surprising that a manager will often be found dealing with groups of, or individual employees. Mintzberg identifies three interpersonal roles – figurehead, leadership and liaison (see Table 10.1).

Informational roles Managers are in a unique position to collect and disseminate information. Subordinates report to them, their own bosses discuss matters with them, they glean information from trade journals and magazines, and they have contacts with outside organisations. There are three informational roles – monitor, disseminator and spokesperson.

Decisional roles In undertaking a decisional role a manager acts as entrepreneur, disturbance handler, resource allocator and negotiator. Once again the manager is in a unique position to carry out this role – this time because of the information that has been collected.

Managerial functions

One of the earliest management writers was a French industrialist Henri Fayol (1841–1925). To him is credited the idea of analysing the job of a manager around functions such as planning, organising, directing and controlling. These functions he believed were used by managers whatever the nature of the organisation or the level of the manager. We will examine these four functions in detail in later chapters. Here we will just make some very general remarks.

Planning is the starting point for all managerial action. If your objectives or goals are ill-defined it is unlikely that you will ever achieve them. Planning also enables you to devise strategies for achieving those objectives. Although all managers plan, this function is most important for senior managers (*see* Fig. 10.5).

Once plans have been devised the manager has to develop an *organisation* structure which will achieve the desired goals. This will involve the creation of departments and the division of work within them as well as establishing communication systems. Although ob-

Table 10.1 Managerial roles

role	explanation	examples
Interpersonal **Figurehead**	Acting as a symbol of the organisation undertaking social or legal duties	Opening new factory; meeting shareholders; presenting long service awards; attending funerals
Leader	Motivation and encouragement of subordinates to achieve organisational goals	Praise; criticism; promotion; dismissal
Liaison	Acting as a connecting link between the organisation and outside bodies who provide information	Relationships with: clients; suppliers; trade associations or the local community
Informational **Monitor**	The manager searches for information on the environment and the organisation in order to more accurately predict future events	Written means include: professional journals; newspapers; subordinates' reports; mail. Verbal means include: discussions with suppliers, customers and other managers
Disseminator	The transmission of information to superiors, peers and subordinates so that correct decisions are made. Such information may be hard ie, factual or soft ie, open to interpretation	Departmental meetings mail, written reports and telephone calls
Spokesperson	Represents the organisation to outsiders or unit to superiors	Meetings with share-holders, bankers; interviews with media
Decisional **Entrepreneur**	Adapts organisation to meet changed environmental conditions	Introduction of new projects/processes; revision of organisational structure
Disturbance Handler	Reacting to unexpected situations	Strikes; breach of contract; customer complaints; material shortages
Resource Allocator	Allocation of resources among various units in organisation	The screening of all decisions with financial implications; annual budgets; allocation of own time to subordinates;
Negotiator	Mediator in internal and external conflicts	Drawing up contracts; industrial relations problems; size of budget.

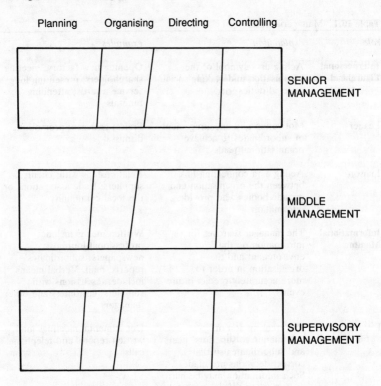

Planning   Organising   Directing   Controlling

SENIOR MANAGEMENT

MIDDLE MANAGEMENT

SUPERVISORY MANAGEMENT

10.5 How management functions change at different levels in the organisation

viously important, organisation takes up proportionately less time than any of the other functions.

The *directing function* is also referred to as *co-ordinating*, leading or motivating. Whatever phrase is used though, it involves finding, training and motivating employees to work in a way which contributes towards organisational objectives. Supervisors with their large span of control (i.e. the number of workers responsible to them) spend more time on 'directing' workers than on any other function.

The manager's final function is *controlling*. This involves watching the organisation's performance and ensuring that actual performance coincides with planned performance.

How managerial functions differ within the organisation

Although all managers perform the same functions – planning, organising, directing and controlling – the emphasis which is placed on each function will vary according to the manager's level in the organisational hierarchy.

Top management. Senior management is responsible for long-term planning and policy decisions within the organisation. Planning involves determining the organisation's profit and growth targets. Organising involves deciding upon the basic structure of the organisation – what divisions or departments to create, whether to organise by product or territory. Directing includes providing the motivation for employees to strive for organisational objectives, while controlling is through measurement of achieved results against objectives.

Middle management. Middle managers are required to implement on a day-to-day basis the policies decided by senior management. Planning requires formulation of plans and procedures to ensure that activity is directed towards organisational goals. Organisation requires the delegation of specific activities to subordinates, the co-ordination of their work, and the development of horizontal relationships (i.e. with other middle managers of equal status). Directing involves creating situations where the employee can satisfy personal goals while at the same time meeting organisational goals. Controlling is based upon a comparison of budget results in relation to plans.

Supervisory management. Sometimes called first-time management, supervisors or foremen these are the managers in daily contact with the workers. Planning by supervisors is limited to developing detailed schedules of work for employees. Organisation requires implementation of these schedules. Directing involves the application of motivation and discipline to overcome employee resistance, the recognition of outstanding work and sometimes acting as friend and counsellor. Control lies in ensuring that work is completed satisfactorily and according to schedule.

For the sake of simplicity we have considered the function of managers separately and not as part of a cycle (see Fig. 10.6). Unfortunately, in reality it is not so simple. First, except in a completely new organisation, the functions will not necessarily occur in the order illustrated in the cycle. Moreover the manager is involved in many projects all in different stages of completion and will perform all functions on a typical day.

Secondly, in practice, it is difficult to distinguish the four func-

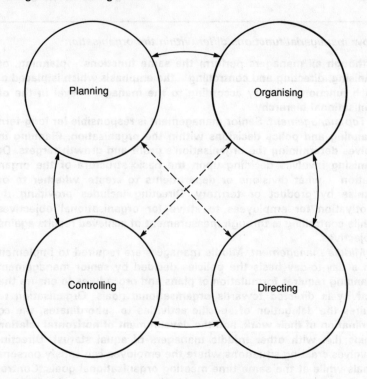

10.6 The relationship between management functions

tions. Plans are used to control employee activity (orgnisation and direction), or control activities may lead to the revision of plans.

Finally, the manager's ability to plan, organise, direct and control is often impaired by resrictions on their authority or the use of resources. It would be extremely rare for any manager to have complete freedom of action.

Examination Questions

1 How will the promotion of a sales consultant to the position of Area Manager change the nature of his work and the skills he uses?
(PSC 1987)
2 What in your view are the essential qualities of a good business manager?
3 Identify the main constituent elements of management?
To what extent does the task of supervisor differ from that of a senior manager?
4 Discuss the difficulties and dilemmas faced by management in the long term as opposed to the short term *(AEB 1989)*.

Chapter 11
Planning

Planning

Planning is the process by which we decide what our objectives are and how they are going to be achieved. The process may be formal or informal. Formal planning occurs where there are written statements clearly defining our intentions and these statements are freely available to others in the organisation. Formal planning is practised by virtually all large organisations. Conversely informal planning is more likely to be found in small owner-managed firms. In many cases the plan is no more than an idea of what the owner would like to happen in the future – it is very general and there are unlikely to be any supporting plans outlining how the objectives are going to be achieved.

The importance of planning

Formal planning benefits the organisation in many ways. Planning attempts to offset environmental uncertainty. Although obviously fraught with difficulty predictions can be made about the future – the size of markets, the nature of competition, the impact of technology, societal attitudes and new laws. The more accurately the organisation predicts the future the more it can develop plans that reduce the risk of failure. Without planning all sorts of unforseen problems can occur. Far greater efforts may be needed to solve these problems than would have been needed to plan effectively in the first place!

Planning is also the means by which we ensure that scarce resources within the organisation are used effectively. Thus:

- The organisation structure can be designed so that all parts contribute to organisational objectives

- It is a means of motivating employees by providing them with targets to achieve

- It enables the manager to direct employee efforts more effectively

- Plans act as a means of control. They can be used to check how far the goals of the organisation, a separate department or an individual have been achieved.

There are also a number of problems which are associated with planning. The cost of planning may be greater than the benefits gained. Planning may take time and delay badly needed action. Plans may be inappropriate in unanticipated circumstances, in which case they are an unwelcome restriction on managerial initiative.

However, despite these problems surveys have shown that firms who plan generally achieve a higher return on capital than those which do not.

Hierarchy of plans

We have already seen that planning is carried on at all levels in the organisation and also that its nature varies according to organisational level. In practice, we can identify a hierarchy of interlocking plans which govern the organisation's activities at all levels (see Figure 11.1).

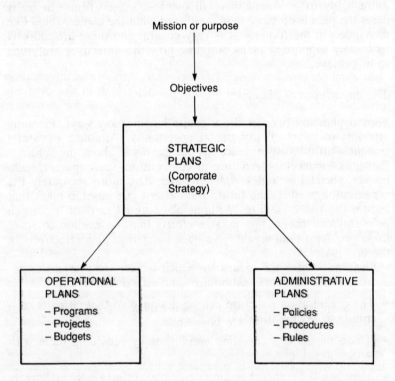

11.1 The hierarchy of plans in a typical organisation

Each of these plans serves two functions. First, it serves as the means of achieving the objectives outlined by the plan at the next higher level. Second, the plan will provide the end objective for plans at the next level down in the organisation. In broad terms this means that a very general plan generated by senior management becomes increasingly more specific and detailed as it works its way down through the organisation.

Defining the mission of the organisation is the starting point for all planning. The mission is the reason why the organisation exists. For companies in the UK it may be found in the Memorandum of Association in the 'Objects Clause', for nationalised industries in the legislation creating them or for charities in the charter or deed setting them up. Such statements are very general.

However, many management writers and leading business people believe that defining the mission of the organisation is all important to its survival, profitability and growth. The classic case is the American railway system which missed its opportunity by failing to re-define its mission as being in the transportation rather than the railway business. Many glass bottle manufacturers have also failed to grasp opportunities available to them as 'liquid container manufacturers'. In the UK the decline of the textile industry can be attributed to a failure to re-define its mission in the context of third world competition, new technology and new cloths.

Statements of mission or purpose do not include any information on how that end will be attained. The next step in the planning process – the setting of objectives tells us how senior managers propose to do this. Common objectives include:
- survival
- sales maximisation
- profit maximisation
- new product development
- higher dividends
- diversification
- social responsibility

There are of course many others. Typically organisations will adopt a number of objectives as long as they are not incompatible with one another.

Organisational objectives reflect the particular situation a business finds itself in. As circumstances change so may the objectives.

Once objectives have been defined managers must plan how to achieve them. Strategies are broad plans based on different sets of assumptions of what the 'environment' will do and how managers will react to this. There may be several strategies which could be used. If our objective is to maximise profits, strategies to meet this could be:
- increase production lines

- introduce factory automation
- horizontal/vertical mergers
- diversification
- increase sales effort
- rationalisation

The generation of alternative strategies and the selection of the best alternative is an important part of the process of planning. Once a strategy has been developed there is a commitment to allocate the resources necessary to implement that plan.

Although strategies are general plans of action they will now be stated in quantifiable terms. Thus the objective 'maximising profits' will become 'to double profits in the next five years', or 'increase market share' will become 'to achieve a 25 per cent market share within the next decade'. We are stating the results we wish to achieve in such a way that we can see how near or far we are from actually achieving those results. The statement in this way can be used for control purposes.

Strategic plans are developed by senior managers as guides to action over a number of years for their subordinates. It is the responsibility of these managers to develop supporting plans. These may be either *operational* or *administrative*.

Administrative plans are devised to guide actions in circumstances which are likely to recur. The aim of such plans is to enable the manager to save time and act consistently in similar situations. There are three types of administrative plan – policies, procedures and rules, all of which are designed to contribute to organisational objectives.

Policies are guides to managerial action. Policies are created where managers have discretion in decision-making and act as limits to that discretionary power. Thus an organisation may have a policy of making senior appointments from employees within the organisation. This is a guide to decision-making and will be followed by managers in normal circumstances. It is not a straitjacket though and managers may decline to follow the policy (in which case they will be required to justify their decision.)

Most policies will be established formally in order to improve efficiency, avoid confusion, ensure consistency of action or to enforce some particular set of values. Examples of policy guidelines include:

- making decisions at the lowest possible level in the organisation

- equal opportunities for all applicants/employees regardless of sex, race or religion

- improving the quality of working life

- to secure the supply of raw materials

- to sell only to those customers who are able to buy in bulk.

Procedures are sets of detailed instructions which have to be followed in a certain situation. In large organisations there are many examples of standard operating procedures to be found, for example:

- ordering office equipment and supplies
- receipt of money or goods
- employee disciplining
- payment of wages
- machine maintenance

Procedures often cut across departmental boundaries. The sale of goods on credit will involve sales, production, despatch and accounting departments. It is vitally necessary that procedures are followed so that the relevant information reaches all the departments involved. Often allied to the introduction of procedures is the development of standard forms.

Rules. Whereas policies are guides to decision-making and leave room for managerial discretion rules replace decision-making and discretion. Rules either enforce or forbid certain types of behaviour. Examples of rules commonly found in organisations include:

- No smoking
- No drinking in this room
- No employee will accept gifts, favours or entertainment from a supplier
- Working hours are from 8.30 am – 5.00 pm
- All cheques over £5,000 must be signed by a director
- Safety equipment must be worn at all times

These rules must be applied by the manager whenever possible. In unavoidable circumstances a manager may suspend the rule, for example if the central heating system breaks down the manager may decide to send employees home. However, if the rule has to be suspended frequently the rule will obviously have to be modified. No one should work under the mis-apprehension that 'rules are made to be broken'.

Operational Plans. A strategic plan to develop a new product – say a car – will call for many subsidiary programmes. These will be developed in the individual departments and sections of the organisation. Thus, in our example of developing a new car a few of the plans which have to be made are:

Research and Development   – to produce and test prototype
Marketing   – to research customer requirement

189

	– to devise promotions' campaigns
	– establish a pricing policy
	– establish retail outlets
Production	– design and install new plant layout
	– enter into contracts for the purchase of components
Personal	– recruitment of new workers
	– training of operatives
Finance	– to provide necessary finance for development and launch of new product
	– to provide system of financial control for new product

There are of course many other plans which have to be developed. But all these plans are interdependent. Co-ordination of activities is very important since a failure to adhere to any one operational plan will delay the whole strategic plan.

These *operational plans* are also sometimes called *single use plans* because they have been devised specifically to help achieve one strategic plan. Other strategic plans are unlikely to require the same supporting plans. The three most common types of operational plans are programmes, projects and budgets.

A programme is an operational plan covering a large number of activities. Programmes are normally long-term plans requiring considerable commitment of resources. A good example is the American moon programme. Most business organisations will have more modest programmes than that! Common examples are:

- the development of new products

- removal of factory/office to new premises

- development and retraining of personnel arising from organisational change

Programmes will identify the steps needed to achieve the objectives, the units or individuals responsible, resources which are required and the order and timing for each step.

A project is more limited in its scope than a programme. Indeed, a project may be a part of a programme. For example, within the general programme of development and training of personnel mentioned above 'manager development' may form a project. This is possible because the programme can be divided into different parts which can be undertaken separately from one another.

Budgets are statements of resources needed (quantified in monetary terms) which are needed to undertake a programme or project. These financial statements are commonly used for control purposes (see p. 352).

The process of strategic (corporate) planning

Recently, there has been a growing recognition of the importance of strategic planning. It is seen as a means of predicting and adapting

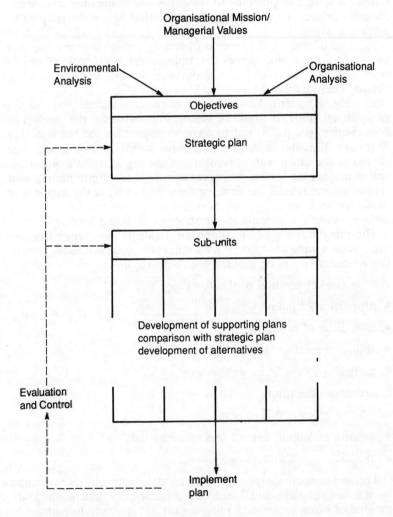

11.2 The process of corporate planning

to environmental change. It is also a means of ensuring that the organisations' scarce resources are best for the organisation. More recently writers have also argued that factors such as the increasing:

- speed of technological change

- complexity of the macro and micro environment

- complexity of managerial work

require a system of planning to cover the whole organisation. Many business failures are the result of not developing a strategic plan or getting it wrong.

Figure 11.2 shows the process of strategic planning. We see that there are three major factors determining the organisation's objectives and strategic plan. The importance of the environment has already been discussed (see p. 55).

Equally important, however, are managerial values and the organisational ethos. It would be almost impossible for the mission of Scott Bader (see p. 28) not to have an impact on the strategy that it adopts. Equally, managers may have strong views on social or ethical issues which will, in turn, affect the organisation's objectives and strategic plan. Other managers may wish to empire build – that is, expand the size of the firm, or their part of it, at the expense of profit, or seek security – by avoiding risky investments. All these differing values are inputs to the strategic planning process.

The third major influence upon the strategic plan arises from an organisation-wide analysis of its strengths and weaknesses. In particular planners will be looking for evidence on:

1. the market position of the company, e.g.

- proportion of industry sales

- reputation of products

- ability to produce new products

- particular strengths or weaknesses

2. cost considerations

- relative efficiency of operations

- security of labour, capital and raw materials

- unique cost advantages eg, patents

The aim of such analysis is to ensure that opportunities presented by the environment and which are attractive to management are capable of being exploited having regard to the strengths and weaknesses of the organisation. The organisation will seek to capitalise on strengths it already has – its 'distinctive competencies'. A shoe shop is unlikely to open a supermarket, or a computer software specialist move into oil refining just because it sees opportunities there.

Why planning fails

1   The process has not been followed properly, e.g. inadequate environmental or organisational analysis.
2   Not all levels of management are involved in the process of planning *or* informed of their contribution.
3   Slavish adherence to the plan. Circumstances may change more rapidly than predicted. It may be necessary to adapt the plan.
4   Failure to implement satisfactory control techniques.
5   Lack of commitment on the part of senior management.
6   Resistance to change by managers and employees.
7   The plan is not worked to once it has been drawn up.

Having developed the strategic plan it is up to managers in the sub-units to develop plans which contribute to the overall objective. In developing these plans these managers, like their superiors, will be influenced by the impact of the environment of their sub-unit, their own values and their sub-unit's strengths and weaknesses.

Once these plans have been developed they will be examined by senior managers to see how far they contribute to the strategic plan. It is unlikely at this stage that the supporting plans will be sufficient to achieve the objective. For example, a strategic plan may call for a reduction of 100 staff or a £1m increase in profits within two years. If the sub-unit's plans do not match this figure a 'planning gap' exists. This must be closed.

The planning gap which has been revealed may be closed in one of two ways. First, it is always possible to modify the strategic plan, in practice though this is the last thing to be considered. Instead, the managers of sub-units will be asked to develop alternative plans which will contribute more fully to the overall objective. This is certainly not impossible in most cases. Figure 11.3 shows some of the options open to managers trying to achieve a £1m increase in profits.

From the alternative plans that are generated, senior management will choose those that close the gap most effectively. It is only at this stage that if the 'planning gap' still remains that the strategic plan will be modified.

Once these sub plans have been agreed the plan is put into operation. All sub-units know how they have to contribute – what time spans they have to work to, what budgets they have to keep within. These plans in themselves act as benchmarks for control.

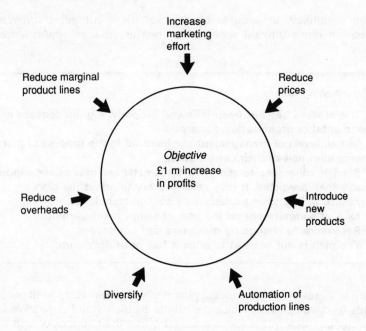

11.3 Ways in which sub units can help achieve a profit goal

Control is an important aspect of strategic planning. It is not unusual for plans to go off course at some stage. What is necessary is for the organisation to set up some system for monitoring the plan – the 2 most common methods are monthly budget reports and regular progress meetings. Of course, not all deviations need to be reported, some are inconsequential, others will be easily corrected, but it is important to see that managers receive feedback whenever significant deviation occurs. It is then for these managers to work with their subordinates and find ways to correct the deviation. In many cases contingency plans to deal with just this situation will exist. However, even if they do not it is unlikely we will have to discard the whole plan. Once again we look to managers to develop alternative courses of action to meet the changed situation. Finally, it is always open to senior management to revise the strategic plan to take account of intractable difficulties.

Decision-making

Decision-making is the selection of a course of action from a number of alternatives. It is a key part of the manager's job. Table 11.1 shows how essential decision-making is in all areas of managerial work. Collectively, these decisions determine the future of the organisation – its objectives and the success with which they are carried out. Consequently, it is important that managerial decisions – which are often made in difficult conditions – are made as objectively as possible.

Table 11.1 Examples of managerial decision-making

Planning
What are the organisation's objectives?
What product/service shall we provide?
How shall we provide it?
When shall we provide it?

Organising
How shall we structure work?
How much work do I delegate?
What is my span of control?
What is the relationship between line and staff departments?

Directing
How do I motivate my workers?
How do I introduce change?
What leadership style will be effective?
How can I improve co-ordination?

Control
Where should I control organisational activity?
How do I control it?
When should I be informed of deviations from plan?

The process of decision-making

We can define decision-making as the process by which we systematically study a problem so as to develop alternatives and select the one which will most effectively achieve our goal. The process is shown in Fig. 11.4. We will look at each step in detail.

1 Diagnose and define problem. There are four common ways that problems are brought to a manager's attention. First, on the basis of past experience the manager may realise that a problem exists. This could be a fall in sales, an increase in customer complaints or a rise in staff turnover. What has gone before is, to the manager, a standard against which current performance can be gauged.

Standards of performance are also provided by plans as well as experience. The second way in which a problem is identified is for a deviation of actual from planned performance to come to the manager's attention.

Thirdly, a manager may be brought problems by other people. For example, the resignation of a key subordinate or a breakdown in industrial relations culminating in a strike. The majority of day-to-day problems a manager faces arise in this way.

195

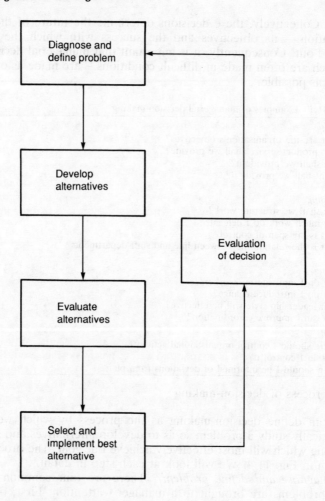

11.4 The decision-making process

Finally, the actions of competitors in producing new products, using new processes or introducing new market strategies may require the manager to make decisions.

However the successful manager will not just wait for a problem to arise but will try to anticipate them and plan how to deal with that eventuality.

Once a problem has been diagnosed the manager must then define the problem. Drucker argues this stage is critical to the decision making process. Define the problem incorrectly and one can never hope to achieve a satisfactory solution to that problem.

Let us take the example of falling sales. It would be easy to define the problem in terms of increased competition. A little more thought though will tell us that there are several other possibilities we should consider before jumping to conclusions. These would include poor quality, obsolete products/changed tastes, unattractive packaging or seasonal patterns of trade. The most obvious solution to a problem is not always the correct one.

2 *Develop alternatives.* The manager's aim is to develop as many different alternative methods of solving the problem as possible. Alternative courses of action most often generated by managers revolve around their own past experience and selective imitation of other managers' actions. Where these are insufficient other alternatives may be generated by 'brainstorming'.

Brainstorming

Brainstorming was first used in the USA in the 1950s to generate new brand names for products and advertising slogans.

This process is designed to aid creative thinking (and the generation of ideas). In essence, brainstorming involves a group of people coming together and stimulating each other's thinking. Any idea is acceptable, judgment is suspended and criticism not allowed. The important thing is the generation of lots of new ideas. Later these ideas will be evaluated (by a different group of people), the vast majority will be rejected but one, perhaps two, will provide a novel answer to the problem brainstormed.

Of course, not all possible alternatives will be considered by the manager when making a decision. Some will not even have been thought of, others will have been ruled out immediately as too costly or contravening organisational policy. In this sense the alternative that is finally chosen may be termed 'satisficing' as it answers the problem reasonably well but is, commonly, not the ideal solution.

3. *Evaluate alternatives.* Once the manager is satisfied that sufficient alternatives have been identified each of them must be evaluated. Again past experience may play a large part in the decision. If the manager has been confronted with a similar problem in the past (is it really the same?) and has dealt with it successfully then similar alternatives will be looked for to provide the solution this time. In unfamiliar situations the manager will evaluate alternatives by two criteria:

- how realistic each is in terms of the objectives and resources of the organisation

- how effectively each alternative deals with the problem.

4. *Select and implement the best alternative.* The selection of one alternative to solve the problem is fraught with difficulties. As we have already noted no alternative is likely to provide the ideal solution. Additionally, each alternative has its own particular set of drawbacks. It is not surprising that some managers find it exceedingly difficult to make important decisions.

Once selection has been made we move to implementation of the decision. As in any kind of plan implementation is critical to success. Subordinates have to be informed of what is required of them, resources must be allocated and a system of periodic reports instituted.

5. *Evaluation of decision.* No problem is solved until the manager has evaluated the success of the decision taken. If the problem has not been solved then the adage 'don't throw good money after bad' should be adopted and another alternative used.

Group decision-making

Many decisions taken in organisations, especially important ones, are taken jointly by a group of individuals. We know that managers spend a large proportion of their time – up to 40 per cent – in meetings. These meetings of groups of individuals are given many names, the most common is 'committee', but task forces, study groups, project teams, advisory panels are also examples of group decision-making. Group decision-making has many advantages. For example:

- *More information.* The old adage is 'two heads are better than one'. Group members can pool knowledge on a topic and thus generate more complete information.

- *More alternatives.* Individuals with their diversity of backgrounds and skills tend to view problems in different ways. They also see different solutions. A group will generate many more alternatives than an individual and is less likely to overlook potential solutions.

- *Improved motivation.* Individuals who are involved in the decision-making process are more committed to ensuring the group decision works. This occurs even when the individual concerned has been unsuccessful in promoting their particular solution.

- *Improved co-ordination.* Individuals who have been involved in the decision making process understand what decision has been taken, why it has been taken, and how they and their department should contribute to the success of the decision.

On the other hand group decision-making has its fair share of problems! These include:

- *Time consuming:* it is often difficult to arrange a meeting time which is acceptable to all group members. This problem increases with the size of the group. Moreover communication within the group is often inefficient. Consequently groups take longer to reach a decision.

- *Individual domination.* Group members differ in rank, communication skills, experience and expertise. It is unusual to find a group where one or two members are not dominant. The final decision may be unduly influenced by this unrepresentative group.

- *Conformity.* Groups are brought together to solve a problem. There is organisational pressure on individuals to compromise their interests. There are, additionally, psychological pressures for compromise in a cohesive group. The individual may be inhibited from speaking his mind for fear of being the odd one out. This pressure is sometimes referred to as 'groupthink'.

- *Lack of responsibility.* It has been suggested that because no one member is personally responsible for the decision taken members are less careful and objective. Additionally, because members do not feel personally responsible for a decision they may not work so hard to correct it should it go wrong.

Although group decision-making has significant benefits for the organisation there are limits to its use. Thus, where a decision commits a large proportion of organisation resources for years to come, where a quick decision is required or where confidentiality is paramount, groups will not be used.

Aids to managerial decision making

As organisations have grown and invested in new technology the complexity and costliness of decision-making has increased dramatically. The manager's job has become far more difficult. For this reason there has been increasing interest in ways in which planning and decision-making can be helped by the application of quantitative techniques. Typically these decision-making techniques involve the use of mathematical models and often the use of a computer. Many of these techniques were initially developed for military use and were later found to have value in other situations. In this section we will look at some of the more popular aids to decision-making being used in organisations today. Other aids to decision-making are mentioned on pp. 311, 320, 354 and 363.

The pay off matrix. This is a method of evaluating the likely rate of return from different courses of action (strategies) in different circumstances.

Let us assume that Lee Mo Yieup Ltd wishes to market a new microwave cooker. However, they are unsure how consumers and competitors will react to this product. Consequently, they devise a matrix which shows both the alternative strategies they can adopt – low, medium and high levels of production and the level of demand.

The matrix drawn up (Fig 11.5) shows that revenue under the poorest circumstances – low demand conditions will be $2 million, and under medium and high demand conditions will be $3 million and $4 million, respectively. A decision to adopt a high production strategy under high demand conditions will generate $4m revenue. But if demand conditions turn out to be low the maximum revenue is only $2 million Lee Mo Yieup Ltd may very well have problems with unwanted stocks of finished foods and components. The risk of this situation occurring can be lessened by market research and forecasting the likelihood of each outcome happening in practice. Each level of demand conditions will be allocated at probability value and by multiplying this to the revenue predictions indicated in Fig. 11.5 we can arrive at an expected value for each strategy. In our example market research indicated the following probabilities for Lee Mo Yieup Ltd: low (30 per cent), medium (50 per cent) and high (20 per cent).

Fig. 11.5 shows the expected revenue for each option taking into account the demand probabilities specified above. The expected value for each strategy is obtained by estimating the expected revenue for each option within a strategy. On the basis of these the company, if it wishes to maximise revenue, will choose a high production strategy as this yields the highest expected value.

Decision Trees This depicts each decision or chance event as a branch of a tree. By ascribing values to each decision and chance event we can reach the same position as with the pay off matrix and compare the results of each strategy. Decision trees have the advantage of having far more visual impact than the pay off matrix. An example of a decision tree, using the same data as before; is shown in Fig. 11.6.

While decision trees (and pay off matrixes) systematically identify the options and likely outcomes open to a manager it is still necessary for the manager to make the decision. Probability technique are based on the assumption that managers will follow their findings. In practice, this is not necessarily so. Thus, if there is a 70 per cent chance of being right logically the manager should adopt this option. Yet if the penalty for being wrong (a 30 per cent chance) was dismissal or demotion how many of us would risk this?

Demand conditions

Production strategy	Low	Medium	High
Low	£2 million	£2 million	£2 million
Medium	£2 million	£3 million	£3 million
High	£2 million	£3 million	£4 million

Payoff matrix

Demand conditions

Production strategy	Low (30%)	Medium (50%)	High (20%)	Expected value
Low	£0.6 million	£1.0 million	£0.4 million	£2.0 million
Medium	£0.6 million	£1.5 million	£0.6 million	£2.7 million
High	£0.6 million	£1.5 million	£0.8 million	£2.9 million

Payoff matrix with expected values

Fig 11.5

Different people have different attitudes towards risks. Senior managers, who often work in situations of high uncertainly, may be more prepared to take larger risks than their subordinates. Other factors may affect the decision too. The manager who is prepared to risk the firm's money on a 70 per cent chance of success may demand something considerably better before risking their own fortune! Equally important is how much money is involved. In general terms, we can say that most of us will be prepared to accept a fairly low probability of success if the sums involved are small.

Operations Research. Sometimes known as OR, operations research can be defined as the 'application of scientific method to the

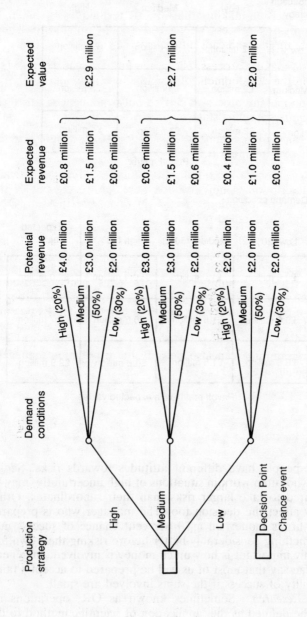

Production strategy	Demand conditions		Potential revenue	Expected revenue	Expected value
High		High (20%)	£4.0 million	£0.8 million	
		Medium (50%)	£3.0 million	£1.5 million	£2.9 million
		Low (30%)	£2.0 million	£0.6 million	
Medium		High (20%)	£3.0 million	£0.6 million	
		Medium (50%)	£3.0 million	£1.5 million	£2.7 million
		Low (30%)	£2.0 million	£0.6 million	
Low		High (20%)	£2.0 million	£0.4 million	
		Medium (50%)	£2.0 million	£1.0 million	£2.0 million
		Low (30%)	£2.0 million	£0.6 million	

Decision Point

Chance event

11.6 Decision tree

analysis of alternatives in a problem situation so as to provide a quantitative basis for arriving at an optimum solution having regard to the goals sought'.

In practice decision-making utilising OR techniques is similar to the decision-making process we have discussed previously. There are, however, three significant differences:

- the decision-making process relies upon human logic whereas OR relies upon the development of a mathematical model.

- the decision-making process is carried out by managers, OR techniques require specialist staff.

- OR staff can only recommend a solution, it is the manager who has power to implement it.

Because OR techniques are often quite complicated mathematically a detailed description is not included here. However, out of the many different OR techniques which are available the four most popular are briefly detailed below.

1. Linear Programming Models
This technique will most often be used to solve allocation problems. It is used where there are linear, that is directly proportional, relationships between a number of factors. Thus, it may be used to determine the number of factories that should be built in order to minimise transport costs between different markets. This is possible because there is a linear relationship between (1) distance and cost, and (2) the number of factories built and building costs.

Linear programming can also simplify the production manager's job in areas such as:

- inventory levels

- product mix

- machine utilisation

2. Game Theory
Game theory has been used for many years by the armed services as a means of predicting how an enemy will react in a specific situation. This is done by simulating reality as closely as possible. Game theory is now also used in business to explain how competitors will respond to an increase in production, an increase in advertising, a price increase, or the introduction of a new or modified product. Anticipating competitors' responses to certain situations enables managers to develop better strategies.

3. Queuing Theory
This is sometimes also termed waiting line theory. It is concerned with the most efficient handling of an intermittent service. By com-

paring the costs of allowing a queue to develop (in, say a restaurant) and comparing these with the costs of eradicating the waiting line, managers can decide whether it is better to reduce waiting line time and if so by how much?

4. *Probability Theory*

By predicting the probability of future events happening managers can reduce business risks. For example, probability theory is used to reduce the likelihood of producing defective products. Statistically, it has been proved that, if a small proportion of total product is tested – say 0.1 per cent and the number of rejects falls within defined limits then the number of rejects in the whole batch will be within acceptable levels. Probability theory is also used by insurance companies in assessing their exposure to risk (e.g. death of applicant for life assurance).

The great advantage of OR techniques is that they can help managers make better quality decisions because:

- a large problem is broken down into small parts enabling easier analysis

- logical systematic analysis rather than intuition, hunch, or rule of thumb is used

- more alternatives (together with their opportunities and risks) are generated and assessed.

Like most techniques though, OR has its limitations. First, the use of such techniques is costly. Many smaller firms are unable to afford the investment in hardware, software and personnel. Second, many decisions need to be made too quickly which prevent them being referred to OR specialists. Third, the number of factors which are present in many managerial situations are so many that present mathematical and computing tools cannot deal with this complexity. Fourth, many of the factors which have to be considered e.g. inter-personal relationships can not be easily quantified. Consequently, these may often be ignored. Finally OR findings may be resisted by managers who have to implement and may be judged on that decision.

Examination Questions

1 What is the purpose of a corporate plan? Describe the various steps in the planning process.
2 Of all the management functions, planning is the most important. How far do you agree with this statement?
3 Explain and describe a logical way which a firm may use to arrive at a selection of alternative strategies.

4 Your directors have recently decided they wish to diversify out of their current range of products. As a member of the team which will have to turn this decision into strategies, draw up a comprehensive checklist of matters which the directors should consider.

5 It is often suggested that planning is only as effective as its implementation and that this is dependent upon commitment and control. How far do you agree with this statement, and how would you go about ensuring commitment and control?

6 Preparation of future plans must be based upon a comprehensive analysis of an organisation's current and past performance. Discuss.

7 Planning places an organisation in a straitjacket and is alien to the enterprising organisation. Examine this statement critically.

8 Explain how corporate planning is likely to differ in
(a) a multinational
(b) a medium sized firm.
What, in your opinion, are the key areas for multinational planning?

9 A company manufacturing machine tools has become concerned at the level of low priced imports entering the UK. Assess the options open to the company to combat this situation.

Chapter 12
Organising

Approaches to organisation design

Before the industrial revolution little thought had gone into organisation design. That was because apart from the Church most organisations were small. However, with the growth of large industry, problems of co-ordination and control increased and the need for research organisation design became obvious.

The classical (or scientific management) approach

Classical writers were convinced that there was only one way to structure an organisation and sought to find a set of principles which if implemented would guarantee an efficient organisation.

F W Taylor (1856–1915) is often said to be the father of the classical school. He was a production engineer who spent his life in the American steel industry. His interest was in work and productivity which he believed could be raised significantly by what is now known as method study and work measurement. As a result of his studies he published a number of books and propounded the four following principles for job design:

- Job design should be undertaken scientifically (see Ch. 17, p. 321 for a detailed description of method study and work measurement).

- Workers have different attributes and abilities – select the proper employee for the job, and ensure they are trained properly in the correct method.

- Workers are motivated primarily by money. The introduction of incentives can increase productivity.

- Each task has both a 'planning' and a 'doing' element. It is the function of the manager to plan, thus allowing the employee to concentrate on doing the job.

These principles may not seem particularly significant to us today, but at the turn of the century they were thought to be revolutionary. They rapidly became standard practice.

While Taylor focused his attention at the base of the organisational pyramid, Henri Fayol (1841–1925) a French mining engineer sought to establish principles could be applied throughout the organisation. They were:

- The principle of the objective – all parts of the organisation must contribute to its objectives, otherwise they are redundant.

- The principle of specialisation – each member of the organisation should be allocated a single role which is well defined in terms of authority, responsibility, and relationships.

- The principle of co-ordination – the structure established should ensure united efforts towards the goals of the organisation.

- The principle of authority – a clear chain of command should exist from the most senior executive to all employees in the organisation.

- The principle of responsibility – a superior cannot avoid responsibility for the acts of subordinates.

- The principle of correspondence – the authority given should always be sufficient to discharge the responsibilities undertaken.

- The span of control – there is a limit to the number of people whose work a manager can supervise. A manager's subordinates should be limited to a maximum of six where their work interlocks.

The acceptance of these principles brought a growing relisation that managerial skills could be learnt, and the subsequent development of management courses in colleges and universities.

Max Weber (1864–1920) provided the third pillar in the development of classical organisation theory. Like Taylor and Fayol, Weber believed that there was a logical framework for organisation which could be used to improve efficiency. He believed such an organisation has the following characteristics:

- Official duties – each employee would be allocated very specialised tasks leading to greater expertise among staff.

- Hierarchy of authority – there are clear levels of authority with the higher positions controlling and supervising those below them. This enables activities to be co-ordinated.

- A system of rules and regulations – all decisions will be based upon the rules which have been established. This ensures uniformity of decision-making.

- Impersonal attitude – rational decision-making is promoted by disregarding all personal or emotional considerations.

- Technical qualifications – employment is based on qualifications and experience (merit). It is expected that organisations will employ workers throughout their working life. Greater expertise is thus developed and employees are more able to resist external pressures.

- Such an organisation Weber termed a 'bureaucracy'. The term, to him, did not have the negative connotations which it has to us today. To Weber it was like a highly efficient modern machine.

Bureaucracies are very much a feature of modern life. Many large organisations and government departments exhibit all the characteristics discussed above. The growth of bureaucracies has arisen because of the following:

1 As the firm increases in size there is a greater specialisation, and the need for more careful co-ordination of activities.

2 The greater complexity of the environment in which the organisation operates, for example the increasing number of ways in which the Government tries to control the activities of business.

3 Their system of rules and regulations, levels of authority, job design, is seen to be efficient.

4 Claims for equality of treatment result in the establishing of rules to be followed in all cases.

The classical approach to organisation theory has been criticised for a number of reasons. First, classical organisation theory takes no account of the individual. Taylor, for example, regarded man as an adjunct to the machine who could be manipulated as management wished. Secondly, the classical writers ignored the impact of the environment upon the organisation. Thirdly, the classical organisation principles seem less valid in today's complex and unstable environment. For example, our bureaucracy with its formalised structure and procedures is unable to respond adequately to rapidly changing conditions. Lastly, in large organisations many principles seem too general. Lines of authority often become blurred with employees receiving orders and being responsible to more than one superior.

The human relations and behavioural science approach

This approach to organisation design arose out of what was seen as the major defect of the classical approach – its dehumanising attitude towards workers. Human-relations researchers believe that organisations should have two objectives – first business efficiency, but also secondly workers' satisfaction.

The first major contribution was made by Elton Mayo (1880–1949) a Scottish psychologist working in America. Mayo conducted a series of experiments at the Hawthorne Plant of the Western Electric Company between 1927 and 1932. These experiments are generally known as the 'Hawthorne Experiments'.

The initial experiment conducted sought to establish a relationship between output and illumination. Researchers found that as illumination increased output rose, but were dumfounded to see productivity rise still further when illumination was decreased (Fig. 12.1).

Further experiments followed in which researchers varied salaries, rest periods, and working days with an experimental group while maintaining normal established working conditions in a control group.

The researchers now found that productivity rose in both the experimental and control groups. Mayo believed that something other than working conditions and financial incentives had affected their motivation to work – these he believed to be social and psychological factors. The interest shown in the groups by the researchers, the group cohesiveness, and the mutual co-operation of the researchers and groups being the major motivators.

But group cohesiveness did not always result in workers striving to achieve organisational objectives. In the bank wiring room at Western Electric Mayo found a group of workers who restricted output, ignored financial incentives, had their own code of conduct, and had selected a leader who was different from the official one. Eventually Mayo concluded:

• Man is motivated by social needs.

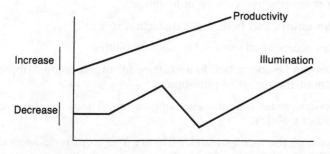

12.1 The Hawthorne Experiments – impact of changes in illumination on productivity

- The division of labour or specialisation had destroyed much of the meaning of work. This now had to be found in social relationships at work.

- The work group will have more effect on worker behaviour than organisational incentives and controls.

- Managers and supervisors concerned with the attainment of organisational objectives must also ensure that the worker's social needs are met.

Mayo's contribution to organisation theory cannot be underestimated. As a result of the Hawthorne experiments a new approach to the problem of organisation design and managerial effectiveness grew up. Many organisations modified their structure and work practices in the belief that satisfied workers would be productive workers. Unfortunately the increases in productivity which were expected often failed to materialise and later writers such as McGregor, Argyris, and Maslow pointed out that the link between organisation design, motivation, and productivity was far more complex than previously imagined.

McGregor, for example, believed that much of the formal organisation structure was based on a set of negative assumptions about workers. These assumptions which he referred to as Theory X were:

- Man dislikes work and will avoid it if he can.

- Man wishes to avoid responsibility and prefers to be directed.

- Above all else man demands security.

The role of the manager therefore is to direct and control their work, if necessary threatening them with punishment should they fail to produce sufficient effort.

Diametrically opposed to Theory X is Theory Y which takes a much more positive view of individuals:

- Man enjoys and finds real satisfaction in work.

- Man accepts and even seeks responsibilities.

- Man can be committed to and strive for organisational objectives without the threat of punishment.

- Modern industrial life uses only a small part of the average worker's ability.

The role of the manager under Theory Y is to provide an environment in which employees can best achieve their own goals while striving to attain the organisational objectives. Thus the organisation would be structured to allow employees more independence, greater communication with managers, and more participation in decision-making.

For the many employees, whom McGregor believed fitted Theory Y, the near-complete control which managers exercised over their activities resulted at best in apathy, or worse still dissatisfaction and frustration. In these circumstances absenteeism and labour turnover were likely to be high, morale low, and the organisation have difficulty in attaining its objectives.

The human relations and behavioural science approach to organisation design, like that of the classicists, has been criticised for several reasons. Like that of the classicists it suffers from the deficiencies of believing there is one best approach to organisation design and ignoring the impact of the environment. Moreover, in practice it is often extremely difficult to structure an organisation so that all jobs are challenging and rewarding, and yet maintain that high degree of efficiency required in today's harsh economic climate.

Contingency approaches

Later approaches to organisation design emphasise that there is no one best method of structuring an organisation. Instead the approach used will depend upon the particular circumstances in which the organisation finds itself. The approach does not reject the classical and human relations approaches – it will draw upon them as appropriate, but believes that there are other factors which have to be taken into account. These would include:

- The strengths and weaknesses of the organisation.
- The objectives of the organisation.
- The external environment of the oganisation.

The formal organisation

The formal organisation refers to the structure which is developed to aid the organisation in meeting its objectives. We can see the formal organisation in the way in which the organisation has:

1. Grouped activities into departments such as marketing, production, and finance.

2. Divided work so that employees contribute fully to the work of the organisation.

3. Defined relationships between employees.

4. Established rules and procedures which are to be followed.

5. Determined where decisions are to be made.

6. Created channels of communication for the passing of information.

The informal organisation

While the formal organisation is an attempt on the part of the managers to structure the organisation and establish relationships which will meet organisation objectives effectively, the informal organisation arises out of the activities and interactions of employees. Virtually all organisations have an informal organisation. It is after all a perfectly natural thing for people within the organisation to be drawn together by job, work, seniority, age, interests, and so on. We can see the informal organisation functioning in the group that always sit and have coffee together, the grapevine that passes information around the office, or the group of employees who restrict output whatever incentives are offered by management.

The informal organisation arises because companionship and social relationships are important to the individual. It is a means by which he shares his own experiences and shares in the experiences of others. It gives him a sense of belonging, a group identity – perhaps making an otherwise boring job bearable. An element of security is also provided by the informal organisation. Workers may agree a common response to new requirements of the formal organisation. They can prevent competition among themselves, which could result in the least efficient workers being laid off. Lastly the competence of the new or inexperienced worker may be increased through the help and advice of the informal group members.

To the organisation though, informal groups are a double-edged sword. They may benefit the organisation through the higher morale of its members. Information arrangements and agreements may also reduce the deficiencies of the formal structure and provide an additional management/employee channel of communication. However, against this must be placed the fact that sometimes informal group objectives run counter to the goals of the organisation. For example, employees may restrict output, or alternatively the ties of the group which bind the members together may limit labour mobility.

The most common method of describing an organisation structure is by means of an organisation chart. This pictorial method is used because of the complexity of most structures and the difficulties of describing them verbally. Let us look at an organisation chart for

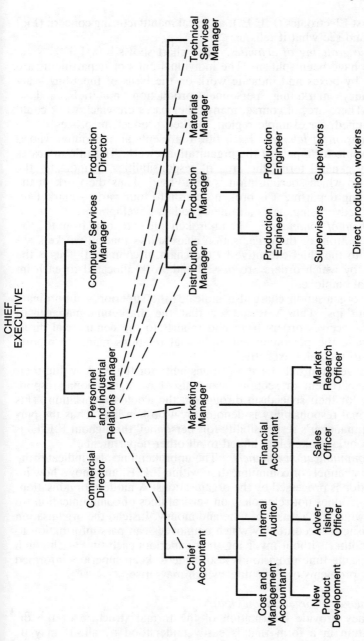

12.2 Organisational chart for Far East Electronics – a typical manufacturing concern

Far East Electronics (F.E.E.), a typical manufacturing concern (Fig. 12.2) and see what it tells us:

1. *The grouping of activities.* The chart shows how F.E.E.'s activities have been split up. The individual units or departments are shown by boxes and indicate work on the basis of functions – accountancy, marketing, personnel, production, materials, and so forth. There are, of course, many other bases on which work could be grouped, for example region, market, product, or process.

2. *Division of labour.* Each title represents an individual who is responsible for a part of the organisation's work. The title indicates in very general terms the area of responsibilities. It indicates the extent to which specialisation is being used. Thus the work of the marketing department is broken down into four parts – market research, advertising, sales and new product development.

3. *Chain of command.* The unbroken line extending from the top to the bottom of the organisation chart shows that all workers are linked to the chief executive by the chain of command. This is the means by which orders are passed and work allocated to each individual employee.

The organisation chart also indicates the superior – subordinate relationships. Thus we can see that the marketing manager of F.E.E. receives orders from and reports to the commercial director, while the personnel and industrial relations manager reports direct to the chief executive.

Managers not only have a responsibility for the work within their own department or section, many also have a functional responsibility for their specialism throughout the whole organisation. This functional responsibility is denoted by a broken line. Thus the personnel manager's responsibility for 'personnel' throughout F.E.E. is shown by a broken line linked to all other departments.

4. *Communication channels.* The unbroken line also indicates the formal channels of communication within F.E.E. and shows how information is processed by the organisations. A modern organisation, however, does not rely solely on vertical lines of communication, to do so would be a waste of time and money. Instead the organisation establishes procedures by which employees can pass information to one another without involving their superiors each time – although at the same time provision is also made to keep superiors informed of any problems or difficulties which may arise.

Advantages of organisation charts

1. They provide information of the formal structure of the organisation in a form that is easily understood by all. It may be displayed on staff notice-boards thus providing a focal point for information on changes in organisation structure or personnel.

2. The preparation of the chart draws attention to organisational

defects, for example areas of conflict, areas of duplication, an excessive span of control or an excessively long line of authority.
3. The organisation chart is also the basis from which any proposed changes to the organisation structure are made.

Disadvantages of organisation charts
1. The chart is a picture of the organisation at a certain time and is rapidly outdated by changes in structure or personnel.
2. The designer faces the difficulty of showing the organisation structure in full, in which case the chart is complex and confusing, or simplifying the structure and thereby presenting an inaccurate picture.
3. The organisation chart may cause employee discontent. Employees often believe status within an organisation is implied by their distance from the Chief Executive, or the size of their box!
4. Organisation charts do not reveal the different degrees of responsibility borne by executives.
5. They do not show the unofficial relationships and chains of communication without which the organisation would not function properly.

Types of organisation chart
The traditional method of portraying the structure of an organisation in the vertical organisation chart. Attempts have been made to show the structure in a different way to avoid the emphasis on status or levels or management. Figures 12.3 and 12.4 depict the upper levels of F.E.E. organisation structure in a horizontal (Fig. 12.3) and circular (Fig. 12.4) fashion. However, the vertical chart still remains the most widely used.

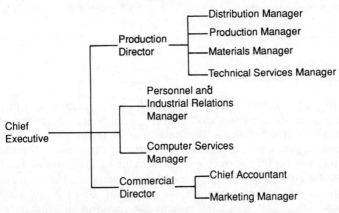

12.3 Horizontal organisation chart for Far East Electronics

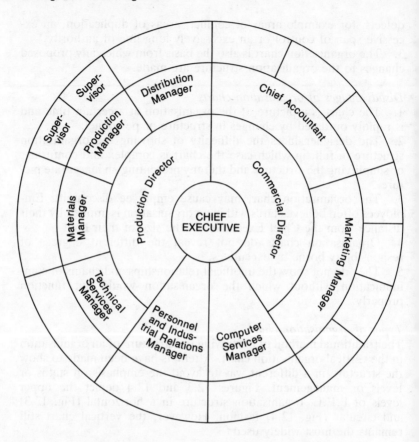

12.4 Circular organisation chart for Far East Electronics

Types of organisation

The formal structure of an organisation is the means by which it co-ordinates its activities and thereby attains its objectives. The structure adopted reflects the particular requirements of the individual organisation. It should not surprise the reader, therefore, that there is no one correct way of structuring activities or that organisation structures will alter as objectives change. However, most structures will fall into one of the following three broad classifications: line; line and staff (including functional organisation); matrix.

Line organisation There are certain activities which are essential if an organisation is going to survive as an efficient unit. These we will term line activities. Other activities carried on within the organisation are designed to improve the efficiency with which line activities are carried out. A line organisation exists when the formal structure of the organisation consists of departments based upon line activities.

Let us consider an engineering firm. Should this business adopt a line structure, what would it consist of? Put another way, what activities are essential in order to achieve its primary objectives (survival, profitability, growth). Certainly the business needs to be able to raise the finance necessary to start or expand the business. It must be able to manufacture the products it plans to sell. The products must, in fact, be sold, while in the longer term the business should develop new or improved products. All other work carried out by the business merely seeks to improve the efficiency of these activities. Figure 12.5 illustrates a line organisation we have described.

Other businesses will of course have different line activities and therefore a different line-organisation structure. Thus a retail organisation adopting a line structure will group its activities around purchasing finance and sales, and an insurance company around claims, sales, finance and underwriting.

The line organisation has a number of advantages:

- The structure is easy to understand.

- Responsibilities are well defined.

- Employees can see the value of their contribution (and other peoples) to the organisation.

- The simple structure makes for few communication problems.

- It aids the development of all-round managers rather than specialists.

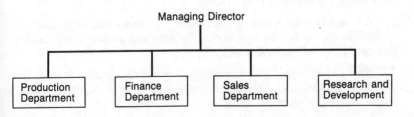

12.5 Line organisation in an engineering firm

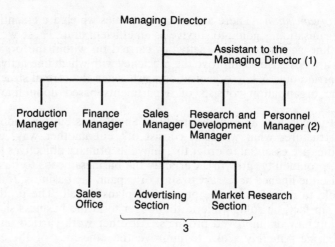

12.6 Line and staff organisation in an engineering firm

Line and staff organisation   A line organisation is primarily suited to the small organisation. As an organisation grows the managers of line activities find that more and more of their time is taken up with peripheral activities. Thus the production manager rather than concentrating on the problems of production will be devoting time to industrial relations, quality control, and the purchasing of raw materials or components. The production managers' attempts to deal with these other problems are a waste of their time and expertise. Such efforts may be being duplicated elsewhere in the firm, while more importantly they may not have the expertise to deal with these problems effectively.

Once we have recognised that the appointment of specialist staff and the creation of specialist departments may aid organisational efficiency, a line organisation no longer exists.

A line organisation becomes a line and staff organisation once the structure incorporates. (Fig. 12.6):

1.   An assistant to a senior executive who does not have line responsibilities – a senior secretary or a personal assistant may adopt this role (termed general staff).

2.   New departments with specialist responsibilities are created, for example, purchasing, personnel, work study, or computer departments (termed specialist staff).

3.   Line departments are modified to accommodate specialist activities, for example the production department may include, as a

distinct activity, purchasing or quality control while the sales department may create sections dealing with advertising or market research (termed specialist staff).

(a) General staff. It is important to distinguish between an assistant to a senior manager, for example assistant to the managing director and an assistant managing director. The latter has line authority – they will have specific duties allocated to them for which they are responsible and will be able to give orders to subordinates. In the absence of the managing director the assistant managing director will take over these responsibilities. On the other hand the assistant to the managing director has no formal authority, duties are those allocated to them by their superior from time to time and they are unable to issue orders in their own name. In organisational terms the difference is illustrated in Fig. 12.7.

The appointment of general staff assistants can be beneficial for a number of reasons:

1. The assistant can relieve the overburdened executive by taking over responsibility for certain parts of their work, or undertaking the detailed work necessary to implement a decision made by a senior executive.

2. The general assistant may also act as a co-ordinator, making arrangements in the superior's name.

3. Alternatively, the role of the general staff assistant may be used to provide a loyal member of staff with employment, rather than making them redundant when organisational change occurs.

4. It may also be used to enable a young executive to learn the job they are expected to take over shortly or to give them support while they are learning the job.

Although we may support the appointment of general staff assistants in principle, careful consideration of all the factors should always be made before making such an appointment.

1. Personal assistants can be something of a status symbol, and the appointment of one to a manager on the same level as you may cause friction if your claims to equal treatment are turned down.

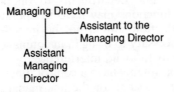

12.7 Example of a general staff assistant

2. The appointment of a personal assistant to a manager may also cause friction within that department. Subordinates may feel the work allocated to the personal assistant should have devolved to them, or that an extra subordinate position should be created.

3. We may question why the manager is overburdened – perhaps they will not delegate – and point out the danger of the manager developing too close a relationship with the personal assistant to the detriment of subordinates.

For these reasons general staff assistants have always been used sparingly.

(b) Specialist staff. Specialist staff are appointed for their expertise, an expertise which it is believed will enable the line departments to do their work more efficiently. Their work within the organisation, whatever their expertise, may be classified as advisory, service, or control. In their advisory function the specialist will advise the line manager on some proposed course of action. The maintenance engineer may advise the production manager against purchasing a certain make of machinery because of the difficulty of servicing or of obtaining spare parts. The personnel manager may advise the production manager on aspects of health and safety legislation. Of course the line manager is not compelled to accept this advice and may already have received conflicting advice to that of the maintenance engineer from the purchasing department, but they will listen carefully and consider all that is said.

Should a staff specialist be convinced that the decision of the line manager is incorrect they may appeal to their superior who then has to mediate between the two. Should the senior manager accept the advice of the staff specialist that advice then takes on the form of a line order from a superior to (in this case) the production manager. Unfortunately, whatever decision the superior reaches the relationship between the two subordinates is impaired.

The specialist's second function is to provide a service from which the line departments may benefit. Thus, the personnel manager may provide a recruitment service for the whole organisation, or the maintenance engineer establish a programme of planned maintenance. But it must be remembered that the service function is not an end in itself. It exists to enhance the efficiency of line departments. Indeed, for line departments to operate with maximum efficiency, service functions may have to operate below this level. For example, production should not be impeded by maintenance work. It may be necessary to bring in maintenance staff on overtime at night or weekends to avoid interference.

Finally, staff departments have a control function. In this capacity they will introduce a system for the line manager's use and ensure that the system is used properly throughout the organisation. Thus the personnel manager may establish the procedure to be followed in the disciplining and dismissing of employees so as to avoid unfair dismissal claims. He or she must ensure that the procedure is in fact understood and followed by all departments.

The major disadvantage of line and staff structure arises from its greater complexity of relationship – a complexity which often causes friction between line and staff personnel. For example:

1. Line managers find their authority and responsibility curtailed by the appointment of the specialist. They feel their status is threatened.

2. Line managers may feel the specialist is being used by senior staff to monitor their work.

3. Line managers feel that specialists have a narrow outlook and are unable fully to understand the problems of line management.

4. Specialists talk a different language and often use highly sophisticated techniques which are incomprehensible to the layman.

5. Specialists may introduce change to justify their position.

The role of the staff specialist within the line and staff organisation is purely advisory; where, however, they are given authority over others in respect of their specialism they are said to have a functional role. Under this form of organisation an employee may be responsible to more than one superior.

The concept was popularised by F. W. Taylor during the early part of the twentieth century. He believed that the work of foremen in engineering workshops demanded so many different skills that one man could not do the job efficiently. Taylor's solution was to divide the work of the foremen into eight different activities, allocating one function to each foreman. The worker thus became responsible to eight supervisors – each for a different part of this job. Although examples of this structure do exist, functional organisation has never been popular largely due to the potential conflicts the worker could face in being responsible to so many different people.

Matrix organisation This structure was developed first in the United States in the aerospace industry. It is an attempt to break down the communication and authority/responsibility barriers which exist in a line and staff organisation by integrating personnel into a project team. Today the concept of the matrix organisation is widely used in the construction industry and also in many other situations where a high degree of coordination is necessary.

Figure 12.8 illustrates a typical matrix organisation. It is in fact two organisations in one. The departments are a permanent feature of the organisation responsible for their specialism throughout the business. Project teams, however, are created as necessary – that is, when a contract calling for a high degree of co-ordination and multidisciplinary skills is obtained.

The members of the project team are drawn from the various

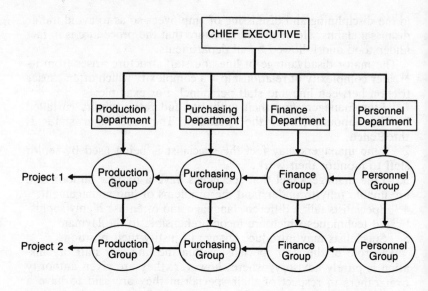

12.8 Matrix organisation

departments and are, for the duration of the project responsible to the team leader. The team members will draw from their parent departments such resources as are necessary for them to carry out their jobs as team members. The project leader is responsible for co-ordinating their efforts and ensuring that the project is completed successfully. Once the project is finished the team members and leader will return to their parent departments until they are assigned to another team.

The matrix organisation structure has several advantages of which the most important is the efficiency with which the project is carried through. Interdepartmental barriers are broken down by the team approach, team members can devote their skill completely to the project, and are more likely to co-ordinate their activities. The appointment of a team leader has the dual advantage of ensuring tighter control of the project and providing a contact to whom the client can always refer (thus ensuring a better client/organisation relationship). Last, the integrated approach to problem-solving aids manager development, and may reduce barriers between the parent departments.

However, matrix organisations are much more complex than other organisation structures, and often result in a less efficient use of resources in the parent departments. Moreover, the assignment of staff to project teams unless carefully planned may disrupt or even prevent staff management development.

Delegation and decentralisation

Delegation

It is unlikely that any manager is capable of making all those decisions which are necessary for the smooth running of their part of the organisation. It is therefore essential that the manager assigns some duties to subordinates. In doing so they are able to concentrate on those tasks which are most important to the organisation. At the same time the assignment of tasks trains and develops the skills of the next generation of managers, while also acting as a powerful motivating influence.

The act of assigning work to subordinates is delegation. Its importance in the modern organisation can be gauged by considering the complexity of the typical organisation chart.

There are three important aspects to delegation – responsibilty, authority, and accountability.

Responsibility In accepting the task a subordinate assumes a responsibility – that is, an obligation to ensure that delegated duties are performed satisfactorily. For delegation to be effective, responsibilities should be clearly defined. The sum total of the subordinate's responsibilities can be seen by referring to the job description for the position held.

Authority For delegation to work the subordinate must have the authority to carry out these duties. This authority could include spending money, using other organisational resources, hiring and firing personnel, or the giving of advice in the name of the superior.

Accountability The subordinate having been given the responsibility and authority necessary for these duties is accountable to the superior for performing the work agreed and the results achieved. This accountability is most meaningful where standards of performance have been established beforehand. However, there is another side to accountability. Managers are not only accountable for the duties which have been assigned to them, they are also accountable for the actions of their subordinates. In this way the chief executive of a company is ultimately responsible and accountable to the shareholders for all that happens within that organisation and may be required to resign when things go wrong.

Although delegation has important advantages for an organisation, in practice there are limits to the extent that it can be used. It is unlikely that highly specialised or highly confidential work will be delegated to subordinates. Equally the greater the potential cost of a decision to the organisation the greater the likelihood that that decision will be made by senior managers.

We must also consider the ability and the attitude of both superior and subordinate to delegation. A manager may experience difficulty in controlling the activities of more than two or three subordinates. V. A. Graicunas suggested that a superior's span of responsibility could not efficiently extend beyond controlling the work of six subordinates whose work interlocks. But many superiors are also unwilling to delegate arguing that 'it's quicker to do it myself' or 'I've got to make sure it is done properly'. Other managers may not be able to plan sufficiently far ahead to delegate. Finally, feelings of insecurity – the idea that a subordinate who does a good job may become a threat to their own position may prevent a superior delegating.

The ability of subordinates to carry out the delegated task is also an important consideration, especially as superiors are ultimately responsible for the actions of their subordinates. Yet while this is a legitimate reason in the short term, in the longer term it is no excuse for the manager should be training their subordinates for these responsibilities. It is also possible that the subordinates are unwilling to accept the extra responsibility delegating imposes upon them. The common reasons for this include wanting a quiet life, fear of making a mistake, or insufficient incentive to take on the extra duties.

Decentralisation

While delegation refers to the extent to which individual managers assign duties to subordinates, decentralisation refers to the extent to which the organisation as a whole pushes authority and responsibility for decision-making down into its divisions, departments, and sections. In a highly centralised organisation power is concentrated in the upper-management levels of the organisation with key decisions being taken by a few top-level managers. In a decentralised organisation lower levels of management will have responsibility for many important decisions. However, no organisation is completely centralised for no one person could take all decisions necessary to run the organisation. Equally, no organisation is completely decentralised; to be so would imply a total lack of control and co-ordination.

The degree of decentralisation present in any organisation structure will be determined by the following factors:
1. *The philosophy of management* – some organisations have a history of centralisation or decentralisation which reflects the philosophy of its chief executive. Thus Henry Ford once boasted that all major decisions in Ford were made by himself.
2. *Method of growth* – firms that have grown through merger tend to adopt a more decentralised structure than those expanding internally.

Centralised Organisations

Benefits	Problems
- Uniformity of decision making	- Heavy strain put on a few managers
- Duplication of effort eliminated	- Communication difficult with senior management (lack of time)
- Highly skilled personnel available to whole organisation not just one unit	- Demotivating influence for all but senior managers
	- Too much power given to a few individuals

Decentralised Organisations

Benefits	Problems
- Reduces workload on senior managers	- Lack of uniformity of decision making
- More managers involved in decision making process	- Unco-ordinated effort between separate units
- Decisions made by managers who 'know the situation'	- Inter-unit conflict may arise
- Power is dispersed	- Managers may not be willing to accept responsibility

3   *The costliness of the decision* – the greater the cost involved the greater the degree of centralisation.
4.   *The influence of the environment* – where the environment is unstable a higher degree of decentralisation is often chosen so that the organisation may respond more quickly to those changes which it perceives.
5.   *Characteristics of the organisation* – the greater the number of products the organisation makes, or markets it serves, the greater the degree of decentralisation forced upon it.
6.   *The ability of subordinates.*

Examination Questions

1   Why is delegation so necessary to the success of a business, and why is it so difficult to carry out? *(AEB 1988)*
2   'The traditional tree diagram is not always an appropriate way to depict the organisation of a firm.' In a report to management *either* (i) outline an alternative presentation of the way an organisation functions, supporting it with a reasoned argument; *or* (ii) show why you think

the traditional approach is still the best, and outline your proposals for ensuring that it works efficiently. *(CAMB)*

3 A colleague at work never delegates and appears to be suffering the stresses and strains of overwork. These are benefits for employer and employee from delegation of work. What arguments could be used to convince someone of the need to delegate? *(PSC)*

4 Management thinking has passed through several phases including classical and human relations. Discuss these briefly and indicate their respective contributions.

5 What factors influence the extent to which an organisation is centralised or decentralised in its operations?

6 'The fundamental dilemma is that delegation is made up of two parts: trust and control.' (N Worrall)
Critically examine this dilemma and analyse its implications for an organisation. *(AEB)*

7 Job enrichment is believed to be a technique that motivates personnel. To what extent can delegation create an environment of job enrichment? What are the essential requirements for its implementation and successful operation?

8 A managing director is considering delegation of some of his functions to a committee.
What are the advantages and disadvantages of delegation?
Draw up some guidelines indicating when it would be worthwhile delegating work to a committee.

9 Distinguish between formal and informal organisation.
How important is this distinction to an understanding of the management process?

10 Explain the term 'matrix organisation'.
What are its advantages and disadvantages over other organisational forms?

11 'Line' and 'Staff' relationships are found in many forms.
Distinguish between the two, and explain how in a large organisation they could create inter-personal problems. How might such problems be overcome?

12 What implications do you see for managers arising from an informal organisation existing alongside the formal organisation structure?

13 How far do you agree with the statement 'there is no one best way of designing an organisation'?

Chapter 13

Directing

Motivation

Motivation is a key subject for managers. Managers are responsible for a job which is too large for them to undertake by themselves. They therefore have to work with and through other people. Thus, the manager needs to understand the behaviour of people and find ways of persuading them to act in ways which are beneficial to the organisation. In practice, this is not as easy as it sounds. There may be factors within the organisation or its environment acting as a demotivational force. Examples would include:

- fear of redundancy or short-time working
- pay and conditions of work
- lack of appreciation
- boring or repetitive jobs
- lack of communication between management and workers
- loss of faith in management

and many of these will be outside the control of the individual manager.

Many writers have contributed to an understanding of motivation, yet there is not one accepted theory of motivation. We will look at two groups of theories – content and process theories.

Content Theories

These theories consider the question 'what causes behaviour'? The answer commonly given is that behaviour is directed towards satisfying needs. At the simplest level it is saying that a search for food is prompted by hunger. The most popular content theories are Maslow's hierarchy of needs and Herzberg's two-factor theory.

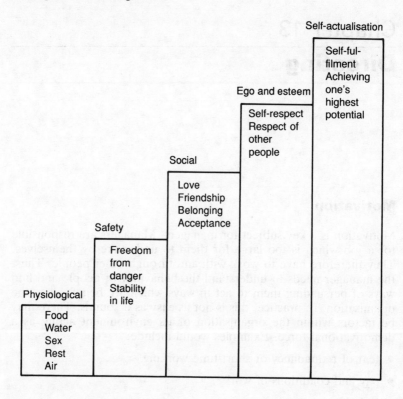

13.1 Maslow's hierarchy of needs

The hierarchy of needs

Maslow argues that individuals have a hierarchy of needs (see Fig. 13.1). Within this hierarchy of needs at any one moment in time there is one need which is dominant – and remains dominant until it is satisfied. Once that need is satisfied it is no longer a motivator. Instead, it is replaced by a higher order need which, as yet, has not been satisfied. Thus the individual whose psychological and safety needs have been met will now seek to satisfy his social needs.

Maslow also suggested that an individual's needs could vary. For example the threat of redundancy may result in the employee seeking to satisfy a safety need and temporarily forgetting about some higher level need.

Although Maslow did not develop this theory to answer the problem of motivating employees the implications are obvious.

Managers must identify the needs of their subordinates and provide the means of satisfying these needs in an organisational context. But how can a manager do this? There are many ways. Examples are shown in Table 13.1 below:

Table 13.1 Methods of satisfying employee needs

Need	Example
Physiological	Pay; rest periods; canteens; holidays
Safety	Health and safety measures; security of employment pensions
Social	Formal and informal groups; organised social events; sports clubs
Ego and esteem	Power; titles; status symbols; merit awards; promotion
Self actualisation	Challenging work; developing new skills

However, the hierarchy of needs should not be considered as a complete answer to the problem of motivating employees. For example:
- satisfaction of needs is not the only motivator of employees. Group allegiances and attitudes towards management may exert a stronger motivational force than anything the organisation can offer
- some people have very low levels of aspiration particularly where their experience of life has been limited
- the hierarchy of needs as devised by Maslow is not applicable to all people – thus creative people may be motivated by higher level needs even when other needs are not satisfied (e.g. the starving artist!)
- higher level needs, for example ego and esteem may be obtained through leisure rather than work related activities (e.g. scout leader or local football team manager).

Herzberg's two-factor theory The theory arose out of a research survey of 200 engineers and accountants. The group was asked to recall events which gave them job satisfaction and job dissatisfaction. From his analysis of their answers Herzberg concluded that job satisfaction and job dissatisfaction tended to be caused by two different groups of factors. These he termed motivating factors and hygiene factors (see Fig. 13.2).

Motivating factors are those factors which encourage an employee to do well. The absence of these factors, however, does not cause job dissatisfaction but just a lack of job satisfaction. Conversely,

229

Motivating factors	Hygiene factors
Recognition	Company policy/administration
Achievement	Supervision
Responsibility	Working conditions
Advancement	Interpersonal relationships
Challenging work	Job status/security
Personal growth	Salary

13.2 Herzberg's Motivating and Hygiene Factors

hygiene factors, if absent, caused job dissatisfaction but even when present did not contribute significantly to job satisfaction.

The other significant finding of the survey was that all the motivating factors arose from the content of the job while the hygiene factors arose from the context of the job – that is the environment in which the job is done.

The significance for managers is that to obtain high performance from employees they must provide strong motivational factors while, at the same time, ensuring that negative hygiene factors (which would detract from performance) are not present.

Herzberg's findings have been criticised as being based on anecdotal evidence and lacking scientific method. Additionally the placing of money as a hygiene, rather than a motivating, factor has been questioned by Herzberg's critics. However his work has had a significant practical impact. Job enrichment programmes developed by many companies were strongly influenced by Herzberg's two-factor theory (see p. 308).

Content theories generally have been criticised for simplifying the complex subject of motivation. In the first place people's needs differ. Not all of a manager's subordinates are going to be motivated by the same need as they are. Moreover, there may be individual differences among subordinates arising from their personal circumstances. Motivating a group of subordinates with individual needs is a task which will tax most managers' ingenuity.

Secondly subordinates will not necessarily act consistently. The motivating factor that works today may fail to motivate them next week.

Process Theories

Process theorists argue that needs are just one factor in determining how a person acts. They point out that a need is not going to motivate an individual if there is no opportunity to fulfil that need. They believe that an individual's expectations of the outcome of a

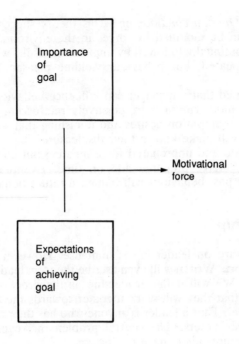

13.3 Vroom's motivational process

particular course of action exert a considerable influence upon that person's actions.

Vroom's value-expectancy theory According Vroom motivation depends on two factors. First, the expectation that increased effort will lead to increased rewards. Second, the value of that goal to the individual (*see* Fig. 13.3). Let us take two examples. The manager will find an individual to be highly motivated where they (a) highly prize the goals or rewards and (b) believe the reward can be achieved without too much effort. In other circumstances the motivational force will be low. If the subordinate does not value the goal – say promotion – (even though it is attainable) or does not believe it is attainable (even though they value the goal) the motivational force will be low.

Expectancy theory plays down the idea that motivation is dependent on needs and desires and suggests that individuals act rationally in deciding whether to strive for motivational goals. However, it is unlikely that people will always act in such a rational way.

Skinner's Operant conditioning This theory suggests that our behaviour can be modified by forces in the environment. Behaviour which is continually followed by unpleasant results will, after a time, not be repeated, but behaviour yielding pleasant results will be repeated.

It is argued that a manager can influence behaviour – it is called behaviour modification – by positively reinforcing that behaviour which the organisation desires and punishing that which it dislikes. Managers will make known their displeasure when the subordinate turns up late and unprepared for a meeting but congratulate them when they arrive prepared and on time. Eventually, the consequences of past behaviour will influence future behaviour.

Leadership

The literature on leadership is immense. However, much of it is contradictory. Writers will even ascribe the term leadership different meanings. We will define leadership as the process of influencing people so that they will work together towards the achievement of a group goal. Thus a leader is anyone who has the power to exercise control over others. The central problem however is why some people and not others have this power.

There are three broad approaches to the study of leadership: trait, behaviour and contingency. We will look briefly at each of these.

Trait Theory

The traditional answer to the question 'What is leadership?' rested on the assumption that leaders were born not made. Leaders therefore must have certain traits or personal characteristics which others lacked. Early research therefore concentrated upon identifying the traits of leaders and followers and then isolating that set of characteristics which made a leader. These research efforts were inconclusive. Individuals who were widely recognised as leaders exhibited remarkably different sets of characteristics.

Attempts to identify individual characteristics associated with leadership were more successful. Intellectual skills, social and interpersonal skills, task-based knowledge, task motivation and dominance are commonly associated with leaders. In fact, nearly thirty different characteristics showed a positive correlation with leadership. Yet no one characteristic could be identified as being essential for a leader!

The trait approach has also been criticised for ignoring the environment within which leadership operates and the needs of the followers.

Behavioural Theories

These theories concentrate on identifying behaviour which would differentiate successful from unsuccessful leaders. The change of approach is significant. If researchers could identify specific behaviour which separated the leader from the led it was possible to teach leadership. Leaders were not born but developed!

Initially researchers concentrated on leadership styles. Lewin's research in the 1930s on small group behaviour identified three forms of leadership behaviour. These he described as:

autocratic – power lies in the hands of the leader who makes the decisions. They are often thought to be hard task masters

democratic – power is shared with subordinates. The group is involved in setting objectives, devising strategies and assigning jobs

laissez-faire – little direction or discipline is exercised by leader. Responsibility lies in the hands of the subordinates.

Lewin went on to devise a number of boy's teams which were structured around these styles of leadership. In the autocratic group, work effort, when the leader was present, was high but quality was low. Work effort also fell dramatically when the leader was absent. The level of conflict was also high and eventually two boys refused to participate any longer.

Work effort in the democratic group was high whether or not the leader was present. Quality was also high.

In the laissez-faire group frustration among group members built up very quickly and work effort was very poor.

The conclusion he reached was that in this situation the democratic style of leadership gave the best results.

More recent studies have confirmed Lewin's views. Likert devised another model of leadership behaviour which considered two factors (1) emphasis on output – job-centred leadership and (2) emphasis on the worker – employee centred leadership. From his practical research he believed that there was a continuum with four major leadership styles (see Fig. 13.4). We will look at these in turn.

System 1 All decisions are made by the manager. Levels of performance are also established by the manager and rigorously enforced. Threats or coercion are used to ensure goals are met. There is little trust between managers and subordinates

System 2 Subordinates may have a marginal input into decision and policy-making. Subordinates have limited flexibility in carrying out orders and may be rewarded for exceeding managerial goals. The manager uses a condescending manner toward subordinates

System 1	System 2	System 3	System 4
Exploitive – Authoritative	Benevolent – Authoritative	Consultative Democratic	Participative Democratic

◄─────────── Job centred ─────────── Employee centred ───────────►

13.4 Likert's Leadership Systems

System 3 Broad or key decisions are made by the manager. Subordinates decide how to implement decisions. Rewards rather than threats are used to motivate staff. The level of trust between manager and subordinates is higher

System Decisions are made by the group. Subordinates are motivated by intrinsic as well as extrinsic rewards. The managerial level of control is low. The level of trust between manager and subordinates is high.

The studies found that departmental leaders who used systems 1 and 2 achieved low levels of productivity from their workers. High productivity departments tended to have a leader who used a participative form of leadership. Likert therefore concluded, like Lewin, that a democratic or participative form of leadership was to be the most preferred.

Although the democratic style of leadership has a considerable following today its success rests on a number of favourable assumptions about the followers and the situation. McGregor's Theory X and Y makes two very different sets of assumptions about the followers (see p. 210). If a manager perceives the workers to fall into the Theory X mould then a democratic participative form of leadership would not work at all. Nor would leaders be 'democratic' when they alone had the knowledge necessary to make a decision, or in an emergency situation. Conversely, a professor dealing with his academic staff, or a manager dealing with a group of research scientists may give them considerable latitude in what work they undertake and the way that it is organised.

Contingency Theory

We have seen that for a variety of reasons trait and behavioural theories have been insufficient to explain leadership. Indeed, researchers today argue that there is no one style of leadership which will work for a manager in all situations. There are circumstances when an autocratic style is necessary even though the feelings of subordinates may be hurt. Equally, other situations lend themselves to a more democratic approach. The question therefore rose as to what factors should affect leadership style, and in what way.

Tannenbaum and Schmidt developed another leadership continuum after studying leader behaviour (see Fig. 13.5). At one end of the continuum is a highly leader-centred leadership and the other end a highly group centred leadership. The authors argue that there are a number of different styles which a leader may use, none of which is best, but each of which may be more appropriate in a particular situation.

The most appropriate style of leadership is seen by Tannenbaum and Schmidt to be a function of forces in the leader, forces in the subordinates and the situation. For example:

Forces in the leaders
1.   Value system. The strength of your feelings on sharing decisions, organisational efficiency/profits and personal growth of subordinates.
2.   Confidence in subordinates. Do your subordinates have knowledge and experience to deal with this situation?
3.   Leadership inclinations. Managers' inclinations may be to be highly democratic. This is a function of education, training and experience.
4   Feelings of insecurity. How well can a manager tolerate the uncertainty arising from delegating decisions to subordinates?

Forces in subordinates
Subordinates will be granted greater participation and freedom in the following circumstances:
– they have a need for independence
– they have a need for responsibility
– they have the ability to deal with the problem
– they identify with organisational goals
– they have expectations of sharing in decision making.

However where any of these forces are missing the manager may adopt a more authoritarian style. This will continue until the subordinates have gained the manager's confidence.

Forces in the situation
1.   The type of organisation. Organisations develop values and traditions e.g. emphasis on results, interest in people
2.   The effectiveness of the group
3.   Time and money constraints
4.   The nature of the problem e.g. importance, complexity

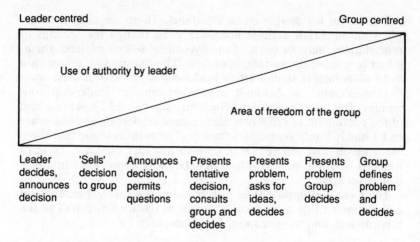

Leader centred   Group centred

Use of authority by leader

Area of freedom of the group

| Leader decides, announces decision | 'Sells' decision to group | Announces decision, permits questions | Presents tentative decision, consults group and decides | Presents problem, asks for ideas, decides | Presents problem Group decides | Group defines problem and decides |

13.5 Tannenbaum and Schmidt's continuum of leadership behaviour

To Tannenbaum and Schmidt the best manager is not one who is autocratic or democratic, but rather one who is capable of adapting their style to the situation facing them.

Co-ordination

One major function of management is to break down work into components which can be handled by departments, sub-departments, sections and eventually individuals. These individuals will concentrate on a small and very specialised part of the organisation's total activities. Yet for successful organisational performance the manager has to re-integrate all the activities of individual, units and sections. An analogy with a football team is useful. The team is made up of a number of individuals who have specialised roles – goalkeeper, forward, midfield and defensive players. The job of the coach or manager is to weld them together into a team with a common goal. Each member's specialist role must be used in such a way that it contributes to the overall performance of the team. That is the function of coordination.

The larger the organisation the more difficult it is to control. Almost by definition larger organisations will have a higher degree of specialisation of activity – different people with different backgrounds and attitudes doing different jobs. We can identify three particular problems of co-ordinating interdepartmental activities:

Differences in attitude. The education and training of managers forces them to perceive problems in different ways. Thus the marketing department will argue that to increase sales you should increase the product range while the production department argues for an increase in quality.

Differences in time horizons. Production managers work to a very short time horizon — often a week or less, accounting departments, a month, quarterly or annually, research and development two or three years.

Differences in control measures. Some departments, for example production, will have very precise methods of assessing performance (e.g. quantity or quality of output) while in other departments the nature of work precludes short term and highly specific measures of performance.

Co-ordination of activity in business is essential. The production department has to liaise with the purchasing department over what types and quantities of raw materials and components to buy. Too little, and the production line may be stopped, too much and there may be storage problems. Equally the production and marketing departments must liaise to ensure that quantities produced are in line with quantities sold.

There are many ways in which a lack of co-ordination will manifest itself. The most obvious symptom is where an organisation fails to achieve its objectives. Equally significant are high levels of interdepartmental conflict and neglected organisational activities.

Methods of co-ordinating activities

Organisational hierarchy. Within any organisation there is a chain of command which links the lowest levels in the organisation with the highest. Each person in the structure is responsible to a superior whose responsibility it is to co-ordinate the activity of this and other subordinates. The organisational hierarchy can also be used to reconcile disagreements between two individuals or even departments. The problem will be referred to a common superior who will take the decision.

Interdepartmental communication. It is all too easy for the vertical communication channels to become overloaded. Ideally, in the interests of efficiency, these channels should be kept for non-routine or non-recurring problems. Standard procedures can be established for dealing with many of the routine activities within an organisation without involving departmental managers e.g. wage payments, sales orders.

Interdepartmental communication can also be achieved by having representatives of other departments sitting on departmental committees, or by having individuals within departments who are responsible for liaising with other departments

Committees A committee is a group of people who have been formally appointed to undertake a specific duty. It is a form of delegation, the members having been charged with responsibility for a task, given the necessary authority, and being accountable to those who created the committee.

Although committees have long been the butt of managerial wit – 'a camel is a horse created by a committee' – they are widely used in business today for fact-finding, problem-solving, co-ordination, decision-making, and advisory purposes.

Standing committees have a permanent role within the organisation and will meet weekly or monthly to deal with their routine business, for example forward planning or finance.

Ad hoc committees are set up for a specific purpose, for example company reorganisation. They have no routine work and once their task is accomplished they are disbanded.

Advantages of committees

Co-ordination. Large organisations often find that activities are insufficiently integrated through the formal vertical communication channels. The committee allows managers of approximately the same level to come together, exchanging information and systematically co-ordinating their activities.

Decision-making. The diversity of expertise a committee can bring to bear on the topic under discussion is far greater than that of the individual executive. It is therefore possible to obtain a more balanced view and avoid biased decisions.

Creativity. Working in a group can stimulate creativity. Ideas put forward by one committee member will be developed by another, or generate a different idea in yet another member.

Consultation. A committee is an invaluable method of obtaining specialist advice from subordinates. It also provides a channel through which the views of subordinates and other staff on a wider range of issues can be made known.

Commitment. Participation in the decision-making process tends to increase an individual's commitment to the decision reached and the desire to implement that decision effectively. Even where a committee member does not agree to the decision taken, they know their viewpoint has been considered, and also the rationale behind the committee's decision.

Disadvantages of committees

Cost. Committees cost an organisation dear both in time and money. Try calculating the cost of a three-hour meeting for five middle-management executives each earning £25,000 p.a. But conversely, you might also consider how long it would take to pass the same information and reach the same decision without the committee!

Quality of decisions. As most committees wish to accommodate the views of all participants, the decision is often a compromise which satisfies no one.

Indecision. Many managers argue if you want to delay a decision appoint a committee. Difficulties in arranging times suitable for all participants, and conflicting viewpoints both preclude the fast decision the organisation often needs.

Accountability. Decisions taken are often more risky because committee members are able to avoid individual responsibility for the outcome. For the same reason they may not work as hard to correct the decision when wrong.

Much of the criticism of committees is a reflection of the way they work. All too often meetings are ineffective because responsibilities are poorly defined, bad chairmanship, or incorrect size or structure of the committee. Careful attention to these matters will ensure that committees function as an effective and integral part of the organisation structure.

Examination questions

1 What does the work of major authorities tell us about employee motivation?
Why in practice is there frequently a failure to meet such expectations? *(AEB 1987)*

2 Examine critically the statement that effective motivation of employees arises as much from an understanding of their needs as from the application of standard textbook methods. *(AEB 1985)*

3 It is claimed that leadership is important for the success of any group activity in business, although the styles of leadership may differ according to the situation.
What is meant by the term 'style of leadership'? Discuss the appropriateness of different leadership styles in a business context. *(AEB)*

4 How far does the style of leadership adopted by management make any significant difference to the way people work? *(AEB 1988)*

5 'The job of a manager is to make decisions rather than to motivate others.'
Discuss this statement with relation to the production manager of a soft drink canning factory. *(CAMB 1986)*

6 The best way to encourage employees to work harder is to pay them more.
Discuss this statement. *(PSC 1985)*

7 (a) With regard to a company's employees what do you see as the motivating influences?
(b) To what extent can the personnel department help implement policies designed to motivate? *(PSC 1987)*

Managers and Management

8 Explain how
   (a) the task to be undertaken
   (b) the subordinates
   (c) the situation
   might influence a manager's leadership style.

Chapter 14

Controlling

By control we mean the process of monitoring organisational activities to see that they are being carried out as planned or that any necessary action is taken to correct a deviation from plan. The definition draws attention to the close relationship between planning and control. The plans provide benchmarks against which the progress of the organisation may be assessed.

In modern organisations control systems are essential. Plans cannot take into account all possibilities. Some plans may work the way management intended but by far the majority of complex plans will deviate. Such deviations may be organisational – the inability of a department to complete its part of a plan on schedule, or environmental – new government regulations on product safety or perhaps the advent of new technology. A control system is necessary to spot these deviations in time thus allowing management the opportunity to take action before serious problems occur.

To be effective a control system must not only report deviations from plan quickly, it must also be simple to understand, accurate and cost effective.

Types of control

Most methods of control fall into one of three groups – forward, concurrent or retrospective.

Forward control requires the manager to forsee problems that will arise and act to ensure they do not prevent the organisation from achieving its objectives. For example, some firms have been actively planning how to overcome the problems caused by the fall in the number of school-leavers in the 1990s. The steps taken have included accelerated programmes for automation and computerisation and training programmes aimed at thc adult (and often woman) worker.

The major problem for the manager in anticipating problems is a lack of information about changes in the environment and organisation. Because such information systems are difficult to develop managers often rely more heavily on concurrent and retrospective controls.

A *concurrent* or *steering control* monitors operations while they are in progress and corrects deviations as they occur and before they become too costly. An analogy with a car driver is useful. The driver, during his journey, will make many small steering corrections to keep the car on the road and avoid accidents. Within the organisation direct supervision is one form of concurrent control. More recently computers have also been used as a form of concurrent control.

Retrospective controls are based on past performance. The reasons for deviation from plan will be analysed and steps taken to ensure the same problem does not recur. Budgeting is one example of a retrospective control. Many people would argue that retrospective controls are of little use – in many situations the damage will already have been done, but the manager may have little option but to rely on these controls. Moreover, retrospective controls are beneficial in that they:
– indicate how successful initial planning was, and
– provide information which can be used to appraise the efforts of manager and workers.

The process of control

Whatever types of control are used the process of control is the same. It consists of a number of steps designed to ensure that planned performance and actual performance coincide. Figure 14.1 illustrates the steps in this process.

Establishing standards of performance is the first step in the process. For the control process to be successful standards of performance should meet two criteria. First, all standards should be stated so that they are measurable. It is insufficient to say 'reply to customer complaints quickly' because we do not know precisely when we have met the desired level of performance. However, if we say 'reply to customer complaints within three days' we have a much clearer idea of how well we are achieving this objective. Second, standards of performance should be established at key points throughout the activity. For example, before raw materials and components enter production; at the end of the production process; and before packaging. In this way corrective action can be taken before the end of the activity cycle and before mistakes become too costly.

The second step is to measure performance. Obviously the measurement used should conform to the standards of performance set eg, quantity, quality and time.

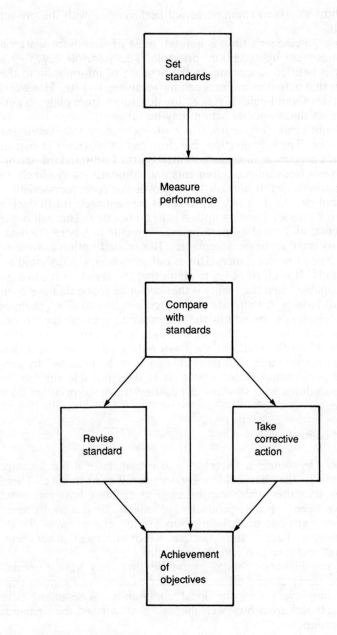

14.1 The control process

The third step is to compare actual performance with the pre-set standards.

Because a manager's time is limited, most organisations work on the 'management by exception' principle. This principle says that a manager is entitled to assume, in the absence of information to the contrary, that activities are proceeding according to plan. However, subordinates should quickly report any deviations from planned performance so that remedial action may be taken.

Significant costs are incurred in both measuring and comparing performance. The organisation therefore has to balance the cost of the control process against the potential costs of substandard performance. Thus frequent measurements and comparisons are likely to be made where health hazards to employees or consumers exist.

The final step in the control process is for management to decide what is to be done. The first option is to do nothing. This will occur where actual and standard performance coincide or where the deviation is so small as to be acceptable. The second option is to alter the standard of performance. This is not an action which should be taken lightly. It is all too easy to claim that the standard is too high or unattainable when the reality is that performance could have been improved. However, there are undoubtedly occasions when changes in the environment or within the organisation prevent the pre-set standard being achieved. The final option is to correct actual performance. Here the manager must not only take immediate action to correct performance, but must also analyse the reasons why substandard performance came about. It is then possible for him to revise procedures with the aim of ensuring the same problem does not recur.

Areas of control

The Total Organisation. Directors and managers of a business are responsible to the shareholders for its overall performance. There are many measures which can be used to evaluate how successful they have been – profit, productivity, morale, or quality to name but a few. Yet none of these measure overall effectiveness. To do this we must go back to the objectives which management set themselves and compare performance with this.

Many organisations though recognise that they have responsibilities to many groups other than shareholders, for example consumers, employees and the local community. Assessment here would be based upon how well management satisfied the demands of each group.

Operations: The production of goods is an important area of control. If an organisation is unable to produce goods or services efficiently it is unlikely to survive. Although the output or quantity produced is likely to be one of the more important areas of control, design, quality, packaging and timing are also of importance. Examples of operations control such as production control, stock control, quality control and work study are dealt with in more detail in Chapter 17.

Marketing: Many of the plans developed by other functional departments – for example production – depend on estimates of sales by the marketing function. For example, a fall in sales, if not corrected, may affect finance (money borrowed), personnel (numbers employed/overtime/short-time) and operations (stocks output, cost of output). In the short term products sales figures are a significant control device while in the longer term market and product research is important. Other measures which are commonly used are market position and product leadership.

Finance. Financial control is often the most critical area for the organisation. In business organisation the key measure will be profit, or return on capital employed.

All organisations are concerned with efficiency and many will have introduced budgetary control systems for this purpose. Cash budgets predicting the flow of money into and out of the organis-

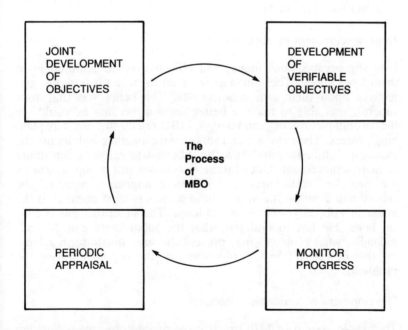

14.2 The process of MBO

ation are particularly important. Ratio analysis and break even analysis are examples of two other techniques which are used as control devices. These are dealt with in Chapter 18.

Personnel. People are the most important resource within an organisation. Poor employee morale can be measured through indicators such as product quality, industrial accidents, absenteeism and labour turnover. Individual control will be exercised by the manager on a day-to-day basis, dealing with problems as they arise. Formal control of the employee is undertaken through performance appraisal interviews and, where necessary, disciplinary procedures or interviews.

Management by Objectives

Management by Objectives or MBO as it is often called has received many accolades. It has been described as 'the best example of participative management', 'the major planning tool' and 'a comprehensive management system'. It is all of these things, but also a means of evaluating and controlling managerial performance and we introduce it here for that reason. There are four stages to the process of MBO (see Fig. 14.2).

Joint development of objectives

In many organisations managerial objectives were imposed upon them from above. These managers would then, in turn, impose objectives upon their own subordinates. The belief was that your superior was able to make a better decision because he could see the 'overall picture' or grand design. MBO rejects this one-way planning process. The manager and subordinate together will discuss the manager's objectives and how the subordinate can best contribute to their achievement. Out of these discussions will be agreement by the two 'key result areas' – 'the most important parts of the subordinate's job' – the areas where success is most needed', if the manager's objectives are to be achieved. The superior's role is critical here. He has to find out what the subordinate can do and, secondly, what problems may prevent the subordinate form achieving that objective (the superior often has the key to removing the problem).

Development of verifiable objectives

The whole system of MBO rests on verifiable objectives. Such an objective is one that is capable of being measured. In some way a quantitative elements has been introduced with the objective. For some departments this will cause little difficulty. The production department could use:

output: 3 million units
cost: an average cost per unit of £1 or less
wastage: a scrap loss of less than 2 per cent
labour: turnover of less than 10 per cent in workforce.

However, in other departments establishing verifiable objectives is, at first sight, more difficult. The key, it is suggested, is to ask the subordinate 'how will you know when you have achieved this objective'. Thus the Research and Development unit may talk about 'producing a prototype product within a year', or the training section 'retraining of 75 per cent of certain operatives within six months'. Once again the superior's role is important. The standard to be achieved has to be agreed with them. It must be realistic. They must counsel against a standard which is too high and therefore unattainable. Equally they must ensure that the standard is not too low.

Monitor progress

Once the superior and subordinate have agreed the verifiable objectives the performance of the subordinate can be monitored. The emphasis here is on self control. MBO is based on McGregor's Theory Y assumptions regarding workers – that they are capable of self direction, seek responsibility and will work towards organisational objectives without coercion. Subordinates by reference to actual and planned performance can see for themselves how well they are doing. If actual and planned performance diverge the subordinate is expected to remedy the situation.

Periodic appraisal

The final phase of the MBO cycle is to evaluate the efforts of the subordinate. Such appraisals will take place once or twice a year. Because specific short term objectives have been agreed by the superior and subordinate, the subordinate's success (or lack of it) is plain to see. The aim of the appraisal interview is not to humiliate the subordinate, but to help analyse what went wrong and take steps to ensure these deficiencies are remedied. Periodical appraisal is not only used as a starting point for the training of managers it is also the basis for rewards – merit rises and promotion and the next round of MBO negotiations.

Benefits of an MBO programme
It improves management. Managers are forced to plan systematically and develop verifiable objectives. This ensures all work is

directed towards organisational objectives and enables managers to prioritise work. MBO also forces managers to allocate time to each subordinate to discuss objectives, monitor performance and appraise results and as a result there is a much higher level of communication between superior and subordinate.

It improves the organisation structure. Discussions between superior and subordinate reveal the ways in which individual parts of the organisation can contribute to overall objectives. Managers are thus able to evaluate the effectiveness of organisational structure in contributing to these objectives identifying those parts where contribution is marginal, integral and under-resource.

It improves motivation. Research shows that subordinate participation in goal setting stimulates higher levels of commitment to organisational objectives. The subordinate has negotiated personal goals with the manager, has been given responsibility for getting those results and will be evaluated on these efforts. Motivation is also improved by the fact that subordinates understand how their work contributes to the achievement of overall objectives.

It improves control. The development of plans with verifiable objectives provides the benchmarks for control of organisational activity. Development of such controls is likely to prevent serious deviation of actual from planned performance before discovery.

Problems of an MBO programme

Organisational ethos. Some organisations have a strong authoritarian flavour. Such organisations and their managers find it hard to adapt to the new participative mood. They will have to develop new leadership and interpersonal skills.

Time. Managers have to devote considerable time to their subordinates.

Frustration. Individuals may become very exasperated where they find that their objectives cannot be achieved because of factors outside their control. Examples include environmental factors, or failings of other subordinates upon whom your work depends.

Frustration may also occur where verifiable objectives set are longer rather than short term and the individual expects to be moved before that period is up.

Reliance on strategic planning. For MBO to be successful, plans and verifiable objectives must stem from the strategic plan. If the strategic plan is not worked to, or has not been properly established, MBO will fail.

Inflexibility. The MBO process is not designed to create an inflexible plan yet once objectives have been stated there is always a hesitancy about changing those objectives. The result may be an organisation working very efficiently towards an outdated or unobtainable goal.

Examination Questions

1 Control is the essence of management. Discuss.
2 Explain the most important facets of reliable and effective management control systems.
3 Why is the setting of objectives so important in the process of planning? Describe the advantage and disadvantages of 'managing by objectives'.
4 In order to achieve effective control of business activity what principles, in your view, need to be adhered to?
5 In business the bottom line is profit – you don't need any other measures of effectiveness. Discuss.
6 The greater the degree of control exercised by a manager, the greater the likelihood that control will be effective. Discuss.

Chapter 15

Communication

A great deal of our time is spent communicating in our leisure activities and at work. It is difficult to imagine a day or even an hour when we are not trying to communicate with someone else or them with us. Think back over the last hour – how many people have you talked to face to face or telephoned, how many different pieces of paper – letters, notices, newspapers, magazines and books you have read. In all these situations communication – the process by which information is exchanged – is taking place.

But not only is communication vitally necessary in our everyday lives, it must be good or effective communication. On many occasions there is a difference between what we say (or intend to say) and what another person understands us to say. How often have you heard people say there was 'a breakdown in communications'? Almost inevitably when people communicate misunderstandings occur causing frustration, anger and distrust. Relationships may be totally severed as a result of a careless remark misinterpreted.

Within an organisation communication is essential – a manager will spend as much as 80 per cent of a working day communicating with others. Yet as organisations get bigger communication tends to deteriorate because:

- we become specialists – use our own jargon which only other specialists understand
- lines of communication get longer
- organisation structures become more complex
- communication becomes impersonal

Effective communication in an organisation is essential so that:

- management has the necessary information for planning, organising, directing and controlling the activities of the organisation
- the activities of the different departments can be co-ordinated and all contribute to the accomplishment of organisational objectives
- individuals understand what is required of them and that they are integrated into the organisation both socially and workwise
- we maintain good relationships with all external contacts eg, suppliers, customers, bankers, unions and the local community.

Barriers to good communication:

1. (a) Vocabulary deficiencies. There are many thousands of words in the English language and the average person will know and use only a small proportion of these. Unfortunately, differences in age, education and environment mean that we do not all know and use the same words. The problem of vocabulary deficiencies is often compounded by the fact that pride stops us from admitting that we do not understand certain words.

(b) Words have different meanings to different people. Even when people use the same words they may use them in a different way. Some words may even have multiple meanings. Consider how many possible meanings there are to the word 'communication'! Once again age, education and background influence the meaning we attach to words. How would you interpret 'the drill is boring'?

(c) Jargon. Specialists – accountants, engineers, lawyers – have their own particular way of expressing themselves. Jargon is a form of 'shorthand' between members of the same trade or profession. It is often incomprehensible to the outsider. The professional must therefore ensure the recipient of the message understands the meaning of all the words used.

2. Perception Our personal feelings will often affect the way we interpret communications. We are more likely to accept information from people we agree with. Perception causes the following problems:

(a) Cognitive Dissonance: We always try to be consistent in the way we think and it is always difficult for us to accept communications which force us to re-evaluate our beliefs. Let us take a simple example. We often create stereotypes – that is we group ideas and experiences together to create a model. One such stereotype is the woman driver. It is a popular fallacy that 'all women are bad drivers' – at least amongst men! Now if you stereotype women in this way seeing a bad woman driver reinforces your belief while the example of a good woman driver is ignored. It does not fit in with a certain type of man's view of the world.

(b) Emotions. The mood of a person will influence how a communication is interpreted. When unhappy or distressed we often respond aggressively and defensively to an innocent comment – our friends would describe us as being 'touchy'. Extremes of emotions, happiness or depression affect our ability to interpret information rationally which is why we are often advised not to make an immediate decision.

(c) Selective attention: An individual may be exposed to many messages or pieces of information over a very short period of time. Much more than can possibly be absorbed. The information which

we take in is commonly what we want to hear – the unwelcome information is filtered out.

3. *Distance (a) Geographical:* We are much more likely to communicate with people who are in close proximity to us. Geographical distance often breaks down family ties and friendships. In an organisation people whose work impinges on each others should be grouped together in an office to reduce the likelihood of poor communication.

(b) Status: The importance of an individual within an organisation determines how information is received. Communications from senior managers will be considered important and significant. Conversely research has shown that people with low status within an organisation find difficulty in communicating with those who have a higher status. Vertical communication channels are, for this reason, often ineffective for feedback purposes.

Symptoms of poor communication:

- **low morale and apathy**

- **an increase in mistakes and misunderstandings**

- **an increase in anxiety perhaps illustrated by:**
  - **unwillingness to make decisions**
  - **an increasing level of aggression and hostility**
  - **need for personal worth to be confirmed**
  - **need for instructions/communications to be repeated**
- **inadequate control of operations.**

---

4. *Manipulation* Individuals may sometimes distort or omit information before passing it on through the communication system. An individual will do this if disclosure of information could damage his interests. Information may also be withheld so as to enhance the power of the holder. In a conflict situation, for example industrial relations, information may be withheld for both these reasons.

5. *Non verbal signals* Non verbal communication is an important way of communicating information. It is often termed body language. Facial expression, hand motions and bodily postures all tell us something about the way a person feels. Research has found that non verbal signals have a greater impact than the words actually spoken. Of course, in normal circumstances, non verbal and verbal communications reinforce one another. However, where the two are inconsistent (as where a manager consults you on a problem but continuously glances at his watch) communication is disrupted.

Organisational Communication

So far we have talked about communication in very general terms. We now turn to the problem of organisational communication. This is more complex because the organisation imposes restrictions in the way, with whom and for what purpose we communicate. In this section we will look at formal and informal communication, communication channels communication nets and methods of communication.

Formal and informal communication

The distinction between the two should not be difficult to understand as we have already talked about the formal and the informal organisation.

The formal organisation is commonly illustrated by the organisation chart which shows the formal hierarchical relationships between different individuals. That chart also shows the communication lines through which information of all kinds is supposed to pass. These communication lines or channels are often slow and inefficient when compared with informal communications networks. We will look at formal communication channels in more detail after we have considered informal communication.

Informal communication arises through the network of social relationships which exist within an organisation. Primarily, the informal communication network exists to satisfy the needs of its members – the need for companionship, to counter boredom, to influence others and provide work related information that is not provided by the formal communication channels.

Informal communication networks are often referred to as the 'bush telegraph' or the 'grapevine'. Managers tend to dislike the grapevine – there is, after all, a possibility that information may be incorrect, malicious or speculative. The information may have an unsettling effect upon employees.

Studies have shown that the grapevine has the following features:

- it is faster than formal communication channels

- much of the information on the grapevine is correct

- the grapevine is active at the place of work but not away from it

- senior managers use informal communication networks more than their subordinates

- staff managers are better informed by the grapevine than their line counterparts.

Managers have to accept that the grapevine will continue to exist and learn to harness its energy for the benefit of the organisation. They may, for example, use it to pass information to the workforce quickly rather than use formal channels. It may also be used as a sounding board for possible changes in working practices. The managers are able to evaluate employee attitudes towards the changes and on the basis of this information decide whether or not to introduce the new working practices.

Indeed, the grapevine is a useful feedback mechanism for managers letting them know what issues are important to, and troubling employees at this moment. Management is then able to respond to these issues as they think fit.

Communication channels

Let us now return to the subject of formal communication – communication which takes place through channels prescribed by the organisation structure. Fig. 15.1 indicates that these channels are vertical, horizontal and diagonal.

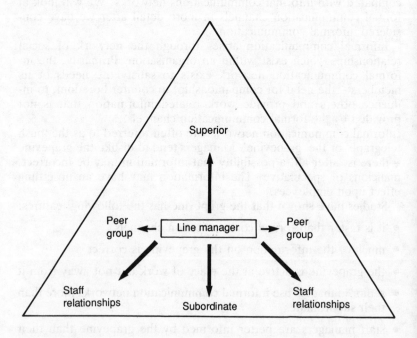

15.1 The manager's communication network – vertical, horizontal and diagonal

Vertical communications may be downwards or upwards. Vertical downward communication follows the organisation's command chain carrying messages from superior to subordinate. This has four purposes:

- to give instructions regarding work to be undertaken

- to give information on organisational policies and procedures

- to inform subordinates about their performance

- to provide information on organisational goals and progress towards them.

Examples of downward communication include: verbal instructions; memos; staff meetings; newsletters; notices and circulars.

Vertical upward communication is needed to pass information to the manager. Such information will cover items such as how work is progressing, and the feelings of their subordinates. The extent of upward communication is extremely variable. We have already noted that differences in status inhibit communication from subordinate to superior. Another important factor is the level of trust. Where trust exists the level of communication is much higher. Examples of upward communication include: progress reports; attitudinal surveys; suggestion schemes; grievance procedures and joint consultation committees.

Horizontal or lateral communication takes place among employees at the same level within the organisation. Such communication may be between members of the same or different departments. Horizontal communication is needed:

- to co-ordinate tasks

- to share information

- to solve problems

- to resolve conflicts

In the majority of cases these relationships are sanctioned to avoid over-burdening the vertical communication channels. Procedures are often established as a way of controlling such communication.

Horizontal communication may also take place to avoid the inefficiencies of vertical communication systems and speed up action. This may cause problems where decisions are taken without the superior's knowledge.

Project groups and inter-departmental committees are examples of horizontal communication.

Diagonal communication, as the name suggests, cuts across traditional vertical communication channels. It occurs most often in line and staff relationships where the specialist staff – say personnel

– are responsible for advising other departments on some proposed course of action, for example disciplining or dismissal. To compound the problem the person giving the advice is not only in a different department but is probably at a different level from the recipient of the advice.

Because such communications are not part of the normal vertical network there are normally built-in controls involving superiors who have been bypassed. Thus a disagreement between two individuals involved in a diagonal communication process will be resolved by their common superiors.

Diagonal communication has the advantages of efficiency and speed but there are obvious dangers in the process. In most organisations its use is limited.

Communication Networks

In an organisation one employee does not communicate with every other employee. The way in which communication takes place – the

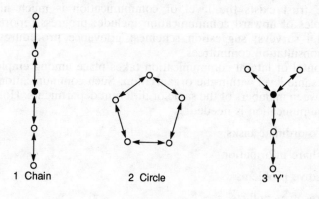

1 Chain   2 Circle   3 'Y'

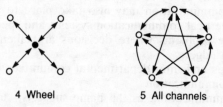

4 Wheel   5 All channels

15.2 Five common networks

network – may have significance for how efficient organisational communication is. Fig. 15.2 shows the five most common networks – each is analogous to command structures found within an organisation.

The chain represents a five-level hierarchy within the organisation with information flowing either up or down the chain of command. The people at either end of the chain can only communicate with those to whom they are linked.

The circle can be likened to three tiers in the organisational hierarchy with the subordinates reporting to their superiors through the chain of command. At the lowest level horizontal communication as well as vertical communication takes place.

If we invert the 'Y' network we see at once this is a four-level hierarchy with two subordinates reporting to a superior at the base.

The wheel illustrates a two-level hierarchy with four subordinates reporting to their common superior.

The all channel network is a situation where all individuals may communicate with whom they please. This network will occur in group work or committees.

Table 15.1 An evaluation of 5 common networks

	Chain	Circle	'Y'	Wheel	All Channel
Speed	Average	Poor	Average	Good	Good
Accuracy	Good	Poor	Good	Good	Average
Morale	Average	Good	Average	Poor	Good
Leadership	Average	None	Average	Good	None

No single network is superior to all other in all situations. The choice depends upon the circumstances. Table 15.1 assesses each network against four criteria, how quickly tasks are completed, the level of accuracy, the morale of team members and the opportunities for a leader to emerge.

The more centralised networks – the wheel and the chain (and to a lesser extent the 'Y') are best for collecting information and routine problem solving. The person in the position marked by the coloured circle is in a key position to influence the activities of the group by selecting the information to be passed on to the others. The dependence of other group members on this one person makes the situation less satisfying for them.

At the other extreme lies the decentralised all channel network (and to a lesser extent the circle). The greater 'free flow' of information is enjoyed by the members, there are greater opportunities for creative thinking (or brainstorming: see p. 197) and the network is generally more suitable for non-routine problems. Against this must be put the fact that it is often slow and error prone.

Methods of Communication

There are three broad methods of communication – oral, written and visual. We will look at each in turn.

Oral The majority of our time, both at work and leisure, is spent communicating orally. It includes:

personal meetings	joint consultation
committees	collective bargaining
conferences	the grapevine
training courses	telephone and tannoy

Oral communication has a number of advantages. First it is direct. Misunderstandings can be clarified quickly and feedback is immediate. Moreover, the message is reinforced by non verbal behaviour.

There are also a number of disadvantages associated with oral communication. There is, for example, no permanent record. Only the parties to the communication actually know what was said. It is always possible to deny this later. [For this reason a permanent record is often made later by a letter confirming a conversation, or the minutes of a meeting.] Second, oral communication does not lend itself to the transmission of large amounts of technical information – the receiver is rapidly in a situation of information overload. A third problem is that where the message is to be relayed further there is the likelihood of distortion. [Do you remember as a child playing the game pass the message and how different the end message was from the start message?] Fourth discussion, question and answer sessions, particularly to a group of people, can be very time consuming. Finally statements made on the spur of the moment without preparation or prior consideration can be dangerous. Spontaneous, ill-judged remarks are often the cause of conflict.

Written Communication This overcomes some of the problems of oral communication. The principal forms of written communication are:

Internal	*External*
memos and reports	letters
agendas and minutes	annual reports
bulletins and noticeboards	sales brochures and catalogues
computer print-outs	recruitment advertisements
in-house magazines	press releases

The major advantage of written communication is that it provides a permanent verifiable record of what has been said. Either party will be able to refer back to clarify points. This is particularly important in long or complex negotiations. Written communication is also less likely to cause misunderstandings as greater thought and care can be put into what is conveyed. Written communications also have the advantage of allowing the recipients to absorb the information at their own speed.

However, written communication also has its drawbacks. It is more costly than oral communication. In many cases the original draft will be altered and there is also the cost of the typist's time and possibly photocopying or reprographic facilities. Quite apart from being very much more time consuming than oral communication, written communication is still liable to misinterpretation and suffers the additional problem of not allowing for feedback and immediate clarification of unclear points. It also lacks the warmth and informality of much oral communication and poses difficulties should the communicator wish to modify information shortly after transmission.

Communication Technology   It is in the area of written communication that communication (or information) technology has had its greatest impact. Advances in technology are such that the old-fashioned office is being replaced by a modern computerised office which has very different methods of preparing and transmitting information.

- Information preparation: Word processing may be carried out on a micro computer or a dedicated word processor. Large amounts of information can now be prepared, edited and stored without using paper. Software packages are available for graphics presentation, direct mailing exercises and form design.
- Information transmission: There are many developments here. They include:
— Faxsimile (Fax): Exact replica copies of documents can be obtained through transmission by data-link using the public telephone system;
— Teletext: Both BBC and ITV have teletext services which are based upon television sets with a teletext facility. News, sports, weather and other items of general interest are provided. The user pays no fee for this service:

The advantages of communication technology

Reduction in costs. Many traditional features of the office eg document creation and filing are reduced through the use of micro computers and word processors. Apart from savings in labour costs savings are also made through using less paper and less space.

- **Quality**. Word processing allows the production of better presented information more quickly and cheaply.
- **Easier access** to more extensive information from data bases and other communication systems.
- **Better management decision making** through more information,

up-to-date information, and better presented information being available.

● *Security*. **Computer storage provides far more effective security than does files.**

— Viewdata: These are systems providing information to a television screen through the public telephone system. Information can also be transmitted by the customer through the viewdata network;
— Electronic Mail: These are systems for sending messages electronically through the telephone system. Messages are 'posted' through electronic office equipment to a central computer which holds the information in a 'mail box' which can only be accessed by the recipient. Large firms have their own systems of internal electronic mail. Externally a national electronic mail system is provided by British Telecom under the name of Telecom Gold.
— Electronic data interchange: This is a system which allows information to be passed electronically from one computer to another. Examples would include price lists, purchase orders, delivery notes, invoices and payment advice. EDI, as it is called, will generate considerable savings in transaction costs and from reducing errors caused by manual processing systems.
— Telex and Teletex: Telex is a system which transmits printed messages over a telephone line. Telex was introduced first of all in the 1930s but became really popular in the 1970s in international trade. Today it is possible to connect any electronic office machine to the telex system thus cutting out many of the costs previously associated with this system (e.g. telex room, specialist operators).
— Teletex was introduced by British Telecom in the mid 1980s and was intended to replace Telex. Teletex has the advantage that transmission speeds are far faster and the costs less.
— Electronic Funds Transfer: Computers can now be used to transfer funds from one person to another e.g. payments to suppliers or from one account to another eg, current to deposit account.

Visual communication   Visual forms of communication include:
   posters   films, slides and videos
   wall charts   closed circuit television
   noticeboards   microfilms
   photographs   visual (statistical) aids
As a form of communication which stands alone the impact of visual communication is limited. Wall charts, posters and notice boards may be used to impart a limited amount of information to a mass audience. They have the disadvantage of being essentially passive and rely on the desire of the individual to absorb that information. They also have a limited impact over a period of time –

frequent changes to the display have to be made if the receiver is not to lose interest.

Visual communication may also be used as an aid to a lecture or presentation. Films, videos, television programmes and visual aids may all be used as a means of reinforcing an oral or written message. In this section we wish to concentrate on the use of visual aids, particularly as a means of presenting statistical information.

There is an old saying – one picture is worth a thousand words. People are able to grasp technical information or complex processes far more easily if that information is presented pictorially. A series of bars on a chart, for example, which are progressively increasing in height immediately implies a rising trend. Similarly a line on a graph which is downward sloping from left to right is recognised as a falling trend.

Information can be presented pictorially in a variety of ways. We will look briefly at a number of ways of presenting information:

Tables. The table is commonly used to present complex information in a way which:
– is orderly
– shows patterns in the information
– summarises those figures.

Table 15.2 which is drawn from *Social Trends 1989* is an example of the type of information which is conveyed in a table. More complex statistical tables can be found in government publications such as the *National Accounts*, the *Annual Abstract of Statistics* and *Economic Trends*. The EEC, OECD and United Nations also publish a wealth of statistical information in table form.

When constructing a table you should take care to:

● ensure there is a clear title explaining the contents of the table

● give sources of data so that it can be checked

● ensure columns and rows are clearly headed

● clearly separate aggregates and percentages from the figures to which they relate

● generally ensure the table is easy to read – for example adequate space between columns or separate them by a line.

Tables have the advantage that a large amount of statistical information can be presented clearly and concisely. However, they have the drawbacks of lacking visual impact and requiring a high level of concentration to understand them.

Bar Charts. This is one way of presenting information with a greater visual impact. As its name suggests it is made up of a number

Table 15.2 Household expenditure on selected leisure items: by household income, 1986

United Kingdom — £ and percentages

| | Gross normal weekly income of household | | | | | | |
	Up to £100	Over £100, up to £150	Over £150, up to £200	Over £200, up to £250	Over £250, up to £300	Over £300	All house-holds
Average weekly household expenditure on (£):							
Alcoholic drink consumed away from home	1.67	3.64	5.23	6.23	7.73	10.63	5.93
Meals consumed out [1]	1.03	2.00	3.00	3.66	4.65	9.43	4.38
Books, newspapers, magazines, etc	1.46	2.13	2.53	2.75	3.10	4.16	2.73
Television, radio and musical instruments	2.09	3.05	4.45	5.79	6.39	7.62	4.85
Purchase of materials for home repairs, etc	0.84	2.01	2.03	2.96	3.63	6.00	3.08
Holidays	0.65	1.75	3.24	4.30	5.26	12.95	5.39
Hobbies	0.03	0.03	0.06	0.07	0.06	0.11	0.06
Cinema admissions	0.03	0.04	0.08	0.09	0.11	0.20	0.10
Dance admissions	0.03	0.06	0.07	0.12	0.18	0.24	0.12
Theatre, concert, etc admissions	0.05	0.17	0.18	0.26	0.25	0.64	0.29
Subscriptions and admission charges to participant sports	0.08	0.36	0.38	0.68	0.86	1.59	0.71
Football match admissions	0.01	0.07	0.03	0.13	0.10	0.14	0.08
Admissions to other spectator sports	0.02	0.01	0.02	0.03	0.05	0.07	0.04
Sports goods (excluding clothes)	0.09	0.14	0.17	0.42	0.28	0.83	0.37
Other entertainment	0.10	0.19	0.31	0.33	0.49	0.86	0.41
Total weekly expenditure on above	8.18	15.64	21.76	27.83	33.15	55.46	28.54
Expenditure on above items as a percentage of total household expenditure	*11.3*	*12.6*	*13.7*	*15.7*	*16.2*	*18.3*	*16.0*

[Source: *Social Trends 1989*]

of bars presented vertically or horizontally, the height or length of which are proportional to the figures they represent.

Simple bar charts such as Fig. 15.3 (which is based on information from Table 15.2) give limited information a highly visual impact. We see that the average family spends considerably more on either drinks or meals out than on home repairs. Such comparisons are

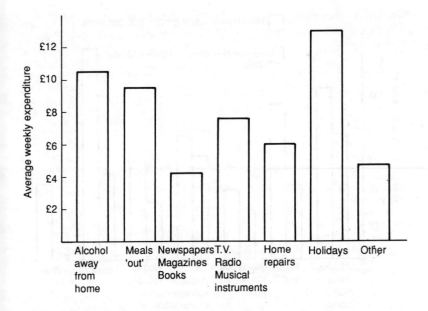

15.3 Average weekly expenditure on selected leisure items by households earning over £300 per week

more readily made, but what is lost in the chart is the precision of the table. It does not tell us the exact difference between 2 items.

More complex bar charts can also be constructed. Fig. 15.4 makes a comparison of the leisure spending of households earning between £250 and £300 and over £300 per week. Other complex bar charts make comparisons over time rather than between products or introduce positive and negative items sometimes termed two-directional bar charts (see Fig. 8.3, p. 133).

Bar charts may also be used for monitoring progress and controlling operations. One popular example of this is the Gantt chart. This defines the level of planned performance and then compares actual performance against the plan. Gantt charts are dealt with in more detail on p. 311.

Histograms. As we can see from Fig. 15.5 a histogram appears to be very similar to a bar chart. Indeed, once constructed, it is read in exactly the same way as a bar chart. There are, however, a number of differences. Let us compare Fig. 15.3 – a bar chart – with the histogram shown in Fig. 15.5. The first thing we notice is that on the horizontal axis of the histogram we are looking at one item – in this case output. On the bar chart we are looking at a number of

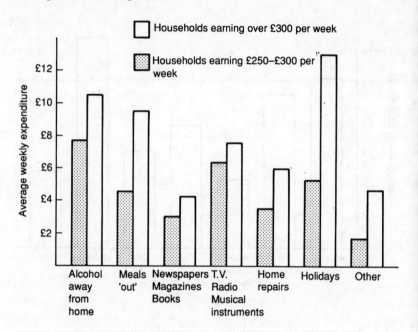

15.4 Average weekly expenditure on selected leisure items

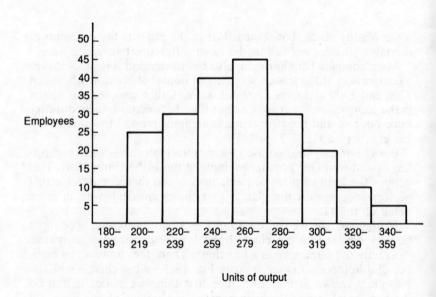

15.5 Histogram of worker productivity

separate items – alcohol, meals, newspapers and so on. Secondly, we see that the horizontal axis of the histogram shows a continuous measurement of the same thing – output.

Finally bar charts usually have gaps between the items – this makes for greater visual impact. On our histogram there are no gaps, nor would any histogram show gaps unless there was a complete absence of 'observations' in one of the range of values shown on the horizontal axis.

Summarising we can say that a histogram is a special form of bar chart showing the frequency of occurrence of the item being studied (in Fig. 15.5 – output) within certain defined limits (e.g. 180–199 units of output).

Pie Charts. This is a circle which is broken into segments of information. Each segment has an area which is equal to the quantity of the variable. An example of a pie chart is shown on p. 131. Pie charts have the advantage of being easy to understand and having an immediate visual impact. Among the disadvantages are that some differences in the size of sectors are too small for the individual to perceive any difference. Second, pie charts just tell us about shares not actual numbers or values. Third, they can be confusing if there are a large number of segments. Consequently pie charts tend to be used where detail is not all that important but rather we wish to draw attention to broad divisions in data.

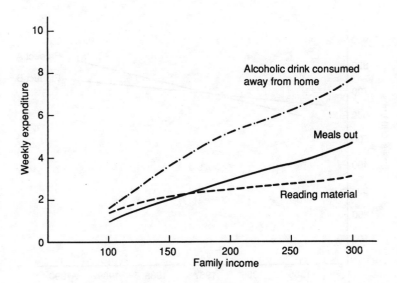

15.6 Line graph illustrating the relationship between income and selected leisure items

In constructing a pie chart the following points should be noted:
– The total value of items making up the pie must be known – in our case – alcoholic drink consumed away from home
– Individual segments of the pie are reduced to percentages which are then converted into portions of a circle (1 percent = 3.6°)
– Each segment of the pie must be labelled clearly and the value of the slice included.

Graphs. Graphs are one of the most frequently used ways of presenting information pictorially. The impact of the line graph compared with Table 15.1 from which it is drawn is clearly shown in Fig. 15.6. The detail of the Table is retained, but trends become clearer and comparisons easier to make. The line graph shows two sets of information (identified in the graph heading and on the axis) which are plotted against one another. On the vertical axis we put that set of information which is dependent or is influenced by the other set of information (the term variable is often used instead of 'set of information').

In Fig. 15.6 as family income rises so does leisure spending, but the level of leisure spending does not affect family income. Thus leisure spending is the dependent variable and family income the independent variable.

Normally the vertical axis starts at zero, but sometimes in an attempt to show trends more clearly or make comparisons easier we

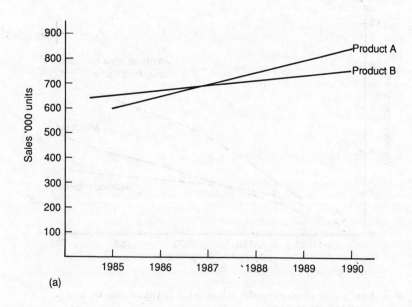

(a)

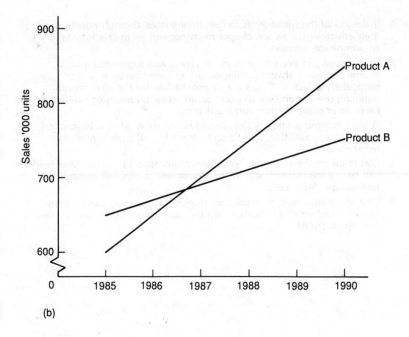

(b)

15.7 Graph (a) showing vertical axis starting from zero (b) misuse of vertical axis

omit the first part of the vertical axis and expand the remainder. Fig. 15.7 (a) and (b) illustrate this. Unfortunately, the power to show trends more clearly may be misused. Fig. 15.7 (b) shows a steeply rising curve for product A – we infer a dramatic increase in sales. The reality is that the annual increase in sales is less than 10 per cent.

Bar charts may also be misused in the same way.

Examination Questions

1 For what reasons can communication break down in organisations? Suggest ways in which the problems you have identified may be overcome.
2 Two members of staff within your organisation seem unable to communicate properly with each other. As a result work efficiency is suffering. Outline the reasons why personal communication may break down and explain how you would attempt to remedy the situation.
3 If people concerned themselves less with communicating and more with working we would have a far more efficient workplace. Discuss.
4 It is often argued that high morale in organisations is dependent upon an adequate level of communication within that organisation. Discuss.

5 If the job of the manager is to 'get things done through people' then their effectiveness as a manager must depend on their ability to communicate. Discuss.

6 At a meeting of departmental managers it was suggested that communication between management and employees was not particularly effective. Prepare a memorandum for the next meeting outlining the importance of good communication and steps which can be taken to improve vertical communication.

7 Formal communication is fine, but to really know what is happening within an organisation, just listen to the informal communication network. Discuss.

8 Comment on the view that better communication in the business world will be the inevitable result of improvements in communication technology. *(AEB 1985)*

9 Describe formal and informal communication systems. Examine the factors which would indicate when the formal communication system is inefficient. *(AEB)*

Part IV
Management in Action

Chapter 16

Marketing

The Institute of Marketing defines marketing as: 'The management process responsible for identifying, anticipating, and satisfying customer requirements profitably.'

Success in business is by no means guaranteed. Within a short period of time highly respected organisations may suffer a reversal of fortunes resulting in dramatic losses or even bankruptcy. Equally, companies which were unheard of a decade ago are now the market leaders.

One major reason for these organisations' changes in fortune arises because our affluent twentieth-century consumer is presented with many ways in which to spend his money. Improvements in international trade, transportation, and technology have greatly increased the quantity and type of goods available for purchase. For manufacturers this has meant that they can no longer rely upon the general scarcity of goods as providing a market for their product, but rather the goods they make must be tailored to the consumer's requirements.

Yet this was not always the situation. In earlier times goods were always limited in supply, nor was there any choice between similar products. It was a seller's market with businesses realising that customers would buy almost everything which they produced. We could say that business was production orientated. Gradually, though, the situation changed. Mass production dramatically increased the supply of many products while at the same time reducing their price. Improvements in transport and the relaxation of international trade controls resulted in larger markets being created and an increase in the level of competition between firms. Consumers used the wider choice available to them to select goods which matched their own particular requirements. The successful firm became one which set out to discover what the consumer wanted or could be persuaded to buy, who then made that product (or provided that service), and sold it at a profit. Such firms are said to be marketing orientated.

The Marketing Mix and Product Life Cycles

As we can see marketing strategy is now more important than it was in the nineteenth century. The strategy adopted will comprise four elements, often called the '4 Ps' or the 'marketing mix'. Fig. 16.1 shows the elements in this mix. We will look at each in turn:

1. Product

The organisation has to identify the products which the consumer wants and consider ways in which its products can be adapted to meet the consumers' needs more successfully. Since the needs of consumers differ this is not as easy as it sounds. In practice, through

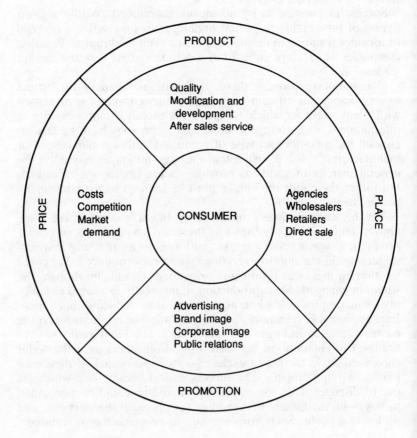

16.1 The Marketing Mix

a process called market segmentation, an organisation can concentrate its efforts on specific parts of the total market.

Market segmentation involves taking a total market and dividing it into a number of smaller markets that have similar characteristics. Potential markets can be identified in a number of ways. Two common methods are (a) demographic – age, sex, race, income, occupation or (b) geographical – urban, rural, inland, coastal.

Market segmentation enables the organisation to analyse the precise requirements of a group of consumers, the size of the market and the level of competition. It is then able to make a well informed decision on which markets it wishes to enter.

2. Price

A balance has to be obtained between the demands of the consumers for 'value for money' and the organisation's requirements for a satisfactory profit. A number of pricing strategies may be used to achieve these objectives. They fall broadly into one of three groups.

- cost
- demand
- competition

Cost orientated pricing may be either a standard mark-up percentage or a target return on capital. Mark-up price is often used by firms dealing with many products where it would be too costly to price each item separately. It involves adding a fixed percentage to the cost of each item. The precise percentage will vary according to industry and product (see Chapter 18, Financial Management p. 347) Target return pricing involves estimating that selling price which will yield a specified return on capital. Nationalised industries and public utilities, who are required to make a reasonable return on money borrowed, will use this method. Target return prices can be calculated as follows:

$$\text{Price} = \text{Product Cost} + \frac{\text{Desired \% return} \times \text{Investment}}{\text{Volume of product sales}}$$

There are various methods of *demand orientated* pricing. Skim pricing sets prices as high as possible. It is used when a product with unique features is first introduced to the market. This strategy relies on the fact that some people are willing to pay a much higher price than others. As this market is saturated, or competition moves in, the price may be lowered.

Penetration pricing involves setting a low price so as to reach a large market quickly. It may be used when goods or services are price sensitive or when you wish to discourage early competition from other organisations.

Price Sensitivity

Some products are far more sensitive to price changes than others. By this we mean that a change in price will result in a more than proportionate change in the quantity demanded. This has important implications for organisations. For example, a firm wishing to raise product prices to cover increased costs may be constrained by the knowledge that an increase in price will trigger a major fall in demand. Factors affecting buyers' sensitivity to price changes include:
- **uniqueness of product**
- **consumer awareness of substitutes**
- **ratio of expenditure to total income**
- **ratio of expenditure to total cost of end product**
- **status or prestige of product**

Psychological pricing. Many retailers will price an item at £295 rather than £300 because consumers will then tend to band it in the £200–£300 rather than the £300–£400 price range.

Many consumers also use price as an indication of quality. This is particularly true of luxury products such as perfume or high performance cars. Thus sales of perfume have been known to rise when prices have been increased! The manufacturer or retailer of luxury products may therefore set prices far in excess of the real worth of the product.

Discriminatory pricing. Different prices are charged for the same product. British Rail charges several different fares for a train journey to London. The student or shopper on a trip to London will be prepared to pay far less than the business person going to a meeting. By charging lower prices to certain groups of people British Rail is able to gain custom which it would otherwise have forgone. For discriminatory pricing to work the total market must be segmentable, the different segments unwilling to pay the same (high) price for the product or service, and higher priced segments unable to obtain the product or service at a lower price.

The third method of pricing is *competition orientated*. This may take several forms:

Follow my leader pricing. Prices are based upon what the competitors charge. There will normally be one firm, dominant in the industry, which will establish a price that is followed by other firms.

In oligopolistic industries, for example oil companies, firms commonly charge the same price and compete in other ways.

Loss leader pricing. A strategy used by some retail stores of pricing some products below the normal price. It is hoped that people enticed into the store by this offer will purchase other items as well.

Discount pricing. Some stores have a reputation for 'value for money' by selling most products slightly cheaper than other outlets. They are able to do this by renting/buying cheaper premises, paying less attention to presentation or having higher product turnover.

Tendering. This is common in the building and construction industry where sealed bids for a job are submitted by interested parties. The contract is awarded to the lowest bidder.

3. Place

Distribution of the product or service is a key part of the marketing mix. Until the item is in a position to be sold all the work done previously is of no effect.

An organisation's distribution strategy is determined by two major factors – coverage and control. Some products require extensive coverage – this particularly applies to impulse purchases, while at the other end of the spectrum spciality goods coverage may be limited to one retail outlet in the area. Control of the distribution channel will be important where personal service is important, for example tailoring or the selling of insurance. It will also be important where the manufacturer believes the display at the point of sale is a key factor in the sale.

A description of different channels of distribution will found on p. 290.

4. Promotion

The purpose of promotion is to generate sales of the product or service by:
- recruiting new customers
- retaining old or loyal customers
- retrieving lost customers

This may be achieved by advertising, sales promotion or sales force. These are dealt with later in this chapter.

The term 'marketing mix' indicates that we can combine these elements in different ways. The aim of the marketing specialist is to combine them in such a way as to optimise sales revenue. However, the strategy or marketing mix adopted is not static but is adjusted to meet the changing circumstances both within the company and the market. For example, where the business experiences increased competition the natural reaction is to place more emphasis on ad-

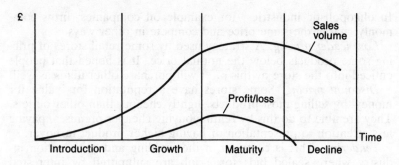

16.2 Product life cycle

vertising and promotion, or perhaps competitive pricing. Equally the introduction of new products by our competitors will intensify our company's research into new products, or the modification of existing products.

One critical factor affecting the marketing mix is the position of the product within its life cycle. Products are said to have a life cycle consisting of four stages, as illustrated in Fig. 16.2.

1. *Introduction.* The product is brought to the market, sales are low. The emphasis will be placed on a promotion strategy designed to inform the public of the product's availability. As sales are low we can be relatively selective as to the outlets from which the product is sold, yet at the same time strive for maximum exposure at these points of sale. The price may be relatively high at this juncture due to the newness of the product and the lack of competition.

Industrial Products

Another critical factor affecting the marketing mix is whether a consumer product or an industrial product is being sold (an industrial product may be defined as one which is used to manufacture, or in the manufacture of other products). The marketing of an industrial product is quite different from the marketing of a consumer product because:

- **The buyer is more informed about the product. He or she will make a rational decision to purchase based on product performance**

- **Many industrial products will be sold directly, without the use of middlemen, to the purchaser**

- **The decision to buy is often taken by someone different from the person seen by sales representatives**

- **The number of potential customers is far smaller than for consumer goods but the average order is far larger**

- **Many industrial products will be engineered to the customer's specifications**

- **After sales service e.g. installation, repairs and maintenance is more important.**

---

2. *Growth.* A period in which there is extremely rapid growth of sales and the first signs of competition arise. Prices may be lowered to attract a wider market and the numbers of outlets are increased. The search begins for products which will eventually replace this one.

3. *Maturity.* Sales and profits reach a peak and eventually decline. The majority of sales are 'replacements' rather than first-time purchases. Prices are reduced further to maintain our share of the market in the face of fierce competition. Advertising seeks to persuade the consumer to buy 'this' rather than the competitor's products. We search for other markets (perhaps abroad) and other uses for this product. The product is examined to see if there are

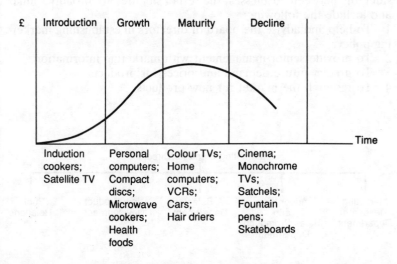

16.3 Stages in the product life cycle of selected goods

any developments or refinements which can be introduced, giving us a competitive edge and putting off the decline in sales. We introduce those other products which will, in the future, replace this one.

4.   Decline.   As new products take over the market, sales decline until it is no longer profitable to continue production. Advertising ceases and prices are reduced to the minimum compatible with profitability to stave off the eventual close-down of production.

In Figure 16.3 we see examples of products at different stages in the product life cycle.

The organisation of the marketing function will vary from business to business. In large organisations the scale of operations may warrant the creation of several departments each specialising in one aspect of the marketing operation. Each departmental manager would report to a senior manager who may very well be an executive director of the company (Fig. 16.4).

Smaller firms, however, may find it uneconomical to develop a similar range of marketing activities within the organisation. They may, for example, place advertising and other promotional activities or marketing research in the hands of an advertising agency, or a marketing research company. But even where smaller firms carry out similar marketing activities to those undertaken in the larger organisation the structure adopted is likely to differ – normally that of a single department headed by a marketing manager responsible to the marketing or some other executive director (see Fig. 16.5)

Although the organisation of the marketing function will vary considerably between businesses, the responsibilities are broadly similar and include the following:

1   To help and advise the board of directors in establishing marketing policy.
2   To provide senior management with marketing information.
3   To predict future demand and prices for products.
4   To research the market for new products.

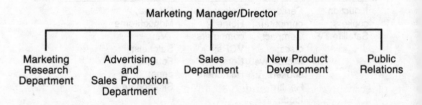

16.4 Division of marketing activities in a large organisation

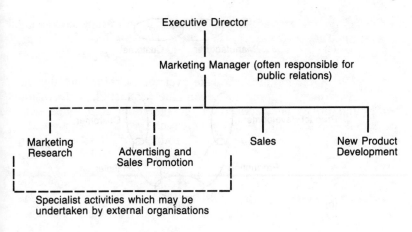

16.5 Marketing organisation within the small/medium-sized business

5   To spearhead the development of new products, or modification of existing products.
6   To co-operate fully with other parts of the organisation so as to ensure coordination of effort.
7   To establish and maintain a good image in the eyes of the public.
8   To promote the organisation's products by advertising and other means.
9   To identify and establish the most suitable channels of distribution for the organisation's products.
10   To administer an efficient and cost-effective function.

We will now consider in detail how these responsibilities are discharged by looking at the work of the marketing function under the headings of marketing research, advertising and sales promotion, sales management, new product development, and public relations.

Marketing research

With the growth of large organisations and the introduction of specialist functions the simple relationship which existed between manufacturer and customer has disappeared (see Fig. 16.6(a)). In its place we have the extended chain illustrated in Fig. 16.6(b). The result of this change is that information on markets and products fails to get to those parts of the business which need to act upon it. Marketing research is designed to fill that gap (see Fig. 16.6(c)).

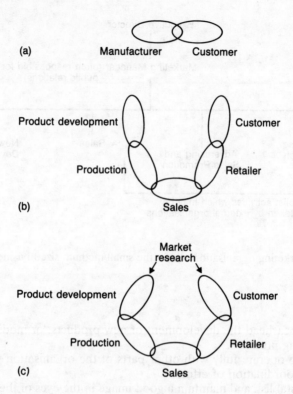

16.6 The need for marketing research

Marketing research aims to provide management with information on which to base its decisions regarding the organisation's future activities. Such information is vital to the success of the organisation, all decisions relating to the marketing mix – products, prices, promotion and distribution – being based upon marketing research. Failure to provide such information leads to an inefficient use of the organisation's scarce resources.

Forms of marketing research

Market research

● Economic, aimed at providing important background information on the country or region under consideration. Examples will include size of population, their income, restrictions on trade, the stability of the government, and business activity. Political and social factors may also be considered.

- More detailed research on a particular market designed to ascertain what products are being purchased at the moment and the trend in their sales. We are also interested in the degree of competition in the market, the strength of the competitors, their market share as well as the structure of their prices. Should the information obtained so far be encouraging, sales forecasts for specific products may be prepared.

Consumer research This aims to build up a profile of the person who buys a particular product. We are interested in discovering the critical attitudes and desires which persuade them to purchase that product. It is then possible to design a product which more obviously meets their requirements, or alternatively to create a promotion strategy which is more likely to persuade people to buy that product.

Product research Product research is concerned to establish the acceptability of new or existing products. It seeks to establish the essential features of the products and the price the consumer is willing to pay for those features. It is then possible to redesign a more competitive product incorporating the essential features, but also reducing costs by eliminating non-essential features or using alternative (cheaper) materials.

Promotional research This seeks to ensure that money spent promoting goods is used to the best effect. By comparing different forms of promotional activity in terms of cost and sales generated it can identify the most efficient promotional strategy.

Market research techniques

Desk research This should be undertaken prior to any field investigation. The research team will analyse information obtained from the sources given below.

1. Internal sources. Those which will cover the organisation's records to identify popular and unpopular products, and trends in sales (including seasonal fluctuations). Such information is of limited value; it cannot tell you what the market size is, why our products are not doing well, or the consumer's needs. However, research of this kind does reveal and clarify the nature of the problems faced by the organisation. Other sources or techniques, though, may now be used to discover the causes and remedies for these problems.

2. Published data. Obtained from a variety of sources, it is the basis of most statistics, trade research, and professional associations, and even everyday newspapers can be used to answer questions on:

- market size and trends;

- how our competitors are doing;
- what products customers are buying;
- what our competitor's costs and prices are;
- the effect of advertising; and many others.

Such information should be collected systematically and analysed regularly. It may very well obviate the need for costly field studies.
Field studies   Field studies are used when desk research fails to provide the information required by the organisation. Three techniques are widely used.
1.   Surveys.   A number of carefully selected people, who it is believed form a cross-section of the market, are questioned. The aim is to establish from their answers the reactions of consumers generally to new or modified products. Such surveys may be conducted personally by telephone or by post.

A personal interview is time consuming and expensive; however, it is possible to obtain more information by this method – supplementary questions may be asked while the interview can also enable other information on the respondent to be obtained merely by observation.

Telephone interviews tend to be shorter and less costly than both personal and postal surveys. However, telephone costs prevent a lengthy interview, follow-up questions are restricted, and the call may be terminated before the end of the interview.

Postal questionnaires are cheap, easy to administer, and speedy. However, the response rate is normally low, the questions asked have to be simple, and it is impossible to supplement answers by additional questions or observation.
2.   Observational methods.   Data is collected by watching an individual's reactions in a given situation. The respondent is normally unaware of the attention being paid to him. By this method consumer reactions to a certain product or group of products may be tested (this could of course be followed up by a personal interview) as may his reactions to certain sales techniques. Alternatively, an interviewer may pretend to be a customer in order to assess the ability of sales staff or discover which products they promote.

Observational methods will tell us more accurately than the respondent himself can, what his actions were at any given moment. However, it gives us little insight into why he acted in a particular way. Moreover, as we cannot control the environment within which the observations are made it is difficult to be sure that the stimuli we are investigating was, in fact, the cause of the reaction we noted. For this reason it may be necessary to use experimental records.
3   Experimental methods.   The most common application is in test marketing. Here a control market is established in which a product

is marketed as before. Test markets are then established in which one of the variables (e.g. price, product, promotional activity, distribution) is varied. It is then possible by comparing sales in the test and control markets to see what effect the change in variables has had.

The great advantage of experimental methods is that it is the only method of investigation which uses the market situation. Yet the results obtained in the test market are of little value if the test market is unrepresentative of the whole market – herein lies the real problem. Moreover, these tests by their very nature are both lengthy and costly. The tests may also be undermined by the actions of competitors in changing prices or promotional activities in test or control areas!

Conducting a market research investigation

Defining the project Normally the object of the investigation will be to find the answer to some problem, perhaps why a particular product is not selling well. Alternatively the object may be to discover if there is a problem. For example, how effective is our advertising, or is our product range adequate?

Background research We have already noted that a large amount of statistical information is available from published sources. Quite apart from the regular study of such information an appraisal of it should be made prior to any field studies. The aim is to become familiar with the literature relating to the research investigation and ensure that the answer to the problem cannot be obtained from these sources. Desk research may also clarify the nature of the problem leading to the formulation of certain hypothesis which can be tested by field studies.

Planning and implementation of field studies Having identified the group of people who have the information needed, consideration must be given to the methods of obtaining this information – personal or telephone interviews, maybe postal questionnaires. Normally the cheapest method of obtaining the necessary information would be selected; however, speed could also be an important consideration.

Once the methods for gathering information have been decided a questionnaire has to be devised and tested. Testing of the questionnaire is undertaken to reveal such problems as ambiguity, words and phrases which would be unfamiliar to the respondent, impertinent and leading questions. Failure to devote sufficient consideration to testing can invalidate the whole study and even result in future plans being based upon false information.

When the questionnaire has been tested, and if necessary

amended, the actual work of collecting the information may begin. *Analysis of results, conclusion and recommendations* Once the data has been collected it has to be collated. Nowadays much of this work would be done by computer, saving time and money. The results can now be analysed and a report drawn up embodying the findings, conclusions, and recommendations.

The advertising and sales promotion department

The advertising department is responsible for all activities involved in promoting the products or services of an organisation. Thus the department is not only concerned with the production and dissemination of advertisements but also with the design and distribution of brochures and catalogues, special offers (reductions in price of 25 per cent or more, free gifts), sponsorship, special displays, and competitions. There are many ways of promoting sales, but those listed above are the most commonly employed.

It was the rise in large-scale production which prompted business to invest heavily in advertising and other promotional activities. Large-scale production (bringing with it the advent of cheaper products, and the possibility of goods which the average person could never have previously afforded) was dependent upon a large-scale market. Business had to make known to the consumers what was being produced and persuade them to buy. A whole industry, advertising, grew up around the possibilities of increasing demand and even creating demand for goods and services. In short, the advertising industry seeks to change people's attitudes towards a service or product in a way which would be advantageous to the seller.

Today advertising falls into three broad classes – informative advertisements, persuasive advertising and institutional advertising. With each class the general aim is to increase sales, but more specific objectives would arise because of the nature of the product and its position in the product life cycle.

The Benefits of Advertising

1 It ensures the level of sales necessary for

- large scale production
- economies of scale
- employee security
- investor confidence

2 The public are informed of new and improved products.

3 Advertising revenue enables other products e.g. newspapers and TV programmes to be provided at a lower price.

4   Advertising encourages competition and results in better products at a keener price.

The Criticisms of Advertising

1   It raises costs.
2   Advertising expenditure may be

- **wasteful**
- **offensive**
- **misleading**

3   It is a method by which large firms may prevent new firms entering the market thereby preserving their 'monopoly' position.
4   Advertising generates desires for things which many can never hope to achieve.

Informative advertisements   Where a new product is brought to the market sales are naturally low at first because few customers know of its existence and perhaps even less its application. Here advertising seeks to inform the public of the product and its uses. Equally, where a product is modified and improved or new uses are found for an existing product, advertising informs the public of these facts.

Other products and services are complex in nature with a large amount of information needing to be digested before purchase is considered. Many industrial products fall into this category, though the purchase of a car or life assurance are also good examples. In these circumstances advertising is designed to highlight the most important or attractive features of the product. Although radio, television, and newspapers are often used for advertising these products, the use of brochures and leaflets is also very common.

Persuasive advertising   This form of advertising will normally be used during the maturity stage of a product's life cycle - a situation where there is normally a high degree of competition with several businesses producing and selling similar products. Experience has shown that the consumers in these situations do not always purchase the same brand of product. Rather they will select the first make of product they see provided the price is right. Persuasive advertising seeks to point the consumer in the direction of a specific product and by that means ensure that sales are maintained at a satisfactory level.

Persuasive advertising is commonly associated with consumer goods. It has been particularly heavily used where the degree of product differentiation is minimal. For example, one make of toothpaste is very like another. Similar comments can be made for soap powders, cans of beans, and many other products which we buy regularly. Persuasive advertising has been criticised for playing too heavily on emotional appeal and exploiting anxieties.

Most advertisements though, are a blend of informative and persuasive communication. Thus an advertisement referring to cut-price petrol (a) informs the market on the details of the offer in such a way that it (b) persuades them this offer is too good to miss.

Institutional advertising Such advertising is designed to improve the image of the advertiser, rather than to sell a specific product. It is very much a public relations exercise. Many large companies try to show by such advertisements how socially responsible they are – what contribution they have made to society. The aim is to engender a positive attitude to the business in the minds of the shareholders, consumers, and employees as well as the general public.

Ensuring that advertising is effective

A marketing executive is reported to have once commented, 'Half my advertising budget is wasted – but I don't know which half'. No doubt the comments are apocryphal, yet a problem does exist. It is undoubtedly true that not all advertising is successful in generating extra sales, yet it is also true that it is difficult to prove conclusively that a particular advertisement has, or has not, achieved the desired results. The fact that sales rose during an advertising campaign may suggest that advertising has achieved the desired result, but it is not conclusive. Other marketing factors or even external conditions could have affected the outcome.

Although techniques have been devised to measure an advertisement's impact none have the degree of authority we would like. The following points must be considered for advertising to be successful.
Business environment. We have already seen that in a recession the level of demand for most goods and services declines. For luxuries though, the drop in demand is much greater and advertising is unlikely to be successful. A similar situation will occur when the Government imposes additional taxes or public attitudes harden against the product advertised.
Suitable media There are many possible media which may be used for advertising, but it is important to select those that are likely to obtain the best results. Thus it is unlikely that an engineering product would be advertised on television. The target audience is more likely to be reached by using specialist magazines.
Adequate background preparation. Advertising is most likely to succeed when market research has previously been undertaken to discover the likes and dislikes of the consumer. Consideration must also be given to the style of the advertisement – informative or persuasive – and the method of presentation. Poor presentation may even create resistance to the product advertised.

Position in the product life cycle. New products will often be launched with a large amount of advertising so as to inform and persuade people to give the product a trial. As a product moves into its growth and maturity stage the ratio of advertising expenditure to sales will fall. In the decline stage advertising will have little effect.

Market conditions. Advertising will be the most effective form of promotion when the market is widespread with many customers in different locations.

The nature of the product. Where a product is tailor-made to a customer's requirements and has a high unit value or is technical in nature, it is best promoted by personal sales efforts. Conversely, where a product is mass produced (standardised) having a low value and has few or no technical features advertising will be cost effective.

Sales management

The primary function of the sales organisation is to produce that volume of sales which will yield the planned profit. It will also be required to undertake other activities as specified by the marketing manager or the board of directors. These could include sales maximisation of certain product lines, export penetration, or the provision of information for marketing research. Although the organisation structure adopted for sales may vary considerably there are normally three facets to its work, namely selling, distribution, and administration.

1. *Selling* – sometimes referred to as the field sales organisation, selling is concerned with the work of the sales force. This will involve aspects of appointment and training together with motivation and control of sales staff.

2. *Distribution* – potentially there are many ways in which a product or service can be sold to the public. The problem which business faces is to determine which of these channels is most appropriate. The final decision will take into account factors such as:
(a) the nature of the goods, e.g. weight, size, fragility;
(b) the nature of the market, e.g. size, distance, competition, profitability.

3. *Administration* – the sales office is responsible for maintaining records and ensuring efficient operation of the administrative system.

Where firms are selling only a small range of products through similar distribution channels a functional structure is often adopted. Figure 16.7(a) shows how specialists responsible to the sales manager are appointed to each of the positions mentioned above.

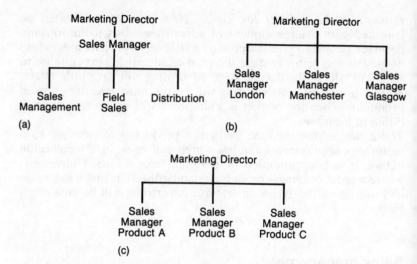

16.7 (a) Functional organisation; (b) area organisation; (c) product organisation

While this structure is popular with small or medium-sized firms, larger firms tend to base their organisation on areas or products.

Area organisations (see Fig. 16.7(b)) are used by many large companies manufacturing relatively few products but which have to be distributed over a wide area. Oil companies, banks, and breweries all adopt this structure, finding it easier to cater for changes in consumer preferences between areas and also to establish and maintain local links.

Industrial companies tend to favour a product-based structure (see Fig. 16.7(c) acknowledging the high degree of differentiation between many of their products and also their technical complexity. The sales organisation will then be responsible for marketing a range of relatively homogeneous products.

Selling

Why do we need sales people? Basically because advertising and other promotional efforts may be unsuccessful in reaching our target group and obtaining a sale. Personal selling, although being far more costly per person reached than advertising, may, because of sales made, be far more cost effective. Personal selling carries with it the opportunity for discussion and clarification on points of misunderstanding, and therefore has far greater persuasive force than other promotional techniques. Moreover, the sales presentation can be tailored to the needs of the individual customer. Yet the employment of the sales force has other benefits for the business too, as enumerated below:

1. It is an invaluable source of marketing research information.
2. Sales staff are able to find new outlets for their company's products, selecting only those which reflect the image the company wants to create.
3 By maintaining a direct link with the customer rather than marketing through an intermediary the company ensures that its products are always brought to the attention of the customer.
4. The sales force will promote new products, whereas intermediaries are more interested in selling products which are already well known – this after all is the easiest way to earn their money.
5. In establishing a personal relationship with customers repeat sales are more likely to be made.

Supervising the activities of the sales force is the function of the sales manager. In conjunction with the personnel department the sales manager will be responsible for the appointment and training of new sales staff. Training is particularly important to ensure that the sales representative is well groomed, and has a good understanding of both the products to be sold and the company's procedures.

Sales managers motivate and control their staff by means of targets and remuneration. Targets for sales, both monthly and annually, are established. The target should be agreed with the salesperson, rather than imposed from above. Skill is needed in setting the target. If it is set too high the salesperson quickly loses heart, too low and the company is not using these services efficiently. The target is used as a means of evaluating the salesperson's efforts from month to month, but may also be used as a means of generating competition between sales staff (who can exceed their target by the greatest percentage?) and calculating pay bonuses.

The system of remuneration which is operated is normally a basic salary together with incentive/commission payments for achieving high results. The system must be fair and take into account all factors affecting the volume of sales they are likely to achieve. For example, should a salesperson in one period be required to spend a large proportion of their time promoting a new or unknown product the value of sales produced during that period is likely to be far less than normal, and their target should reflect this.

Sales administration　The primary function of the sales office is the maintenance of an adequate set of records, they will include:

1. *Salesperson's records* – showing areas worked in, sales achieved, salary, bonus, and expenses paid.
2. *Customers' records* – showing names of contacts within the firm, orders taken in the last few years, discounts given, any special re-

quirements, and credit rating. Records on past and prospective customers will also be kept.

3. *Sales representative's reports* – sales reps spend most of their time away from the office working by themselves. Reports are essential, therefore, to discover how their time has been spent. The report form must be designed so that the maximum information can be obtained in the minimum time, but should indicate the number of calls made, the name of the person met, details of the discussion, orders obtained or the state of negotiations, and any information on competitors.

4. *Statistics* – records on products sold over time and by area should also be maintained.

The sales office will also handle enquiries, orders, and complaints. All must be dealt with speedily. Enquiries and complaints will require individual attention by either the sales manager or the salesperson who is normally responsible for maintaining contact with that business (or in whose area the firm is situated). Standard letters for quotations and orders enable information to be supplied promptly – perhaps aided by a word processor, while also facilitating the keeping of records.

Distribution

Traditionally, distribution has been outside the control of the marketing function; however, distribution is an important element in the marketing mix and the marketing department is keenly interested in this area. This paradox may be explained by considering distribution at two different levels.

The marketing department's interest in distribution lies in what channels should be used to obtain an advantage over their competitors, for example whether to sell direct to the consumer or to intermediaries. The marketing department has not the same degree of interest in the physical distribution of the goods, for example scheduling and routeing of deliveries, control of stock, and transportation.

Moreover, the blend of skills needed to run such a system efficiently is not normally found within the marketing department. They are more likely to be found within the production department. Again, as distribution follows on naturally from production it is logical to place it within the ambit of the production department.

Channels of distribution
Direct selling. There are many examples of direct selling to the consumer. Avon and Tupperware are always mentioned, but double glazing and insurance are also examples of selling to the consumer in his or her own home. Another variation is where a producer owns and runs a retail outlet, such as Singer Sewing Machines or the

Burton Group, but the list could also include shoe manufacturers and bakeries. Many industrial products are also sold in this way.

The major benefit arising from direct selling is that by using your own staff and retail outlets you can be sure your product will be properly promoted. Competing products are not at hand to divert the customer's attention and sales staff are fully conversant with the products they are selling. The above points also apply when the place of contact is in the customer's home, with the added advantage that the salesperson has a semi-captive audience!

The major disadvantage of direct selling is that selling costs are likely to be high – rent and rates where retail outlets are established, and a higher sales force cost where home canvassing is employed. However, these extra costs are to some extent offset by a higher profit margin.

Producer to retailer. Very much a compromise between direct selling and selling to intermediaries, this method is adopted by large firms selling a number of products to the same kinds of retail outlets. Frozen-food firms and bakeries both have their own distribution network. A large, costly sales force is needed to ensure that orders are obtained from retail outlets; however, this has the advantage that the firm has some control over the way their products are displayed. Indeed some firms will even assist in the presentation of their products within the retailer outlet to ensure that their point of sale display is the equal of, if not better than, their competitors. One particular problem experienced both with retail and wholesale distribution is that new products (because they generate less sales per unit of sale space) are not promoted sufficiently.

Producer to wholesaler. This is often chosen by firms who have a small or incomplete product range and are unable to afford the high costs associated with an extensive distribution network and large sales force. The major advantage is avoiding the high selling/distribution costs associated with the methods described above, though we hasten to add that some kind of distribution network must be maintained and some sales staff will be employed. Yet there are major problems associated with this method of distribution. First, the producer has no control over the retail outlets – as to how the products are displayed, or even whether they are stocked at all. Secondly, new products do not receive the promotion they deserve, and finally the profit margin tends to be lower than in either of the other two methods of distribution.

Franchising. A franchise is a concession given by the owner of patents relating to goods or services to another person allowing them to produce and sell those products/services. Generally the franchiser – that is, the person giving the concession – provides a well-known trade name together with technical and administrative training. The franchisee – the person to whom the concession is given – undertakes in return to sell only the franchiser's products and conform to specified standards.

Franchising is attractive to the franchiser because it allows them to expand their sphere of influence without any more capital investment. Indeed franchising may result in an injection of capital into the firm. The franchiser will also benefit from contributions to overhead and operating costs from the franchisee. Moreover, the franchisee may be contracted to purchase certain goods from the franchisor. Against these advantages must be put the fact that it is difficult to control franchisees, and that an unsuccessful franchise arrangement may detract from the image of the franchisor.

To the franchisee – often a person new to running a business – it offers a proven product, training in all aspects of the business, help and advice with administrative matters and the advantage of being part of a well known group. However, the franchisee may feel that the constraints placed upon them – what they can sell, hours of work, pricing policy – in reality the ability to run the business the way they want to, irksome.

Franchising should not be regarded simply as a distribution technique but as an increasingly important method of running a business.

The British Franchise Association has been set up to vet franchisors and protect the interests of individual franchisees.

New product development

So far we have concerned ourselves with the marketing of existing products. Yet our discussion earlier on the product life cycle will

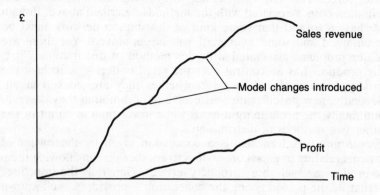

16.8 Effect of product modification on sales and profit

have told us that no business can rely upon existing products to provide an indefinite future for the firm. For many businesses the search for new and improved products is a continuous process. Product development encompasses two ideas: first that an existing product may be modified, and secondly the development of a new product.

Product modification

The aim of product modification is to prolong the life of a product by changes in its quality and features. Consider how motor manufacturers change specifications and styling at regular intervals after the introduction of the original model. The effect can be seen by considering Fig. 16.8.

Once the original model has been introduced the search begins for modification which would improve the car's standing with consumers. Marketing research is closely involved in this process. Sales of the model are closely monitored and modification will be introduced to coincide with the peaking of demand for the original model. Renewed interest will then cause a further expansion in sales. Production modification may eventually result in the marketing of a model which is totally different from that which was first introduced.

Product development

Product modification does no more than put off the day when a product has to be phased out. Product development is therefore essential to the survival of the business. But although most firms recognise the importance of product development, actually producing a new product which is commercially successful is by no means easy. Even large well-known companies achieve a success rate of less than 50 per cent on the introduction of new products. Fig. 16.9 illustrates the stages in the development of a new product and re-emphasises that few new product ideas will actually become commercially successful. The following section outlines the procedure for new product development.

Generation of ideas. Ideas for new product development tend to fall into three categories. Products may be entirely new, that is, something for which there is no substitute, for example video-cassette recorders. Other products may replace existing products and yet be significantly different from those earlier products, for example tinned peas replaced dried peas and frozen peas replaced tinned peas. The third category of new product is purely imitative – it apes a product already on the market in the hope of capturing part of that market.

Maintaining the flow of new ideas is both a major problem and a necessity to the business. All departments, but especially marketing

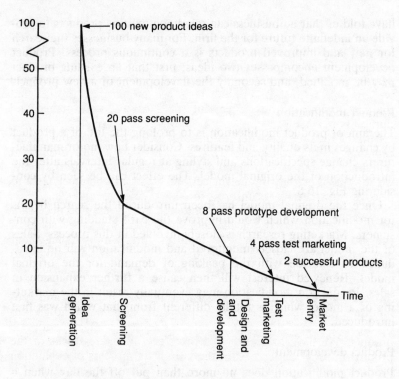

16.9 Stages in the development of a new product

and production, have a contribution to make. In some businesses a technique referred to as 'brainstorming' is used.

Assessment of new product ideas. As development costs escalate sharply once we have passed the assessment stage it is vital that we consider the following:

1. Is there sufficient market demand?
2. Is the product compatible with other products which we produce? In particular do we have the necessary technical expertise, can we use our present sales force and our channels of distribution, and is the product compatible with our business image?
3. Is this product going to be profitable and do we have sufficient finance for its development?
4. Do we have the physical capacity and time to deal with this product?

It is obvious from the questions which have to be answered that new product development draws upon the expertise of the whole firm.

Design and development. By the end of this stage a prototype will have been produced. Technical problems involved in its production will have been identified and ironed out. We are able to cost the finished product more accurately. Again we evaluate the product in terms of the criteria established in the assessment section above.

Market and product testing. Now that a prototype has been made we are able to test it. Product tests are designed to ensure that the prototype conforms to certain standards of performance and durability.

Market tests are designed to discover whether the product is acceptable to the consumer. This may involve asking groups of potential consumers to use and evaluate the product. Alternatively, we may market the product in certain areas and conduct tests to discover how closely it conforms to consumer requirements.

As a result of the information obtained here it may be necessary to revert to the design and development stage to change some of the product's technical or style features. But senior management now has as much information on the product as it is ever likely to have and must shortly make the decision whether to market the product commercially.

Market entry. Before entry, decisions relating to prices and promotion are made. We have to buy plant and machinery and go into production. The sales force has to be fully conversant with the product. We have to ensure that there are adequate stocks of the product in retail outlets. After the launch the process of evaluation begins again. In what ways can we modify the product so that it more closely meets customer requirements? Is it possible to improve our marketing mix? We will also be considering what other ideas are worthy of our attention. Product development is very much a continuous process.

Studies have revealed there is no one best method for organising product development. Often a separate department is created reporting directly to senior management. The department would be responsible for all aspects of development and would only hand over responsibility for the product to the marketing department after a successful launch.

Alternatively, a committee structure, normally with members from finance, marketing, production, and research may be used. This has the benefit of drawing directly on the expertise held in other departments and involving the whole business in the process of product development.

Public relations

Public relations work is often confused with advertising. This is not surprising as the end result of a public relations exercise may very well be an advertisement extolling the virtues of the organisation. Yet just as advertising is only one form of sales promotion it is also just one facet of public relations.

Public relations can be defined as presenting an acceptable image of the business to members of the public. Through public relations the business seeks to:

1 Persuade customers or 'would-be customers' that it is an organisation with whom they are happy to be associated – thereby indirectly promoting its products.

2 Provide the investing public with information which presents the activities of the business in the best possible light – thereby encouraging investment in the business now through the Stock Exchange, or later when it is necessary to raise capital.

3 Inform employees of the firm's activities, emphasising the contribution of all employees to the success of the business – thereby strengthening employee interest in the business and raising morale.

In a large organisation public relations may form a department in its own right while in smaller organisations either the marketing manager is responsible for maintaining a positive business image, or a public relations officer with a background in journalism may be appointed. The methods used to maintain and develop public relations cover the following range:

- Press releases and conferences.

- Participation in exhibitions or trade fairs.

- The sponsorship of sports and other events.

- Literature – house magazines, annual reports and accounts, recruitment literature.

- Information to employees of the firm's activities, emphasising the contribution of all employees to the success of the business – thereby strengthening employee interest in the business and raising morale.

Consumer Protection

Consumer protection in Britain is very much a twentieth century phenomenon. In the past, the attitude of the law is best summarised by the legal maxim 'caveat emptor' or 'let the buyer beware'. The assumption was that parties were of equal bargaining power and entered into the contract with their eyes open – no one could force you to accept defective goods or onerous terms in a contract. The onus was on the buyer to ensure he got what he wanted. The law would not intervene just because he made a bad bargain.

Yet in the nineteenth century the sale of defective goods and adulterated foodstuffs was rampant. Moreover, the consumer had little remedy against the seller – first because he lacked the resources to pursue his claim and second because he lacked the knowledge of how to pursue it.

We could also add that the manufacturer and retailer with their greater financial resources were willing to spend large amounts of money to avoid liability. Failure to avoid liability could, after all, open the floodgates to many actions of a similar kind.

Today the consumer is in a much stronger position. Both the Government (through legislation) and the judges have intervened to protect their interests. Voluntary bodies such as the Citizens' Advice Bureaux, Consumers Advice Centres and Law Centres are able to advise the consumer.

This is just as well because:

- the imbalance of power between seller and buyer is greater than ever

- faults in many products are not discernible at the time of sale

- many consumers don't know their rights or how to obtain redress.

In the following pages we will look at some of the ways in which consumers are protected.

Defective goods

The term goods covers the purchase of visible tangible items such as cars, computers, machinery, foodstuffs, toiletries – the list is endless. It also includes crops, livestock, and services in which a major element is the supply of goods, for example a restaurant meal.

The Sale of Goods Act 1979 is the key piece of legislation protecting consumers. The Act covers all purchases of goods from traders who would normally sell that type of product. It implies with every contract for the sale of goods three rules. They are:

- Goods should correspond to their description. For example a suit which is made of man-made material should not be described as 'all wool'

- Goods should be of 'merchantable quality'. This means they should be reasonably fit for their normal purpose, taking into account any description, the price paid and the nature of the goods. For example, if shoes let in water the first time you wear them they are not of merchantable quality. If, however, they had been purchased cheaply off a second-hand shoe stall at the local market and they leaked the legal position would be very uncertain.

Consumer safety standards

By law certain consumer goods must conform to minimum safety standards before being sold. Examples include children's anoraks, babies' dummies, cosmetics, crash helmets, furniture and drugs. There are many more.

The legal safety requirements are often based on the work of the British Standards Institution (BSI). The BSI has also suggested minimum quality or safety standards for many other products, and where manufacturers produce to these specifications they are allowed to use the BSI Kitemark (see below).

BS 857

To the consumer it is a guarantee of acceptable safety standards.

– Goods should be fit for a particular purpose. Where the buyer tells the vendor what the product is required for and relies upon the vendor's skill and judgment in selecting something suitable the item selected must be suitable for the buyer's purpose.

Where there has been a breach of one of these implied terms the buyer may reject the contract and demand his money back, or request compensation. This right of action is against the person with whom you contracted – the seller of the goods. However these rights could be lost if:

- the defect complained of was drawn to their attention at the time of the sale

- the fault was obvious

- the buyer keeps the goods for a reasonable length of time and fails to tell the vendor that they are not perfect

- the goods were a present (the actual purchaser has the legal right to redress).

It is important to emphasise that in the absence of a breach of an implied term the supplier has no legal obligation to exchange the goods or refund money.

Defective Services

The Supply of Goods and Services Act 1982 states that there is an implied term that the supplier of a service acting in the course of a business will carry out that work with reasonable care and skill. If a client feels that this is not the case he may sue the service supplier for breach of this section. Thus if a plumber comes to repair a leaking pipe and it starts leaking again shortly after the work is completed the client may sue.

The 1982 Act also covers the situation where goods are supplied in the course of a service contract. Here the person who supplies those goods is under a duty to see they are of merchantable quality and fit for a particular purpose, just as if it had been a contract for the sale of goods. So our plumber is unable to avoid liability by claiming that the leak is caused by faulty materials used in the repair rather than faulty workmanship.

Exclusion Clauses

An exclusion or an exemption clause is a method by which a seller of goods or services seeks to limit their liability to a purchaser should things go wrong. For example:
- we are not liable for loss or damage howsoever caused – cars are parked here at the owner's risk
- all sale goods bought as seen – no refunds will be made
- this guarantee replaces any conditions or warranties, expressed or implied

are all examples of exclusion clauses which have been successfully used in the past.

The scope of exclusion clauses today has been severely curtailed by the Unfair Contract Terms Act 1977. The Act says that certain exclusion clauses are not allowed, and others allowable only if fair and reasonable in all the circumstances of the case. The following exclusion clauses have no effect whatsoever:
- clauses seeking to avoid liability for death or injury to consumers arising from the seller's negligence
- clauses in consumer contracts which seek to avoid the implied terms of the Supply of Goods legislation
- clauses by which the seller seeks to avoid liability for negligence in the manufacture of goods.

The following exclusion clauses are effective if the courts believe them to be reasonable:

- clauses avoiding responsibility for misrepresentations
- clauses enabling a seller to perform a contract in a substantially different way from that which was intended
- clauses enabling a trader to avoid liability for loss of profits caused by their negligence.

In deciding what is fair and reasonable the courts will consider factors such as the relative bargaining power of the parties, any inducements which were given to accept the exclusion clause and whether the purchaser knew or should have known about the existence of the exclusion clause. The burden of proof regarding reasonableness is placed upon the person seeking to rely on it.

Of course banning the use of exclusion clauses is of little use if traders can convince purchasers that they have no rights. For that reason it is now a criminal offence to attempt to mislead consumers into believing they have no rights.

Guarantees

There are two completely different situations to consider. First, the agreement between the trader and purchaser may include a guarantee. For example, this often happens when you purchase a second-hand car from a dealer. Once upon a time this was the way traders actually limited their liability to the purchaser. By signing a contract and guarantee form, purchaser agrees to many of their legal rights being taken away! As we have seen this is no longer possible in a consumer contract and while such a guarantee may give you no other rights than those you have under Sale of Goods legislation it certainly cannot take those rights away.

A second situation arises where a manufacturer gives a guarantee to the purchaser of their product even though they are not a party to the contract of sale. The guarantee will normally give the right to repair or replacement of the product free of charge if it goes wrong within a specified period (often a year). Here the guarantee gives the purchaser rights in addition to those under the Sale of Goods legislation. A purchaser with a complaint may aproach either the retailer (under the Sale of Goods legislation) or the manufacturer (under the terms of the guarantee).

Trade Descriptions and Misrepresentations

Trade Descriptions.   Under the Trade Descriptions Act 1968 it is a criminal offence to make:

False statements about the nature of goods
eg hand-made   (manufacture)
    real leather   (composition)

will not stain   (performance)
one careful owner   (previous history)
False statements about the nature of services
eg qualified instructor available   (provision of service)
   open 7 days   (manner of service)
   a short stroll into town   (location of service)
   heated pool   (nature of service)
False statements about the prices of goods
eg stating price is less than MRP (manufacturer's recommended price)
   advertising goods at a price lower than that at which they are really offered
   indicating that prices have been reduced.

While the major thrust of Trade Descriptions legislation is the prosecution of offending traders it is of indirect help to consumers. Where a prosecution is successfully brought by the Trading Standards Officer the court may award compensation to the consumer. However, this is not automatic and the court may take the view that it does not have the knowledge or experience to make a just award. Even so, evidence of a criminal conviction would be very useful evidence in a future civil case for compensation.

Misrepresentation. A representation is a statement of fact made in the discussions before contract and which influenced your decision to enter into that contract. A false statement of fact is called a misrepresentation. There are three types of misrepresentation and because they have different remedies it is important to distinguish between them.

A *fraudulent* misrepresentation arises where the trader makes an untrue statement knowing that it is untrue.

A *negligent* misrepresentation occurs where a statement is made by a trader, he has no grounds for believing it to be true and it is in fact untrue.

An *innocent* misrepresentation is a statement which is made and believed to be true, but which in fact is untrue.

Generally speaking you are able to rescind (reject) the contract whether the misrepresentation was innocent, negligent or fraudulent. However, this remedy will not be available where a contract of service is partially performed or goods have been used for some time. Rescission (rejection) is only available where both parties can be returned to their previous position. Where cancelling the contract is not available the other remedy is damages. This is available for both fraudulent and negligent, but not for innocent, misrepresentation.

Fair trading

The Office of Fair Trading (OFT) was created by the Fair Trading Act 1973. It is headed by a Director General of Fair Trading who is appointed by the Secretary of State for Trade and Industry. While the OFT is not concerned with individual complaints, it has a wide-ranging duty to monitor and control the activities of traders. The Director General will take action against traders who consistently act in a way which is unfair to consumers. For example, a motor car dealer was convicted under the Trade Descriptions Act of changing the mileage reading on cars eight times in 6 months. The Director General obtained promises from him that this action would stop.

In respect of dealings between consumers and traders the Director General has five functions;
- to publish information and advice which will be of use to consumers e.g. rights under consumer legislation, how to obtain consumer rights, obtaining credit
- to persuade trade associations to develop voluntary codes of conduct. These have no legal standing but are guidelines on the way in which dealings with the public should be conducted e.g. British Code of Advertising Practice
- to monitor complaints of consumers to Trading Standards Departments, Citizen Advice Bureaux, Environmental Health Departments and, where necessary
- to report bad trading practices, and recommend action to be taken by the Secretary of State
- to take action against traders who persistently act in a way detrimental to consumers.

Consumer credit

There are many different ways of borrowing money, for example bank loan, bank overdraft, credit sale, chain store credit account and hire purchase. All these, and others, are covered by the Consumer Credit Act 1974. The aim of this Act is to protect the interests of the consumer by ensuring 'truth in lending'. The Act is extremely complex and so we will only deal with it in outline.

The Consumer Credit Act covers all credit agreements where the amount of credit is not more than £15,000. The Act is enforced by Local Authorities through their Trading Standards or Consumer Protection Departments, but the Director General of Fair Trading has overall responsibility for the working of the Act.

Any trader who wishes to arrange or give credit requires a licence. The Office of Fair Trading will only grant these if they believe the applicant is fit to be in the credit business. Although licences are issued for 10 years they can be cancelled at any time.

One major aim of the Act was to ensure that there was truth in lending. Consumers should know the real cost of borrowing money and be able to compare one source of credit with another. This has been done by requiring traders to calculate the cost of credit in a particular way – the APR (Annual Percentage Rate) – and controlling advertisements relating to credit.

Many firms try to assess a consumer's financial standing before granting credit. As part of this process they will often consult a credit reference agency. Credit reference agencies are also controlled by the Act. Agencies need licences to set up in business and the Act lays down procedures for an individual to correct faulty information about himself.

Taking action

In many cases when a problem is brought to the attention of a trader they will be anxious to put the matter right. At times though the purchaser of goods or services may not obtain satisfaction from the trader and it will be necessary to take the matter further. There are several avenues to consider.

Trade Associations. Many trade associations have laid down standards of service required of their members. These are usually termed 'codes of practice'. There are, for example, codes of practice for package holidays, car repairs, funerals, double glazing and dry cleaning. Compliance with the terms of the code by members is voluntary – the standards do not have the force of law. However, members are supposed to comply with these standards and risk expulsion if not. Where the code has been approved by the OFT it will have a complaints procedure. Some associations go further and provide a conciliation and arbitration service.

The media. Television, radio and the press all have an interest in consumer affairs. Stories of injustice at the hands of traders would obviously be of interest to them. Moreover no firm is going to enjoy the experience of trial by mass media!

Small Claims. As long as claims do not exceed £500 there is a special procedure using county court arbitration. The procedure discourages the use of solicitors by not allowing claims for costs. Details of the procedure to be followed can be found in a booklet 'Small Claims in the County Court' which is available from court offices or consumer advisory bodies.

Examination questions

1   Discuss the elements beyond a firm's immediate control which may influence its marketing decisions. *(AEB 1987)*

2   How far do the marketing and production functions have to compromise their objectives in order to accommodate each other? *(AEB 1986)*

3   How far can break-even analysis help to determine the price at which a product should be sold? *(AEB 1985)*

4   A business is about to launch a new product. Identify and discuss the information it will require before deciding on a pricing strategy. *(AEB 1985)*

5   Explain and comment on the influences which will help to determine the choice of distribution channel for a product. *(AEB)*

6   Outline the main aspects of consumer protection provided by the law and discuss the consequences of such protection for the consumer. *(AEB)*

7   Distinguish between *cost-based* and *market based* pricing methods. Discuss the relative merits of each group of methods and suggest where they would be most appropriately used. *(CAMB 1988)*

8   How might the manufacturer of a new chocolate bar decide to market the product? *(CAMB 1987)*

9   'The role of advertising is to awaken customers to wants that they never had.' Discuss. *(CAMB 1986)*

10 What do you understand by the concept of the 'marketing mix', and what are the main elements of a typical 'mix'? Show, by reference to the marketing of a new video game produced by a firm new to the business, how the elements of a mix must be inter-related if a product is to be marketed successfully. *(CAMB)*

11 A firm's Research and Development Department suggests an idea for a new product as a result of research into an existing one. What are the considerations that would have to be taken into account when deciding whether to market the new product or not? *(PSC)*

12 'The pricing of products is easy. All you have to do is work out your costs, add a percentage of profit and that's it!'
    Why do you feel this quotation is a gross oversimplification of the factors a company would take into account when deciding on the price to charge for its products? *(PSC 1986)*

13 Why is the concept of the product life cycle important for business planning and budgeting?

14 In what ways would you expect the marketing mix of a consumer product and an industrial product to differ?

15 Briefly describe
    (a) the means by which marketing research information is obtained and
    (b) how it can be used to aid the efficiency of a firm.

16 An enterprise is aware that the decisions to buy its product are made at the point of sale. How does this affect the marketing strategy of such an enterprise? *(AEB)*

17 To what extent is advertising the key to successful marketing? *(PSC 1985)*

Chapter 17

Production

Production is the process by which we produce a finished product from raw material. The role of the production function is to ensure that this transformation process is carried out efficiently. The decisions which have to be taken are similar whether we consider an organisation employing 50 or 5,000 people. What differs is the number of roles that individuals have to undertake. In a small firm one person may undertake several jobs, whereas the larger firm is able to employ specialists in each of these activities.

In broad terms the activities which have to be undertaken within the production function fall into one of three categories. First, those relating to the manufacturing process itself – decisions concerned with where to produce, what to produce, and the methods and techniques which should be used. Secondly, there are the ancillary or service activities – those which are designed to ensure that the manufacturing process proceeds smoothly without interruption. Finally, we have the control or advisory activities which seek to ensure that the process is carried out as efficiently as possible (see Fig. 17.1).

In the following pages we will use this classification to discuss the workings of the production function in more detail, but first a word of warning. The production department does not act in isolation and decisions taken will be based upon information received not only

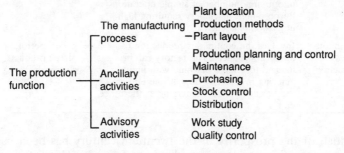

17.1 Activities undertaken by a typical production department

from sources within the function but also other departments in the organisation. Thus decisions regarding what to produce will be taken in conjunction with the marketing department, the personnel department is required to engage employees with the correct skills, while the finance function is required to provide information on costs which may be used for control purposes.

The manufacturing process

Production methods

Production methods fall, broadly, into four groups. The method used is determined by the nature of the product and the amount required. These are detailed in Table 17.1.

Table 17.1 Flexible manufacturing system

Method	Description	Examples
Job (unit) Production	Often a contract to produce one item to a customer's requirements. Often requires a large technical sales force, general purpose machines, skilled workers, sophisticated production planning and control procedures	ships, bridges machine tools overhaul and repair of cars, boilers etc
Batch Production	The production of small or large quantities of an article. Will produce many different articles at the same time. Relies upon general purpose machines, skilled craftsmen and sophisticated production planning and control procedures	books, steel, clothes and furniture
Mass or line Production	All operations involved in product manufacture are carried out continuously. It requires a highly standardised product with few variations from the basic product. The production process is broken down into a large number of simple operations. Purpose-built machinery requiring high utilisation is needed	cars, cookers, washing machines, TV sets and radios
Continuous/ Process Production	Involves the continuous production of identical products. The factory can be likened to a large machine with inputs entering in a steady flow at one end and the finished product emerging at the other end	paper, petrol, plastic products, chemicals

Much of the prosperity of the twentieth century has been based upon automation and mass production of goods. This increase in productivity has caused the unit cost – and therefore the price – to fall dramatically. There are, however, many thousands of products, both consumer and industrial, for which mass production is unsuitable. The majority of these will be manufactured using a batch production system. Flexible manufacturing systems (FMS) exist where robots, computer controlled tools and wire controlled work carriers are used to perform a wide variety of tasks. FMS potential lies in its ability to reduce the cost of goods which are made in small quantities by:

- quicker production
- reducing change-over time

Large-scale production is said to depend on two factors – specialisation and simplification. Let us look at these in turn.

Specialisation, or the division of labour, was first drawn to our attention by Adam Smith an economist who in 1776 published a book titled *An Inquiry into the Nature and Causes of the Wealth of Nations*. He proceeded to describe the process by which a pin was traditionally made with one worker undertaking all operations. He concluded that by this method it was impossible for that worker to produce more than twenty pins a day. Where, however, making the pins was divided into eighteen different operations and workers specialised in one or two distinct operations output per worker was increased to 4,800 pins per day! That process of specialisation has been taken to its logical conclusion in flow production today where one worker with specialist machinery is responsible for a very small part of the whole production process. The advantage of specialisation is not only the increased output, but also the reduced investment in tools, machines, and materials for each worker. Specialisation, however, requires a stable market and technology, sudden or rapid movements in demand or technology may cause business severe organisational problems and financial loss.

Product simplification is the process of eliminating marginal lines in the organisation's output. A motor-car manufacturer, for example, may examine sales and find that one particular model is not selling rapidly. The decision to cease manufacture is an example of product simplification. The business will in future concentrate on its most successful product, obtaining longer production runs, reducing its investment in people, materials, and machines, and simplifying organisational administration. The consequent savings may be passed on to the consumer in the form of lower prices. Simplification often brings the production function into conflict with the marketing group who would like to see the organisation provide exactly what the customer requires. This, as previously indicated, is not consistent with flow production or low prices. Some degree of compromise is often achieved, however, by slight variations of the basic design.

The term 'simplification' is often confused with standardisation. The confusion arises because the process of simplification is often

extended to the components and materials used in manufacture. The car manufacturer may simplify stockholding by using the same door handles, plugs, carburettors, etc. on many of his models. His use of components has been standardised.

However, standardisation is really the process of obtaining agreement on a standard to be applied to a product and the implementation of that standard. The standard agreed may relate to performance or method of manufacture as well as dimensions or composition. Hence, although standardisation may result in simplification this is not always the case.

The success of flow production lies in being able to maintain a high and continuous level of production. Great emphasis is placed on ensuring that materials and components are always available, plant maintenance to ensure that breakdowns on the machines on the line itself are kept to a minimum, and the prevention of labour disputes through good industrial relations.

Flow production techniques have undoubtedly led to major improvements in productivity in many industries. However, it has been suggested that these obvious benefits may be outweighed by the high labour turnover and absenteeism resulting from breaking down the manufacturing process into small repetitive tasks. Behavioural scientists argue that workers seek more than money and security from their work. They are motivated as much by a sense of achievement – a difficult job well done – and recognition of their importance to the organisation. Moreover, the trend of work rationalisation runs counter to the higher educational levels of today's school-leaver.

Numerous attempts have been made to provide more interesting, varied and challenging work; for example job enlargement allows employees to carry out a wider range of activity, so reducing boredom and perhaps allowing the employee to complete one small part of the production process. An alternative to loading the employee with more tasks of the same degree of difficulty is job enrichment. Here the scope of the job is widened by giving employees greater responsibility for decisions relating to their work. Thus they may be responsible for deciding how to carry out their work, or for ensuring that the quality of their work is up to standard. Job enrichment unlike job enlargement requires employees to use skills they have not used before.

There are many recorded instances of jobs being redesigned so that they are enlarged or enriched. Almost without exception they report a reduction in turnover, absenteeism, and other behavioural problems. However, job enlargement and enrichment are not the panacea to all industrial ills. Often the tasks undertaken by workers in the production process are highly specialised and difficult to enlarge or enrich while still maintaining the high level of productivity. Moreover, even where it is possible to maintain high productivity while redesigning jobs difficulties may occur – trade-union opposition to the breaking down of the barriers between skills, or claims by the employees for pay rises to reflect their greater responsibilities!

Plant layout

While the precise nature of the plant layout in an organisation is dependent upon the product being produced and the production capacity required, in general terms it will conform to one of two basic types.

Product layout This is associated with the production of standardised goods in large quantities. The most obvious example is car production. It is sometimes also referred to as line layout. Its essential feature is that each unit of production will undergo a similar sequence of operations which starts with the drawing of raw material components from stores and ends with the finished product. The success of product layout depends upon maintaining a high output and thus reducing manufacturing costs per unit. Considerable emphasis is placed upon 'line balancing' so that the machines at each stage of operation are just sufficient to deal with the workload. Such balancing prevents bottlenecks occurring at certain stages of production and under-utilisation of machinery at other points.

Considerable use of work study is made to speed up and automate the movement and operation of the production line. This has the advantage of reducing the amount of material in the production process at any one time and the unit labour cost. Product layout also has the advantage of being easier to control than process layout because of simpler routeing of materials and fewer variations of product. Against the undoubted advantages of the product layout must be the problem of inflexibility. A breakdown in any part of the production line inevitably affects the rest of the line. Line balance will also be affected should the marketing department require changes in product design or specification.

Process layout Normally associated with firms producing small quantities of product to a customer's order or for stock, for example furniture. Firms will produce a variety of products all requiring slightly different manufacturing operations. Process layout requires machines doing a similar job to be grouped together.

The major advantage ascribed to process layout is its high degree of flexibility. The layout can accommodate the production of several different products at the same time, each following a different

309

production route. Moreover, the disruption caused by a machine breakdown affects only one person and may also be minimised by the holding of buffer stocks.

Service of ancillary functions

Production planning and control

Planning and control lie at the heart of the production process. Because the two activities are so closely related they are normally undertaken by a single section within the production department. The responsibility of this section is to:

1. Bring materials, machines, and labour together in the most efficient way thereby ensuring the elimination of bottlenecks and space capacity.
2. To enable good delivery periods to be offered and complete orders on time.
3. To develop a system of controls for the monitoring of performance.
4. To take whatever corrective action is necessary so that production continues according to plan.

It is difficult to overemphasise the importance of this function to the organisation as a whole. The inability to deliver customers' orders on time resulting from poor production planning and control will quickly rob the firm of its reputation and customer goodwill. Moreover, high production costs arising from frequent production changes, operational delays, and overtime will greatly reduce profitability.

Production planning Information received from the sales or marketing department on the likely future demand for the organisation's products provides the data from which a production plan is designed. Production planners will not only need information on what to produce but also the quantities required and the date required for completion.

The production plan is drawn up by determining the process which has to be followed in manufacturing the finished article and thereby establishing the workload for each group of machines. Production is then 'routed' so that each product or group of products moves logically from stage to stage through the production process. Production is also 'scheduled' so that sufficient time is allowed to complete each operation before it is required at the next stage, and the final operation is completed before the goods are required by the customer. The production plan is then broken down into very precise instructions to each work process or group of machines explaining what work has to be done, when it has to be done, and which work stations it should be transferred to when finished.

Charts are often an important tool in the planning and control of work. The most widely used is the Gantt chart, an illustration of which is shown in Fig. 17.2. The chart shows a product going through three stages of production planned over a period of ten days. The planned time for each process is indicated by the horizontal broken line against each process. Thus process 2 is planned to take three days and finish on day 6. Once production starts we indicate the present day in the process by a pointer at the top of the chart. The pointer indicates we have just finished day 6 of the production process. Our actual progress is shown by the dark horizontal bar against each process. Figure 12.2 shows that process 1 was completed as planned, but that process 2 which should have finished on day 6 will not be finished to schedule.

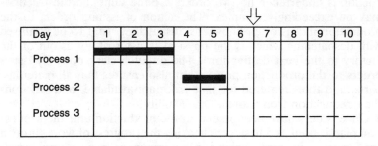

17.2 Gantt chart

The advantage of such charts is that they show both the plan and present progress in a form which is easily and quickly understood. Production controllers can rapidly identify these jobs which will require their attention each day.

Production planning requires liaison with many other parts of the organisation. It is necessary to ensure that raw materials will be available when required for use in the production process. The raw material requirements, which are based upon the sales estimates, will be passed to the purchasing/materials management section within the organisation. Production engineers – concerned with the design and operation (rather than the management) of the production system – need to be informed of products to be produced so that the necessary tools and patterns are produced. It may also be necessary to purchase additional plant and equipment for the production process. Yet again we may need to consult with personnel so that the correct mix of labour skills is available, or so that piecework rates (if applicable) where not previously established are calculated and agreed upon by management and unions. Lastly the costing department may be involved in establishing standard costs or prices for any work undertaken.

Considerable skill and compromise is required by production planners, as it is unlikely that sufficient resources, labour, materials, and machinery will be available to meet all demands made upon them. In these circumstances it may be necessary to agree some form of priority for the work which is to be undertaken.

Production control Once the production plan has been drawn up it is put into effect by issuing detailed instructions to all those involved in the production process. In flow production industries the instructions might be quite simple as all items of manufacture will go through the same process. However, where job or batch production is undertaken no two orders are the same, and instructions may be exceedingly complex. The action of issuing orders to the production unit is often known as 'dispatching' (not to be confused with despatching which is the physical transfer of goods out of the factory to the next destination). The dispatch clerk not only issues orders to the production process but also ensures that all materials, parts, and tools required for that order are available, and sanctions their requisition from stores.

Once orders have been issued to the production unit the production plan is used as a basis for checking the progress of work through the factory. This work which is often known as 'progressing' is normally undertaken by the dispatch clerks, though some firms may use a separate group of employees known as 'progress chasers'.

Where orders are proceeding according to plan there is little to be done. Unfortunately, this state of affairs does not normally exist for very long. Where work does deviate from plan it is the dispatch clerk/progress chaser's job to discover the cause of the problem (e.g. lack of or substandard materials, machine breakdown, labour difficulties) and then:

(a) help in removing the cause of the problem; and

(b) adjust the production so as to bring work back on to schedule, or alternatively revise the production schedule.

In this work the progress chaser is aided considerably by inspection staff concerned with quality control.

Many of the production planning and control tasks we have mentioned are now undertaken by computer. These include: production scheduling; machine scheduling; raw material and tooling requisitions. The use of computers in this way (and for maintenance schedules and stock control) is said to result in the:

- better utilisation of plant and equipment
- reduction in costs of holding finished goods or work in
- progress
- more efficient use of labour
- reduction of production times

Maintenance

Maintenance is defined as work which is undertaken by a person or organisation in order to keep and restore every facility to a reasonable standard. The importance of maintenance to the average organisation lies in the large amount of money it has invested in land, machinery, plant and transport. Without maintenance this investment would rapidly diminish in value. Maintenance of machinery is also required to ensure that breakdowns are kept to a minimum. This is of the highest priority in flow production where the breakdown of one machine can stop the whole manufacturing process, or alternatively in job or batch production where if little spare capacity is available any breakdown will cause an immediate bottleneck.

It must be obvious that in many manufacturing situations it is too costly to wait until a machine breaks down before repairing it, but rather we must plan maintenance to prevent or minimise machine failure. Such a policy is often referred to as 'planned maintenance' or 'preventative maintenance' and a measure of its success is its ability to keep plant running or to repair breakdowns as quickly as possible.

For planned maintenance to be successful an inventory of all plant and equipment must be kept. The inventory should show:

- the type of plant – uses, design, and manufacture;
- its age;
- spares required/carriage/sources;
- likely causes of breakdown;
- a record of past breakdowns;
- the record of planned maintenance.

A schedule of inspection and overhauls (the maintenance plan) will also be drawn up indicating how often a machine has to be inspected and how long can elapse between major overhauls. This information can also be useful in determining the size of the workforce and the skills needed by the maintenance department in order to carry out its work, though some element of overmanning is required because breakdowns will still occur despite all efforts.

Once the maintenance plan has been put into operation it should be revised as experience dictates. Thus it may be possible to extend the intervals between inspection and servicing of certain machines, while others will require more frequent overhaul than originally anticipated.

Planned maintenance has been criticised. Often it involves replacing items which are in perfect working order because statistically it has been calculated that this is the optimum time to replace that item. The alternative is to replace items only when they actually fail with results which we have already noted.

Although by far the most important responsibilities of the maintenance department are to develop and implement a system of planned maintenance there are other important aspects of its work. Many machine breakdowns are caused by the operator using the machine in an improper manner, and in conjunction with training staff the department has a responsibility to instruct operatives in the correct method of use. Similarly the department has a duty to advise the production manager on the replacement of plant and equipment. The advice given will relate to the timing of the replacement purchase and the maintenance cost of different types of machinery.

Where planned maintenance fails to bring a reduction in the number of machine breakdowns two major causes have been identified. First, schedules of inspection and overhaul designed to prevent breakdowns may be defective. Alternatively, the cause of breakdowns may not be covered by planned maintenance, for example metal fatigue in essential parts of a machine.

Purchasing

The role of a purchasing department will vary according to the type of business. In manufacturing over half the total costs may be attributable to raw materials and components. Similarly, in retailing a large proportion of all expenditure will be on goods bought in for resale. Supermarkets and discount stores, in particular, rely on astute purchasing to provide a reasonable profit margin while retaining their competitive edge. However, a service organisation, for example an estate agent or insurance broker, will not require the sophisticated purchasing function demanded by the manufacturer or retailer.

For many organisations though, the purchasing function may have an appreciable effect on overall profitability. Consider the effect upon the organisation when goods of the wrong type or quality are purchased or where too high a price is paid. Buying too large a quantity leads to an excessive investment in stock and a potential obsolescence problem, while purchasing too little may result in costly production stoppages.

A successful purchasing policy will avoid the problems mentioned above and will take account of factors such as those listed below.

Estimates of future demand. The level of stocks held by either a manufacturer or retailer will reflect the marketing department's prediction of future sales. Consider the extra stocks held by retailers during the Christmas period.

Price. The aim of the purchasing officer must be to buy as cheaply as possible. Price may, however, have to be sacrificed should any item be needed urgently, though this should only happen on rare occasions. In all circumstances though, care should be taken to ensure that quality is not sacrificed.

Quality. Substandard raw materials or components may be purchased cheaply, but in the long run will injure the organisation's reputation with the customer. A system of checks should be instituted to ensure that materials and components ordered are of the quality required and that those received are of the quality ordered. It is equally bad for the organisation to purchase items which are of a higher quality than needed. The organisation will then be paying a higher price than is necessary for quality which is not required.

The supplier. The reputation of the supplier in terms of price, quality, service, and reliability should be assessed. Alternative sources of supply should always be identified for all essential raw materials and components.

Quantity. The quantity purchased should always be sufficient to meet current demand. Regular purchases of small quantities minimises stockholding costs, but precludes the negotiation of lower prices for buying in bulk.

Delivery. All contracts should specify a delivery date, and the importance of adhering to this date should be made clear to the supplier. Lists of alternative suppliers should be maintained in case of non-delivery.

The method of purchase. This will not be the same for all items used by the organisation. Where it is necessary to ensure continuity of supply, as in flow production, a contract to purchase an agreed amount over a specified period will be entered into. As part of the agreement it may be stipulated when deliveries are required, thus reducing stockholding costs. Such an agreement may also be used where there is little likelihood of variation in the price of the items ordered over the period of the contract. Apart from ensuring continuity of supply, the organisation is also able to estimate accurately its cost of production for the forthcoming period.

Should market prices of items contracted for fall during that period the organisation will be at a competitive disadvantage compared with other organisations who made 'spot' purchases. Consider the case of the independent oil companies who have been able to purchase surplus oil cheaply on the 'spot' market and pass this saving on to the consumer in the form of lower petrol prices. 'Buying as required' would normally be limited to non-essential items or those for which there is a continuous supply. There is, however, an element of risk as prices may rise as well as fall.

It is also possible to extend the element of speculation by 'purchasing futures'. This is a practice adopted in certain commodity markets, for example copper and cocoa, to purchase a commodity in advance of it being needed or harvested. The belief is that future price rises will result in a saving being made by buying now, or that the commodity can be resold at a profit later. The element of speculation in purchasing futures is great. Extremely large sums of money have been both gained and lost in estimating the future demand and therefore the price of the commodity.

The organisation of the purchasing function varies widely. Where the cost of materials is a high proportion of total cost the purchasing organisation is likely to be complex and its senior executive have similar status to other departmental heads. Alternatively, purchasing may be part of the production department where the purchasing of materials and components for the manufacturing process forms the major part of its work, or the marketing department where, as with the retailer, goods are purchased for resale.

The organisation for purchasing may also be centralised or decentralised, but as a firm grows in size the movement is towards centralisation. The major reason for this is the possibility of bulk buying and obtaining substantial discounts. However, other advantages include:
1. Different departments will often have similar needs, e.g. stationery, furniture.
2. Centralisation establishes a standard procedure for ordering purchases.
3. It is easier to obtain control over the total purchases expenditure of the organisation.
4. Quality is more easily controlled.
5. The needs of one department may be satisfied from a surplus of another department.
6. Specialist buying staff can be utilised.
   However, against this must be put:
1. Delays in obtaining purchases and increased paperwork.
2. Specialist requirements of a department are better met by direct negotiation by that department and the supplier.
3. Dealing with local suppliers leads to a stronger relationship and a greater commitment to service on the part of those suppliers.

In practice the answer to the problem of centralisation or decentralisation is normally a compromise. The majority of items are purchased centrally, but each individual unit (whether it be a factory or a department) has the authority to purchase certain items or items to a specified value without the sanction of the purchasing department. Details of such purchases would be transmitted to the purchasing department as a matter of course.

Stock control

This section of the production department is responsible for the control of all purchases made by the organisation from the time of receipt until their issue to the production process or other department. Its work follows logically on from that of the purchasing function, and in some organisations this has led to the creation of a combined department (materials control) embracing both activities. Stock control involves not only controlling and issuing stock but also the inspecting and reordering of stock and checking the accuracy of stock records. We will examine each of these activities in turn.

On receipt of stock items the stores clerk will check what has arrived against the purchase order. This is not a detailed check of individual items but is intended to ensure that the correct number of cases, cartons, etc. have arrived. The materials will then be passed to the appropriate store where, after inspection, they will be entered on the stores records. The purchasing department will be informed on their arrival. The stores records maintain a running total for each item of stock with 'receipts in' being added to the existing balance and 'issues out' deducted. The information in the stores records is duplicated by the use of 'bin cards' which are found with the storage containers in which the stocks are physically located.

Prior to the goods being placed in their appropriate bins or entered on to the stores records, detailed inspection of the order takes place. It is, after all, too late to discover that the goods are substandard once they have been issued to production. The nature of the inspection varies according to the item concerned but could include weight, dimensions, colour, hardness, or chemical composition. The inspection may take the form of checking a random number of items which will, statistically, guarantee the remainder or a detailed inspection of each item.

Issue of material to the production process is made against a materials requisition form. The requisition will indicate the materials and the quantities required and to which job their cost is to be charged. Rules should be laid down as to whom may authorise the withdrawal of stores as this is an important element in proper stock control. The information on the materials requisition form will, after the issue of the materials, be transferred to the stores records and the bin cards, and the costing department informed of the amount withdrawn.

As materials are withdrawn from stock for the production process the level of stock held declines. One of the storekeeper's most important tasks is to see that there is always sufficient stock available to meet production's needs. Minimum stock levels are established by ascertaining the length of time it normally takes to re-order stocks – this is commonly referred to as 'lead' time – and calculating how much stock will be required before the order is delivered so:

Re-order level = Average consumption rate × lead time

Once materials requisitions take the balance on stores records below the re-order level, stock should be ordered automatically.

As an extra safety device the re-order level may also be indicated on the bin holding stock by a white line painted on the inside – when the white line is exposed it is time to re-order. Alternatively, lead time stock may be kept in a sealed container – when the seal is broken it is time to re-order.

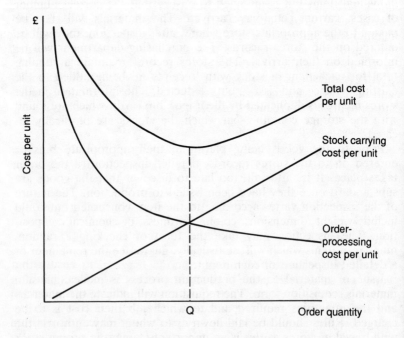

17.3 Economic order quantity

A decision also has to be taken as to how much of a product to order. To determine the most economic order quantity we need to compare order processing costs and the costs of stockholding. Fig. 17.3 shows the order processing cost per unit falling as the order quantity increases. This is because ordering costs are spread over more units. Conversely, stockholding costs per unit rise as orders increase in size because each unit remains in stock for a longer period of time. From this information we can create a total cost curve. The lowest point on this curve represents the economic order quantity (EOQ).
The formula for the economic order quantity is as follows:

$$EOQ = \sqrt{\frac{2\,P\,d}{S}}$$

where P is the ordering/handling cost
d is the consumption rate
and S is the storage cost per time period.

Our discussion of stock control has so far concentrated on the receipt and issue of materials and components to the production process. In practice, stock control is also responsible for the storage and safe keeping of other stocks of articles which the organisation owns. These would include work in progress, finished goods, and maintenance and repair items, and in some organisations office, canteen, and welfare items. The principles of stores control outlined above apply equally to these other stocks.

All organisations hold stocks of 'materials' against future demand and in many cases the cost of doing so is high. A good system of stores control may reduce this cost considerably by ensuring:

- stocks of each item are not too high or too low

- poor stores layout does not result in excessive lighting and heating bills, or deterioration of stock, for example through rusting or breakages

- pilferage is kept to a minimum.

Distribution

It is the responsibility of the distribution function to ensure that goods get to the right place at the right time, in the correct quantity and condition, and at the lowest cost commensurate with adequate service to the customer. In practice, a compromise is always necessary – few firms can afford the luxury of a 'Rolls-Royce' distribution service. In order to minimise costs the distribution manager will be considering the following points.

What level of finished stock should be maintained? Remember, distribution is responsible for getting the goods to the customer at the right time. Where goods are made to a customer's order the level of finished goods held will be low. Finished goods will be inspected for quality and soon after transported to the customer. A more difficult situation arises where goods are not produced to a firm order but for stock. Here the level of finished stock held will be based on what has been found necessary in the past, adjusted as required by the current sales forecast.

Stock levels are often a source of conflict between the production and marketing department. The marketing department, with its emphasis on serving the customer would wish to see stock levels sufficiently high to satisfy all customer requirements as and when they arise. Yet a large investment in stock is expensive, and the production department would prefer lower stock levels even if customer's requirements cannot be met immediately and some sales are lost.

How shall we transport goods to the customer? Air, sea, rail, road, canal – all have their own particular advantages. Sea is cheaper than air but takes longer. The decision taken will depend on a large number of factors including the nature of the goods to be transported (weight, fragility, perishability), the importance of the market, the level of service given by competitors, as well as cost.

Where, as in many cases, distribution is by road the manufacturer also has the option of owning or hiring transport. Often there is no clear-cut answer because the level of orders in a certain area justifies the use of company transport, but in other areas does not. The distribution manager will also have to consider whether there are any special factors which preclude the use of outside carriers (fragility or perishability) or whether the image of the firm will be impaired by not having its own transport fleet to deliver goods. It is also worth remembering that the delivery man is often the only contact the customer has with the seller apart from members of the marketing department.

Often the decision is to own and run a transport fleet which is slightly smaller than necessary. This has the advantage of ensuring that the fleet is used to the full. Outside contractors will then be employed for the work which is surplus to capacity. Transport costs can be considerably reduced by careful routeing and scheduling of deliveries. Lorries should never leave the factory premises half loaded. Empty return journeys may also be avoided by collecting deliveries of materials or components to be used in the production process.

Advisory activities

Work study

'Work study' is a term which covers a number of techniques designed to improve the efficiency of the organisation and help in the control of costs. We will consider the two main techniques, method study and work measurement.

Method study is concerned with how the work is carried out. It looks at existing procedures with a view to improving them. In essence it answers the question, 'Is there a better way of doing this job?' Work measurement, on the other hand, questions how long a job should take. By scientific methods it determines what time should be allowed for a task and thereby provides an important element in labour cost control. Work measurement follows logically on from method study, for it is only after we have established the best method of doing a job that we can calculate how long it should take. We will consider method study first.

Method study   The procedure has six stages namely: select; record; examine; develop; install; maintain.

1.   Select the job to be studied.   The request for an investigation will normally come from management within the production department who perceive problems such as:

- bad-quality work;

- high labour turnover and absenteeism or accident rates;

- production bottlenecks or under-utilised machinery;

- excessive overtime.

Once a job has been selected and authority has been obtained for its investigation the most important task before moving on to the next stage is to inform all those who will be affected by the study. Explaining the reasons for the study prior to its commencement will prevent misunderstanding and increase the likelihood of worker co-operation. However, it would be unwise to conduct method study in parts of the factory where there are bad labour relations.

2.   Record the present method.   A detailed analysis of present methods is necessary before we can move on to seeing what improvements are possible or desirable. The investigator will record details of the existing system under the headings of purpose, method, sequence, place, and person.

3.   Examine the existing method;   and

4.   Develop the new improved method.   The existing method which we have now investigated forms the basis for our search for new improved methods. In fact as we chart the existing method we find ourselves quite naturally questioning what we see, but during this stage we carefully question all that we have recorded. Each of the aspects we previously recorded we now challenge, ask for alternatives, and finally decide what action is to be taken. Figure 12.3 shows one particular form that is often used for this purpose. It is important that this stage is done systematically and that all alternatives are considered, however impractical they seem at first. For example, few people uninitiated in method study would think of questioning why a particular activity is done at all, or if it can be eliminated. Yet this has proved to be one of the most effective ways of improving methods.

Eventually, out of the critical examination will come the ideas for the improved method. These will be discussed with management in the department concerned. Perhaps after these discussions ideas have to be amended or even dropped, but the work study officer must be satisfied that the criticisms are sound, for even managers are known to dislike and resist change!

At this stage it is also necessary to draw up a formal report which will outline:

- the changes recommended;
- the cost of those changes;
- the savings which will result;
- the time needed to institute the changes.

The report is presented to the management who instigated the investigation and once their approval is obtained we move to the next stage.

Present facts		Alternatives	Decision
What is done	Why?	What else?	What should be done
How it is done	Why that way?	How else?	How it should be done
When it is done	Why then?	When else?	When it should be done
Where it is done	Why there?	Where else?	Where it should be done
Who does it	Why him?	Who else?	Who should do it

17.4 Critical examination sheet

5. *Installation of the improved method*. Work study personnel must pay particular attention to two aspects of installation. First they must persuade everyone concerned of the need for change. A successful installation needs the co-operation of all staff. Secondly the installation will involve considerable planning. Liaison with the purchasing department to buy any new plant, equipment, or materials required, with the personnel department for the training or retraining of employees, with the maintenance department for installing or repositioning plant, and with production planning for the issue of new production orders.

6. *Maintain the new method*. The introduction of the new method will not be without its difficulties, but it would be wrong for work study personnel to consider changes immediately. It will take some time before all employees are fully conversant with the new method and reach the expected level of productivity. Indeed, work study personnel will be monitoring the new system for several months after it has been introduced to see that planned savings are achieved in practice, or whether any refinements are possible, but also – and very important – to guard against unauthorised change by operatives. Perhaps these changes are improvements, in which case they should be officially integrated into the new system, but it is all too easy for operatives to slip back into old ways or into new but bad habits.

Resistance to change

Men and women are creatures of habit – all of us are guilty of resisting change at some time or another in both our personal and professional lives. This is so even when, to the unbiased observer, it seems that the proposed changes will benefit us. Thus most of us would agree if asked that technological change – greater automation, the use of computers or word-processors for example, were necessary. Yet what we are seemingly unable to accept is that our personal situation should be disturbed in any way by these changes. The main reasons for resisting change are listed below:

- possible loss of job or transfer to another job;

- skills become redundant;

- reduction in status or pay;

- social groups at work may be broken up;

- worries about establishing new friends or learning a new job;

- dislocation of social life by new working arrangements.

As we can see, the question uppermost in most people's minds is, 'how is this going to affect me?'

Yet it is imperative that management reduce the level of resistance. Investments in new technology or new methods will not yield the expected benefits without the co-operation of the workforce.

Much of the answer lies in the degree of trust that has been developed by the management with the unions and the workforce over a period of many years – is the organisation one which 'cares for' and 'plays fair' by its employees?

However, the degree of resistance may be reduced if the principles below are followed:

1 A proper manpower plan is developed, identifying new skills which will be required and offering retraining to those who may be displaced by the change. Reduction in the workforce should be planned in advance so that natural wastage and voluntary redundancy reduce the necessity for compulsory redundancy.

2 Do not keep the planned changes secret, the organisational grapevine can do more harm than the truth by exaggerating the scale and effects of the change. Tell people what their position will be, let them get used to the idea and give them time to plan their future.

3 Change is more acceptable if people participate in the making of those plans which affect their working lives rather than having it imposed upon them.

4 Change is more acceptable where work/social groups are not disturbed.

5 Employees who suffer financially should be compensated, e.g. removal and selling expenses where a house move is required, guaranteeing previous income for a period when moving to a lower-paid job, or generous redundancy payments.

6 Where possible introduce the changes slowly so that they are accepted and understood by those that are affected.

Work measurement   Work measurement seeks to establish how long a particular job should take. It is necessary that this calculation be made so that we do not either over- or underestimate the total amount of work which we can carry out in any period of time. Overestimating the amount of work we can do means we fail to deliver on time and lose the goodwill of our customers, while an underestimation means that men and machines which could be earning money are lying idle.

There are several techniques by which we can measure work and establish a reasonable time for the job. The best known of these is 'time study', sometimes termed 'stop-watch studies'. By this method an operative is studied working at their normal job over an extended period of time. Each operation carried out is timed and retimed so as to arrive at a basic time for the job which represents the normal rate of working. It is not unknown for the subject of the study to deviate from normal work methods in an attempt to make the job look more complicated and obtain a larger time allowance for that job. For this reason it is necessary that method study has previously established the correct method for the job and we now require the operative to conform to that method.

Time studies are made on a number of workers undertaking the same activity, and it is not unusual to find that the observed times vary considerably as each worker has their own pace of work. So as to establish a basic time for the job we therefore have to rate each worker in terms of the effort which they have expended. A scale is established from 0 to 100 with 0 representing zero activity and 100 representing the normal worker. We may then, for example, rate a slow worker at 80 and a fast worker at 120. Our next step is to adjust the observed time by the rating we have allocated to the worker:

$$\text{Basic time} = \text{Observed time} \times \frac{\text{Rating}}{100}$$

Let us for example assume that we have studied two workers over the same operation. Worker A took four minutes to complete the activity and was rated at 120, while worker B took six minutes and was rated at 80. Our basic time for worker A is

$$4 \times \frac{120}{100} = 4.8 \text{ minutes}$$

and for worker B

$$6 \times \frac{80}{100} = 4.8 \text{ minutes}$$

If our rating of worker effort is correct the adjustment to observed time will result in a very similar basic time in each case.

A description of work measurement so far has assumed that it is necessary to time study each job individually to establish the basic time. However, over a period a large number of different jobs will be timed and that information stored. Now many jobs will have certain activities or operations in common, and it is possible to obtain much of the information we need more quickly and cheaply from our records.

The basic time that we have calculated assumes that the worker can carry on working at the same speed all day. This is not so. All workers will relax their efforts from time to time, perhaps to talk to the supervisor, their workmates, to visit the toilet, to light a cigarette, and so on. To the basic time already calculated we add relaxation allowance. This may be as little as 10 per cent, or for highly fatiguing work over 100 per cent of the basic time. The resulting figure is known as the standard time for the job. It is defined as 'the rate of output achieved by a qualified worker naturally without over-exertion provided he adheres to the specific method and applies himself to his work'.

Standard times are used in a variety of ways throughout the organisation. Within the production department it is used to establish a reasonable workload for people and machines in the forthcoming period. Standard times can be used to monitor the times of individual workers. The personnel department will use standard times in determining future manpower requirements and in establishing incentive schemes. The accounting function will use standard times in the preparation of budgets, against which actual performance can be compared.

Quality control

Quality control is the system by which management ensures that goods produced conform to a predetermined standard.

Greater emphasis than ever before is placed upon quality control. The advent of the discerning consumer and the growing competition among manufacturers has had a widespread impact. Certain industries, food and drugs, are required to maintain high standards of quality by law. Others, concerned with assembling a product from a large number of components (e.g. the car industry) demand that less than 1 per cent of any component used be defective. This near-perfect reliability of individual components is required to guarantee the operation of the finished product.

As our definition implies, there are two parts to any quality-control system. First, the establishing of standards which we require the production process to conform to, and secondly, a method of inspection to see that this standard is adhered to.

Quality Circles

A quality circle is a group of employees who meet together regularly to discuss work-based issues which are of common interest. These will, for example, include the level of output, rejects and safety issues. The aim of these circles is to devise ways of overcoming the problems identified and implementing the proposed solution.

There are several benefits resulting from the use of quality circles:
- employee involvement in decision–making taps a hitherto tapped source of company knowledge and expertise
- employee involvement in decision–making improves factory morale and motivation
- improvements in productivity, quality, safety etc

– production workers have a greater knowledge of and interest in company problems

What quality do we require our products to conform to? To the layman quality implies some degree of excellence, yet this is not always required by the consumer. For example if we asked what standards of quality the average driver required for their family car it would be unusual for them to demand the standard of a Rolls-Royce. Pressed further they would probably say it should be capable of cruising at 70 miles an hour, not consume too much petrol, and not be too expensive to repair and maintain. It is these factors that the manufacturer is interested in: quality may be defined here as the product being fit for the purpose of the average consumer.

The question of quality is critical to the manufacturer, higher quality means higher costs and all too often we find that people are unwilling to pay the extra price associated with quality. This can be seen from Figure 17.5.

As we raise the quality of our product the manufacturing cost increases. Up to point C the selling value (i.e. the price we can charge) increases more rapidly. However, increase in quality beyond point C will raise manufacturing cost more rapidly than sales value and profitability therefore declines. Thus our manufacturer will seek to establish quality standards at point C because at this point the gap between costs of production and sales revenue is largest.

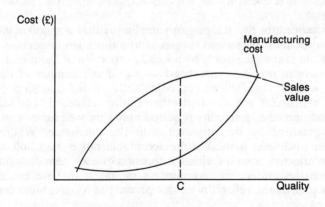

C = the point of maximum benefit to the manufacturer

17.5 Comparison of manufacturing cost and sales value at different quality levels

Once quality standards have been decided upon, a system of inspection is developed. This system may be used in two particular ways. First, as a means of controlling the production process. Let us take for example a company which has to achieve certain standards of accuracy in the dimensions of the product it is producing. Variations are bound to occur. The quality of material used may differ, one machine may have more play on it than another, even operatives may have an 'off' day. But by examining work at each production stage regularly we can ensure that standards are maintained.

Today many quality control devices are micro-processor based. The measurement and analysis of foodstuffs, drugs, beverages and many other industrial and consumer products is undertaken in this way. Once set up these control devices are easy to use and lack the capacity for human error of previous methods.

Records of failures in quality should be kept so that over a period of time we should be able to spot consistencies in quality failures – establish the cause whether it may be people, machines, or materials, and take action to remedy the problem – perhaps retrain the people, introduce more rigorous maintenance schedules for machines, or change our material supplier. As we can see, inspection not only serves the immediate need of controlling the quality of the production process but also a longer-term aim of improving the process.

Although process control will uncover many failures in quality the vast majority of organisations still sample the finished product further to ensure its reliability. This is termed 'acceptance sampling' (and although we are referring here to the sample of a finished product it is relevant to the inspection of raw material and work in progress).

The procedure for acceptance sampling is that a random sample of the product is taken and subjected to a thorough inspection. The size of the sample may only be a small proportion of the total batch, but has been precisely calculated so that if the number of defects is below a certain level we can confidently predict that 95 per cent of the remainder will also be to the required standard. The sample size and degree of reliability required may very well have been previously agreed by the producer with the purchaser. Where the number of defects is outside the acceptable range the whole batch will be rejected or an individual inspection of each item undertaken. The great advantage of acceptance sampling is that we can confidently predict the reliability of our product at a reasonable cost.

Examination questions

1 The management of a large scale manufacturing organisation has decided to centralise the buying function.
   Comment on the factors which should have been considered in coming to this decision. (AEB)

2 Change is a critical element in an organisation's ability to survive and grow. Why, then, is change often resisted, and how might the process of change be eased? (AEB 1988)

3 (a) Differentiate between work measurement and method study.
   (b) What do you consider to be the main problems likely to be caused by the introduction of a work study unit to a manufacturing firm?
   (c) Discuss the usefulness of data collected by the work study team and suggest to whom it should be made available. (CAMB 1988)

4 (a) What factors should determine the level of stock held by a company?
   (b) How might you use ratios or other methods to achieve satisfactory control of stocks? (CAMB 1987)

5 (a) What are the principal types of production system?
   (b) How would the management of a catering establishment choose between them?
   (c) What problems might arise in moving from one system of production to another?

6 (a) What are the objectives of stock management?
   (b) How might each of these objectives be achieved? (CAMB 1985)

7 How does the process of production planning and control aid the flow of high quality products? (PSC)

8 Briefly describe the following:
   (a) stock control
   (b) quality control
   (c) production control.
   How does each aid efficiency within the manufacturing organisation? (PSC 1985)

9 The following are details of the movements in the stock level of a product which is purchased for resale:

Date	Purchases (Units)	Purchase Price per unit £	Issues (Units)	Balance (Units)
1986				
1 June B/Forward	—	—	—	300
8 August	200	8.00	—	500
15 September	—	—	500	—
17 September	500	8.25	—	500
1987				
5 January	—	—	100	400
8 January	—	—	200	200
16 March	200	8.75	—	400
31 May	—	—	200	200

   (a) Explain the meaning of the following terms:
       (i) FIFO
       (ii) LIFO
   (b) Using the available information, calculate the value of the closing stock on 31 May 1987:

      (i) if the method of valuation is FIFO

      (ii) if the method of valuation is LIFO.

(c) The budget for the current year contained a figure for the purchase price of £8.35 per unit. Calculate the average price actually paid.

(d) Actual results usually exceed or fall short of budgeted targets. Why then do firms bother to budget? *(AEB 1987)*

10   Your company, Singapore Tech, proposes to extend its manufacturing operations but is unable to do so on its present site. Write a report to the directors explaining the factors which should influence their choice of alternative sites.

11   The works manager of Luk Kee Computers Ltd a small manufacturing concern, is responsible for all aspects of the production function within the company. So that he may concentrate more on the manufacturing process it has been decided to relieve him of some of his duties. Select two specialist activities which are normally carried out as part of the production function and explain the benefits that Luk Kee Computers can expect to gain having appointed staff to these positions.

Chapter 18

Financial management

The history of the accounting function goes back many hundreds of years. The art of bookkeeping – that is, the recording of financial transactions, can be traced back to the early fourteenth century. It was not until the nineteenth century though, that accountancy emerged as a profession. The Industrial Revolution and the growth of large-scale enterprise was fertile ground for the embryo accounting profession. Shareholders, not involved in the day-to-day running of an enterprise in which they had invested their money, required the managers of these companies to account for the use of their money. But in many cases misuse of investors' money still occurred. This eventually led to legislation requiring companies to submit to an annual independent audit of their records by a professionally qualified accountant. At the turn of the century the typical accountant in business was employed to:

- establish a sound system of bookkeeping;

- establish a system of internal check (audit);

- prepare the final accounts (profit and loss account, balance sheet).

This remained very much the role of the accountant in business until after the Second World War. Gradually though, accountants came to realise that the details of financial transactions which were so carefully recorded by bookkeepers could also be used to monitor the progress of the organisation against a predetermined objective – often termed 'control accountancy'. Later still accountants developed other techniques which enabled business to evaluate alternative uses of capital, or determine whether a project should or should not be undertaken. This was termed 'decision accounting'.

In business today the financial accountant's work corresponds broadly to the traditional role of accountancy with its emphasis on bookkeeping, auditing, and the presentation of financial results. An accountant who is involved in control accountancy or decision accountancy, on the other hand, is normally called a management

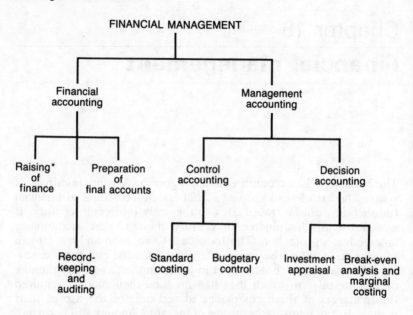

18.1 Work typically undertaken within the finance function

accountant. The work of the financial and management accountant is shown in Fig. 18.1.

Financial accounting

Bookkeeping and internal audit

The recording of all transactions entered into by an organisation lies at the heart of the accounting process. Details of sales, purchases, and expenses are required so that bills may be paid on time, debts can be collected, and the values of assets recorded. The same information may be used in the control of business activities through standard costing and budgetary control techniques. Lastly it is by relating expenditure to income that we calculate the profit or loss for the period.

Internal auditing of the bookkeeping system is undertaken to test the efficiency of that system. Internal audit seeks to ensure that transactions are processed quickly and cheaply, that a high level of accuracy is maintained, and lastly fraud, theft, or other irregularities are minimised. Characteristically, checks undertaken will fall into one of the following categories.

1. *Analysis of the accounting system*. This has the aim of improving efficiency through revision of procedures and training of staff. Additionally, such analysis will seek to ensure that the system is proof against fraud or theft on the part of staff operating the system.
2. *Verification of records*. It is obviously impossible to verify the accuracy of all transactions recorded by the business. Instead a small number of transactions will be selected at random and checked for accuracy. Should the check reveal inaccuracies further investigation will be undertaken. Additionally, where the business holds stocks of raw material, components, or finished goods the balance shown in the accounts may also be verified by means of a physical check of those stocks.
3. *Psychological checks*. Certain checks may be instituted so as to create an environment whereby misappropriation is discouraged by the possibility of discovery. For example irregular or spot checks may be made upon petty cash holdings, National Insurance and postage stamps. Alternatively, staff may be compelled to take annual holidays or accept transfers to other jobs.

The 1948 Companies Act requires all companies registered in Britain to present an annual report to shareholders and other interested parties (such as debenture holders). This report must contain the following:
1. A statement of profit or loss arising from the past year's trading.
2. A balance sheet as at the year end.
3. A director's report giving details of dividends, directors, director's shareholdings, employees, and total remuneration, together with charitable and political contributions.
4. An auditor's report affirming that the final accounts give a 'true and fair view of the state of affairs of the company' at the end of the financial year.

It is also normal, though not required by law, for the annual report to contain a chairman's statement on the company's activities during the past year and its prospects for the future.

Accounting conventions

In preparing the financial accounts of a business there are certain conventions which accountants follow. These conventions are not based on law but the agreement of the majority of accountants. The advantage of these conventions lies in the uniform manner in which information is recorded and the degree of comparability within the same firm over a number of years and with other firms. However, as we will see, these conventions have been criticised because they do not always serve the information needs of external users.

The entity convention Requires that the accounting information presented relates to the activities of the business alone and not to its owners. Thus the balance sheet reflects the firm's indebtedness to its owners, and how it has invested that money.

The money measurement convention   The information which is incorporated in the accounts relates to the financial affairs of the business. Information which the accountant cannot measure in money terms will not be communicated to the owners or external users. In practice, this means that many important facets of a firm's activities, e.g. poor industrial relations, new product developments or the collapse of established markets will not be reported.

The money measurement convention has also been criticised for failing to take account of changes in the value of money. The high inflation rates of the 1970s and early 1980s forced the accounting profession to face this particular problem.

The going concern convention.   Assets in the business will be valued on the assumption that the business will continue. As a result there may be differences in the 'book' value of assets and their open market value. For example a £10,000 car with a life of five years may have a book value of £8,000 after one year's use but if sold may only realise £6,000.

The cost convention.   The value of an asset to a business is shown by its cost of acquisition less any depreciation. However, valuing assets on the basis of historic cost does not necessarily reflect their current value because of inflation e.g. land and buildings. Nor does it provide a satisfactory base for developing profits. Let us take our example of a car again. The car cost £10,000 and the firm writes off its value over five years at £2,000 per annum. Yet when the car is replaced it may cost – say £15,000. Income over the past few years has been overstated by £5,000 – the difference between the depreciation provisions and what was actually required to purchase a new car.

The realisation convention.   This follows closely the cost convention. Just as the value of an asset to a business is determined by the cost of purchasing it, so any change in its value will only be recognised at the time of its sale. Accountants argue that as the market values of assets fluctuate it would be wrong to anticipate any gain which might be made on its disposal.

The accrual convention.   In the same way as the cost convention argues that it is wrong to anticipate any gain in the value of an asset before it is sold the accrual convention states that a business cannot anticipate the right to receive or pay cash. For example, under a contract money may be payable to a firm on 1 May. The firm cannot anticipate the legal obligation to pay that money and enter it in the accounts before 1 May. However, on that date the receipt of cash, or the right to receive cash (the creation of a debtor) will be recorded in the accounts. Similar rules apply to expenses.

The matching convention.   In drawing up the final accounts this convention says that it is important to ensure in calculating the income of a period all expenses incurred in earning that income are included. Thus the fact that an expense for a period (e.g. rent) has not been paid is irrelevant when calculating income for that period. The expense was incurred in earning that income and must be matched against that income.

The periodic convention. Periodic reporting of results must be made to the owners of the business. Today, this is enshrined in company law which requires directors to make annual reports to the shareholders. There is no good reason why the period should be 12 months, and many companies will report to their shareholders at far more frequent intervals than this.

The consistency convention. In order that we may compare financial information between years or companies, it is necessary that we are consistent in the way financial reports are drawn up. Changes in the treatment of stock or depreciation may affect the income reported for that period. Thus where changes are made the firm should indicate to the owners that (1) a change in accounting methods has been made and (2) the impact of that change.

The conservation convention. The accountant is required:
- not to anticipate income but to provide for all possible losses and
- where there are two methods of valuing an asset, the one which results in the lower value should be taken.

This convention has been criticised as contravening the accrual convention in respect of expenses, and the going concern convention in respect of the treatment of assets.

The balance sheet

The balance sheet can be likened to a photograph. It provides a picture of a firm's financial position at a given point in time. It is constructed from the bookkeeping records of the business and shows how the company obtained the finance necessary for its operations and how that finance was utilised. Traditionally, balance sheets were presented in a two-column format showing liabilities (or sources of finance) on the left-hand side, and assets (applications of finance) on the right-hand side. The balance sheet in Fig. 18.2 uses that format and shows the subheadings commonly used.

Balance sheet	
Liabilities	*Assets*
Shareholders' funds	Fixed assets
Loan capital	
Current liabilities	Current assets

18.2 Layout of a balance sheet in traditional form

By convention, liabilities are shown in order of permanence to the business. Thus shareholders' funds – which provide the permanent capital of the business – are listed first. Shareholders' funds consist of ordinary and preference share capital together with reserves of undistributed or retained profits. Our second heading on the liabilities side of the balance sheet – loan capital – refers to money lent to the business for long-term financing. Examples would include debentures, mortgages, and bank loans.

Current liabilities are short-term borrowings which will normally be repaid within a year, and will include creditors – that is, amounts owing to suppliers of goods and services – and also bank overdrafts.

Moving to the right-hand side of our balance sheet we see that the money raised is invested in either fixed or current assets. Fixed assets refer to items that the company has acquired for use (rather than sale) in its business. Land and buildings, plant and machinery, and vehicles are examples of fixed assets.

Current assets consists of stocks, debtors – that is, amounts owed to the business by customers – and cash owned by the business. They are sometimes referred to as short-term or circulating assets due to the fact that they constantly change as the firm conducts its business.

There is no legal requirement as to how the business presents its final accounts. While the format adopted above has the advantage of grouping assets and liabilities together the modern trend is to present the information in tabular form as in Fig. 18.3 so as to highlight the long-term financing of the business together with the net assets.

In reality the only difference with this presentation is that current liabilities, instead of being included with the other sources of finance, are deducted from current assets. This has the advantage of showing the extent to which the business can meet its short-term liabilities from short-term assets without recourse to borrowing or sales of other assets.

(a)	Longer-term financing of the business	Shareholders' funds + Loan capital
		=
(b)	Net assets of the business	Fixed assets + Current assets − Current liabilities

18.3 Presentation of balance sheet in vertical form

Figure 18.4 shows the balance sheet of an imaginary company, Far East Electronics plc, as at 31 December, 19–8 in the columnar fashion described above. Comparative figures for the previous year, as is the normal practice, are also shown. Explanatory notes on the balance sheet (and the profit and loss account) would again be included in the annual report. Most of the terminology used in the balance sheet should be familiar, but it is necessary to explain the following items:

1 *Reserves.* Reserves may be either revenue or capital. A revenue reserve arises when some of the profits are retained in the business at the end of the year and not distributed to shareholders. We sometimes use the term 'ploughed back' profits. Capital reserves arise

Far East Electronics plc Balance Sheet as at 31 December 19–8

		19–8 (£'000)		19–7 (£'000)
Capital employed				
Ordinary share capital		4,000		2,500
Reserves		15,792		13,248
Shareholders' funds		19,782		15,748
Secured bank loan	2,050		2,050	
Minority interests	591	2,641	591	2,641
		22,423		18,389
Employment of capital				
Fixed (tangible) assets – Less depreciation		9,239		6,817
Intangible assets		1,421		1,421
Subsidiary companies		4,008		4,008
		14,668		12,246
Current assets				
Stock	8,833		6,639	
Debtors	4,492		4,806	
Cash	1,830	15,155	816	12,261
		29,823		24,507
less *Current liabilities*				
Creditors	6,284		4,061	
Bank overdraft	123		532	
Taxation	825		1,388	
Proposed dividend	168	7,400	137	6,118
		22,423		18,389
Goh Eng Kim Chan Ah Kow	Directors			

18.4 Illustration of a typical company's published balance sheet

where profits are made from activities other than trading. For example, if fixed assets are re-valued and an increase in worth is revealed, a capital reserve will be created. Similarly, if a business sells its own shares for more than their face value the surplus will be held in a capital reserve called the 'share premium' account. It is important to distinguish between revenue and capital reserves as dividends to shareholders can only be paid out of revenue reserves.

Many people confuse reserves with cash. This is wrong, the terms are fundamentally different. Reserves indicate that the value of the business has grown, but that increase is not necessarily held in cash. Indeed, the expanding company, even though it has large reserves, may be short of cash because of new investments in plant and machinery, stocks and debtors.

2 *Minority interests.* Many public companies quoted on the Stock Exchange are groups of businesses which have been formed by merger and take-over activity. Sometimes, not all shareholders are willing to trade their investment in the original business for a stake in the newly combined group. It is then necessary to show what amount of the subsidiaries' assets belong to shareholders outside the company. Thus the value of the subsidiary companies' assets in Far East Electronics plc balance sheet is shown as £5,429,000 of which £591,000 belongs to 'outsider' shareholders.

3. *Depreciation.* At the end of 19–8 fixed assets in Far East Electronics were valued at £8,239,000 after deducting depreciation. Depreciation is deducted so that the balance sheet gives a 'true and fair' view of the affairs of the business. If an asset through use, age, or obsolescence is now only worth, shall we say, 40 per cent of what it originally cost that fact must be shown in the balance sheet. Similarly, if an asset is used during any financial period to earn profits and through use suffers a diminution in value, that reduction in value is an expense which should be set off against revenue in determining the true profit of the period.

There are several ways of calculating depreciation. The most commonly used methods are the straight line and reducing balance depreciation formulae.

Straight line depreciation is calculated as follows:

$$\text{Annual Depreciation charge} = \frac{\text{Purchase price} - \text{residual value}}{\text{anticipated asset life}}$$

This method reduces the value of the asset by a fixed amount each year of its working life. At the end of its working life only the scrap value is left in the accounts. Straight line depreciation is criticised because it fails to reflect the fact that the greatest loss in the value of an asset occurs in the first year of its life.

The reducing balance method of calculating depreciation involves deducting a constant percentage of the asset balance so that at the end of the asset's working life the asset balance equals the scrap or residual value. To find the constant percentage which should be deducted the following formula is used:

$$\text{Depreciation rate} = 1 - \sqrt[n]{\frac{\text{residual value}}{\text{original cost}}}$$

where n is the number of years working life

Although the method of depreciation chosen by a firm is to some extent arbitrary, it may have a significant impact upon reported profits. As we can see from Fig 18.5, the reducing balance method will result in a far higher depreciation charge in the early years and a corresponding reduction in profits.

4. *Intangible assets*. These are non-physical assets of the business which provide some long term competitive advantage to that business. Goodwill is one common example. This occurs when one firm pays more for another company than is justified by its net assets. The higher price may be justified because of the firm's location, reputation, skills and good relationship with customers, staff and suppliers.

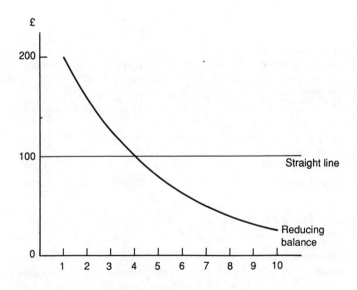

18.5 A comparison of depreciation charges for an asset with an original cost of £1000 and a life of 10 years

Other examples of intangible assets include: patents; trademarks: copyrights and franchise agreements (providing a monopoly right to trade in a certain area). Research and development costs are also sometimes 'capitalised' and treated as a fixed asset.

5. *Stock*. The law requires (1967 Companies Act) that where stocks form an important part of a company's assets that the method of valuing stocks should be stated in the Annual Report. Manufacturing companies will carry three types of stock – raw materials, work in progress and finished goods. Retail organisations will normally only carry finished goods, but these may also be a substantial proportion of total assets. The most common method of stock valuation is to take either its cost or net realisable value whichever is the lower.

We would normally expect stock to be valued at its cost to the business, but the concept of net realisable value may be important where stock is obsolete or has deteriorated. Net realisable value may also be important if a business holds stocks of commodities e.g. copper, tin, sugar, cocoa as the price of these may fluctuate wildly.

The value of stock in the balance sheet may also vary according to the method by which purchases are transferred from stores. As we will see (Fig 18.7) the decision is significant because of its impact upon profits. There are two methods in general use – FIFO and

	FIFO £	LIFO £
Opening stock 1,000 units at £12	12,000	12,000
Purchases 1,200 units at £13	15,600	15,600
	27,600	27,600
Stock sold 1,000 units at £12 1,000 units at £13	12,000	13,000
Closing stock	15,600	14,600
Sales 1,000 units at £16 Stock sold 1,000 units at £12 1,000 units at £13	16,000 12,000	16.000 13,000
Profit	4,000	3,000

18.6 Comparison of FIFO and LIFO stock valuations

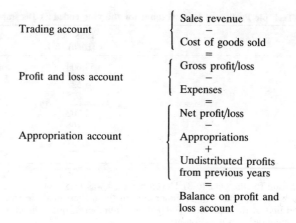

Trading account
{
Sales revenue
−
Cost of goods sold
=

Profit and loss account
{
Gross profit/loss
−
Expenses
=

Appropriation account
{
Net profit/loss
−
Appropriations
+
Undistributed profits
from previous years
=

Balance on profit and
loss account

18.7 The sections of the profit and loss account

LIFO. FIFO or First In First Out assumes that goods which came into stock first go out first. LIFO or Last In First Out assumes the last stock in is the first to go out. Under the FIFO method the value of closing stock is similar to the replacement cost (when prices are rising) but profits are higher than under the LIFO system. This is because stock sold is charged out at a higher price under the LIFO system thus reducing the profit available for taxation. However, under conditions of rising prices the value of closing stock will be understated.

6. *Taxation and proposed dividend.* Although neither of these items are liabilities arising from F.E.E.'s trading activities, both will need paying during the forthcoming year and in consequence are grouped with current liabilities.

The profit and loss account

In order to calculate the profit earned by a business all expenses which have been incurred in earning the sales revenue of that period must be charged against that revenue. The profit and loss account is divided into three sections (see Fig. 18.7). First, the trading account in which gross profit is calculated by deducting the cost of goods sold (labour, raw materials, and other production costs) from sales revenue. In the central section which is termed the profit and loss account, the net profit is arrived at by deducting all business expenses for that period from the gross period. This is the figure which is normally quoted in the financial press. The final section,

Singapore Tech plc Profit and Loss Account for the year ended 31 December 19–8

	1988 (£000)	1987 (£000)
Turnover	53,000	42,300
Net profit	3,527	3,312
Taxation	825	1,032
Profit after tax	2,702	2,280
Dividends	168	137
Retained profits	2,534	2,143

Notes:
1 Depreciation for the year to 31 December 1984 was £1,531,000.
2 Director's emoluments. The remuneration of the highest paid director was £68,000 and that of the Chairman £40,000. The number of other directors in each range of remuneration was as follows:

	1988	1987
Nil–£15,000	4	4
£15,000–£20,000	—	1
£20,000–£25,000	2	1
£25,000–£30,000	2	2

3 Emoluments to employees earning in excess of £30,000 were as follows:

	1988	1987
£30,000–£35,000	2	—
£35,000–£40,000	1	2

4 Interest paid on loans

	1988	1987
Loans repayable over more than five years	£311,000	£327,000
Short-term borrowing	31,000	98,000

18.8 Illustration of a typical company's published profit and loss account

the appropriation account, shows the way in which the profit is used – how much is to go in paying corporation tax, what dividends are to be paid this year, leaving the residue to be added to the retained profits in previous years. In practice much of the detailed information contained in the profit and loss account could be useful to competitors and consequently companies are not required to show full details. The profit and loss account of Singapore Tech (see Fig. 18.8) shows the details which have to be published by law.

Inflation accounting

In Chapter 6 we noted that inflation – a rise in the general level of prices – has been with us for most of this century, certainly since the end of the Second World War. We also noted that even a modest rate of inflation – say five per cent could have significant impacts on costs and asset values over a period of time (see p. 88). For many years the impact of inflation on company accounts was ignored by the accountants, but the high inflation rates of the 1970s provoked a debate about whether historic cost accounts provided a true and fair view of a company's financial affairs.

To accountants preparing financial statements inflation caused a number of problems. These were:

- the real value of fixed assets was not stated in the balance sheet

- investments in debtors and cash lost value over time

- provisions for depreciation were insufficient for the replacement of assets

- the value of stock was understated

- profits were overstated where depreciation and stock valuations were based on original cost

- too generous wage increases being given as a result of profit over-statements

Many large companies have made attempts to quantify the effects of inflation by producing supplementary statements. Fig. 18.9 shows the current cost profit and loss account for F.E.E. plc. From the historic cost profit deductions are made for depreciation, stock and working capital. The depreciation adjustment arises because

	£	£
Historic cost profit		3, 527
deduct		
(1) adjustment for depreciation	273	
(2) adjustment for stock	146	
(3) adjustment for working capital	180	599
Current cost operating profit		2,928
add back		
(4) gearing adjustment (15%)		90
		3,018

18.9 Far East Electronics plc current cost profit and loss account for the year ended 31 December 19–8

depreciation is now calculated on the replacement, rather than the original, cost of assets. Similarly extra money needs to be put aside to purchase replacement stock, and to cover the additional credit given to customers through higher prices of goods sold. The gearing adjustment indicates the proportion of total deductions (£599) which will not be borne by the owners of the company.

The current cost balance sheet values all assets at their present – or current replacement cost. Where, as a result of this, assets are greater than liabilities a special reserve – the current cost reserve – is created and credited with the surplus thrown up on revaluation.

The interest in current cost accounting has waned somewhat in the 1980s because the rate of inflation has fallen.

Additionally, current cost accounting has never been popular among users of financial information or company accountants who experienced great difficulty in calculating the adjustments necessary.

Who uses the annual report?

Although the annual report is by no means the only source of information on a business which is available to interested parties it is the most easily obtainable, and is therefore the normal starting-point for research into any company. The annual report will provide information on:

- *Profitability*: e.g. the trend of profits, adequacy of profits in relation to capital employed; are profits sufficient to finance further growth?
- *Solvency*: can the business pay its debts when they fall due, is the working capital sufficient, does the business have the financial resource to survive an unforeseen crisis?
- *Finance*: who provides the finance for the business, is the relationship between the long- and short-term sources of finance correct, is the gearing ratio correct, can the business issue more shares?
- *Security*: what assets are available to satisfy creditors if debts are not met, is the ordinary share dividend safe, how far do profits have to fall before debenture interest cannot be paid?

Shareholders Existing shareholders automatically receive a copy of the annual report, and potential shareholders may also obtain a copy by writing to the company at its registered office. Both groups will be interested in the trends of company profits (many companies now provide summaries of the past five or ten years' financial results as part of the report) and future prospects of the business. Apart from comments made in the press, the annual report is often the only source of information that small investors receive on the company they have invested in.

Employees and unions Employees, like shareholders, have a vested interest in the success of the business and the annual report is one method of passing information to them. Many large companies produce an annual report especially for employees. Here the emphasis is on presenting information in a way which can be easily understood by the employees. Figure 18.10 shows an alternative way

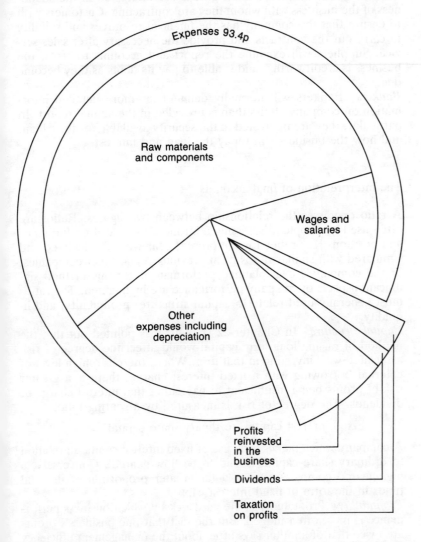

Expenses 93.4p

Raw materials
and components

Wages and
salaries

Other
expenses including
depreciation

Profits
reinvested
in the
business

Dividends

Taxation
on profits

18.10 Far East Electronics Plc – results at a glance: how each £1 of sales revenue was spent

in which the information in the profit and loss account of F.E.E. plc could be presented to employees.

Employees and their representatives will be interested in how much profit has been made – this after all may be used as a tool in the annual wage negotiations, and the company's plans for the future with its implications for employment.

Customers and creditors Both groups are interested in the soundness of the business with whom they are contracting. Customers wish to ensure that the company has the financial resources and stability to carry out the contracts and provide the necessary after-sales service. Suppliers will examine the report and accounts to see if the business is creditworthy, and is able to pay its debts as they become due.

Bankers Bankers will normally demand far more detailed information on company affairs than is provided in the annual report. In particular, they are interested in the security available for their loan, and how the business will repay the loan and interest.

The interpretation of final accounts

A ratio expresses the relationship between two figures. Ratios are often used by people in assessing a business's financial performance and position. Key ratios for the present year will be calculated and compared with similar ratios from previous years, other companies, or the company's own planned performance. By this method significant aspects of company performance are highlighted. The ratios most generally used relate to capital structure, profitability, and liquidity.

Capital structure In Chapter 22 (p. 440) it is pointed out that the method of raising long-term capital would affect the degree of risk associated with investing in that firm. Where there is a high level of external borrowing with a fixed interest charge, there is a greater risk of profits being insufficient to pay either that interest charge or dividends. The degree of risk is measured by a gearing ratio:

Fixed interest capital : ordinary share capital

A company which makes little use of fixed interest capital in relation to ordinary share capital is said to be 'low geared'. Conversely, a high-geared company obtains a far greater proportion of its total funds in the form of fixed interest capital.

Profitability Profitability is the yardstick by which business performance is most often judged. But the fact that one business's profits are twice that of another says little about the management efficiency in the use of resources. Profitability and performance are therefore assessed by comparing the profitability against the resources which were used to obtain those profits. This ratio is termed the 'return on capital employed' and is calculated thus:

$$\frac{\text{Net profit before tax}}{\text{Capital employed}} \times 100$$

where capital employed is total assets *less* current liabilities. Being expressed as a percentage the ratio can easily be used for purposes of comparison, and answers investors' questions such as, 'Is the management making good use of the firm's resources?', and 'Could I obtain a better return by investing elsewhere?'

The return on capital employed may be subdivided into two further ratios by comparing net profits and capital employed, in turn, against sales. The first, the net profit percentage, is measured as follows:

$$\frac{\text{Net profit before tax}}{\text{Sales}} \times 100$$

It is a measure of management's efficiency in keeping costs down.

Second, asset turnover measures how effectively capital or assets are used to generate sales. It is measured as follows:

$$\frac{\text{Sales}}{\text{Capital employed}}$$

A return on capital employed of 15 per cent may be earned in many different ways. A company may have a profit margin of 5 per cent, but turn its capital over (and earn the profit margin) three times during that period. Alternatively, the same return of 15 per cent could be obtained by turning assets once, but having a net profit of 15 per cent, or an asset turnover ratio of 2 and a $7\frac{1}{2}$, per cent profit margin.

The nature of the relationship between profit margin and asset turnover is often determined by the industry in which the firm works. Heavy engineering industries, being capital intensive and with contracts often taking months if not years to complete, have a low asset turnover ratio but a high net profit percentage. Conversely, a supermarket will work on a very low profit margin but aim to turn its assets over very many times during the year.

Liquidity and solvency There are many recorded cases of businesses trading profitably and yet because of a shortage of funds being forced to curtail their activities if not go into liquidation. Therefore, the management of working capital is of as much importance as profitability to shareholders, employees, and all the other interested parties.

By 'working capital' we are referring to those assets which may be rapidly converted into cash and used to pay the debts of the business. Working capital is also used to acquire the labour, materials, power, and other items needed before the fixed assets can operate, and to finance the business's sales activities. In balance sheet terms working capital is shown as the difference between current assets and current liabilities. For F.E.E. plc working capital was £7,755,000 in 19–7 and £6,143,000 in 19–8.

When working capital is inadequate the following difficulties may occur:

1. An inability to take advantage of favourable terms for settling indebtedness (e.g. discounts for prompt payment).
2. An inability to pay debts when they become due, with a consequent loss of goodwill and creditworthiness.
3. Stocks may be withheld by suppliers until payment is made in cash, thus damaging production schedules.
4. The business may be forced to purchase the goods that it needs in small and uneconomic quantities.
5. The firm may be forced to sell at reduced prices or to give excessive discounts so as to obtain funds quickly.

The best test of a business's ability to pay its debts when they become due is to be found in a cash budget. Unfortunately this information is not available outside the company and we are therefore forced to use information from the published accounts. One measure which is commonly used is the 'current ratio'. This examines the relationship between short-term assets and liabilities. It is often termed the 2:1 ratio, indicating the margin of safety which is generally accepted as being necessary to meet the uneven flow of receipts and payments. The current ratio is calculated as follows:

$$\frac{\text{Current assets}}{\text{Current liabilities}}$$

Although a ratio of 2:1 is normally recommended a marked degree of difference is found between industries. Heavy engineering, for example, tends to have a higher than average current ratio because of the large amount of capital tied up in raw materials and work in progress. However, our supermarket (which trades mainly for cash) can operate on an exceptionally low current ratio.

Two other ratios also tend to be widely used. The stock turnover ratio:

$$\frac{\text{Sales}}{\text{Stock}}$$

indicates the speed with which the company turns over its stock. A fall in the stock turnover ratio may be caused by a fall in sales – raising questions regarding marketing policy. Alternatively, an increase in the level of stocks held raises questions regarding stock control and purchasing policy.

The debtor turnover ratio, which shows the average number of days customers take to pay their bills measures the efficiency of the company's credit control system. Obviously the faster debts are collected the better. It is calculated as follows:

$$\frac{\text{Debtors}}{\text{Sales}} \times 365$$

There may, of course be perfectly adequate reasons for changes in these ratios. A decline in the stock turnover ratio may be due to a stocking-up process prior to an expansion in sales. Changes in the debtor turnover ratio may reflect a different management policy on credit trading. What is important with these ratios is that they focus attention on issues vital to the company's survival and profitability.

Interfirm comparison

The value of ratio analysis lies in its comparison with information of a similar kind. Traditionally, the comparison has been made with data from the same organisation for previous years. Yet even greater benefit can be obtained if comparison is made against the performance of other firms in the same industry.

Demand for such information has led a number of trade associations to develop schemes facilitating interfirm comparison. Individual companies within the industry supply information on their performance to the trade association on the understanding that it should be treated in strict confidence, and will only be revealed to other members in the form of industry averages.

A similar scheme, the Centre for Interfirm Comparison, was also established by the British Institute of Management in 1959. This seeks to cover those industries whose trade associations do not run an interfirm comparison scheme. Details of industry averages are again supplied, together with the range of performance. Comments on the strengths and weaknesses of the particular firm are also made.

Both trade associations and the Centre for Interfirm Comparison lay down rules for a common presentation of accounts and also specify methods by which assets should be valued or depreciated, thus ensuring comparability of performance.

Funds flow analysis

In addition to the balance sheet and the profit and loss account which are required by law, firms have also included in their annual

Condor plc Sources and Application of Funds for the years ended 31 December 19–8

	£'000	£'000	£'000	£'000
Opening cash position				816
Sources of funds				
Ordinary share capital		1,500		
Net profit	3,527			
Add back depreciation*	1,531			
		5,058		
Debtors	314			
Creditors	2,223			
		2,537		
			9,095	
Disposition of funds				
Purchase of fixed assets		3,953		
Stock	2,194			
Bank overdraft	765			
Tax paid	1,032			
Dividend paid	137			
		4,128		
			8,071	
Excess of sources over applications				1,024
Closing cash position				1,830

*Depreciation, which has been charged as an expense in the profit and loss account, does not result in a flow of funds out of the business.

18.11 Illustration of a typical company's published funds flow statement

report a 'funds statement'. In Britain this is often called the 'sources and applications of funds statement'. The statement aims to explain what sources of funds have become available during the past year, and how these funds have been utilised.

The technique for constructing a funds flow statement is relatively simple. A comparison is made of the business's balance sheet at two different dates, and the differences noted. Thus if examination reveals that creditors have increased during the period, it means that they are financing more of the business than previously, and represent a source of funds. Conversely, if the value of fixed assets has increased, the increased investment represents an application or disposition of funds. The rules for constructing a funds statement are summarised as follows:

- profits from trading are sources of funds

- increases in liabilities are sources of funds
- decreases in assets are sources of funds
- losses on trading are dispositions of fund
- increases in assets are dispositions of funds
- decreases in liabilities are dispositions of funds

Figure 18.11 shows the sources and application of funds statement for Condor plc which is based upon the final accounts for 31 December 19–7 and 19–8. It has been designed so as to explain the differences in the cash balance at the beginning and the end of the period. There is, however, no one standard format for such statements. The presentation may be adapted to explain why in a year of successful trading, the business is suffering a cash crisis, or alternatively to explain the changes in working capital. In this way a funds flow statement fills an important information gap for management, investors, and other interested parties.

Management accounting

So far we have concerned ourselves with financial accounting, the main aim of which is to record all transactions of the organisation and at the end of the year summarise the results of trading in the profit and loss account and balance sheet. We have also seen how ratio analysis and funds flow statements can be used further to explain the performance and results of the business. But while such information is useful to management in the control of their operations it suffers from two defects. First the information is not always readily available. Traditionally, the final accounts are only drawn up at the end of the financial year. While some firms do produce these statements half-yearly and quarter-yearly, information for control purposes is needed very much more frequently. Secondly the information presented in the final accounts is of little use at the operational level of the business. Management needs cost information for product pricing, to ensure departments do not overspend, and to control the labour and material used in production.

Management accounting seeks to fill this gap and provide managers with the information they need to manage effectively. But, of course, let us be clear that cost information alone is insufficient for decision-making purposes. Managers will also draw upon their knowledge of the firm's environment – economic, political, technical, and social, and also the organisation's strengths and weaknesses. Indeed, often managers may ignore cost considerations and make their decisions upon other grounds; for example employee morale or customer goodwill.

Control accounting

Budgetary control Budgetary control is undoubtedly the most widely used management accounting technique. On a personal level we are all familiar with the idea of budgeting – we have to plan our student grant or wage packet so that we do not run short of funds before next pay-day. On a national level the Chancellor of the Exchequer estimates government revenue and expenditure, and presents his proposals to Parliament in the form of a budget.

A company budget is much the same; it represents an attempt by the business to predict future income and expenses together with their effect upon profitability and the balance sheet. Equally importantly though, budgeting is seen as a means of ensuring that:

- decisions about the use of scarce resources and priorities can be made on the basis of sound information

- important steps which the organisation needs to take are highlighted e.g. raising new finance

- departmental responsibilities are clarified

- challenging but realistic targets can be set for departments, sections and individuals

- early warning of deviations from plans allows corrective action to be taken

- inter-departmental conflict is reduced

Budgeting is part of the overall planning process within the firm (see Fig. 18.12). Senior management will have considered a variety of strategies, and eventually decided the long-term or corporate objectives of the organisation. These objectives could be expressed, for example, in terms of profitability, sales revenue, new product development, or growth. However, it should be noted that corporate planning is a continuous process, not an activity to be undertaken, say, once every five years. Corporate objectives may very well be redefined as either environmental or organisational factors change.

Budgets are normally prepared on an annual basis and cover all aspects of the firm's activities. The process of drawing up a budget will start well before the year to which it will relate. Managers in conjunction with their supervisors will establish objectives for themselves and their departments. It is essential that managers are involved in this process, otherwise objectives may be rejected as unrealistic. Such objectives must, of course, be consistent with the

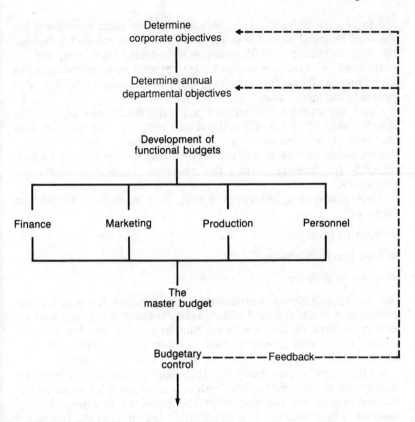

18.12 Simplified budgeting process

overall strategy of the organisation and also flexible enough to accommodate unforeseen changes in corporate objectives.

Additionally, these departmental objectives must also be consistent with those established by other managers. For example, it would be nonsensical for the sales department of an engineering firm to budget for a sales volume greater than production capacity. In practice, we will find that there is one factor – the 'limiting factor' – which shapes or determines all other budgets. Often the limiting factor is sales, with the firm being unable to sell as much as it can produce. The production budget in this case would be based on what the marketing department believed they could sell.

The establishing of departmental objectives is considered to be one of the most important facets of the budgetary process. Managers are forced to sit back and systematically plan their operations for the next financial year. Co-ordination of effort is enhanced through the interdependence of departmental budgets. Moreover, the involvement of managers in the budget process not only establishes their responsibility for achieving the agreed objective but also provides the motivation.

Once departmental objectives are established and agreed the development of functional budgets can begin. In conjunction with the budget accountant – a senior accountant with the firm – departmental managers will draw up statements (or budgets) which quantify (in financial terms) the resources needed to attain the objectives.

Thus production objectives which were previously defined in terms of

- what to produce
- how much to produce
- when to produce

will be broken down into monthly requirements for people, materials, and machines, and subsequently translated into the cost we expect to incur under each head. Similarly, sales cost budgets will detail, on a month-to-month basis, expenditure on advertising, market research, new product development, or administration.

At this stage responsibility for the budget process passes from the departmental managers to the budget accountant who develops the master budget for submission to the board of directors. Master budgets, which are based on information drawn from the functional

Production Department

| Item | Period 3 | | | | Year to date | | | |
	Budget £	Actual £	Variance £	%	Budget £	Actual £	Variance £	%
Labour	33,000	36,000	+ 3,000	9	99,000	95,000	− 4,000	4
Materials	50,000	45,000	− 5,000	10	155,000	140,000	− 15,000	10

18.13 Extract from a budgetary control statement

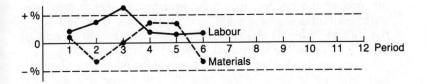

18.14 The graphical presentation of budgetary variances

budgets, are normally presented in the form of a profit and loss account and balance sheet. This has the advantage of showing the financial projections for the forthcoming year in a form familiar to the board and which facilitates comparison with the results of previous years. Should the budgeted results be deemed unacceptable the functional budgets will be referred back to the departmental managers for adjustment. This process will continue until the master budget is accepted by the directors.

Now we look at the budget as a means of control. The annual budget is divided into shorter control periods normally based on the calendar month or a period of a few weeks. Shortly after the end of each control period managers will receive a statement comparing actual results with budgeted figures.

Presentation of the information is important. Attempts should be made to highlight significant differences between actual and planned results (what constitutes a 'significant difference' will have been established previously – perhaps ±10 per cent from budget). A common method used is shown in Fig. 18.13. Alternatively, actual costs may be shown as a percentage variation from budgeted costs on a graph (see Fig. 18.14). The dotted lines indicate percentage levels of variations which are considered significant and should be investigated.

However, while care must be taken with the presentation of budgetary information this does not guarantee effective control. Managers should be required by their superiors to investigate and report upon all significant variations from budget. The report to the superior will be in two parts. First an explanation of why the variances have occurred, and secondly what action is being taken regarding those variances over which the manager has some control. As a result of these investigations and reports departmental and organisational objectives may also be questioned, and if necessary revised. Although budgetary control has many advantages it does have some drawbacks. These include:
- treating the *budget as a regulator*. Some managers will argue that no expenditure outside the budget can be allowed. This is not the

function of the budget, it is a monitoring aid. There may very well be situations where additional expenditure over and above the budget is highly desirable from the organisation's point of view. It is up to the individual manager to argue the case.

– *'spending up'* the budget. It is not unusual for managers who have surplus funds in their budget near the end of the financial year to incur unnecessary additional expenditure. This will happen where the budget for the forthcoming year is based on what has been spent in the past year, rather than trying to establish realistic budgets.

– *fluctuating prices*. The budget is drawn up on a whole series of assumptions about prices – raw materials, labour, power and so on. Fluctuations in prices, or rises in inflation above those anticipated will make budgets rapidly out of date. In these situations firms may adopt 'flexible' budgeting which can, to a certain extent, allow for price changes.

Standard costing Standard costing, like budgeting control, aims to provide a basis for the control of costs. However, where budgetary control creates targets for the various departments within the organisation, standard costing seeks to establish a check on each process or operation within an individual department. Standard costing is therefore a very much more detailed system of control.

To establish a system of standard costs an operation or process within a department will be broken down into its constituent parts. Each of these will be allocated a cost based upon certain clearly defined assumptions. For example, where materials are used the expected or standard cost for materials will be calculated by establishing:

- the amount of material used;

- any allowance for wastage;

- cost per unit of material.

In the same manner a standard labour cost will be based upon the (standard) time allowed for the job and wage rate for that class of labour. Standard costing thus establishes what the cost of an operation should be, rather than what it is expected to be.

As with budgetary control it is the comparison between actual and standard costs which forms the basis of control variances being investigated and where necessary acted upon.

Standard costing is widely used in industry, and because of its similarities with budgetary control is often incorporated into it.

Decision accounting

Break-even analysis This is one of the most widely used decision-making techniques. Break-even analysis recognises that profit is a function of price, costs, and output. It allows managers to determine the effects of changes in these variables on overall profit.

Breakeven analysis is based upon appreciating that costs may be either fixed or variable. Certain costs do not vary with the level of business activity. The rent and rates for the business premises have to be paid whether or not we actually produce anything. The same could also be said for debenture interest or management salaries. These costs are called 'fixed'. However, the point must be made that it is not true to say that fixed costs never alter. They will do, rents and rates will increase from year to year, and loan interest may be affected by changes in the interest rates, but they do not alter as a result of a change in the level of business activity.

Variable costs, on the other hand, are costs which change or vary with the level of the firm's activity. Thus if we increase output by 25 per cent we would expect expenditure on the raw materials, power, and labour involved in the production process to also increase by 25 per cent.

Marginal Cost Pricing

This method of pricing is based upon the distinction between fixed and variable costs. For example a business with spare capacity receives an order for 10,000 widgets at £25. On looking at its cost structure it finds that to make a profit it would have to charge £32. It would seem that the firm's response should be to turn the order down. Indeed, it certainly would if there were other orders for which it could charge a 'full cost' price, but, in the absence of such orders, the firm may be wise to accept this 'loss-making' order.

We find that fixed costs per unit are £12 and variable costs £20. As a result of taking this order we cover all our variable costs and receive a contribution towards our fixed costs of £5 per unit. If we refuse the order we deny ourselves this contribution to fixed costs and thereby increase our losses. In this way marginal cost pricing tells us to do something different to full cost pricing.

One example of marginal pricing is the hotel industry which earns sufficient revenue in the summer or peak period to cover costs and make a profit allowing them to charge off peak holidays at a marginal cost – the cost of accommodation and food. In reality they will probably obtain a contribution to fixed costs as well.

There are also some costs which do not fit neatly into either of the categories 'fixed' or 'variable'. In Britain, for example, telephone bills comprise a fixed element which has to be paid regardless of usage, but also a variable element based on the number (and length) of calls made. While it is possible to divide our telephone bill into its fixed and variable components by observation, this is not possible in many other cases. There are, however, simple statistical methods which may be used for this purpose.

The importance of the distinction between fixed and variable costs can best be seen through a simple example illustrating the impact of fixed costs on overall profitability and profit per unit (see Table 18.1). We note that as output increases unit cost decreases. The reason for this is that fixed costs are divided between units of production. When output is 500 units, each unit has to bear 1/500 of the fixed cost – that is, £8 per unit, but when we reach a production level of 1,500 units each unit bears only 1/1500 of that cost – £2.67 per unit. Variable cost per unit remains constant throughout this range of business activity at £6 per unit.

Table 18.1 Profitability at different levels of output

Units of output	500 costs £		1,000 costs £	1,500 costs £
Labour £3 per unit	1,500		3,000	4,500
Materials £2 per unit	1,000		2,000	3,000
Power £1 per unit	500		1,000	1,500
Total variable cost	3,000		4,000	9,000
Rent and rates		1,000		
Administration		2,000		
Loan interest		1,000		
Total fixed cost	4,000		4,000	4,000
Total cost	7,000		10,000	13,000
Revenue £15 per unit	7,500		15,000	22,500
Profit	500		5,000	9,500
Cost per unit	£14		£10	£8.67
Profit per unit	£1		£5	£6.33

Fixed and variable costs can easily be presented graphically, and when combined with information on sales revenue form the basis of what is known as the 'break-even chart' (see Fig. 18.15).

On the graph variable cost is shown as an upward-sloping line starting from the origin of the graph, since at zero activity variable costs will be nil. On top of the variable cost we have fixed costs

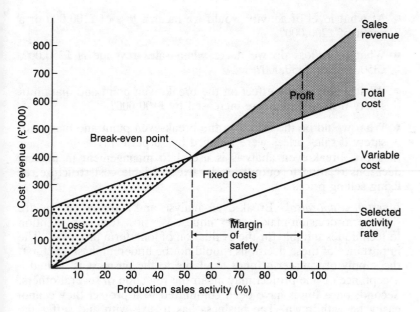

18.15 The break-even chart

giving us a line for total costs. The line for total cost lies above but parallel to the line for variable cost, reflecting the fact that fixed costs do not vary with output. To these two lines we may now add a third – sales revenue. Once again the line starts from the origin of the graph, for when sales are nil so is sales income; and afterwards rises proportionately to volume.

It is now possible to read off from the chart total costs and income for any level of activity. The break-even point on the chart indicates the level of activity where neither profits or losses are made, where total costs and total income are the same. The break-even point is of importance to the firm because it indicates the minimum level of production and sales needed to ensure the survival of the firm in the long run. While sales may occasionally drop below this level, and the firm survive, on balance the business must operate above this point. The margin of safety shows the amount by which sales would have to fall from the selected activity rate before we reach a loss-making situation.

The break-even chart can be used to answer the following types of question (which readers may try and answer for themselves):

• What is the profit or loss at activity levels of 30, 50, or 80 per cent?

- At what level of activity would we incur a loss of £100,000 or a profit of £200,000?

- What profit/loss do we make when sales revenue is £250,000, £350,000, or £450,000?

- What would be the effect on the break-even point and margin of safety if fixed costs were increased by £100,000?

- What would be the effect on the break-even point and margin of safety if sales prices were reduced by 10 per cent?

In short, break-even analysis is useful to management in making decisions relating to output levels, fixed/variable cost structure, or fixing selling prices.

Investment appraisal Break-even analysis and marginal costing are short-term decision-making techniques. We now turn our attention to techniques suitable for the evaluation of long-term proposals. The importance of these decisions should not be underemphasised. First, the supply of long-term funds available to the business is limited – acceptance of one project may mean the rejection of several others. Second, once funds have been committed to a project they cannot easily be withdrawn. The business has to live with and suffer the consequences of that decision – for better or worse!

The aim, therefore, of investment appraisal (or capital budgeting as it is sometimes called) is to ensure that funds are allocated correctly. The criterion which is normally used is profitability – the rate of return on capital employed in that project.

But not all projects can be assessed in strictly financial terms. New sports facilities and staff canteens are hard to justify financially – there is no obvious return on the investment. Yet many firms, believing that there is a definite, though unquantifiable, benefit in terms of employee motivation and loyalty to the business, continue to invest large sums in such projects. Similarly the erection of a new office block will show no obvious return in the profit and loss account. Yet improvements in administrative efficiency, and their effect on customer goodwill (in addition to the possible need to expand the administrative unit in future) may prove to be a very cogent argument for the building of the office block.

However, our concern here is with those projects which can be assessed by normal commercial criteria. There are many methods in investment appraisal used by business organisations. We will briefly consider three – pay-back, return on investment, and the present value method (discounted cash flow).

One of the most widely used methods of making investment decisions is the 'pay-back' method. This method does not take account of the overall profitability of the project but seeks to discover how long it is before the project pays for itself. The popularity of the pay-back method stems from two factors. First, most companies have limited financial resources, the shorter the pay-back period the sooner those funds can be reinvested in another project. Secondly, the shorter the pay-back period the shorter the risk to shareholders funds through, for example, unforeseen changes in the business environment.

Table 18.2 gives information on two potential investments, both requiring the same capital expenditure and having a similar life but with very different cash flows. On the basis of the pay-back period we would favour project A as it takes just three years to repay the initial investment compared with over four years on Project B.

Table 18.2 The comparison of two projects by means of the payback period

	Project A		Project B
Required investment	£20,000		£20,000
Estimated cash flow	£		£
Year 1	6,000		2,000
Year 2	6,000		5,000
Year 3	8,000	pay-back	6,000
Year 4	6,000	period	6,000
Year 5	2,000		10,000
Year 6	2,000		7,000
Estimated total cash flow	30,000		36,000

The major criticism of the pay-back period method of appraising projects is that it favours projects showing a quick return on capital and ignores those projects where the greatest return is made in later years. In project B profits do not reach their maximum until year 5, and should we consider the projects over their total life span the decision (to adopt project A) could very well be changed.

The return on investment method takes account of this criticism by comparing cash flow with investment. The average annual cash flow for projects A and B is £5,000 and £6,000 respectively. Assuming the investment has no residual value at the end of year 6, the average investment for both projects is £10,000. The return on investment is therefore:

$$\frac{\text{Average annual cash flow}}{\text{Average investment}} \times 100$$

Project A:

$$\frac{5,000}{10,000} \times 100 = 50 \text{ per cent}$$

Project B:

$$\frac{6,000}{10,000} \times 100 = 60 \text{ per cent}$$

Our decision on changing the criteria would be to undertake project B rather than project A.

Return on investment has the advantage of emphasising the importance of profitability in any investment decision. Its drawback is that it fails to distinguish between the value of £1 of profits in each of the years of the project.

The present value, or discounted cash flow method of appraising capital projects has become increasingly popular over recent years. This stems from the fact that it encompasses the most important features of pay-back and return on investment, namely the timing of cash flows and overall profitability.

This method of evaluating projects is based on the fact that the timing of cash inflows affects their values. Consider which you would rather have, £1,000 today or in a year's time. The answer is £1,000 today because it is possible to invest it so that in a year's time it is worth considerably more than the initial £1,000. Using the same principle we can also answer the question, 'How much is next year's £1,000 worth today?' by calculating how much we should have to invest now to produce £1,000 in a year's time. For example, if we can invest the money at 10 per cent per annum we would need £909.10, while at 20 per cent per annum we would need £833.30. Put another way, we can say that the *present value* of £1,000 in a year's time is £909.10 when discounted at 10 per cent and £833.30 when discounted at 20 per cent.

In order to evaluate capital projects the principle of present values is extended so that we consider how much we have to invest now to yield a given sum in three, four, five, or more years from now. Let us see how this works in practice by considering our two projects, A and B again (Tables 18.2 and 18.3). The assumption made in comparing projects A and B is that money can be invested to earn a rate of interest of 10 per cent. The discount factor shows the amount which would have to be invested now at 10 per cent to yield £1 at the end of years 1 to 6. By multiplying the estimated cash flow for each year by the appropriate discount factor we arrive at the present value of that cash flow. By converting all cash flows to present values and totalling the results we can see that the present value of project B is greater and should therefore be chosen.

By means of these and other techniques the accountant is able to provide management with information on which to base investment decisions. Yet the calculations made by the accountant are only as good as the information on which they are made. In estimating cash inflows and outflows the accountant is drawing upon the knowledge

Table 18.3 The comparison of two projects using discounted cash flow

	Project A			Project B		
	Cash flow (£)	Discount factor (10%)	Present value (£)	Cash flow (£)	Discount factor (10%)	Present value (£)
Year 1	6,000	0.9091	5,454.6	2,000	0.9091	1,818.2
Year 2	6,000	0.8264	4,958.4	5,000	0.8264	4,132.0
Year 3	8,000	0.7513	6,010.4	6,000	0.7513	4,507.8
Year 4	6,000	0.6830	4,098.0	6,000	0.6830	4,098.0
Year 5	2,000	0.6209	1,241.8	10,000	0.6209	6,209.0
Year 6	2,000	0.5645	1,129.0	7,000	0.5645	3,951.5
Total	30,000		22,892.2	36,000		24,716.5

and expertise of many other members of the organisations. During this process many assumptions will have to be made regarding the firm's environment – the future level of economic activity, demand for products marketed, the degree of competition, changes in technology or products, and so forth. Assumptions will also be made on other factors internal to the firm, for example the expertise we have available, or the availability of people, materials, machinery and money. The accountant should therefore qualify the conclusions made by drawing to the attention of management the quality of information on which the calculations were made.

Examination questions

1 (a) What is the role of the *Average Rate of Return* when evaluating investment projects?
   (b) When might the *Pay Back Period* be a better technique?
   (c) What advantages and disadvantages would the *Discounted Cash Flow* technique have over other methods when evaluating investment decisions? *(CAMB 1986)*

2 (a) In what ways would accounting information, when prepared for internal management, differ from that compiled for the use of other interested parties?
   (b) What kind of information would a supplier require of a new customer ordering £1 million worth of raw materials on a regular basis? *(CAMB 1986)*

3 (a) How might inflation distort the annual accounts of a company?
   (b) Briefly propose a way for overcoming these problems.
   (c) How might your suggestion affect the conventions that 'consistency of treatment' and a 'true and fair view' should always characterise the published accounts of a company? *(CAMB 1985)*

4 (a) What is meant by Full Cost Pricing?
   (b) In what circumstances would you advise the use of Marginal Cost Pricing, and why?
   (c) Why is the profit earned on a product important? *(CAMB 1985)*

5　What is budgetary control?
　　Explain how it aids planning, co-ordination and control within the organisation.

6　What are the quantitative techniques of investment appraisal? Assess the extent to which they should be used by firms to plan future capital investment. *(AEB 1987)*

7　State the reasons why companies prepare financial statements and accounts.
　　Comment on their usefulness. *(AEB 1987)*

8　To what extent would Ratio Analysis enable you to draw meaningful conclusions about the performance of different public companies? *(AEB 1986)*

9　Briefly describe the reasons why an accounting profit is important to a private sector enterprise. Comment on the problems encountered in measuring and evaluating profit from an accounting standpoint. *(AEB)*

10　The following is an extract from the balance sheet of a public limited company.

ORDINARY SHARES	£
Authorised 300,000 at £1 each	800,000
Issued and fully paid 700,000 at £1 each	700,00
General Reserve	50,000
LONG TERM BORROWING	
Debentures 10% (2010)	250,000
Capital employed	£1,000,000

The company now wishes to raise an additional £500,000 to finance the development of a new product. Assess the implications of the relevant alternative sources of finance. *(AEB 1986)*

11　A shareholder finds certain aspects of a company's activities recorded in the annual report and accounts. To what extent do the details supplied allow him to make an assessment of the state of his investment? *(AEB 1988)*

12　A manufacturer produces a single product for an industrial market. At full capacity the following data applies:

Fixed costs	£10,000
Variable costs	50p per unit
Output (at full capacity)	100,000 units
Selling price	90p per unit.

(a) Using these figures draw a suitable break-even chart. State the volume of output at which the enterprise will break-even.
(b) State the anticipated profit
　　(i)　at full capacity
　　(ii)　when output is 50,000 units.
(c) What, in this context, is meant by the term 'contribution'?
(d) The overall level of demand in the industry falls and the enterprise must limit its output to 30,000 units. If this happens and costs and selling price remain unchanged
　　(i)　express variable costs as a percentage of total costs
　　(ii)　calculate the contribution at this level of output
　　(iii)　give *one* reason why, despite the reduced level of output, the enterprise can continue to operate.

(c) What would be the position if output fell to 20,000 units, again
without a change in costs or selling price
   (i) In the short term
   (ii) in the long term? (*AEB)*)

13 The data given below refers to the book value per annum of a machine
over a period of ten years after allowance has been made for
depreciation using the reducing value method. The original cost of the
machine was £10,000.

Year	Book value shown on balance sheet at end of year £
1	8705
2	7578
3	6596
4	5742
5	4999
6	4351
7	3788
8	3297
9	2870
10	2500

(a) What is meant by the term 'book value shown on the balance sheet
at end of year'?
(b) State the residual book value of the machine if the enterprise
decides to replace it at the end of ten years.
(c) From the data given and using the same axis draw graphs to
illustrate the effect on the written-down value of using
   (i) the reducing value method of depreciation
   (ii) the straight line method of depreciation
assuming the same residual value in each case at the end of ten
years.
(d) What would be the book value of the machine at the end of four
years if the straight line method of depreciation was used?
(e) Give *two* reasons for using *either* the reducing value method of
depreciation *or* the straight line method of depreciation.
(f) As a result of technological change the useful life of a machine is
reduced from ten years to six years. State and explain *one* possible
effect on an enterprise of this occurrence.
(g) In what way does the incidence of inflation undermine the
usefulness of the above methods of providing for depreciation?
(*AEB 1983*)

14   Ratios extracted from one company's accounts are virtually useless
without additional information. What other information would you
need in order to make them valuable? (*AEB 1989*)

Chapter 19

Personnel

The success of any organisation depends upon the efforts of its employees; employees who differ in their abilities, aspirations, and emotions. Employees, therefore, are more unpredictable and uncontrollable than any other input into the production process. The result is that special attention has to be paid to this particular input.

Personnel management, in so far as it deals with people within the organisation, is the responsibility of all managers and supervisors, yet many have little or no expertise in this area. The function therefore of the personnel department is to aid other managers and supervisors in their dealing with people, ensuring that most effective use is made of this valuable resource.

An effective personnel function will ensure:

- people *doing* the right job
- people *trained* to do their job efficiently
- people *paid* according to their contribution and effort
- people *protected* form danger and unnecessary hazards
- people *motivated* in their job
- people *satisfied with their employer*
- people *remaining* with the business

The work of the personnel function is shown in Fig. 19.1. We will discuss each of these items in turn.

Manpower planning

Both the cost and difficulty of obtaining the right kind of labour have convinced management that labour is a resource for which careful planning is required. The function of manpower planning is to ensure that the organisation is not prevented from achieving its objectives because the correct mix of human resources is unavailable. The process involves considering our present manpower re-

19.1 The work of a typical personnel department

sources, our future requirements, and identifying those courses of action necessary to ensure that our future requirements are met. Figure 19.2 shows this process in detail, and makes the point that manpower planning is part of a wider plan – often termed 'corporate strategy' – involving the whole organisation and determining the organisation's long-term objectives.

In order to produce a strategy for an organisation it is necessary to consider:
1. *The environment in which the organisation operates.* The environment – economic, social, political, and technological – is constantly changing and provides threats and opportunities for any organisation. Some changes may have little effect upon the organisation, whereas others will have serious implications.

2. *The external position of the organisation* – its strengths and weaknesses, for example the ability to raise new finance, to develop new goods and services, or fight off competition. Out of this analysis will be developed a corporate strategy indicating what products are going to be made and what markets served, including the timing and sequence of major steps.

The organisation's future manpower requirements will stem directly from the corporate strategy. Discussions will take place with all departments to discover what their future manpower requirements will be, having regard to that corporate strategy. To avoid problems such as 'empire-building' such estimates should always be backed up by supporting evidence. It may also be possible to use other techniques to determine future requirements. For example if six sales representatives generate £3 m. worth of sales revenue, a projected 50 per cent increase in sales revenue will require another three salespeople. However, such techniques should be used with care; economies of scale or diminishing returns may effect the relationship between salespeople and sales revenue. By these methods a picture of the organisation's future requirements in terms of employee numbers, qualifications, and experience is drawn up. This is often termed the demand forecast.

The basis for the supply forecast – that is, the labour that will be available to meet the demand forecast is the current workforce. From personal statistical information held within the personnel department it is possible to predict for example:

- How many people will retire in the next few years.

- What percentage of new employees will remain with the firm.

- What percentage of other employees (by skill) will find other jobs.

- How many new managers and supervisors we will train.

Projecting this information forward a number of years it is possible to make broad statements about the size of the workforce in different departments, their qualifications, and experience. These forecasts are of course very tentative – they assume past experience on labour movements is a reasonable method of predicting future changes in the workforce. More importantly the forecast also assumes that external forces do not change, yet the expansion or closure of other firms in the area (to give but one example) will very probably affect the supply forecast.

By comparing the supply and demand forecast for individual departments and skills within those departments it is possible to predict where the shortages and surpluses are likely to occur. The

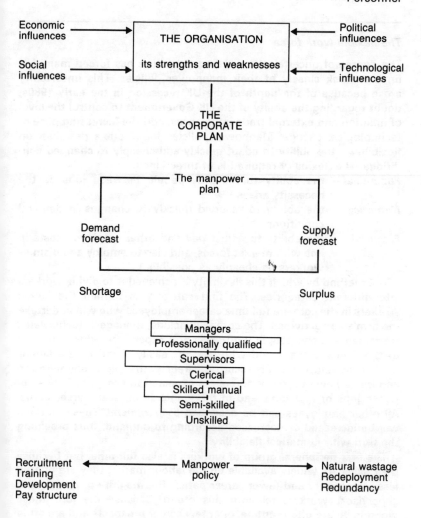

19.2 Determining manpower policy

manpower plan is then drawn up so as to ensure that the predicted shortages and surpluses do not in fact occur, but that rather – through policies of recruitment, training, redeployment and redundancy – the manpower requirements of the organisation are met with the minimum of cost to the company and friction among employees.

The flexible work force

The degree of uncertainty regarding the future has forced many UK firms to look closely at their manpower policies. This uncertainty arose because of the depth of the UK recession in the early 1980s, doubt regarding the ability of the UK Government to control the level of inflation and external trade imbalances, and the increasing pace of technological change. Manpower policies today put a premium on flexibility – the ability to adapt quickly and cheaply to changed conditions. The flexibility required is of three kinds:

Functional – the ability to redeploy people between jobs as the necessity arises

Numerical – the ability to respond quickly to changes in demand conditions

Financial – the ability to adjust pay and other employee costs in line with market forces, and also to employ and dismiss workers as cheaply as possible.

The method by which this flexibility is achieved is to divide workers into different categories. The first category is termed the *'core'*. Workers in the core are full time career employees who will undertake the firm's key activities. The core will include, managers, technicians, craftsmen – those people with skills and experience which are vital to the firm's success and who are not easily found in the labour market. In return for job security, career paths, high renumeration and fringe benefits core workers are expected to accept switches between jobs or locations, and in the longer term, even career paths. All other employees can be described as *peripheral*. These workers will be increased or decreased according to demand, thus providing the firm with numerical flexibility.

The first peripheral group of workers is also full time, but because their skills are widely available on the labour market they are offered less job security and fewer career paths. The majority of clerical and supervisory workers fall into this group. Because the jobs these workers do are often routine, offer few career prospects and are often aimed at women, labour turnover tends to be high. This provides the element of numerical flexibility which firms require.

To provide even greater functional and numerical flexibility a second peripheral group of workers is often employed. Part-time workers provide the best example of this group, but it also includes short term contracts, job sharing and subsidised trainees.

Finally, if the firm needs work undertaken that is either very specialised or very routine, for example systems analysis or office cleaning, it is also open to buy these services from the market rather than providing them from within the firm. Many firms, particularly those in London where office space is at a premium, find considerable

savings can be made in overheads and labour costs by buying-in specialist services.

Recruitment

Traditionally, recruitment lies at the heart of the personnel department's work. Except in extreme circumstances the organisation depends upon a continuous flow of new employees to replace those lost through death, retirement, resignation, or dismissal. Figure 19.3 illustrates the process by which a vacancy is filled. Once a vacancy has been notified to the personnel department the immediate task is to undertake what is termed job analysis in order to draw up two other documents, namely the job description and job specification.

Job analysis is the method by which all facts relating to a job are identified and recorded. With manual jobs the information will normally be obtained (if it is not already on file) by direct observation of the job. Where the task is more complex, techniques used may include an interview with the job-holder, the job-holder maintaining a diary of tasks undertaken in a given period or filling in a questionnaire. The information so obtained is then used to write up a job description outlining the content of the job. Items mentioned would include:

- *Basic details*: the title and grade of the job, the department concerned.

- *Job summary*: outlining the purpose of the job, identifying main tasks, secondary and occasional roles, the standards to be maintained. Information on the social and work environment.

- *Responsibilities*: clarifying the position in the organisation struc-

19.3 The recruitment process

ture. Identifying subordinates for whom the job holder will be responsible, and those to whom the job holder will be responsible.

- *Conditions of employment*: salary, holidays, hours of work, pension schemes, welfare and social facilities, trade-union membership.

- *Training*: facilities for training to bring new employees up to standard. Attitude to/facilities for staff development.

- *Promotion*: opportunities for promotion, career structure within the organisation.

Once a comprehensive description for a job has been drawn up that information may be used in a number of ways. It may be adapted to form the basis of the recruitment advertisement, it may be used in wage and salary administration, measuring each job's level of difficulty and thereby deciding the salary to be paid. Job descriptions also tell us the skills, abilities, and knowledge we need to develop in training programmes. In the recruitment process job descriptions are used as the basis of the job specification. This identifies the qualities and qualifications of the person most likely to fill the job, and equally importantly fit into the organisation.

The formats adopted for a job specification may vary widely. This reflects the specific requirements of different jobs. Thus in some occupations physical attributes may be important, while in others aptitudes for languages or dealing with people may be emphasised. Job specifications may also distinguish between what are considered to be essential and desirable features. Areas which are commonly covered include:

- *Physical*: age, health, and appearance.

- *Attainments*: academic education, professional qualifications, training.

- *Experience/Knowledge*: a general statement on the likely background of the successful candidate – the positions held, the knowledge gained.

- *Aptitudes*: mechanical, verbal, to work alone, ability to work under pressure, etc.

- *Domestic circumstances*: ability to move for the job, to spend time away from home, etc.

At the same time as the job analysis is being undertaken the personnel department is also considering how the vacancy should be filled. The two possibilities are to promote an existing employee or to bring in a new employee from outside.

Should the organisation have employees who have the necessary qualifications and experience there are distinct advantages from recruiting internally. Employees will be better motivated where the organisation has a policy of promotion from within. The fact that career paths exist within the organisation will tend to result in a lower labour turnover. A present employee is known to management and has proved himself in his present job. Promotion from within is quicker and cheaper. However, against these advantages should be set the fact that a new employee will bring with them different ideas and methods – 'the new broom' which may very well be beneficial to the organisation.

Moreover, the conflict and rivalry that may arise between individuals vying for the same post may have adverse effects on departmental performance. Training and development costs may be higher than the costs of recruiting a trained person externally. Finally, recruitment from within may lead to complacency among staff that the job is theirs – this is often referred to as the 'complacent heir apparent'.

Where it is decided to recruit externally the sources normally considered will include:

- Careers offices
- Private employment agencies for clerical and professional workers
- Professional bodies, employment registers
- Links with higher and further education institutions and schools
- National and local advertising

The choice of the correct source is important to attract as many potentially suitable candidates as possible.

Much of the advertisement itself can be drawn from the job description. Information on the job, its duties, qualifications, experience, salary, conditions of employment, and special requirements are all drawn from there. It remains to provide information on the organisation itself and the method of application.

While telephone applications may be asked for in unusual circumstances (perhaps the need for a replacement member of staff is urgent) the normal methods are letter of application or standard application form. A standard application form has the advantage that all candidates have to answer all the relevant questions, to a standard format which is convenient for comparison and administration. Letters of application, may, however, be used for senior positions because an application form does not provide sufficient room for all information.

Once applications have been received the process of short-listing commences. Although critical to the selection process this task is sometimes entrusted to junior office staff! The filtering process is best conducted by reference to attributes identified in the job specification. Normally applicants are divided into three categories, suitable, not suitable, and marginal. It is with this last category that most care has-to be taken. A rigid interpretation of the job specification may exclude one or more excellent candidates.

When the initial screening has finished unsuccessful candidates. should be informed of the result as soon as possible. Candidates being called for interview should be sent interview details and their references taken up.

The final selection process seeks to establish, first will the candidate perform the job satisfactorily, and second they will fit into the organisation structure? The methods by which the candidate can be selected are numerous. Quite apart from the information contained in the application form and references there are a whole host of tests – aptitude, personality, and IQ being three of the more important ones which may be used. Consideration of these tests is, however, outside the scope of this book. We turn instead to the one common element in all final selection processes – the interview.

It would be wise for the interviewers to prepare themselves for the interview. The preparatory work which has to be undertaken includes making oneself conversant with the candidate's background, determining what questions should be put to each candidate, and in the case of a panel of interviewers, who should put those questions. There are several interview plans which seek to aid the interviewer; with all plans, however, the real benefit lies in forcing the interviewee to prepare adequately prior to the interview and systematically consider all points raised in the job specification.

The interview itself will normally begin with a few opening remarks and questions designed to put the candidates at their ease. Thereafter questions put are designed to explain or amplify points made in the application form. The role of the interviewer is to listen and evaluate. Anything which prevents this – such as the interviewer talking too much, or only half listening while taking copious notes – may result in a poor selection being made.

Care should be taken to see that questions asked are open-ended – that is, cannot be answered merely by 'yes' or no'. The use of words such as 'why', and 'how' often enables the interviewer to determine the reasons behind the candidate's actions and their methods of overcoming difficulties.

The interviewer will normally end with the candidate being asked whether they still wish to be considered for the vacancy, and if they have any questions they wish to ask. If selection is not being made immediately after the interview has taken place, candidates should be informed when they may expect to hear the result.

The necessity for a professional approach to recruitment and selection cannot be overemphasised. The future of the organisation depends upon the ability of managers, with the help of the personnel department, to select the right candidates.

Wages and salaries policy

Wages and salaries are an important element in the total cost of many organisations. Service industries including local government and the Health Service can find that 75 per cent of their expenditure is on labour. Wages and salary policy therefore has as its aim the attracting and retaining of the right-quality staff at a cost that can be afforded by the organisation.

It is customary to divide a consideration of this topic into two: first remuneration for hourly paid workers, second remuneration for clerical, professional, and managerial staff. However, the distinction between the two groups has caused bad feelings in the past – best epitomised by 'them and us' attitudes of one group to another. For this reason and in an attempt to improve labour morale many progressive firms (encouraged by the Government) have given staff status and its associated benefits (pension schemes, better sickness and holiday arrangements) to all staff.

Wages and salary policy is intimately linked with motivation. The assumption of the earlier management writers, for example Taylor and Gilbreth, was that people were essentially passive, if not negative in their attitudes to work. The results of this assumption were that their output could be increased by properly designed system of incentive payments. Since that time other writers, for example Herzberg and Maslow, have emphasised that money, although important in encouraging workers to greater effort, is only one factor in the 'motivation mix'. Other factors include:

- *Security of employment* – many of the restrictive labour practices seen in British industry have their roots in the fear of unemployment.
- *Comparative income* – the absolute level of income earned is often less important than how it compares with that received by workers in similar occupations. Consider how jealously wage differentials are guarded!
- *Status* – where an occupation is valued highly by other workers, management, and society generally, entrants will be attracted even if financial rewards are not great.
- *Group acceptance* – a person is a 'social' animal working within a group, and being accepted by that group is highly important. Individuals may sublimate their own interests to obtain group acceptance.

375

The degree of job satisfaction is not only affected by the factors mentioned above, there are many others. For example the fact that the work is interesting and challenging, the knowledge that there are promotion opportunities and a sense of achievement. The recognition of these factors affecting motivation has led to a consideration of other techniques of motivating employees. The problem faced by employers is that because people's physiological and emotional make-ups differ the factors that motivate them also differ. Some employees will emphasise the need for social relations, others status, security of employment, and so on. Some will obviously emphasise the importance of money while the vast majority would place it high on the list. In the absence of other universal motivating factors money still remains the most obvious if not the most effective factor in the motivation mix.

But exactly how much money should we pay the secretary, the accountant, the production worker, or their supervisor? In practice, the remuneration reflects both external and internal considerations. External considerations are those items affecting the level of remuneration which are outside the control of the organisation. For example a nationally negotiated wage settlement, the rates paid by competitors for similar skills, the level of unemployment in the area, or the employees' opportunities of obtaining another job. The primary internal consideration is to devise a system of payments which reflects the value of the job to the organisation. An important secondary consideration is to see that the wages/salary structure accords with the employees' views of fairness and justice. The method used is job evaluation.

For job evaluation to be undertaken information has to be available on the precise content of each job. In many cases such information is already available in the form of a job description – if not it is obtained in the manner described previously. The job description is then considered by a panel of trained evaluators who consider each element of the job in turn and allocate a numerical value to it according to its complexity. To help them in their task they may have available a senior member of staff from the department whose jobs are under consideration. Once evaluation has been completed the values of all the different elements are summed, and our secretary, accountant, production worker, or supervisor, and indeed all other workers will find themselves allocated into certain salary bands.

Although the numerical value on which the salary grading is based gives a semblance of objectivity, job evaluation is not a particularly scientific or objective way of calculating wages and salaries. Factors which are thought important and therefore emphasised by management may be entirely different from those considered important by the employee. Moreover, employees are apt to forget that it is the job and not themselves that are being evaluated. For these reasons it is important that trade unions or other worker representatives are involved throughout the process.

The personnel department not only has to consider what it is going to pay each worker, decisions also have to be taken on how to pay the worker. We will consider three major remuneration systems – flat rate, incentive, and measured day-work – in turn.

Flat-rate schemes. This provides for a basic wage to be paid where a previously agreed amount of time has been worked – hourly, daily, per week, or month. Beyond this period overtime, often at an enhanced rate, may be paid. Higher-paid salary workers may sometimes receive time off work instead of overtime pay. In its purest form flat rates are extremely easy to administer and result in a minimum of worker misunderstanding.

This system is often adopted where remuneration cannot be related to output, perhaps because the employee cannot control the pace of work (e.g. maintenance man, typists, telephonists) or maybe because of the unwelcome side-effects of payment by results schemes (consider the effect of paying policemen by results!). Flat-rate payments are said to be an act of trust on the part of the employer in that they expect a 'fair day's work for a fair day s pay'. However, in an effort to see that trust is not relied upon too much, supervisors, often with certain sanctions at their disposal, allocate and control the work of the employee.

Flat rates are often modified by an employer to provide some form of incentive for the employee – to work harder or to remain with the organisation. For manual workers bonuses may be awarded for good time-keeping and long service; similarly, salaried workers may benefit from merit awards (where the worker's effort is assessed as above average by the employer) or age/experience-related pay scales. All workers may benefit from other indirect incentives such as profit-sharing or issues of shares.

Incentive schemes. Such schemes are also known as payment by results or piece-work (arising from the days when the worker received so much per piece or product produced). The logic behind these schemes is that workers should be rewarded for individual effort and that if incentives are high enough it will encourage them to work harder. Normally such schemes work by establishing an output norm (let us say 75 units of production per hour) for the average conscientious worker without extra financial incentive. Basic wages are set at this level and should the worker produce more than 75 units per hour then he is rewarded by bonus payments. If, say, he say, 100 units per hour are produced the wage may be up to one-third higher than the basic wage. The advantages of incentive schemes are:

1. If well designed it will result in an increase in productivity.
2. The work study undertaken prior to the introduction of the in-

centive scheme may itself yield savings in the more efficient use of labour and equipment.

3. The more intensive use of plant and equipment results in a lower fixed cost per unit of output.

4. Supervision costs are reduced as the employee is more motivated to undertaking hard work.

The *disadvantages* associated with such schemes are:

1. Schemes are often complicated and easily misunderstood by workers.

2. They are often the cause of discontent among different groups of worker's because:

- workers may believe another base rate is easier to achieve than their own;
- indirect workers upon whom the direct production workers rely do not benefit from the incentive scheme;
- production workers may very well end up earning more than their supervisors and other salaried staff.

3. Unofficial agreements are often made by the men to restrict output regardless of the incentive so as to reduce the likelihood of unemployment, group disunity, and tighter rates.

4. Workers, over a period of time, will come to rely on the incentive as part of their basic earnings – even though the opportunity for earning the bonus may not always be available.

5. Workers may tend to disregard quality and their own safety in an effort to earn the incentive payment.

To overcome some of the criticisms of individual incentive schemes some organisations have introduced group incentives. Again the principle is that in establishing a base in which bonus payments are made the organisation and the workers can benefit from higher productivity. The group involved can be small or large, it may even cover the whole organisation. The bonus paid to the group may be split in proportion to basic pay, or alteratively, equally. Such schemes are advantageous because:

1. People naturally like working in groups.

2. It fosters a team spirit.

3. It includes indirect workers.

4. In their keenness to prevent bottlenecks and to achieve the incentive employees are more likely to adopt a flexible attitude to moving jobs.

Group incentive schemes do, however, also have problems. In particular the size of the group if too large may prevent the necessary team spirit developing, nor may individual workers see how their efforts contribute towards the attaining of the bonus. The development of team spirit may also be hampered where labour turnover is high or where there are wide variations of ability within the group.

Measured day-work. This system seeks to bridge the gap between flat-rate and incentive schemes. The employer and employee agree a level of output, which the employee believes (and past experience shows) can be maintained. The employer agrees to pay the employee for this level of output regardless of short-term variations in productivity, while the employee is on trust to achieve the target agreed.

The *advantages* of measured day-work are:
1. Workers are able to predict and budget upon a stable wage.
2. The employer is able to predict productivity more accurately and therefore output and cost per unit.
3. As employers are employing at the 'high rate' regardless of the level of output they will strive to reduce delays/breakdowns to a minimum, thus enhancing the efficiency of the production system.

Disadvantages of measured day-work are:
1. Differentials in wages are highlighted – which may cause industrial unrest.
2. How to control/discipline those who consistently fail to achieve their previously agreed target.

Education and training

Traditionally the attitude of the Government to education and training of workers has been that this was the responsibility of industry and commerce. While large firms have both the facilities and expertise to train their employees, the sole contribution of many small- and medium-sized organisations was to encourage the new worker to learn the job by watching the more experienced worker.

This haphazard nature of training was sufficient while the level and differentiation of skills was low, but during the twentieth century an increasing imbalance between the demand for trained labour and its supply has been noted. These bottlenecks in labour supply have prevented the UK industry from adopting new and improved technology, and expanding production in times of rising demand (thereby causing inflation and greater imports). It has also produced an élite of industrial workers who are able to demand extremely high wages, and resentment among those workers whose skilled jobs did not yield the same level of pay.

By the 1960s it had become apparent that Government intervention was necessary and to ensure an adequate supply of properly trained *manpower* and an improvement in the quality and efficiency of training programmes. Since then Government has played an important if changing role in industrial training.

While the interest of the Government in industrial training was on the effects of manpower shortages on the working of the economy, industry's interest arose because labour had become both scarce and expensive. Training had the primary objective of ensuring that employees had the skills and knowledge necessary to carry out their duties.

But training also had the advantage of:

- improving production and quality/reducing mistakes
- reducing customer complaints
- reducing labour turnover
- acting as a motivator
- increasing flexibility of work force
- improving its reputation among potential employees

An effective system of training will cover the whole organisation from top to bottom. While inefficiencies in labour skills on the shop floor may be more obvious, the lack of necessary skills on the part of supervisors, clerical, executive, and managerial staff will have exactly the same adverse impact on the organisation. Moreover, there is no reason for assuming that there is a lesser need for training at these levels. The following approach to training (see Fig. 19.4) can be applied to any level of the organisation.

Initial identification of a training need lies very much in the hands of departmental managers and supervisors who will inform the personnel department. Their first task is to establish that the need for

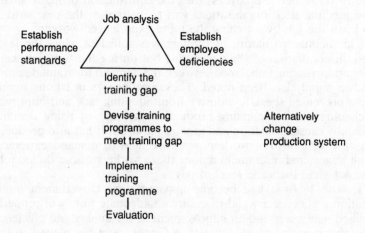

19.4 Determining the training programme

training does actually exist. This falls naturally into two parts: first through job analysis identifying the performance requirements of that position (this may already be available having been prepared for recruitment and selection), and secondly establishing the existing skills, knowledge, and aptitudes and those which new employees bring to the job. The comparison of these two elements will then reveal the nature and extent of the training gap.

The presumption normally made, having identified the training gap, is that a training programme should be devised to remedy the deficiency. This may well be so, but does not automatically follow. Thus redeployment of existing workers and recruitment of new employees with the right qualities could be considered. It is also open to the organisation to adapt the system (equipment and procedures) to suit the worker. Which of these methods is adopted will depend upon cost and feasibility.

The organisation may, having considered the options, decide to embark upon a training programme. The first stage in designing the training programme will be to identify precisely those skills and aptitudes that need to be developed. Decisions must also be taken on whom to train and whether that training is best conducted on or off the job. The training scheme is then drawn up and implemented. Finally the success of the training programme has to be evaluated. This may be done by checking to see whether the required performance standards are now being achieved. Alternatively the benefits accruing from the training in terms of higher performance standards may be compared with the cost of providing that training. If the benefits outweigh the costs the training programme has been to the advantage of the organisation.

Forms of training

Induction The cost recruitment is high and research shows that a high proportion of new employees leave within six months of joining the organisation. The reason for this high turnover is thought to be the difficulty the new entrant (especially the school-leaver) faces in understanding and adapting to the organisation, and more specifically their job within the organisation.

Most entrants will know little about the organisation which they have joined – it is all new (and very confusing). Induction training therefore tries to provide some of the background information, for example the company's history, its objectives, the organisation structure, the products made, and the markets supplied. Tours of the factory and offices may highlight the points made.

Information on the job to be undertaken clearly begins with a tour of the department and introduction to those members with whom the new employee will have to work or to whom they are responsible. It is also worth while explaining the work of the department and how the employee's efforts contribute to this. Departmental rules will also be explained. With manual jobs induction will also cover familiarisation with any machinery which has to be used.

Obviously the amount of information which the new employee has to absorb is vast. Indeed, trying to tell the employee everything about the organisation may have precisely the opposite effect to that intended. The secret of successful induction training lies in identifying what is essential for the employee to know and presenting it to them in a way that can be understood.

Apprentice Traditionally, apprentices have picked up their skills in a haphazard fashion through watching the time-served craftsman. There was little attempt at systematic training. In most trades now, though, the situation has changed, with a blend of academic and practical training designed to ensure that skills are learned. Systematic training has also had the effect of reducing the length of the apprenticeship in many cases.

Operative Training of operatives is usually carried out by the organisation itself. In small organisations the training will normally be 'on the job', that is, undertaken in the normal work situation using the everyday tools and equipment. Such training is less costly than 'off the job'; it has the advantage of the worker becoming familiar with both the environment and the tools normally used. Large firms often have training centres away from the place of normal work. The training conducted in these centres is termed 'off the job' – as would training in a technical or higher education institution. It has the advantage of using specialist instructors, training in correct methods, away from the noise and pressure of the work environment.

Supervisor All too often the person appointed supervisor has the necessary technical skills, but has not developed the interpersonal skills needed to motivate and control subordinates, and additionally to deal with senior management. Before undertaking any form of training though, it is important to identify their training needs in an attempt to adapt training to their particular requirements. Larger firms may very well run courses internally. However, the majority of firms are content to leave this training to the local technical or higher education institution where the supervisors can study for the National Examination Board's Certificate in Supervisory Studies.

Management development This will normally be provided by means of courses run in the management departments of polytechnics and colleges of technology. There are many courses run, all of which lead to widely recognised qualifications. In some cases though a lack of discussion between the college, student, and employer results in courses being studied which meet neither the needs of the student nor the employer. Once more an analysis of training needs is vital to the success of the training programme.

As much of the training carried out within the organisation is 'on the job' and therefore under the control of the individual manager, it is difficult to divorce that line manager from some responsibility for training within their own department. However, the ultimate responsibility for training within the organisation rests with the personal department. Larger firms often appoint a training officer or manager having special responsibility for all aspects of training within the organisation. Duties would normally include:

1. Developing in conjunction with senior management an agreed training policy.
2. Consulting with all departments within the organisation and advising on training needs.
3. Developing and implementing in-company training programmes.
4. Liaising with colleges and polytechnics in the development of training programmes.
5. Advising on external courses available at colleges and polytechnics.
6. Maintaining training records.

Industrial relations

There are many potential sources of conflict between workers and employers, for example workers wish to sell labour at the highest price possible while the employer wishes to engage labour at the least possible cost. Other sources of conflict include the relativities that exist between different groups of workers, which groups of workers should be allowed to undertake certain duties, the nature of the work itself, the working conditions, and more generally, how much control workers should have over decisions which affect their working lives – for example the closure of factories or the introduction of new technology.

Yet at the same time both parties appreciate that it is in their common interest to work together in harmony. Without labour business cannot provide the products or services on which it relies for survival, and labour relies on business to provide employment and thereby the means to satisfy their demands for goods and services. Industrial relations is concerned with the way these two parties interact. More importantly it is concerned with the means by which disputes are avoided or overcome.

The parties to the industrial relations process are described below.

Trade unions

The Trade Unions and Labour Relations Act of 1974 defines a trade union as an 'organisation of workers whose principal purpose is the regulation of relations between workers and employers or employers associations'. There are over 300 trade unions representing in excess of 10 million working people in the UK. Traditionally, union members have held manual occupations; however, we have recently seen the rise of professional (or 'white-colour') unions as these groups too have seen the benefits of organised labour, as itemised below.

- improvements in remuneration, working conditions and status
- protection against unfair practices and arbitrary management decisions
- security of employment and income
- involvement in the decision-making process at organisational and national levels
- The ability to take joint action

To these the TUC (in its evidence to the Royal Commission on Trade Unions and Employer's Associations [1966]) have added

- full employment and national prosperity
- improved social security
- fair shares in national income and wealth
- a voice in government
- improved public and social services
- public control and planning of industry.

More often than not the attitude of management to trade unions has been hostile. Management has seen trade unions as challenging and circumscribing its right to manage. Yet there are benefits which the organisation itself obtains from the organisation of labour. For example where management actions are likely to be questioned and have to be justified, decisions are taken more carefully. In particular, management is forced to consider the effect of its actions upon the workforce and its motivation. Moreover the trade union is the means by which information can be passed to the workforce, changes in wages and working conditions may be negotiated, and disputes settled.

Trade unions tend to be classified in four ways, though the classification does tend to be somewhat arbitrary with few unions precisely fitting their classification.

In 1979 trade union membership was nearly 13.5 million – over 50 per cent of the total work force. By 1988 that had slipped to just over 10.5 million members and 40 per cent of the work force. There are many reasons for the decline. They include:

- unions have suffered heavy losses in their stronghold – manufacturing

- unions have failed to attract new members in the fast growing service industries.

- women now form a larger proportion of the work force but, traditionally, are less likely to be union members

- the growth in part-time employment

- the ability of non union members to obtain the benefits of union collective bargaining

- the growth of legislation designed to curb union influence.

The total number of trade unions is also decreasing. In 1973 there were 519 unions, in 1988 – 330. The decline is due to the process of mergers and amalgamations reflecting the changed industrial structure. In 1986 there were 30 local and craft unions transferring to national unions.

Even though the number of unions is falling due to amalgamation, over 50 per cent of all unions have less than 1,000 members. That should be compared with the 31 unions with over 50,000 members encompassing 86 per cent of all union members.

Craft unions These unions have as the basis for classification a common skill which may be used in many industries. Thus the Amalgamated Union of Engineering Workers (AUEW) seeks to represent all engineering workers wherever they are employed and whatever their engineering skills. Many of the craft unions have their origins among the medieval trade guilds, but most have changed considerably by either amalgamating with related crafts, or accepting workers with lower levels of skills. Consider again the case of the AUEW which started life as the Amalgamated Society of Engineers but now includes among its membership foundry and construction workers, draughtsmen, and labourers. Such unions tend to border upon our second category, that of industrial unions, and thereby provide a sharp reminder of the difficulties of classification!

Industrial unions Industrial unions seek to recruit members within a specific industry whatever their grade or occupation. The National Union of Mineworkers (NUM) and National Union of Railwaymen

(NUR) are normally cited as examples. Neither have been completely successful in their aims. For example the National Associations of Colliery Overmen, Deputies, and Shot Firers (NACODS) and the Associated Society of Locomotive Engineers and Firemen (ASLEF) recruit substantial numbers in their respective industries. Although this form of union is not popular in Britain many unions in the United States and West Germany are organised in this way.

Occupational unions As is implied by their name occupational unions are those who seek to recruit members who have a similar occupation often, but not always, in the same industry. The National Association of Local Government Officers (NALGO), for example, has members not only in local authorities but also in the nationalised industries, and the health and water services. The National Union of Teachers (NUT), the Union of Shop, Distributive and Allied Workers (USDAW), and the National Union of Public Employees (NUPE) are also often cited as examples of occupational unions.

Most white-collar unions can be included in this classification. A white-collar union can be defined as a union with its members working in clerical, professional, or administrative occupations. While trade-union membership generally has been declining in the last decade the growth of white-collar unionism has been dramatic. White-collar workers now account for approximately half of all union members. There are several reasons for this growth. Previously white-collar workers had believed themselves to be immune from the effects of a recession. Recent attempts to cut back public expenditure in the UK have increased the feeling of insecurity among these groups. White-collar workers have also felt that their financial position has been eroded compared with other groups of workers. They have looked to unionisation and the growth of collective bargaining to remedy the situation. With the growth of large and often impersonal organisations white-collar workers have experienced a loss of status and control over their working conditions. Through representation they seek once more to be involved in that decision-making process.

General unions These unions seek to unionise all other groups of workers which are not covered by the above categories. Traditionally, these unions are associated with unskilled workers in industries where other groups of workers are already unionised, or those industries which either because of recruitment difficulties or newness have no history of unionisation. However, unions such as the Transport and General Workers Union now organise both skilled and unskilled labour.

The Trades Union Congress

The TUC was formed in Manchester in 1868 with the aim of representing the interests of trade unions and their members. Today most major unions are affiliated to it and it can claim to represent over 10 million workers. It is an extremely powerful organisation. In the period 1971–74 it organised and led the very effective opposition to the Industrial Relations Act – opposition which was partly responsible for the fall of the Heath Government.

The TUC also enjoys considerable power through its relationship with the Government of the day. It is consulted on major issues, not only those relating to trade unions or industrial relations. For example the TUC makes representations to the Prime Minister or the Chancellor of the Exchequer each year prior to the budget. Members of the TUC also serve on most government committees or commissions.

A major function of the TUC is to represent the interests of its 10 million members. At its annual conference in September many resolutions are passed and these together form the economic and social policy promoted by the TUC General Council between congresses.

Other aims of the TUC include:

- To give aid and assistance to workers in other parts of the world in their attempt to raise living standards.

- To give aid and assistance to other organisations with similar objectives to themselves (e.g. the Labour Party or unions in other countries).

- To help in settling disputes between (a) trade unions and employers (b) trade unions and their members; (c) trade unions themselves.

While the aims of the TUC are remarkably wide its power over the affiliated unions is limited. Each remains completely sovereign and implements or conforms to TUC resolutions as it thinks fit.

In very exceptional circumstances the General Council may exclude a union from membership of the TUC, but this power is rarely used.

Employers' associations

The national federations have a number of functions in the industrial relations sphere, they:

- Ensure collective action on the part of their members with trade unions.

- Negotiate with trade unions at a national level making: (a) procedural arrangements – e.g. the procedure for negotiating a wage change or settling a dispute; and (b) substantive agreements on wages, working conditions, holidays, etc.

- Provide information on industrial relations to their members.

However, the Donovan Commission on Trade Unions and Employers' Associations indicated that their functions were considerably wider. Some of the other more important functions identified were:

- Provision of trade and technical information to members.

- Representing and negotiating with Government and other bodies on behalf of their members.

- Advice on and development of training schemes.

- Provision of management consultancy services.

The concerted action of workers through trade unions brought a response from business in the form of employer associations, the employers' counterpart to the TUC being the Confederation of British Industry (CBI). Its objects are:

- To represent industry's views and influence opinion on economic, political, social, and technical matters.

- To encourage efficiency in British industry – where necessary providing services to that end.

However, unlike the TUC (and the CBI's counterparts in other countries) it has no specific function in the field of industrial relations other than to draw up a general manpower policy to be put in effect by its members.

Towards better industrial relations

The Trade Union and Labour Relations Act 1974 lays down a code of practice for maintaining good industrial relations. The code lays the primary responsibilities for good industrial relations on management. This involves establishing a policy for industrial relations covering:

- The relationship between the organisation and trade unions. For example the organisation's attitude to unionisation, or what unions the organisation will recognise for bargaining purposes.

- The establishment of collective bargaining and dispute-handling procedures.

- The establishment of procedures for communication and consultation with the workforce including employee representation.

A consideration of the first point, that is, the relationship between the organisation and the trade union, is outside the scope of this book. Let us give our attention instead to the institutions designed to maintain and better industrial relations.

Collective bargaining

The fact that approximately three-quarters of the workers in the UK have their wages and working conditions established by some form of joint negotiation illustrates the importance of collective bargaining. Collective bargaining can be defined as the process by which workers through their trade union representatives negotiate changes in pay and working conditions with their employer or their employer's representative.

The argument entered into by the parties falls broadly into two parts. Procedural clauses cover the methods by which the parties conduct their relationship. They will cover:

1 The composition and character of the negotiating body.
2 The matters which can be considered by the negotiating body.
3 The means by which:
   - bargaining is carried out;
   - disputes are settled;
   - information is passed to trade union members or their representatives.

Industrial action

We often hear of negotiations between employers and employees breaking down and the threat of industrial action by employees. Although most people immediately think of the strike there are many other forms of bargaining sanction, and the strike is more often a sanction of last rather than first resort. Other forms of action include: work to rules; overtime bans; go slows and general lack of co-operation with the employers. These other forms of industrial action impose costs on the employer while being relatively cheap to the union and its members.

A breakdown in industrial relations may also manifest itself through low morale, poor quality work, absenteeism and high labour turnover.

Employers are also capable of imposing sanctions, for example the refusal to negotiate, lock-outs and ultimately dismissal.

Substantive clauses refer to the terms of employment established through the bargaining procedures outlined above. The items detailed below are by no means a complete list but are used to illustrate the scope of the substantive negotiations:

- Wages/salaries, incentive payments, overtime pay.
- Working hours, shift working, place of work.
- Holidays, layoff and redundancy provisions, pensions.

The precise nature of the agreement covering each industry, firm, or group of workers will have evolved over a number of years. Normally the agreement is reviewed annually, but it is unlikely that the parties will wish to renegotiate the whole agreement. In practice the annual negotiations will revolve around remuneration, working hours, and holidays with other clauses being negotiated as and when the parties feel necessary. Moreover the freedom of the parties to negotiate may be curtailed by legislation. Thus for most of the period between 1964 and 1979 free collective bargaining over wages was limited by government-backed policies of pay restraint.

Within the UK collective bargaining takes place at two different levels. First as a product of the inter-war years, we have a system of bargaining and negotiating procedure at national levels. At the time such national agreements were beneficial to both parties, providing workers with minimum wages and working conditions and the advantage of protecting employers from price competition arising out of other employers paying lower wages.

While the system of national agreements continued after 1945, the advent of full employment created a situation where employers found difficulty in obtaining the labour they needed. The national agreement over wages and conditions of work rapidly became a minimum which could be improved upon by employees and their representatives in bargaining at a local level. Today many groups of workers still have their terms of employment determined nationally; however, in both the manufacturing and engineering industry local bargaining is now more important.

Not all workers have terms of employment determined by collective bargaining. Over 2.7 million workers are in fact covered by Wages Councils. These statutory bodies exist because the growth of unionism has been insufficient to protect the interests of the workers. Wages councils exist in the hairdressing, catering, and retail sectors where: (a) the large numbers working in small independent establishments; and (b) the large proportion of women (who tend to be more apathetic towards trade unionism) make unionism difficult to establish.

Wages Councils consist of equal numbers of worker and employer representatives together with three independent members (one of whom is elected chairperson). The proposals of the Wages Council on wages and all other conditions of employment become the subject of a wages regulation order and thereafter are the minimum which may be applied in that industry. To ensure that the new terms of employment are enforced in all establishments affected by the order employers are required to display the proposals so workers may read them. Additionally the Wages Inspectorate has the power to check on any firm's records and may prosecute where the proposals have not been affected.

Under the Employment Protection Act 1975 a procedure exists whereby a statutory determination of terms of employment may be phased out in favour of free collective bargaining. Initially, a Joint Industrial Council is formed in place of the Wages Council. The structure and the function of the Joint Industrial Council is precisely the same as that of the Wages Council with one exception – there are no independent members. Once the Secretary of State for Employment believes that free collective bargaining is working properly then the Joint Industrial Council may be abolished.

Terms and Conditions of Employment

The law relating to employment is complex. During the past 20 years many aspects of it have been affected by legislation. This legislation has been designed to give employees a floor of rights and to some extent remedy the imbalance of bargaining power between the two parties. Indeed, even before the contract of employment has been entered into, the prospective employee has rights provided by legislation. These include:

- the right not to be discriminated against on the grounds of sex or race

- the right of the ex-offender not to disclose past convictions after a rehabilitation period if no further offences are committed. The period of rehabilitation varies according to age and the seriousness of the offence, for example:

Sentence	Rehabilitation period
probation	1 year
fine	5 years
under 6 months imprisonment	7 years
under 18 months imprisonment	10 years

these periods are halved for juvenile offenders. There are also many exceptions. For example you have to disclose your conviction if you are applying for a job as a doctor, policeman, social worker or teacher.

- employers with more than 20 workers must, normally, take on a proportion of disabled workers – three per cent of the total work force. Certain occupations – lift and car park attendants – are reserved for the disabled. Where employers have less than their statutory quota of disabled workers they are not allowed to fill a vacancy without exemption.

When an offer of employment has been made and accepted a contract of employment is created. This is really a statement about the conditions on which the parties agreed to contract. In practice, the contract of employment falls naturally into two parts, first those terms and conditions which are expressly agreed and second those that are implied by law. We will look at each in turn.

Express Terms. Within 13 weeks of starting employment an employee should receive a written contract of employment from their employer. This embodies the terms which the parties expressly agreed to. It includes, job title, pay, pay interval, pension rights, working hours, holidays, sickness/injury provisions disciplinary provisions and notice – far more than could ever be agreed to in an interview! In fact there are two sources of express terms other than what has been agreed in the interview. First, there are those terms which are included because of a collective agreement, and secondly, those arising from company rules (these are often, though not necessarily, set out in an employee handbook).

We often find that the contract of employment does not refer to all these terms directly but simply points our way to the document where these terms can be found. Nevertheless, they are part of the contract. For example, in *Dalton v Burtons Gold Medal Biscuits Ltd* (1974) an employee handbook referred to in the contract of employment made the offence of falsifying a time card punishable by instant dismissal. It was held that Dalton, who had falsified a fellow employee's time card was validly dismissed.

Implied Terms. For many years the express terms embodied in a contract of employment have been supplemented by the Common Law placing duties on both employer and employee. More recently legislation has been passed, in some cases embodying common law rules, but in many others introducing entirely new obligations.

Common law obligations on the employer include:

To pay wages when they fall due. Where an employer fails to pay wages due, an employee can, in most circumstances, treat the contract as at an end. You are also entitled to be paid in cash if you wish.

To make only authorised deductions. Certain deductions e.g. tax and National Insurance Contributions are required by law, but fines and other deductions from pay for bad workmanship, stock deficiencies or misconduct are not allowed without the written consent of the employee.

To provide work. Although a judge in 1940 said 'Provided I pay my cook her wages regularly she cannot complain if I choose to take all or any of my meals out,' there are situations where employees may complain if work is not provided. For example, those who are paid on commission or by results.

To take reasonable care for the safety of employees. This has been almost entirely overtaken by Health and Safety at Work legislation. However, at common law the employer must provide a safe system of work including plant, tools and materials, trained personnel and adequate supervision.

To obey the law. Basically am employer must comply with the provisions of common law or statute and not require any employee to undertake an unlawful act.

The common law obligations of the employee include:

The duty of obedience. An employer has the right to expect you to undertake lawful and reasonable orders. Thus when a gardener refused to put some plants in, saying he 'couldn't care less about [his employer's] bloody garden or sodding greenhouse' it was held his dismisisal was justified. Equally, conduct may be tantamount to a rejection of this duty. In 1972 when rail unions disrupted the railways simply by working to the rule book Lord Denning said that it was a breach of duty to construe them unreasonably.

To take reasonable care in doing their job. Though we might add – not so much care as to render their doing the job futile – as in the railway unions case! Thus where a sales rep left their employer's property in their car overnight and that property was stolen they were liable to their employer for the loss. Where an employee claims some special skill (e.g. knowledge of accountancy, first aid, engineering principles) a higher standard of care will be demanded.

The duty of good faith. Employees should act with honesty and integrity and avoid situations where their own and their employer's interests might conflict. For example, the taking of bribes in return for contracts, setting up a competing business or revealing confidential information.

In addition to these Common Law rules Parliament has seen fit to intervene in almost every area of employment law to provide employee rights which would have been unthought of 40 years ago. In all cases the legislation is complex and open to change through the courts and industrial tribunals. The more important legislation includes:

The right not to be discriminated against on the grounds of race. Direct discrimination occurs where a person is treated less favourably for training, promotion, transfer or other benefit than another person on the grounds of race. Indirect discrimination arises where a condition or requirement which appears to apply equally to all, but actually has the effect of preventing the majority of one racial group being able to comply. Lawful discrimination is allowed where there is a 'genuine occupational qualification' (GOQ) for the job. Thus in acting a person of a particular racial group may be required. The same principle applies to modelling or for work in, say, a Chinese restaurant.

The right not to be discriminated against on the grounds of sex. The law again uses the idea of direct and indirect discrimination. Thus it was a case of direct discrimination where a lady was not allowed to join a male decorating team because of 'problems in the past'. Indirect discrimination has extended from the jocular 'bar staff who must wear skirts' to the more subtle making part-time workers redundant before full time workers where most part-timers are women. However, there may be circumstances where the sex of a person is a genuine occupational qualification for example in acting, entertainment for decency or privacy.

The right not to be unfairly dismissed. To claim damages for unfair dismissal or reinstatement a person must have been employed for over two years with the same employer and prove that the grounds for dismissal were unfair. Fair dismissal will occur where an employee

- is unable to carry out their job properly, for example the airline pilot who made two attempts to land a passenger aircraft safely, the second of which demolished the nose wheel structure

- is unable to achieve the level required on a training scheme

- acts improperly e.g. dishonesty or drunkenness

- is genuinely redundant, though dismissal may still be unfair if it was not reasonable to select this employee

- is legally disallowed from working e.g. travelling sales rep losing their driving licence

- has other substantial reason e.g. damage or disruption to business. Thus an employee's marriage links with a rival firm, or refusing to work new shifts may be sufficient.

An employee will be unfairly dismissed if the employer's action does not fall into one of the above categories, or where even though the dismissal was fair the manner in which it was carried out was unreasonable (e.g. no opportunity to give their side of the case or no right of appeal).

The right to redundancy pay. To claim redundancy pay an employee must be over 20 years of age and have had two years' service with the employer from whom they are claiming. A redundancy situation occurs where

- the employer has ceased/intends to cease that business for which the employee was engaged

- where the employee has ceased/intends to cease business where the worker was employed

- where the demand for that business for which the employee was engaged has diminished/is expected to diminish.

The right to equal pay. In fact the legislation requires equal pay and conditions for equal work or work of equal value. Whether or not work is of equal value can be established by a job evaluation exercise. Although the Equal Pay Act applies to both sexes it was intended to ensure women were not paid less than men where the work undertaken was similar.

Joint consultation

Often termed 'worker participation in management', this idea of consulting workers and allowing them to participate in the decision-making process within the firm is not new. It dates back to the Whitley Committee of 1916 which suggested that, quite apart from the negotiating arrangements which should be established at a national level, works councils or joint production committees should be created. These would provide a platform for the discussion of those many other issues which are of common interest to the employee and employer alike. Today joint consultation is said to provide a two-way communication channel allowing:
1. Management to inform employees of the firm's progress, plans, and policy.
2. Workers to have a say in the decisions that affect them.
3. Suggestions to be made by workers for increasing productivity.
4. The development of a greater degree of understanding between the two parties.

The degree of consultation which takes place will vary enormously between countries and organisations. Thus in West Germany the law requires:
1. Every company with over five employees to have a works council set up to resolve disputes within the firm.
2. Every company with over 100 employees to have an economic committee which meets to discuss any matters which may adversely affect worker interests, for example, mergers, changes in production, technology, or company structure. Works councils have the responsibility of resolving conflicts occurring in the economic committee.
3. Where a company employs over 2,000 workers board-level representation for workers is provided for by the creation of a two-tier board. An upper supervisory board comprises of worker and share-

holder representatives (five each) and an independent member agreed by both. The lower board is made of management representatives.

In Britain consultation is by no means so far advanced. Experiments with worker directors have been tried – for example on the group boards of the British Steel Corporation. Moreover, worker co-operatives illustrate a very complete form of worker participation in management. But when the Bullock Committee of Enquiry on Industrial Democracy (1978) proposed a system of board representation for workers very similar to that in West Germany, the adverse reaction from both management and unions resulted in the proposals being quietly shelved by the Government.

More success has been achieved in Britain through 'semi-autonomous work groups' which allow a large element of discretion and employee responsibility on items such as:

- Allocation of tasks between group members.

- Ordering of materials.

- Supervision.

- Quality control.

Those who support joint consultation argue that:
1. It makes greater use of the large body of knowledge and skills existing among the organisation's workers.
2. The more people involved in the decision-making process the better the decision.
3. It generates greater worker interest in the organisation.
4. It improves industrial relations.
5. It is morally right that workers should be involved because they have contributed to the prosperity of the organisation and, moreover, it is their livelihood.

Joint consultation has its fair share of problems. There are for example many management decisions where the employee will have little or nothing to contribute. Joint consultation is time-consuming (some would even say time-wasting). Many employees show little interest in participating, while trade-unionists are worried that their bargaining position with the organisation may be eroded by non-union representatives negotiating matters which they believe to be the proper subject of collective bargaining.

The role of the State in industrial relations

Traditionally the State has played a passive role in industrial relations, believing that free collective bargaining is the best means to

settle disputes. Increasingly though, the Government has seen fit to intervene by:
1.   Legislation to protect certain groups of people – handicapped, women, ethnic minorities, low paid.
2.   Legislation providing ground rules for the conduct of industrial relations – often restrictive upon trade-union activity.
3.   Providing institutions to arbitrate between the conflicting interests where the dispute becomes intractable:

- The Advisory Conciliation and Arbitration Service (ACAS), which is an independent but state-financed service. There are three aspects to its work: (i) conciliation – bringing the disputants together; (ii) mediation – providing grounds for settlement; (iii) arbitration – help in providing an independent mediator to settle the dispute.

- The Central Arbitration Committee set up under the Employment Protection Act (1975). It deals with trade-union recognition problems, disclosure of information to trade unions for bargaining purposes, equal pay, and references on arbitration from ACAS.

- Industrial tribunals. These deal with a majority of cases arising out of employment legislation. The cases relate to unfair dismissal, discrimination, equal pay, safety. Although the decisions of the tribunals are legally binding, unlike a normal court their proceedings are less formal and legal representation is not required.

Welfare, health, and safety

Dangers are bound to exist in an industrial environment and each year many workers are either killed or maimed in accidents at work. Today greater emphasis than ever before is being placed on an employee's health and safety in an attempt to reduce these injuries. A majority of workers in the UK are covered by either the Factories Act (1961) or the Offices, Shops, and Railway Premises Act (1963). These Acts lay down for the workers covered:
1.   Minimum working conditions, e.g. lighting, heating, ventilation, sanitation, and overcrowding.
2.   Safety requirements, e.g. the guarding of machinery with moving parts, maximum loads for lifting machinery, fire precautions.
3.   Welfare provisions, e.g. washing and cloakroom facilities, first-aid facilities.
4.   Women and young persons (under 18), e.g. limitations on night and shift work, overtime and maximum hours worked.
The Health and Safety at Work Act (1974) further provides that:

1.   The organisation must have a written safety policy indicating not only what that policy is but how it is to be implemented, e.g. training and supervision on health and safety matters.

2.   Employers must not charge for safety equipment or clothing.

3.   Safety representatives forming a committee are to be appointed by trade unions. They are entitled to demand information on accidents, to inspect new premises, and make recommendations to the employer on safety matters.

Legislation relating to health and safety is enforced by the Employment Medical Advisory Service and the Factory Inspectorate who are entitled to enter and inspect any premises. Where breaches occur an inspector is entitled to issue an Improvement or Prohibition Notice. An Improvement Notice requires the offending organisation to remedy the situation within a given time. Alternatively, where the inspector believes the breach imposes a continuous danger upon employees and may result in injury, a Prohibition Notice forbidding that activity (until the breach is remedied) may be issued.

Sanctions may also be imposed on persons responsible for the breach of Health and Safety Regulations. Crown Courts may fine such persons up to £1,000 in addition to a maximum of two years' imprisonment.

Breaches of Health and Safety Regulations, however, have far wider consequences than outlined above. Industrial injuries may result in the dislocation of work schedules, legal claims for compensation, and bad publicity. For these reasons many firms employ a specialist safety officer within the personnel department. His duties will encompass:

1.   Inspecting all parts of the organisation to ensure that all health, safety, and welfare requirements are complied with.

2.   Ensuring that all employees are well versed in safety procedures through lectures, training, and advertisements.

3.   Responsibility for advising on the health and safety aspects of office and factory layout, new machinery, and new working methods.

4.   Maintaining records of all accidents within the organisation, investigating their cause and taking preventive measures.

5.   Liaising with the Health and Safety Inspectorate, fire service, etc. to minimise the likelihood of accidents and/or their severity.

Examination questions

1   A pay system for salaried staff incorporates automatic annual increments but no opportunities for additional payments. The shop floor workers are paid on a piece rate system subject to annual negotiations to determine the rate.

(a) How important do you think money is as a means of motivating workers?

(b) Why do you think these two different systems exist?

(c) Comment upon the appropriateness of each of them as a means of paying the people to whom they apply. *(CAMB)*

2   What organisations are involved in ensuring that there is an adequate supply of trained manpower? Explain:
(a) their role
AND
(b) how the training is undertaken. *(PSC)*

3   Comlon International plc with a head office at 4 West Street, London, is a medium-sized retail company. During the last few years John Smith, the personnel manager, has seen his workload increase greatly. The Board has agreed that a personnel officer should be appointed to assist him.
(a) Draft an advertisement for this position suitable for inclusion in a national newspaper. The advertisement should indicate some examples of the type of work involved and the skills and qualities required, as well as the general terms of employment.
(b) Outline *TWO* LIKELY REASONS WHY John Smith's workload has increased so much. *(PSC)*

4   The managing director of Comlon International plc, a medium-sized retail company, has asked the Personnel Officer to prepare a report on the training of staff with particular reference to:
(a) What benefits might be gained by the company from training.
(b) How and where such training should be implemented.
What would you expect the report to contain? *(PSC 1986)*

5   To what extent have such factors as growing industrial democracy, improved communications and protective legislation changed the role of trade unions in today's business? *(AEB 1987)*

6   Analyse the role of the personnel department in a large organisation. *(AEB 1986)*

7   The managing director of your company has expressed interest in the introduction of a measure of worker participation in the decision making process within the company. As personnel officer prepare a report, using a suitable format, outlining:
  (i)   the advantages and disadvantages of worker participation
  (ii) the varying ways in which such participation may be implemented
  (iii) the problems which might be encountered in establishing a system of worker participation. *(AEB 1985)*

8   Define the term 'free collective bargaining'. Evaluate the advantages and disadvantages of this system to a manufacturing company. *(AEB)*

9   A trade union may be defined as an organisation whose main function is to advance and protect the interests of its members. Identify and discuss the constraints which a trade union may experience in attempting to achieve these objectives. *(AEB)*

10 Discuss the implications for a business enterprise of a decision to remunerate all manual employees on the basis of time rates alone. *(AEB)*

11 The Chief Administrative Officer of a hospital employing 500 domestic and manual staff is concerned at what appears to be a high level of labour turnover among this group of workers. As a member of the administrative staff of the hospital, you have been asked to prepare a report for submission to the Chief administrative Officer under each of

the following headings:
(a) possible causes of labour turnover
(b) costs incurred by the hospital as a result of high labour turnover
(c) recommendations for the reduction of labour turnover.
Under each of the above headings
   (i) list *three* relevant factors
   (ii) provide a *brief* explanation of each factor listed
   (iii) indicate what causes or costs are within the control of the
      hospital. *(AEB)*

12 A proposed reorganisation of production at your factory would result in the redundancy of 400 employees. As personnel officer, prepare a report in suitable form for the Board of Directors indicating, with brief explanations:
   (i) *four* possible effects of redundancy on the company
   (ii) four principles on which the scheme should be based to preserve good industrial relations
   (iii) any Acts of Parliament known to you which contain provisions relating to redundancy. *(AEB)*

13 Explain how job satisfaction in a business may be improved and consider the limitations on achieving greater job satisfaction for all the employees in a factory. *(AEB)*

14 As leader of a Union negotiating team, which has just had an initial pay claim for an 8% increase in wages (3% more than the current inflation rate) rejected by the Board of Directors of a Cross Channel Ferry Line, prepare a discussion document for other members of your team outlining alternative dispute procedures and their likely effectiveness. *(CAMB 1986)*

15 A large firm in your town allows job appointments to be made on the basis of family connections. What benefits and problems do you foresee arising from such a policy?

16 A company has recently moved its traditional site in the centre of a town to a newly opened industrial estate on the outskirts of the town. Following the move there has been a sudden increase in the level of labour turnover.
(a) As personnel manager, write a report to the managing director, using a suitable format to cover the following areas.
   (i) how labour turnover may be calculated.
   (ii) why the company should be concerned about the recent increase in labour turnover.
   (iii) Possible reasons for the increase.
(b) What steps would you, as personnel manager, need to take to establish clearly the nature of the problem? *(AEB 1987)*

17 In what ways might the functions of a firm's personnel department be affected by falling levels of unemployment? *(AEB 1989)*

Part V
Services to Business

Chapter 20

Insurance

Risk is a part of life. Some people are more at risk than others – the fisherman for example has a far more hazardous job than the office worker. The old and defenceless are more likely to be attacked and robbed than the physically fit. Equally, certain types of goods, for example fragile or perishable, run a greater risk of damage or deterioration than most.

Some of these risks we accept. After all the consequences may not be serious. Equally we may be ignorant of our danger,or it may be impossible to avoid the risk. But just as there are many risks we accept, there are many we avoid by taking precautions. The precautions may be as simple as looking both ways when we cross the road, or putting on a seat belt.

Firms also take precautions to avoid risks. Risk management involves identifying and assessing all the risks which may affect the firm, its performance, the health and safety of its employees and the satisfaction of customers. Once this has been done it is possible to devise a strategy to avoid, minimise or finance these risks.

There are some risks which cannot be avoided. The firm has to accept environmental uncertainty – for example, changing products, markets, social attitudes, laws and technology. However, all company plans should be sufficiently flexible to be able to adapt to changed circumstances.

Another group of risks are capable of being minimised. Stringent procedures for monitoring production and the production process will reduce customer complaints and improve employee safety. Not only will this reduce insurance premiums, but also will improve the standing of the firm in the community.

Other risks are financed internally. Many firms argue that it is not cost effective to insure predictable losses, e.g. bad debts, because any insurance premium will, in the long run, have to cover the loss plus the insurance company's administrative cost and profit. As a result firms may create an internal reserve against loss rather than insure.

The final method of risk management taken by both firms and individuals is insurance.

The basis of insurance is that in return for a small premium financial loss is borne, not by the individual to whom the misfortune occurs, but by an insurance fund created from the premiums of the whole insured community. To be fair on all participants the premium paid must reflect the risk of a claim being made, and also the likely size of any claim. A motorist with a bad driving record should obviously pay more than one who has never had an accident. In the same way, other things being equal, the premium required to insure a Rolls-Royce will be greater than for a Mini.

It is easy to underestimate the importance of insurance today. Yet many families within the UK will have insurance covering their house, its contents, and their car. A substantial number will save for the future with an insurance policy. The firm, too, will need to insure its premises, and their contents. It may also wish to insure itself against liability for injury to its employees, or third parties, against loss of profits, or any of many other eventualities.

To all these individuals and firms insurance removes the worry of misfortune causing financial disaster. Insurance imparts a confidence in the future without which many new business ventures would never start. But insurance benefits society in other ways. For example:

1. It aids the more efficient use of capital by releasing funds for investment which would otherwise be kept on one side to guard against unforeseen eventualities.

2. The accumulated insurance fund is an important source of finance for both industry and government.

3. The UK balance of payments benefits considerably from the export earnings of the insurance industry.

4. Costs of accidents and injury which would otherwise be borne by society through the social services will in many cases be met by insurance (e.g. car accidents).

5. By their advice and actions insurance companies play a positive part in the reduction of loss. Bad drivers are encouraged to mend their ways through higher premiums. Similarly, firms with bad accident records. Advice may be given on ways to avoid or minimise the extent of loss. Thus firms may be encouraged to install burglar- or fire-alarm systems.

The principles of insurance

Underlying the contract of insurance are four basic principles. These are insurable interest, good faith, indemnity, and proximate cause. They are part of every insurance contract whether or not explicitly stated in the agreement and can only be varied by a clear statement of that fact in the policy.

Insurable interest

Before a legally binding contract of insurance can be formed the insured must show that he has an insurable interest. It is the insurable interest which distinguishes the insurance contract from gambling – an agreement which is unenforceable in English law. An insurable interest exists where there is:

- an object of insurance – person, property or liability which is capable of being insured; and

- a recognised interest in the subject-matter of the insurance so that the insured suffers loss by its death, damage, destruction, by the creation of a liability or loss of a right.

Let us consider a few examples. A creditor may insure the life of his debtor, for if the debtor dies the creditor stands to lose the loan. But the policy could only be for the amount of the loan. It is common to find partners insuring the lives of their co-partners as the co-partner's death or incapacity may cause the firm financial loss. By common law a husband and wife have an unlimited insurable interest in each other, but this does not extend to other members of the family. A man may insure the lives of his children or his parents only if there is some particular financial loss which may come as a result of their death.

An insurable interest in property will obviously arise where it is owned by the insurer. Where there is joint ownership though, insurable interest is limited to the value of the individual share. Ownership is not the only basis for an insurable interest in property. People holding property as agent for the owner may be liable for its loss or damage and thus have an insurable interest. A similar situation arises where you use property (e.g. a motor car) with the agreement of the owner.

A person may also insure himself against the civil consequences of a criminal act. For example the injuries which an employee may suffer as a breach of health and safety regulations, or where another road user suffers as a result of negligent driving by the insured. Equally, an insurable interest exists where a right or financial interest of the insured is capable of being disturbed. Thus a businessman may insure against embezzlement by employees and customer bad debts.

Good faith

Insurance contracts are said to be *uberrimae fidei* – that is, 'of the utmost good faith', whereas for the vast majority of other contracts the common law principle *caveat emptor* – 'let the buyer beware' applies. In ordinary commercial contracts each party is expected to use their skill and judgement to decide whether the agreement is one into which he really wishes to enter. Thus your co-contractor is not obliged to point out all the defects in the car you are buying (but they must answer any questions put to them truthfully and not fraudulently conceal the defects). If you make a bad bargain the law provides no remedy!

Insurance contracts are different though in the sense that one party (the insured) has all the knowledge relevant to the agreement. The other party (the insurer) relies upon the insured to reveal all facts, whether or not the information is specifically requested, which would influence the decision or the premium to be charged. This responsibility rests heavily on the insured and should he fail to discharge it the insurance policy is of no effect. In the event of a claim the insurer has no obligation to make any payment whatsoever.

The duty to disclose all material facts exists until the contract has been entered into. At common law you are not required to inform the insurer of any change in the material facts. Many policies, especially motor and personal accident, do, however, insert a clause requiring such changes to be reported to the insurer.

Indemnity

The aim of insurance is to place the insured party in the same position after the loss to that which they were in before the loss. The insured is not allowed to make a profit out of misfortune, claims are limited to the loss that has been suffered. The insured could therefore not expect to receive the price of a new carpet when the one destroyed was five years old. A deduction will be made for wear and tear.

The extent of the indemnity may be further reduced where the insurance policy is based upon the assumption that the sum insured represents the full value of the property. Many householders inadvertently under-insure the contents of their house. If the house contents are under-insured by, say 20 per cent then any claim for partial loss will also be reduced by 20 per cent.

Mention must also be made of two further points allied to the principle of indemnity, namely:

1. *Subrogation* – once the insurer has indemnified the insured for any loss he has suffered, he is entitled to exercise any rights or remedies available to the insured. Where a motorist's car is damaged by the negligent driving of another person a claim may be made to receive compensation from the insurers. Through subrogation of rights the insurers may then proceed to recover the amount of the indemnity from the negligent motorist or their insurers. Sim-

ilarly where stolen goods, which formed the basis of an insurance claim, are later recovered they are the property of the insurers.

2. *Contribution* – this allows an insurer to require other insurers to share in the cost of meeting an insurance claim. The right arises where there are two or more insurance policies which cover the same claim. Such a situation may occur where an item like binoculars is included on the 'all risks' section of house contents insurance, yet is also insured under a motor insurance policy when carried in the owner's car. If the binoculars are stolen from the car the insurance company, from whom an indemnity is sought, may claim a contribution from the other.

Proximate cause

It is essential to discover the cause of a loss to determine whether or not the insurer is required to give an indemnity under an insurance policy held by the insured. The policy will clearly cover some 'perils', a personal accident policy will clearly cover a pedestrian injured or killed by a car, a fidelity guarantee will cover theft by dishonest employees. But some perils are in fact uninsured. Should our pedestrian have in fact tried to commit suicide any claim under the personal accident policy would fail.

Difficulties really arise though where there are a number of causes which together have produced the loss upon which the insurance claim is based. Some of these causes may be insured perils, others uninsured. The rule of law then is to find the 'proximate' or most immediate cause of the loss. The insurer will then not be liable unless the proximate cause was an insured peril. Let us consider the situation where a fire leaves a wall standing in a dangerous state. A few days later a high wind causes the wall to collapse and damage some other property. Is the owner of the wall entitled to obtain an indemnity for that damage under a fire policy, or is the high wind the immediate cause? In similar circumstances (*Gaskarth* v. *Law Union* 1876) it was held that the fire was only a remote cause of the damage, a new intervening event – the high wind – was the proximate cause.

Classes of insurance

There are in fact several ways of classifying the various categories of insurance. We will adopt the traditional classification of marine, life, fire, and accident considering each in turn.

Marine insurance

This is believed to be the oldest form of insurance. Mediterranean traders are known to have used insurance as early as 1000 BC. In the UK though, the earliest signs of development did not occur until the fifteenth century. But the growth of the insurance industry was rapid, and London soon became the major centre for marine insurance throughout the world.

The potential liability arising from marine insurance is so great that normally the risk is spread among many underwriters.

Life assurance

While all other forms of insurance are intended to indemnify the insured against financial loss in the event of an unforeseen occurrence, with life assurance the event (e.g. death) must occur at some time. Such contracts are normally long term for a period of ten years or more, with a level premium being paid each year. In Britain the premiums normally qualify for tax relief. (In his 1984 budget the Chancellor of the Exchequer abolished tax relief on policies taken out after 5th April 1984.) There are a vast number of policies which are available, but the majority come within the following categories.
1.   *Term assurance* – this is the cheapest form of assurance available. It guarantees a sum of money if, but only if, the assured die within the specified period. It may be used by business people preparing to take a business trip to provide their dependants (in the event of their death) with a lump sum, or to cover a loan (e.g. an outstanding mortgage on the house).
2.   *Whole of life assurance* – as the name implies these policies provide cover throughout the life of the assured. On death a fixed sum is payable to the assured's dependants or into their estate. If such a policy is taken out while the assured is relatively young a substantial sum assured is obtained for a relatively small monthly payment.
3.   Endowment assurance – is by far the most popular class of assurance. It provides for a sum to be paid either upon the death of the assured or upon expiry of a fixed term of years. It has the advantage of providing for dependants in the event of death, yet benefiting the assured should they survive the term of the policy by providing them with a lump sum.

Both endowment and whole of life assurances may be 'with profits' or 'without profits' policies. The standard contract available guarantees the assured a fixed sum on death, or alternatively in the case of endowment assurance on expiry of a specified period of time. For an extra premium this may be converted into a 'with profits' policy which entitles the assured to share in profits made by the life assurance fund. There is no guarantee that such profits will materialise (they are called bonuses by the insurance industry), but in practice policy-holders are seldom, if ever, disappointed. Where bonuses are 'paid' they are added to the value of the assured policy and inflate the sum to be received on death or policy maturity.

Industrial life assurance

Endowment and whole of life assurances are also provided by industrial life offices – the biggest and best known being the Prudential. The origin of industrial life assurance goes back to the years of the Industrial Revolution. Few working-class people could afford the annual premium for life assurance. Yet the desire to provide for one's dependants, or at least ensure a decent burial for themselves was there. To meet this demand policies were created upon terms which would appeal to these classes. The premiums which were paid weekly by the policy-holder to a collector who called at his home – 'the man from the Pru'– were for small amounts. The sum assured was correspondingly small. Today these offices not only transact whole of life and endowment assurance but many other forms of insurance as well. In many cases the premiums are still collected weekly at the policy-holder's house. The collector often has the power to issue cover notes for motor insurance and settle small claims.

---

4. *Annuities* – these are not truly contracts of life assurance. In return for a lump sum the assurer agrees to pay the annuitant a sum of money – the annuity for the rest of their life. An annuity may be 'deferred' in which case the payments will not start now but at some agreed future date.

Fire insurance

The scope of basic or standard fire policy is extremely limited. It will compensate where property has been burnt in the course of a fire which was accidentally started. It does not, however, normally cover a situation where the proximate cause was lightning, earthquake, explosion, or riot. These, and many other perils may be added to the fire policy for an additional premium.

Fire policies are becoming increasingly linked with other forms of accident insurance (e.g. burglary, public liability) in what is commonly termed a combined policy. One particular policy which is often linked in this way by business people is for consequential loss. This policy seeks to compensate firms for the disruption of their business. Dependent upon the precise terms agreed, it can compensate for loss of net profits, fixed costs payable during the period of disruption and any extra expenses necessarily incurred to put the firm back upon a business footing (e.g. temporary accommodation).

Accident insurance

This is very much a mixed bag of insurance policies which have very little in common except the fact that they all developed considerably later than marine, life, and fire insurance. For the most part they are products of the nineteenth century. We will confine our attention to fidelity guarantee, employer's liability, public liability, credit, motor, and engineering insurances.

1. *Fidelity guarantee.* This policy exists in several forms. In its commercial form it seeks to protect an employer from the dishonest acts of his employees. Local government, too, may take out such policies in respect of specific officials. The guarantee in this case not only covers loss through dishonesty, but also through mistakes made by the persons guaranteed.

2. *Employer's liability.* During the nineteenth century the attitude of society towards industrial accidents and injuries was callous in the extreme. In accepting the work it was said, the employee accepted the risks which went with the job. By law if he was injured by a fellow employee, or if he had in some way contributed to his own injuries he had no claim against his employer. Today these restrictions on an employee's right to compensation for an industrial accident no longer exist. Employer's liability protects the employer against claims made by his employees for injuries suffered at work. The policy may also cover the legal expenses incurred in dealing with the claim – these may be extremely heavy where court hearings are involved. By reason of the Employer's Liability (Compulsory Insurance) Act 1969 an employer is now required by law to obtain this insurance cover.

3. Public liability. This provides compensation to the insured in respect of claims made by members of the public. Claims may be made against the negligent pedestrian or cyclist who causes a road accident, against the firm or householder whose property in some way injures third parties (e.g. the collapse of a wall, falling slates, etc.), against businesses for the sale of faulty products or the provision of a substandard service, and even against sportsmen.

A public liability clause is often included in a policy covering the building and contents of a house.

4. *Credit insurance.* This is often called 'bad debts' policies and protects the firm against default by customers who have obtained goods on credit terms. By far the greatest risk of default on debts occurs in the export trade though, and it is the Government through the ECGD which provides protection for the exporter.

5. *Motor insurance.* It is an offence to use any motor vehicle

without having basic insurance cover which indemnifies the motorist for death or injury of third parties arising out of the use of that vehicle. It is more common for motorists to obtain cover extending the indemnity to the property of the third party, and to loss or damage of the motor vehicle caused by fire or theft. Such policies are often termed 'third party, fire and theft'. The broadest form of insurance cover available is known as 'comprehensive' and among the more important clauses included is an indemnity for accidental damage to the insured vehicle.

6. *Engineering insurance.* This is not required by law. The law does, however, require many types of plant to be inspected by a competent engineer. That service is often undertaken by specialist engineering insurance companies. As their name implies these firms also provide insurance covering damage to plant and surrounding property, third-party liability and consequential loss.

The insurance market

London is the world centre for insurance. There are nearly 850 companies carrying on insurance business in London. Three hundred and fifty of these are overseas based, but have been attracted by the large international market. It is estimated that 20 per cent of the world's general insurance business is placed on the London market.

The bulk of insurance in the UK is conducted through three insurance organisations – mutual companies, profit-making companies, and Lloyd's underwriters.

Mutual companies

Such companies have no shareholders. The policy-holders are the owners of the organisation. They share in the profits of the organisation, but less well realised is that they may be required to make good any losses. Although many specialise in life assurance they are free to deal with other clauses of insurance if they wish. Many profit-making insurance companies today are drawn from the ranks of mutual companies. Some still retain the word 'mutual' in their title.

Profit-making companies

These have shareholders who as owners of the firm are entitled to the profits made after the deduction of expenses. Policy-holders are not required to contribute to losses made by the company, nor do shareholders have any liability normally beyond the amount they have paid for their shares. Should the company run into financial difficulties it may have to go into liquidation.

Lloyd's underwriters

Lloyd's underwriters derive their name from the coffee-shop run by Edward Lloyd in the late seventeenth century where they first used to meet to transact their business. Today, Lloyd's is a corporation which was created by Act of Parliament in 1871. Lloyd's provides the facilities wherein underwriters carry on their business. Lloyd's itself does not transact insurance and incurs no liability on the contracts entered into by its members.

To be accepted as a member of Lloyd's an individual must find six existing members to support their application, and satisfy stringent financial and other conditions. The majority of members will form themselves into syndicates (these vary greatly in size) and specialise in one particular type of insurance. Each syndicate will appoint one of its members as underwriting agent, and it is the person who acts on behalf of the syndicate and arranges business. Technically Lloyd's underwriters are sole traders in business on their own behalf, even though they may be members of a syndicate. They are therefore personally liable for all risks underwritten, and may be made bankrupt if they are unable to meet the claims arising from the underwriting. Should any member be unable to meet his commitments the policy-holder may be compensated from the 'Central Fund' created out of the contributions made by all members of Lloyd's.

Members of Lloyd's do not transact directly with the public, but deal only through a recognised broker. The business of 'underwriting' actually occurs when a broker acting on behalf of client prepares a brief statement of the risks to be covered and invites underwriting agents to accept a proportion of the liability (for an agreed premium). The underwriting agent on accepting the risk will sign the name of his syndicate, detailing the premium and proportion of liability accepted below the statement of risks. The syndicate is only liable for the proportion of the risk it has opted to underwrite. Later a policy will be prepared for the policy-holder from the information on this slip of paper.

Brokers and agents

Insurance brokers and insurance agents are the intermediaries of the insurance industry acting as a link between the client requiring insurance and the organisation providing it. In strict terms neither is necessary (the exception being, of course, should you wish to deal with a Lloyd's underwriting syndicate), most large insurance companies having branches throughout the country. However, in practice, the majority of insurance business is channelled through these intermediaries.

Insurance intermediaries are only allowed to call themselves brokers when they have satisfied the Insurance Brokers Registration Council that they have the necessary combination of qualifications and business experience to give the public impartial advice on all classes and aspects of insurance. Transacting insurance business is the full-time occupation of the insurance broker. The broker has contacts with many insurance companies – the larger firms with Lloyd's underwriters as well. Remuneration is received by way of commission from those companies with whom clients take out insurance. Brokers are expected to use their skill and judgment to get the best possible deal for the client.

Insurance agents are not normally engaged in insurance as a full-time occupation. Their appointment as agents arises out of their position to introduce new business to the insurance company. Thus a garage proprietor may have an agency with several companies specialising in motor insurance, or the bank manager and solicitor with insurers dealing with life assurance or pension plans. Like insurance brokers, agents receive commission from the insurance company for their services.

Examination questions

1   On what principles does the existing *world pattern of insurance operate*? Refer in your answer to practical examples. *(PSC)*
2   Briefly outline the types of insurance which would particularly interest the following business organisations:
    (a) a sole proprietor owning a single corner shop;
    (b) a public limited company operating an international passenger airline fleet;
    (c) a medium-sized manufacturing company producing garden and agricultural chemicals and fertilisers. *(PSC)*
3   Which types of insurance is a medium-sized manufacturing company of electrical consumer goods likely to be interested in? For each type of insurance you mention, fully explain the various risks covered. *(PSC)*
4   Describe the work of the following people involved in insurance:
    (a) underwriter (b) broker, (c) agent.
5   What is the purpose of insurance and how does it benefit business and society?
6   (a) Outline the work of the following **three** people involved in insurance:
        (i) underwriter
        (ii) broker
        (iii) agent
    (b) How does insurance benefit business and society?
    (c) Does an insurable interest exist in the following circumstances?
        (i) A business person wishing to insure their company premises against fire.
        (ii) A business person wishing to effect a life policy on their daughter's life from which they will benefit.

Chapter 21
Banking

The origins of our commercial banking system today go back to the activities of goldsmiths in the seventeenth century. Goldsmiths who worked with and traded in gold found other people, particularly merchants, wishing to deposit their holdings of gold with them for safe keeping. The goldsmith would give the depositor a receipt for the gold received, which could be used to redeem the gold (though it was very seldom the same gold) by the holder of that receipt. Over a period of time merchants took to the habit of paying debts with these receipts rather than gold – it was after all far more convenient and safer.

Soon the goldsmiths came to realise that the gold which was lying idle in their vaults could be put to better use – that is, lent out at suitable rates of interest to merchants and other groups wishing to finance business operations. But the loan was made, not in gold (though a request for gold would have been met), but by means of promissory notes which were indistinguishable from the receipts issued against the custody of gold. Later goldsmiths came to realise that only a small proportion of these promissory notes were likely to be presented for payment in gold at any one time. The total amount of gold in their vaults could therefore finance lending on a far greater scale than hitherto considered – the system hinging on the public's confidence in the goldsmith's (or banker's) ability to pay.

Today the basic function of the commercial banking system remains much the same – the borrowing of money from current account or deposit account holders and the making of loans, or 'advances' as they are sometimes termed, to individuals and business.

But in other ways the banking system has changed dramatically. Commercial banks no longer have the right to issue (promissory) notes, they have developed many other services for the benefit of their customers, there are other private financial institutions who play an important role in the provision of finance, while the Bank of England carefully monitors the activities of the whole sector.

In 1988 there were over 600 banks operating in the United Kingdom. They included 18 retail or commercial banks offering a full range of services to their customers, 34 merchant banks, eight discount houses, 184 other British banks and 367 foreign banks.

In this chapter we shall consider the role of the principal financial institutions – that is the commercial and merchant banks, the discount houses, building societies and the Bank of England. We turn our attention fist to the retail or commercial banks.

Retail or Commercial Banks

By far the greatest proportion of commercial banking business in the UK is carried out by Barclays, Lloyds, Midland, National Westminster and the TSB group. Other important retail banks include Bank of Scotland, Clydesdale, Royal Bank of Scotland, Co-operative Bank and Yorkshire Bank. Approximately two-thirds of all British adults have a cheque book account.

The Association for Payment Clearing Services is the organisation by which banks settle whatever claims they have against each other. These claims arise out of the cheques drawn by the banks' customers on their various branches throughout the country and which are payable to the customers of another bank. Membership of APCS is not only open to the banks mentioned above but to any organisation having a minimum level of transactions to clear. As a result, several building societies are now also members.

The functions of a commercial bank

The receipt, safe-keeping, transfer, and encashment of money Money may be placed with a bank either on a deposit or current account. The larger amounts of funds placed with banks are in deposit accounts. These are interest-paying accounts, where one normally puts money that is not going to be needed for some time. For that reason they are sometimes termed 'savings' accounts. Although banks may demand notice before withdrawal from a deposit account, this requirement is normally waived.

Traditionally, deposits on current account made up the bulk of the funds deposited with a banker. However, today people are financially more aware of the loss they incur keeping large sums of money on current account and now tend to place their surplus funds into an interest-bearing account. Current accounts though, are far more useful than deposit accounts because apart from the receipt and safe-keeping of money the facilities detailed below are also available:
1. *The use of a cheque-book.* The vast majority of payments are made this way.
2. *Standing orders.* Instructions to bankers to make a periodic payment from your account direct to the account of another person or

organisation until such time as you countermand payment. Many people use standing orders (or bankers' orders as they are sometimes called) to make the monthly payment of mortgage interest to their building society or charges to the local authority.

3. *Credit transfers.* Used by individuals to pay a sum of money (which could not be determined in advance) direct to the current account of the creditor, for example the quarterly gas bill. Businesses often use credit transfers to pay the salaries of their employees, debiting their own account by means of a single cheque.

4. *Bankers' cards.* These may be either a credit or a guarantee card. Where an individual holds a credit card goods may be purchased without immediate payment. Instead the shopkeeper records details of the transaction and the credit card on an invoice which the customer signs. At the end of the day the shopkeeper will pay the invoice into the bank with the rest of their takings – the total amount being credited to their account. At the end of the month the shopkeeper's customer receives a statement from the bank itemising all credit transactions for the last month and requiring payment.

A guarantee card does not allow the holder to obtain goods on credit, but makes payment by cheque more acceptable to the shopkeeper. By noting the guarantee card number on the back of the cheque, and comparing the signature on card and cheque for similarity, a shopkeeper is guaranteed payment of any cheque up to £50 where the drawer of that cheque defaults.

5. *Cash withdrawal.* Stocks of coins and notes are kept on hand at all branches and may be drawn as needed (subject to current account balance!) by customers. Most branch banks have also installed automatic cash dispensers to enable customers to withdraw cash outside banking hours.

6. *Night-safe and safe-keeping facilities.* Cash takings received by traders outside banking hours may be deposited in the bank's night-safe in a sealed leather container (wallet). The following morning bank cashiers in the presence of the customer will check the amount deposited. Banks are also used as repositories of valuables. Thus the bank may hold bearer bonds, share certificates, or other valuable documents on behalf of the business or individual customer. Equally the items deposited may be jewellery or precious metals. These items, which are held under lock and key at all times, will only be released to the order of the customer.

7. *Customer references.* While bankers are under a duty of secrecy not to reveal any details of customers' accounts they are often called upon to vouch for the reliability of that customer. Thus, a trader who is unsure of the financial standing of one with whom they trade may approach their own bank and request that an 'opinion' be obtained. This bank will then approach the other person's bankers who will provide information of a very general nature. The banker must

in no circumstances disclose the balance on any customer's account.
Loans and overdrafts   By far the most important function of the
bank is the granting of loans and overdrafts to current-account
holders. Let us consider the case of a manufacturing business borrowing money from the bank to buy better plant and machinery.
The economy benefits through the immediate increase in economic
activity and reduction in unemployment and additionally, in the
longer term, from the growth in productive potential. The lending
creates extra work and profits for the firm making the plant and
machinery while our manufacturing business itself will become more
profitable through the use of more efficient machinery. Lastly, customers benefit through lower prices and often better-designed and
made products.

When a customer obtains a bank loan a separate account is
opened and debited with the amount of the loan. The customer's
current account is then credited with that amount. Interest will be
charged on the full amount of the loan regardless of the state of the
customer's current account. Since the bank has agreed to lend the
money for a specific length of time it cannot call in its loan unless
the borrower defaults on one of the terms of agreement.

Where the bank agrees to make overdraft facilities available, the
customer is allowed to overdraw their current account up to the
agreed amount. Interest is calculated daily on the overdrawn balance
of the account. The borrowing must be regarded as temporary as
the bank reserves the right to demand payment of the outstanding
amount at any time. In practice though, the bank would only do
this if it believed the borrower to be in financial difficulties and that
the situation could only worsen by continuing to lend the money.

The traditional view of banking has been that of taking deposits
from individuals and re-lending that money, short term, to business.
Recent statistics suggest that the picture is changing. Whereas in
1980, 67 per cent of bank loans were made to business that had
fallen to 44 per cent by 1987. Several factors were at work. Rising
profits had enabled firms to finance expansion internally. Businesses
also raised more money through the issue of shares and other
securities (particularly on the Eurobond market) and the borrowing
of foreign currency.

In the same period loans to individuals have risen from 18 per
cent to 32 per cent of total bank lending. Banks have expanded their
long term lending to individuals through housing loans (mortgages)
– holding nearly 20 per cent of the market, and credit cards.
Banks find lending to individuals more profitable than lending to
business.

The other major area of growth has been in loans to 'other financial institutions' including investment/unit trusts, insurance
companies and pensions funds. The increase in lending from 15 per

cent to 24 per cent of total bank loans reflects the bouyancy of the 'city' during this period.

Ancillary activities   As a result of changes in the law, retail banking has become increasingly competitive since 1980. This trend of increasing competition – particularly between banks and building societies – is expected to continue. Banks have therefore established or bought into leasing, factoring finance houses, securities dealing through their merchant bank, subsidiaries, insurance companies and unit trusts as well as providing the following wider range of services for their customers:

1. *Foreign business*. The growth of world trade has encouraged banks to play a more active role. The bank can provide information for the would-be exporter on overseas markets, tariffs, documentation required, and exchange rates. Banks have invested heavily in the technology necessary to transfer money speedily between financial centres as well as providing the travellers' cheques and foreign currency so necessary for business trips.

2. *Investment advice and management*. Bank managers often provide advice to their customers on stocks and shares. They may also purchase, hold, or sell shares on their customer's behalf.

3. *Executor and trustee services*. Banks will act as executors to wills, obtaining probate and distributing the estate. They will also act as trustees to estates – holding and managing property for the benefit of others. A trust is often used by the well-to-do to ensure that their wealth is used in a particular way after their death.

Banks and credit creation

Do banks actually create money? The answer is yes, and is based upon the fact, which seventeenth-century goldsmith-bankers discovered, that not all depositors demand or withdraw their money at the same time. Obviously the banker has to keep a certain proportion of assets in cash to meet demands for cash, but the rest may be invested in some way to earn money. Consider the case where a banker discovers over time that prudence dictates that the bank should keep 10 per cent of deposits in cash. Let us also assume that the banker has received a deposit of $100 cash from a member of the public. The balance-sheet is shown in Fig. 21.1. Now, our banker knows that depositors are only likely to demand 10 per cent of their deposits in cash. The bank's $100 cash will therefore support liabilities not of $100 but $1,000. Taking advantage of this, the balance sheet would be as shown in Fig. 21.2.

The bank acquires extra liabilities by agreeing to lend customers $900. This amount is credited to their loan accounts. But the bank also has claims against these borrowers for the repayment of their loans and this appears as an asset in the balance-sheet.

	$	
Assets		
Cash	100	The deposit of $100 with the bank is a liability, since it is a debt owed to the customer. The cash which is now held by the bank is an asset which may be used to repay the liability.
Liabilities		
Deposit	100	

21.1 Balance sheet XYZ Bank Hong Kong

	$	$
Assets		
Cash	100	
Advances	900	1,000
Liabilities		
Deposit	100	
Deposit (loans)	900	1,000

21.2 Balance sheet XYZ Bank Hong Kong

But what would happen if our initial depositor decided to withdraw not $10 but $50 in cash? The remaining $50 cash would not be sufficient to support bank advances of $900. Assuming that our banker still made the maximum loans possible what would his balance-sheet look like? Try filling in the missing figures in Fig. 21.3.

	$	$
Assets		
Cash		
Advances	——	——
Liabilities		
Deposit		
Deposit (loans)	——	——

21.3 Balance sheet XYZ Bank Hong Kong

In practice to avoid the obvious loss of goodwill caused by the curtailment or recalling of loans bankers normally have a second line of defence, 'liquid assets' – that is, assets which may be quickly converted into cash. For many years banks were required to maintain an 8 per cent cash ratio and a 30 per cent liquidity ratio (this includes the 8 per cent cash ratio). Today, these requirements are no longer in force. Commercial banks are required to hold ½ per cent of their deposits in non-interest-bearing accounts at the Bank of England, but that is all. At the present time though, banks are maintaining a liquidity, or near cash, ratio of approximately 20 per cent.

The structure of assets that a bank maintains is a compromise between profitability and liquidity. This is because the more liquid the asset the lower its yield. Consider, the yield of cash is zero, on bank advances 12–15 per cent. As Fig. 21.4 indicates, advances constitute the greatest (and most profitable) bank's asset portfolio.

Liquid assets comprise cash, bills, and market loans. Cash is held either in the till to meet the daily requirements of customers or at the Bank of England. Bank of England used to settle interbank indebtedness and can, for practical purposes, be treated the same as cash in the till.

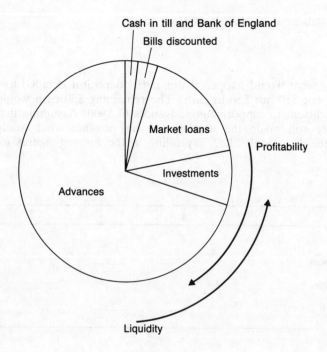

21.4 The relative importance of different assets in a bank's balance sheet

Bills discounted are relatively liquid assets, the majority maturing within two months of purchase. They are normally obtained from the discount houses, and fall into one of two categories – trade or Treasury bills. Trade bills were a popular method of financing overseas trade, and formed the greater proportion of discounted bills held by the banks until the First World War. Today the majority holding is of Treasury bills, that is, bills issued by the British Government to finance current expenditure.

In recent years the workings of the old-established discount market have been overshadowed by the growth of 'parallel' or 'secondary' money markets. Secondary money markets now deal with a greater amount of short-term funds than the discount markets. Bank holdings of market loans, varying between 15 and 20 per cent of their total assets, reflect the growing importance of the secondary market. The most well established of the secondary markets is 'money on call or at short notice'. These are surplus funds which the bank lent primarily to the discount houses but also to other financial institutions in the City, subject to the proviso that it is returned on the day on which the demand for payment is made. This is the most liquid of the banks' investments but carries only a low rate of interest.

A second market deals with sterling certificates of deposit (CDs). These acknowledge the fact that a sum of money has been deposited with the bank issuing the negotiable instrument (CD), and that this principal plus interest will be repaid upon a stated date.

The London Money Market

The London Money Market is part of the total capital market in the UK which facilitates the movement of money between lender and borrower. It specialises in the provision of short and medium-term finance. The Money Market comprises the commercial and merchant banks active in the City of London together with the discount houses and the Bank of England.

There is in fact no actual market-place. It is in the relationship between the interested institutions and the act of negotiating the raising or investment of capital that the market can be said to exist.

The commercial banks provide most of the funds for investment, often for very short periods of time and always at low rates of interest. The biggest individual borrower is the UK Government which finances current expenditure by the issue of Treasury bills. However, in total, private sector borrowing by discount houses and firms is greater than that of the public sector.

In practice, the period for which banks borrow these funds may be up to five years. It is a useful method of financing longer-term borrowing and yet because they are so easily sold in the market provide additional valuable liquidity.

A third market is the sterling interbank market. This consists of the majority of banks – commercial, merchant, British, or overseas acting in the UK. Its members deposit surplus funds with one another for periods ranging up to five years. For banks accepting the deposit it provides valuable cash funds which can be used to cover cash withdrawals by customers.

Fourthly, the currency movements of central banks, multinational corporations, and private individuals (especially from oil-producing states) form the basis of the Euro-currency market. Euro-currencies can be defined as funds denominated in a different currency to the currency of that country where they are deposited. For example dollars held by a Japanese multinational may be deposited with a London bank. These funds then become available for lending by that bank on the Euro-currency market for periods normally not exceeding three months.

Finally, two smaller markets also exist based upon finance houses (hire-purchase specialists) and local authorities raising money for up to a year.

All assets discussed so far are easily converted into cash, or mature within one year, and are therefore termed 'liquid'. We now turn our attention to those assets of the bank which are relatively illiquid – investments and advances. These are often termed 'risk assets' reflecting the risk of losing money if the banker were forced to sell investments before maturity, or a customer defaulted on an advance.

Investments held by a commercial bank are normally bought on the open market. The vast majority are government securities with up to ten years to run until maturity. These yield a higher return than Treasury bills. Banks will ensure they carry a balanced portfolio of investments so that at any time some are near to maturity and will provide a steady stream of cash. By far the largest proportion of bank assets though are loans and overdrafts in customers – perhaps as high as 70 per cent of total assets. These are the most profitable of the banks' assets earning a return of 1 to 4 per cent above their base lending rate. The precise rate reflects the length of the loan, the creditworthiness of the customer, and the security offered.

Merchant banks

The origins of merchant banks go back several hundred years to a time when they were merchants who specialised in overseas trade. Their knowledge and experience of overseas markets quickly drew them into the work of providing finance for international trade and accepting bills of exchange. While this is still an important part of the business of merchant banks, they have successfully diversified their activities into other areas such as acceptance, new issues and corporate advice. More recently some have become part of larger financial conglomerates – the four major high street banks all have merchant banking subsidiaries – providing a far broader range of financial services. This trend is excepted to continue, with a handful of firms dominating the financial services sector by the year 2000.

Acceptances

One major problem which has always existed in international trade has been finance. Briefly, exporters want their money as soon as they ship the goods to the importers, while importers cannot afford to pay until they have received and sold the goods. The method used to surmount this problem was the bill of exchange. When our exporter was ready to ship the goods a bill of exchange (as shown in Fig. 21.5) was drawn up. This would be sent to the importer together with documents verifying that the goods had been shipped. On receiving the bill our importer acknowledged liability by signing it across its face. The bill was then returned to the exporter who

<table>
<tr><td>

Exporter's Address
1 Jan 1984

<u>£5,000</u>

At 90 days after date pay to the order of 'Exporter' on his order £5,000, for value received.

(Signed) Exporter

To Importer
Importer's address

</td></tr>
</table>

21.5 A commercial bill of exchange

could hold the bill to maturity, or more usually discounted the bill (i.e. sold it to another person). But potential buyers of the bill were often deterred by the fact that they knew neither the exporter nor the importer.

A bill exchange may be defined as 'an unconditional order' in writing addressed by one person (the exporter) to another (the importer) to pay on demand or at some fixed or determinable future time, a sum certain in money to, or to the order of, a specified person or bearer.

To discount the bill our exporter had to find someone who would, for a consideration, personally guarantee that the bill would be paid if the importer defaulted. This was the role of the bank who, by placing its name on the reverse of the bill, was said to have endorsed or 'accepted' the bill. By accepting the bill the merchant bank does not provide the exporter with any funds, it merely enables the bill to be discounted. Bills carrying the name of a well-known merchant bank, a member of the Accepting Houses Committee (e.g. Barings, Rothschild, Schroder Wagg, Hambros – there are sixteen members in all), are eligible for discount at the best rates by the commercial banks and the discount houses. However, before a merchant bank will commit its name to any bill the creditworthiness of the importer is ascertained.

As an extension of their work in overseas trade merchant banks have also become foreign exchange dealers and important members of the London Gold Market. Some will also help with export and import documentation. Additionally, through their knowledge and experience of short-term financial markets, they have become active in the secondary money markets – giving advice and buying and selling securities on behalf of their clients, as well as being involved in the factoring of company debts.

New issues

Merchant banks who undertake work connected with the issue of shares or stock are members of the Issuing Houses Committee. In recent years though, their monopoly of new issue work has been challenged and broken by other financial institutions, particularly commercial banks.

The basic function of an issuing house is to help find finance for those companies wishing to expand, but the merchant bank is also prepared to, and in normal circumstances will, undertake the administrative work concerned with an issue of stocks or shares. Thus it will prepare the prospectus or other documents required for the issue, arrange the underwriting, handle the applications, determine the allocation of shares where the issue is oversubscribed, and arrange for a Stock Exchange listing. Additionally, it has the connections to place shares with institutional investors such as pension funds or insurance companies.

For the smaller, relatively unknown company wishing to issue shares for the first time the help of a merchant bank is invaluable. It is the act of the bank in allowing its name (and therefore its reputation) to be associated with the issue that ensures success. Sometimes the issuing house will take over the whole issue itself and resell to the public.

Issuing houses offer a similar service to that described above to foreign firms and governments wishing to raise capital in London. The importance of these overseas customers, especially multinationals, has encouraged merchant banks to develop and extend their traditional links with banks in other countries, participating in the development of multinational banking consortia, and to set up offices in other major financial centres around the world.

Advice

The relationship between merchant bank and client built up during the share issue often continues after the event. Sometimes the bank will maintain the company's statutory registers on members, directors, director's interests, mortgages, and charges. They will help their clients make best use of their assets by advising on finance, organisation, and management. But it is with the number of firms seeking to obtain the benefits of economies of scale, reduced competition, greater competitive strength, and enhanced status through mergers and take-over bids that they have become well known. As adviser to the firm wishing to expand through merger or take-over their work involves identifying those businesses which fit the requirements of their client. They will estimate the value of these businesses to their client, and therefore the price to offer per share. More generally they will consider what defensive arguments may be raised against the take-over bid and how best to counter these. In the same way, the advisers to the firm defending itself against an unwelcome take-over bid will be devising the best tactics and presentation of information against the merger.

Many merchant banks have also developed large investment advisory services for clients. By far the greatest number of these clients are institutional investors such as pension funds, local authorities, investment and unit trusts. Some banks have gone further and now offer a complete investment management service, taking over the day-to-day running of the investment portfolio, acting as market maker, buying and selling securities as they think fit.

The discount houses

The discount market consists of financial institutions who are involved in the purchase, or sale of, commercial and Treasury bills. The work of the discount house is central to this process.

The function of the discount house is to borrow funds (which are not being used by their owners) for short periods and make these funds available to government and business for longer periods. The commercial banks are the major source of funds to the discount houses – providing over 90 per cent of all funds in use at any one time.

These funds are used in two ways. First, the funds are used to purchase Treasury bills which are made available for weekly tender by the Government. The discount houses tender for these bills in competition with one another, and other bidders. The price tendered is lower than the maturity value of the bill (i.e. it is discounted – hence the name 'discount houses'), and establishes the market rate of interest. Today the discount houses undertake to purchase whatever bills are left after the allocation to other bidders. In return they receive a slightly more advantageous discount rate, and the right to turn to the Bank of England (as lender of last resort) for help should they run short of funds.

Attempts by governments to reduce their dependence on short-term borrowing, and the consequent reduction in Treasury bills available has forced the discount houses to find other homes for their short-term funds. Treasury bills now account for approximately 10 per cent of their assets, the remainder being split in roughly equal proportions between commercial bills of exchange and short-term investments on the secondary money markets (see p. 318).

The willingness of the discount houses to purchase commercial bills of exchange depends upon their quality. In this respect the work of the acceptance houses is important. Bills accepted by these houses obtain the best discount rates in the market. Where a bill has not been endorsed by the acceptance house it will only be marketable if the credit standing of the importer responsible for payment of the bill upon maturity is well known, and then only at a substantially higher rate of discount.

Discount houses do not always hold the bills to maturity. Often they are parcelled together on the basis of maturity dates and rediscounted to the commercial banks. The commercial banks' objective is to build up a portfolio of bills with a proportion maturing each day.

Although the discount house policy of 'borrowing short, lending long' seems a certain recipe for disaster it is not often that the market is left short of funds. While commercial banks may be left short of funds at the end of a day's trading and have to demand repayment of 'money on call and short notice' from the discount houses, this is normally offset by another bank having a surplus which it is willing to lend out. In practice it is more likely that discount houses will be left short of funds as part of government policy to influence short-term interest rates than for any other reason. Yet, even where the discount houses have insufficient funds they are always able to borrow from the Bank of England as lender of last resort. But whenever possible they try to avoid this remedy for the rates of interest charged by the bank are high, and they normally lose on the transaction.

In most other countries there is no comparable institution to the discount houses. Banks lend direct to the Government. But while some would argue that the discount houses are superfluous and that the cost of short-term borrowing could be reduced through their demise, both the commercial banks and the Bank of England have argued for their retention. To the commercial banks it is a means of maintaining money in an extremely liquid form, but at the same time earning interest. To the Bank of England it provides a mechanism for exercising control over short-term interest rates. Finally, through its agreement to absorb whatever portion of the weekly lender of Treasury bills is left unsold, the Government is certain that its short-term borrowing requirements will be met.

Building Societies

A building society may be defined as a mutual institution which takes short term deposits from individuals (normally they can withdraw their money at any time) and provides long term loans to house purchasers against the security of that property.

It is only recently that we have come to regard building societies as part of the banking system because, until recently, building societies were:

- a relatively small part of the retail savings market

- offering a very limited range of services to their members

- only lending to a very specialist market

- not subject to banking regulations.

However, by 1986, when the new Building Societies Act came into force, the situation was very different. Building societies held 50 per cent of the retail savings market and 75 per cent of the large mortgage loan market. Banks were competing fiercely with building societies for a share of the mortgage market, and building societies were offering a greater range of savings, products and services – including cheque book accounts – and insurance related to a mortgage loan.

Indeed, it was this increasing level of competition which convinced many that societies had no long-term future unless they were allowed to compete with banks on more equal terms. The 1986 Building Societies Act moved in this direction by allowing diversification into:

- general banking services
- investment services including fund management
- insurance, including life assurance company ownership
- trustee and executorship
- land services including conveyancing, surveys, valuations and the ownership of estate agencies.

The significant power stemming from the Act though, is the power to make unsecured loans. Building societies are expected to remain the major providers of home mortgage loans with a minimum of 90 per cent of their commercial assets (total assets − liquid and fixed assets) being invested here. Of the remaining 10 per cent, five per cent may be used to make unsecured loans or used to invest in ownership of land and property or subsidiaries.

The low proportion of commercial assets which may be invested in unsecured loans is seen as a compromise by Parliament between the need to give building societies the ability to compete with other financial institutions in the non-housing loan market and the need to ensure these extra powers did not lead to an increased risk for building society investors. Traditional lending – small sums on the security of property – by comparison is seen as low risk.

Building societies are now also supervised more closely through a Building Society Commission whose aims are to protect savers' interests, ensure financial stability of individual societies, administer a system of regulation, and, where necessary, make recommendations to the Treasury on matters relating to building societies. The key element in the Commision's control over societies is the requirement that they should maintain 'adequate reserves' of capital. Because of the safe nature of mortgage lending this was as little as 1.25 per cent of assets over £1,000 million. Now, the Commision is requiring societies to maintain a reserve capital level of approximately 3.75 per cent.

The Bank of England

The Bank of England was founded by Act of Parliament in 1694, and was nationalised in 1946 because of its importance to the Government in the implementation of monetary policy – a position it had held for almost 200 years. Its position is that of a State bank, more often termed 'central bank', epitomising the position of such a bank at the hub of the system of banking and other financial institutions in market economies.

A central bank differs from a commercial bank first because it does not operate for profit, rather it is operated by the Government in (what it perceives to be) the national interest. A central bank will normally have no private customers – the Bank of England has a few, dating back to the days before nationalisation, but will open no new accounts for private individuals or organisations. Such a bank provides a lead to the commercial banks. It establishes rules of good conduct and ensures that they are adhered to. Finally, it is the institution through which monetary control is exercised.

Functions of the Bank of England

Note issue The Bank Charter Act 1844 removed private banks' right of note issue. This applied where new banks were established or where two or more existing banks amalgamated. By 1929 the Bank of England had emerged as the sole note-issuing authority in England and Wales. The Bank Charter Act did not apply to Scotland and Ireland, and a number of these banks still issue their own notes. At one time note issue was limited by the amount of gold the Bank of England held. This is not so today, only a small fraction is covered by gold holdings, the rest – the fiduciary issues – is backed by the issue of government securities.

Banker to the Government It was first through accounts which eighteenth- and nineteenth-century governments held at the Bank of England that its role as central bank developed. Today as the government banker it still maintains the most important accounts. It arranges financial assistance through the issue of Treasury bills or Ways and Means advances should the account become overdrawn. Government borrowing, long and short term, is arranged by the bank, and administrative arrangements relating to the keeping of stockholders' registers, the payment of interest, and redemption of stock are also entrusted to it. Finally the bank gives advice to the Government. Working closely with the Treasury the bank examines and forecasts changes in economic indicators, and gives advice on whatever changes in monetary policy or control that it thinks necessary.

The bankers' bank Commercial banks use the Bank of England in a similar manner to a business using its bank account. The commercial banks maintain large deposits of cash at the bank – a minimum of $\frac{1}{2}$ per cent of their eligible liabilities, and also special deposits (i.e. assets which the Bank of England has demanded to reduce the banks' liquidity and which are not available for use). The former are used to set off any interbank liabilities which arise as a result of the day's trading. The Bank of England is also in a position of influence *vis-a-vis* the commercial banks – so much so that even informal requests, say to reduce lending or concentrate lending in certain sectors, are a powerful lever.

External affairs Movements international currencies for investment or trading purposes may cause considerable fluctuations in the value of sterling. Where the Bank of England believes that fluctuations do not reflect underlying market trends, it may intervene to stabilise the exchange rate by buying or selling sterling. The Bank of England, on the instructions of the Treasury, is also empowered to control the movement of sterling into other currencies. This is normally effected through issuing instructions to the commercial banks. Today few restrictions exist on the transfer of currencies, but as recently as 1978, restrictions on sterling/foreign currency transactions were in force. (Many developing countries use exchange controls as a means of limiting imports and avoiding balance-of-payments difficulties.)

The Bank of England liaises closely with other central banks and international monetary institutions, with the aim of ensuring greater stability in the international monetary system. Many of these countries or organisations hold their sterling balances in accounts at the Bank of England.

Monetary policy By far the most important function of the bank though, is its role in implementing the monetary policy of the Government. It is the Government's wish to control the level of economic activity within the economy so as to attain objectives such as a high and stable level of employment, stable prices, satisfactory economic growth and balance of payments. The Government has a number of weapons at its disposal: fiscal policy, incomes policy, and monetary policy. We will consider here the techniques which the Bank of England may use to implement monetary policy.

In practice, there are two main ways in which the Bank of England can affect the economy through monetary policy. The first is by controlling the supply of money. We have already seen that the commercial banking sector has the ability to create money – an ability that is dependent upon the amount of money customers deposit with them. Therefore, the central bank may, by affecting their cash (and other liquid assets), enhance or impair their ability to increase money supply. The second method of control is also designed to affect the quantity of money, but this time through the operation of interest rates, which is believed to affect borrowers' willingness to borrow.

1. *The cash ratio.* Since 1981 all banks with eligible liabilities of more than £10 m. are required to hold ½ per cent of those liabilities in cash with the bank. These balances are non-interest earning and

therefore provide a source of revenue to the bank. Commercial banks often maintain higher balances though, to cover interbank indebtedness.

Before 1981 the Bank of England influenced bank lending through the wider base of liquid assets. Commercial banks were required to hold 12½ per cent of their liabilities in eligible reserve assets. Broadly, these were the more liquid of banks' assets such as cash, money on call or at short notice, or Treasury and commercial bills. These requirements were discontinued simply because they were considered ineffective – commercial banks will always maintain a proportion (often in excess of 12½ per cent) of their assets in relatively liquid assets merely as a matter of prudence.

2.   *Open market operations.* The Bank of England is active in the money market, buying and selling securities each day. Its actions are designed to offset the large and often unpredictable flows of funds between the public sector and the banking system – fluctuations which, if unchecked, would leave the banking system alternatively short or with a surplus of liquid assets. The bank can therefore affect the liquidity of the commercial banks by its actions in buying or selling securities. Should the bank in accordance with government policy wish to restrict bank credit, it may increase its sales of securities to the private sector. Payments to the Bank of England for these securities will reduce the level of deposits held by the commercial banks, causing them to restrict their loans and advances.

The bank may also affect the liquidity of the clearing banks by funding – the process of converting short-term into longer-term securities. Treasury bills and other government stocks with less than a year to run to maturity, form part of the stock of liquid assets held by the commercial banks. Should the Bank of England issue fewer Treasury bills (and even perhaps purchase them on the open market) and in their place issue long-term government stock, the structure of the commercial banks' assets is changed. Liquid assets have been replaced by investments. To maintain their ratio of liquid to total assets the banks will reduce advances.

3   *Lender of last resort.* But not only do open-market operations by the central bank lead to a reduction in lending by commercial banks, they may also be used to engineer an increase in interest rates. Open-market operations work by affecting the commercial banks' balances at the Bank of England. In an effort to restore these balances, the banks will demand repayment of their 'money on call and short notice' from the discount houses. It is the discount houses which are now starved of funds, and they must turn to the Bank of England as 'lender of last resort', for help. They will offer to sell the bank some of their Treasury, local authority, or commercial bills, stating their price. If the price is consistent with the monetary policy which it wishes to pursue, the bank will purchase the bills.

But if the bank wishes to see, say, an increase in the short-term rate of interest, it may refuse the bills, leaving the discount houses to make further offers at lower prices (i.e. discount them at a higher rate of interest). Now the discount houses rely on a small difference between the rate at which they borrow and discount bills to make a profit. The raising of interest rates by the Bank of England has eliminated that profit margin. The discount houses will restore that margin by raising the rate at which they will purchase bills in the market.

Conversely, when the bank wants the rate of interest to fall, it will increase the price at which it is prepared to purchase bills from the discount market.

4. *Directives and special deposits.* It has already been noted that the Bank of England has considerable moral influence over the whole banking sector. This can, for example, be seen in the directives which the bank issues to the clearing banks. Such directives will normally require the banks to limit lending generally, but perhaps also restrict certain groups even further (e.g. property dealers) or exempt others (e.g. exporters). These instructions on how the commercial banks are expected to help aid economic objectives, do not carry the force of law, yet have never been openly disobeyed even though bank profits will often be adversely affected.

However, in recent years the practice of issuing moral suasion has fallen into disfavour. It is argued that too many directives would weaken the authority of the Bank of England, and in any case the same result can be achieved through market forces and interest rate policy.

Special deposits act to reinforce the banks' control over liquidity. Commercial banks are required to deposit a specific proportion of their liquid assets in a special account at the Bank of England. Interest is paid upon these deposits but they do not form part of the commercial banks' holdings of liquid assets.

Examination questions

1 What are the sectors of the English banking system? How are they linked? *(PSC)*
2 Outline the major functions of each of the following, clearly illustrating their distinguishing characteristics: (a) commercial banks; (b) merchant banks; (c) central bank. *(PSC)*
3 (a) Is it a sign of a healthy economy when businesses overdraw their current accounts?
  (b) How do (i) the customers of businesses, (ii) the banks themselves, benefit by the banks making loans to businesses? *(PSC)*
4 Does the asset structure of a commercial bank provide an adequate picture of its activities?

5   What services do commercial and merchant banks offer to industry regarding the provision of capital?

6   Explain the role and functions of the Bank of England. How may it influence monetary conditions within the economy?

7   In the last decade merchant banks have experienced considerable growth. Comment on this growth and the range of services offered nationally and internationally by the merchant banks.

8   How do commercial banks reconcile the conflict between profitability and liquidity?

9   Explain the function and importance of the discount market in the City of London.

10 Explain how banks can create credit and discuss the factors limiting their ability to do so.

11 In what ways can the banking system aid economic activity?

12 (a) Clearly state how
        (i) a bill of exchange differs from a cheque
        (ii) export houses aid international trade
    (b) Mr B Lee, who trades in Singapore, purchases goods worth £10,000 from Comlon International in the United Kingdom. The parties agree that payment should be made by means of a 3-month Bill of Exchange. Outline the procedure which will be followed until settlement.

Chapter 22

Sources of finance

Capital is needed by all organisations to finance their business operations. In many organisations capital is required even before business commences. Money has to be invested in fixed assets – land,
buildings, machinery, and vehicles. Once business has commenced
money is needed for working capital – raw materials, finished stock,
and debtors. Employees have to be paid, as do the rent, rates, lighting, and heating bills. Moreover, as a going concern the organisation
may require extra capital – to cover a temporary cash-flow crisis, to
purchase new improved machinery, or simply to expand.

Sources of finance are usually classified by time into long,
medium, and short term. Long-term finance is defined as money
raised for a period in excess of five years, medium-term any period
from one to five years, and short-term as borrowing of less than one
year. Long-term capital should be used to finance the permanent
needs of the business – that is, its normal investment in fixed assets.
Medium- and short-term sources will be used to finance its investment in current assets. The distinction has a practical importance.
Permanent needs should never be financed from short-term sources
of funds, for the business may find difficulty in renewing that
resource at the end of the loan period. Similarly, with long-term
capital costing more than short-term we must be sure that any expansion of operations is permanent before exchanging short- for
long-term finance.

Not all potential sources of finance are external to the firm. Often
the best sources of capital are to be found hidden in the business's
own balance-sheet. Let us consider fixed assets. Land and buildings
may be surplus to requirements. We may own land which we have
never developed. Alternatively, we may be producing in five locations when two would do. By employing a policy of simplification
we may reduce the product range, thus releasing land and buildings,
plant and machinery. Perhaps we may question why we purchase
plant and machinery at all when we can lease these assets? Similarly,
investments in other companies may be realised rather than raising
capital from expensive external sources. Yet again current assets provide a potential source of funds through better inventory or credit

control. Finally, consider the business's dividend policy. Shareholders may be prepared to accept lower dividends now in return for the promise of increased capital growth and dividends in future years. Undistributed or 'ploughed-back' profits have traditionally provided the bulk of funds needed for expansion.

Long-term sources of finance

Ordinary shares

The holders of these shares are the ultimate risk-takers. It is only after all expenses have been paid and other classes of shareholder have received their due that ordinary shareholders are entitled to their share in the profit. The amount which they receive will vary from year to year, reflecting the changes in the company's fortunes. They may even, in bad years, receive nothing at all. Similarly, should the business be put into liquidation, ordinary shareholders will not receive repayment of their investment until all other creditors have been paid in full. In many cases, where the business has been trading unsuccessfully for a number of years they will receive little or nothing. Where, however, the business is successful ordinary, or equity shareholders as they are sometimes called, stand to benefit most from high profits and the appreciation in the value of the company.

As owners of the business, ordinary shareholders control its activities. They have the right to attend and vote on all resolutions made at the annual and other general meetings. They appoint directors to act for them, and should they disagree with the director's policy or actions they may terminate that appointment.

Preference shares

Holders of these shares receive priority over ordinary shareholders in two respects. First, they are entitled to a fixed rate of dividend each year before the ordinary shareholders may participate in profits, and secondly they are normally entitled to priority of repayment of capital should the business be wound up. However, although preference shareholders are members of the company they do not normally participate in the control of the business, but receive only those rights accorded to them in the Articles of Association.

Preference shares may be cumulative, participating, or redeemable. Cumulative preference shares carry the right to have arrears of dividend paid to them before ordinary shareholders receive a dividend. All preference shares are cumulative unless stated otherwise. Participating preference shares are entitled to receive a fixed dividend together with some further addition should the dividend to ordinary shareholders exceed a certain percentage. For example, the preference shareholders' fixed rate of dividend may be 10 per cent, but where the ordinary share dividend exceeds 20 per cent they may be entitled to receive one per cent extra for each additional two per cent received by the equity shareholders. Where a company issues redeemable preference shares it gives itself the right to repurchase those shares on or after a specified date. This is the only form of non-permanent share capital which exists.

Debentures

A debenture is a document issued by a company acknowledging a debt. Normally the debenture holder will receive a fixed rate of interest on the loan and will be given a security for that loan. The security may be by way of a fixed charge over land and buildings, plant and machinery, or a floating charge over working capital. Debentures receiving the security of charge on company assets are termed 'mortgage debentures'. Debentures issued without security are termed 'naked' or 'simple'. The debenture deed will also give details of when the loan has to be repaid and the rights of the holder should the company default on payment of interest or repayment of capital.

From the debenture-holder's point of view debentures are attractive because their loan is secure and their interest guaranteed even when the company makes little or no profit. To the company the advantages are that the debenture holders are not members of the company and therefore cannot take part in the management of the company, the rate of interest payable is generally lower than that paid to preference shareholders due to the greater degree of security of capital, and such capital may be redeemed out of future profits. Finally, inflation reduces the real burden of paying debt interest and repaying capital.

However, an issue of debentures is not advantageous in all circumstances. Debenture interest must be paid whether or not the company makes a profit. Default on either interest or capital payments may allow the debenture holders to appoint a receiver, thus removing control of the company from the shareholders. Again a charge on the assets of the company reduces the ability of the company to use those assets as it thinks fit.

In recent years some companies have been issuing convertible debentures or loan stock. Often this is unsecured but gives the holder the right to exchange their stock for ordinary shares at some specified date in the future. This conversion is often allowed at advantageous prices so as to reduce company reliance on fixed-interest loans.

Mortgages

Most of us are familiar with the term 'mortgage', as it is the recognised method by which many people purchase their houses, but mortgages are also an important source of finance for the industrial and commercial sector. Mortgages may be granted to businesses wishing to purchase land and buildings by institutional investors such as pension funds, insurance companies, and investment trusts who use the property as security for their loan. Businesses may obtain a loan of up to two-thirds of the purchase price of the property which may be repayable over twenty or twenty-five years.

The distinction between a mortgage and a debenture lies in the fact that a mortgage is a debt owed to a single lender, a debenture is a loan obtained from a number of people or organisations.

Sales and lease back

Businesses owning property may raise money by selling that property – normally to an institutional investor and at the same time negotiating to lease that property back at an agreed rental (subject to periodic revision) for time spans of up to 100 years. The purchaser will wish to ensure that the vendor has a good profit record, and that in the event of default on the lease it will be reasonably easy to obtain alterative lessees.

Sale and lease back has the advantage of releasing funds locked up within the business for other purposes while guaranteeing long-term occupation of the premises. However, the company loses an asset which is likely to appreciate in value over time, which would provide security for loans, and the loss of which substantially increases the level of fixed costs which have to be paid by the business.

Methods of issuing shares and debentures

When a firm wishes to raise new capital by the issue of shares or debentures it has a number of options open to it: (a) issue by prospectus; (b) rights issue; (c) offer by tender; (d) offer for sale; (e) placings.

Although the method of issuing shares may differ, most firms, including large ones, find it beneficial to obtain the help of intermediaries such as issuing houses, merchant banks, and specialist departments of clearing banks. These will advise on the benefits of the different methods and on the timing and pricing of a share issue.

For smaller firms the appointment of such an intermediary is a necessity in order to gain the interest and confidence of the investor.

Issue by prospectus

Shares are offered directly to the public by the company at a stated price. This is probably the most well-known form of share issue as the prospectus will appear in several newspapers. The prospectus contains information on:

- company activities past, present, and future;
- directors, management, and staff;
- the company's financial record, profits, dividends, prospects for the future.

The prospectus also invites potential shareholders to apply for shares as prescribed therein.

The cost of raising money by this method is high. For an established business it is unlikely to be less than 5 per cent, while for a smaller, unknown business it will almost certainly be substantially higher, perhaps as much as 15 per cent of the capital raised.

A significant proportion of the extra costs incurred by the smaller company arises from the higher cost of underwriting the issue. Underwriting is the process by which issuing houses agree to guarantee that all shares offered for sale are in fact sold. In the event of the investing public subscribing for, say, only 60 per cent of the shares offered, the issuing house will purchase the remaining 40 per cent. The company is thus assured of the success of the issue.

Rights issues

Many of the costs associated with issues by prospectus can be avoided by selling extra shares to existing shareholders. New shares are offered to shareholders in proportion to their present holding, often at a price which is less than that currently quoted on the Stock Exchange. Thus a company may offer existing shareholders two new shares for every five already held at a price of 80p per share when the market value of the shares already issued is 90p. The shareholder has the option of either taking up the offer, or alternatively selling their 'rights' on the Stock Exchange to third parties.

Issues by tender

The procedure followed is similar to where shares are issued by prospectus with one important exception. Investors are invited to subscribe for shares at a price above a specified minimum and investors who wish to hold these shares may be willing to pay significantly more than this. The price at which shares are finally sold will be the highest possible commensurate with selling all shares.

Tenders are often used when market conditions are uncertain, or where there is no share already quoted on the Stock Exchange which can be used to establish a reasonable price. Although the company is unsure of the exact amount of capital (above the minimum) it will raise, this uncertainty is offset by the potential premium it can obtain if the issue is successful.

Offer for sale

By this method a company, probably medium-sized and making its first issue of shares to the public, will sell the share issue to an issuing house. It will then offer the shares to the public at a price higher than that which it paid for them, thus covering its expenses. The offer for sale by the issuing house will, as with an issue by prospectus, give full details on the business – its history, financial record, current position, and future prospects.

Placings

A private placing of shares will be used where the size of the company and the capital required are insufficient for a Stock Exchange quotation. An issuing house will approach investment trusts, insurance companies, and pension funds who it believes will be interested in holding shares in this type of business. A high rate of return (and therefore a low purchase price) will be required by these institutional investors to offset the lack of marketability and the high degree of risk of the investments.

A public placing of shares is used where less than £350,000 is being raised, but the company requires a Stock Exchange quotation. The procedure by which shares are sold is similar to a private placing with the exception that 25 per cent of the share issue must be made available to the general public through the facilities of the Stock Exchange, and the placing must be advertised nationally thus helping to create a market for the shares.

Capital gearing

As we have seen, long-term needs of a company can be satisfied in a number of ways – perhaps by an issue of ordinary shares or preference shares, alternatively by the issue of debentures. Gearing indicates the relationship that exists between ordinary share capital and other forms of long-term finance (fixed-interest capital). The company will be described as high geared when it has a high proportion of fixed-interest capital compared with ordinary share capital, and conversely as low geared when there is little fixed as opposed to equity capital. Gearing is normally expressed as a ratio. The effect of gearing upon a company is shown in Table 22.1. Companies A and B have raised the same amount of long-term finance but have different capital structures. Company A is low geared having a ratio of 1:9 (£100:£900) whereas company B which makes for greater use of debentures is said to be high geared with a ratio of 9:1.

Table 22.1 The impact of gearing upon profitability

	Company A (£'000)	Company B (£'000)
Ordinary shares	900	100
Debentures (10%)	100	900
Total long-term finance	1,000	1,000
Situation 1		
Profit	100	100
Debenture interest	10	90
Residue available to equity shareholders	90	10
As a % return on ordinary share capital	10% $\left(\frac{90}{900}\right)$	10% $\left(\frac{10}{100}\right)$
Situation 2		
Profit increases by 10%		
Profit	110	110
Debenture interest	10	90
Residue available to equity shareholders	100	20
As a % return on capital	11%	20%
Situation 3		
But what would happen if profits decline by 10%?		
Profit	90	90
Debenture interest		
Residue available to equity shareholders		
As a % return on capital		

In situation 1 where both companies make £100,000 profit, ordinary shareholders receive a return of 10 per cent on their capital after payment of the debenture interest. But in situation 2 where the profits of both businesses have increased by £10,000, shareholders in company A which is low geared receive a return of 11 per cent while in company B the return has doubled from 10 to

20 per cent. The increase in profits in the high-geared company has benefited the ordinary shareholders far more than in company A.

The logic of high gearing then is that if we can borrow fixed-interest capital and earn a return in excess of the interest charge this will go to the ordinary shareholders. Moreover the higher the gearing the fewer the shareholders to spread the excess among, and the more dramatic will be the increase in the return on ordinary shareholders. A subsidiary benefit of high gearing will be that it enables the business to increase its long-term finance without reducing the shareholders' control of the company.

While high gearing benefits the ordinary shareholders in prosperous times, a fall in profits will have an equally dramatic effect on their return. Readers may like to consider what would happen in situation 3 if profits declined by 10 per cent from those in situation 1. There is a real risk that in one year profits may be insufficient to pay the interest on debentures and preference shares. The prudent company will therefore allow itself a margin of safety for fluctuations in profit, and it is recommended that profits should normally cover fixed-interest charges at least three times.

The Euro-currency market

Quite apart from the national market for business finance there exists an international market in Euro-currencies. Euro-currencies are deposits of funds with European banks in a currency other than that of the host country. For example a UK company exporting to the United States may invest the dollars it receives in France or West Germany.

The origin of the market lies in the high rates of interest offered in Europe compared with the United States after the Second World War and the chronic United States balance of payments deficit which greatly increased the availability of the dollar internationally.

As the major currency available is the United States dollar the market is often referred to as the 'Euro-dollar market'; it would, however, be more correct to refer to it as the 'Euro-currency market'.

Euro-currencies have traditionally been used as a source of short-term finance for international trade. More recently though, government and local government agencies have used the market to cover their short-term indebtedness.

It is also possible to borrow longer term from the Euro-currency market in a manner similar issuing a debenture. Such loans are termed 'Euro-bonds'. This is becoming increasingly popular for both foreign and British firms. Euro-bonds are now as important as bank credit and the Stock Exchange for UK companies wishing to raise finance.

Medium-term sources of finance

Hire-purchase

By this method a firm may obtain assets which are needed in the business immediately, but spreads the cost of payment over a period of up to five years. Normally a down payment of between 20 and 35 per cent of the cost of the asset is required with the remainder, together with interest on the loan, being repaid monthly.

The major attraction of hire-purchase is that no form of security is required for the loan. Instead the asset remains the property of the hire-purchase company until the final payment is made. Moreover, once the finance has been arranged it is impossible to alter the terms of the agreement and the hirer is protected from changes in interest rates.

However, while the cost of hire-purchase facilities will vary from firm to firm it will often be twice that of overdraft facilities. For that reason it is popular with small firms who, without security, are often unable to obtain finance from other sources.

Leasing

It is possible to lease most forms of plant and equipment today. Examples include computers, office machinery, aircraft, dental equipment, and commercial vehicles. In many ways leasing is similar to hire-purchase – the business has the use of an asset which it does not own and has to make regular payments to the lessor under the agreement. The most fundamental distinction between the two is that under a leasing agreement the asset never becomes the property of the business hiring it.

The lessor, who may be the manufacturer, a finance house, a merchant or commercial bank, normally divides the agreement into primary and secondary periods. The lessee is not allowed to repudiate the agreement during the primary period without penalty, for it is during this period that the lessor expects to recover the investment. Thereafter, during the secondary period, the lessee may rent the asset at will and may repudiate at any time without penalty. The rental charged is nominal during this secondary period.

Among the more important advantages claimed for leasing are the following:
1. There is no demand on existing cash resources, nor are other assets tied up as security for the loan.
2. The rental may be paid from income generated by the use of the asset.
3. It is particularly beneficial where assets may become obsolescent rapidly.

4. The lease is a fixed contract, the facility cannot be withdrawn or its terms altered because of changes in the economic climate.

Bank loans

Traditionally, banks have preferred to lend short term; more recently though they have extended their operations into medium- and long-term finance. An agreement is entered into between the bank and its customer whereby a specified sum of money is borrowed for a stipulated period up to a maximum of ten years at a cost of 2–4 per cent above market rates of interest. The agreement will also cover other points such as security, repayment of the loan, and penalties for failing to adhere to the terms of the agreement.

In 1981 the Government introduced a loan guarantee scheme which is designed to encourage banks to provide extra finance for small firms. The scheme is likely to benefit new enterprises lacking security for loans. Under its provisions the Department of Industry will guarantee loans of up to £75,000 made for periods of between two and seven years. The Department of Industry charges the borrower three per cent of the guaranteed amount for this service. In the event of the borrower failing to repay the loan the Department of Industry will reimburse the bank.

Short-term sources of finance

Bank overdrafts

This is by far the best known and most popular source of short-term funds. Although commercial banks moved into the medium- and long-term finance markets they still regard themselves primarily as short-term lenders financing borrowing for purposes such as seasonal trade; finance for a specific contract, or to cover the non-payment of a debt.

In deciding whether to grant an advance the bank manager will consider many factors including:

- The proposition – its viability. How much money will be required? How will the advance be repaid?

- The borrower – what degree of ability and experience does the borrower have? How much personal money is the borrower investing in the proposition?

- Security – in the event of the proposition failing how will the bank recoup its advance?

Technically an overdraft is an agreement by which the customer may draw cheques on their current account to a stipulated limit. Interest is charged daily on the outstanding amount, and the bank will normally require some form of security from the business. Where the business has no assets to offer as security, the owners may be required to give a personal guarantee that the debt will be repaid.

The temporary nature of the overdraft facility is emphasised by the fact that the bank manager may require the overdraft to be repaid on demand. In practice, this rarely happens, and although bank advances are normally only made for six months they are often continually renewed by the customer thus providing an almost permanent source of funds.

Factoring and invoice discounting

Delayed payment by customers is often disastrous for small- and medium-sized firms. Poor cash flow will inevitably hinder growth and may in extreme cases force the business into liquidation. Yet it is precisely these firms which, lacking industrial muscle, are likely to find debtors taking an extended period of credit. Factoring and invoice discounting remedy this problem by advancing cash against debtors, thereby turning a credit sale into a cash sale.

Factors actually purchase the book debts, take over administration of the sales ledger, and assume the risk of non-payment. The factor also assumes responsibility for collecting the debts and deals directly with debtor customers.

The benefits of factoring lie in:
1. Providing immediate cash in return for debts thus aiding liquidity.
2. The fact that factoring is not borrowing and therefore does not affect the ability of the business to borrow.
3. The clerical and administrative savings arising from the factor taking over debt collection.
4. The reduction in the risk of bad debts.

With invoice discounting the business again sells its debts, but this time is responsible for collecting those debts on behalf of the specialist financier and also for bearing the loss arising from bad debts. Up to 75 per cent of the value of the invoices will be paid immediately, the remainder when the debts are paid.

Invoice discounting, like factoring, has the advantage of providing immediate cash, and not affecting the borrowing potential of the business. It also has the advantage of not revealing to the customer that book debts have been discounted – historically a sign of imminent bankruptcy.

Factoring and invoice discounting provide an important source of immediate funds to many medium-sized firms; however, the cost which is 1–3 per cent of turnover is significantly higher than interest on bank advances.

Venture Capital

While medium-sized and large firms with good profit records and prospects have little difficulty in raising the funds they need, it has long been recognised that smaller firms may experience difficulties in raising the finance needed to expand operations. While some small firms rely on short- or medium-term sources of finance, especially bank advances or hire-purchase simply through ignorance of other sources, there are some sources which are just not available – the business may be too small to raise money by means of a share issue, or it may not have the assets needed to pledge as security for a loan. Alternatively the cost of finance reflecting risk and administrative expenses may be too high.

Recognising the importance of small firms to the economy the Government and the financial institutions have created a number of bodies designed to bridge the funds gap experienced by this sector of industry.

Venture capital can be defined as the provision of finance to growing companies. Much of this money will be equity risk capital. Venture capitalists in return may demand the distribution of profits by way of dividend, the appointment of a director, management changes and the right to realise their investment after a specified period. Venture capital will be used to provide firms with:

- 'start up' capital: to develop and market a product
- 'second round' capital: to expand production range
- development capital: to develop a new range of products or diversify through acquisition and merger.

There are now over 150 different firms providing venture finance in the UK. Probably the best known is Investors in Industry or '3 i' which is jointly owned by the Bank of England and a consortium of commercial banks. 3i has had some spectacular successful investments. For example, in 1967 it took a twenty per cent £$\frac{1}{2}$ million stake in Oxford Instruments. This was valued at more than £100 million when the firm came to the Stock Exchange in 1983.

Of course, not all investments by venture capitalists are so wildly successful. Experience suggests that 20 per cent of investments are highly profitable, 20 per cent fail and the remainder at least break even and probably yield a reasonable return on the investment.

Government Aid

A wide range of aid and financial help is provided for industry and commerce by the Government. This is available at a national, regional and local level.

National incentives Under the Industry Act of 1972 grants are available to businesses which undertake investment projects deemed to be in the national interest. Assistance, which is by way of grant, is highly selective and will need to exhibit some of the following criteria:

- substantial impact on productivity

- substantially improved products

- involving a high level of technical innovation or new labour skills

- a general improvement in the competitiveness of UK companies

Under its scheme 'Support for innovation' or SFI the DTI will also offer grant assistance for R and D projects where the project is a significant advance for the UK industry, which if successful, will result in major commercial successes. The grant assistance will not exceed 25 per cent for a single firm, but for a collaborative venture for more than two firms the rate may be 50 per cent.

Regional incentives Regions which have, in the past, suffered higher than average unemployment may benefit from government grants under section 7 of the 1972 Industry Act. Assistance, which is in the form of a grant towards the cost of fixed and current assets, and also training of labour is dependent on new jobs being created or the safeguarding of existing employment.

Firms with less than 25 employees may also benefit from Regional Enterprise Grants. These are designed to encourage investment and innovation by small firms.

Additional help may be available from government agencies such as the Scottish Development Agency, Welsh Development Agency, the Northern Ireland Industrial Development Board or the Council for Small Industries in Rural Areas (COSIRA). For example, the Scottish and Welsh Development Agencies provide both equity and loans for projects, or alternatively may guarantee a commercial loan. These agencies also provide a broad range of advisory services.

Local incentives Special tax advantages can be obtained from starting your business in an Enterprise Zone (e.g Newcastle, Salford, Speke, Dudley, Corby, Belfast, Wakefield, Clydebank, Swansea Valley). Benefits include:

- the cost of purchasing any new building can be set against profits in the year of purchase

- complete exemption from local property taxes

- simplification of the planning process

- fewer demands for statistical information.

The International Stock Exchange

Our discussion so far has concentrated on the primary markets for funds – that is, the specialist institutions who provide finance – long, medium, or short term for business. There is also, however, for long-term funds, a secondary market – a market for existing stocks and shares which aids the transfer of securities between investors. This is termed the International Stock Exchange.

In the UK the major centre is the London Stock Exchange. There are also a number of provincial exchanges dealing in stocks and shares of companies generating local rather than national interest. The functions of these Stock Exchanges are to:

1. Provide a market for stocks and shares. Without this market neither the public nor financial institutions would so readily provide finance due to the difficulty of realising their investment.

2. Aid the issue of new securities by granting companies a Stock Exchange quotation.

3. Provide a means of valuing securities.

4. Provide protection for investors by:

- vetting those companies seeking to obtain a Stock Exchange quotation;
- requiring full information to be given to investors by quoted companies;
- providing compensation to any investor who has suffered loss through a broker failing to meet their obligations;
- establishing rules of conduct for members of the Stock Exchange and quoted companies, e.g. the City Code on Takeovers and Mergers.

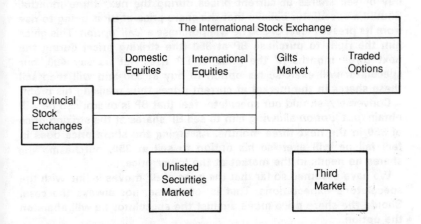

22.1 The International Stock Exchange

In practice, the International Stock Exchange is made up of a number of different markets (see Fig 23.1). The domestic equities market is the place where company shares – ordinary and preference – are traded. Ordinary shares are divided into three categories. The premier group (alpha stocks) are the 50 or so leading UK shares. Market makers are expected to provide firm prices at which they will deal throughout the day. There is less market interest in beta and gamma stock and up-to-date prices are less likely to be available.

An international equities market has existed in London for a long time. In 1989, over 600 firms' shares were traded and it was estimated that turnover exceeded £1 billion daily. The international market ensures leading foreign equities can be bought and sold easily outside their home country at competitive prices. The success of this market is encouraging many large overseas companies to raise equity capital in London also.

The term 'gilts market' is something of a misnoma. While at one time virtually all the markets' business was dealing in UK Government gilt edged securities, it now also deals with stocks issued by UK local authorities and foreign government as well as fixed interest industrial debentures.

The traded option market has grown dramatically in the last few years. It is the largest option market outside the United States. Many market traders and broker–dealers use options as a method of reducing the risks to which they are exposed by holding equities.

Traded options

Option dealing is a form of speculation. An option gives the right to buy or sell shares at current prices during the next three months. Should a speculator believe that the share price of BP is going to rise from its present level of 350 he will purchase a *'call' option*. This gives him the right to purchase BP at 350 (the striking price) during the next three months. If the price of BP rises, let us say 400, our speculator will exercise his option to buy at 350 and will then sell these shares in the market at current prices thus realising his profit.

Conversely, should our speculator feel that BP is overpriced he will obtain *'put' option* allowing him to sell BP shares at the striking price of 350 in the next three months. Assuming the share price does in fact fall he will exercise his option to sell at 350, purchasing the shares he needs in the market at the lower price.

We have assumed so far that the price of BP moves in line with the speculator's expectations. That is, of course, not always the case. Should the share price move against the speculator he will abandon the option.

In 1980 the Stock Exchange created a second tier market called the Unlisted Securities Market (USM). The USM offers smaller firms, who are not ready for a full listing on the domestic equities market, the opportunity of raising cash for expansion and, at the same time, creating a market in their shares. The procedure for joining the USM is a similar but simplified procedure to that of joining the senior market. The cost – approximately £70,000 – is significantly less than for obtaining a full listing. In 1989 there were 410 companies trading on the USM.

In 1987 the International Stock Exchange started its new Third Market. The aim is to extend the possibility of raising risk capital to a greater number of young and growing companies. The Stock Exchange believes it will be of interest to firms who:

- are too small to join the USM

- are unable to demonstrate one year's trading results but can show fully researched projects with the prospect of significant revenue within 12 months

- have been trading for less than three years, and therefore are unable to join the USM

- have been trading for three years but have some defect in their accounting records, and are therefore unable to join the USM

There are 59 companies trading on the Third Market.

The International Stock Exchange is not an open market on which private individuals can transact their business personally, instead the business is transacted through its members.

Until 1986 the Stock Exchange consisted of some 5,000 individual members, commonly working in partnership who acted as either a jobber – dealing in shares, or a broker – acting as link man between the investor and the jobber. There was strict separation of roles. However, as a result of government pressure the system has changed. There are three major differences. First, all stock exchange firms can now act in a dual capacity. Thus brokers are now able to act as jobbers – or market-makers as they are now called. Secondly, market makers are now able to deal with investors directly in addition to their dealings with other market makers and brokers. Thirdly, regulations limiting stock exchange membership have been relaxed – opening the way for commercial banks, merchant banks and financial conglomerates to operate in the market.

The introduction of dual capacity – one firm taking on a number of different roles – has important implications for confidentiality and conflicts of interest. Thus a bank or financial conglomerate may, in relation to one company be acting as adviser, lender, provider of equity capital, investment manager and market maker in its shares.

Insider Trading

The 1985 Act which covers insider dealing prohibits deals in a company's securities by someone, termed an insider, who has gained price sensitive information. The legislation covers several situations. First, a director, or any other employee of a business, who has price sensitive information e.g. a fall in this year's profits, must not use that information until it is announced in the press. Secondly the term 'insider' also covers the situation where an official in a government department has access to price sensitive information relating to a company – perhaps the referral of a takeover bid to the Monopolies Commission. Finally, the term 'insider' even covers the situation where an individual with price sensitive information passes that information to another person so that they may buy shares.

In order to prevent abuse of knowledge and power in these situations a separation of functions is achieved through 'Chinese walls'. In essence this means dividing the work of the business so that information in one part of the business is not available to any other part. This method is widely used in America and Australia.

Stock Exchange procedure

Let us now consider a typical transaction to see how the Stock Exchange works. Our investor, Mr Average, instructs his stock broker to sell 500 Condor plc 'at best', that is the highest price possible. Mr Average may, in fact, not know a stockbroker and give these instructions to his bank instead. Mr Average's intermediary will then use the computerised price information system – seaq (Stock Exchange Automatic Quotation) to find out which of the market makers is offering the best price. Market makers quote two prices – the higher for selling, the lower for buying. Keen prices in the market are guaranteed because market makers are competing against one another for business, and also because they have to quote both buying and selling prices

Prices quoted by the market reflect the supply of and the demand for each individual share. Should the market maker receive more orders to sell than buy Condor plc shares he will adjust his prices downwards. He aims to strike a price at which orders to buy and sell Condor plc broadly match one another. In doing so he ensures that he is not left with too many (or too few) Condor plc shares on his hands. But the adjustments made to the prices of the shares by the market maker do not always reflect buying and selling orders. Sometimes he may feel that there is no good reason why shares should be unpopular and will maintain the present price despite a number of orders to sell. In doing so he reduces the temporary fluctuation in price which may occur due to the lumpiness of transactions, but lays himself open to loss if he has read the market feeling incorrectly.

The broker will return to the market maker offering the best terms, confirm that the prices quoted still hold and then reveal that he wishes to sell Condor plc stock. For small transactions market maker is required to adhere to the prices quoted. If, however, the order is so large that it could depress or raise the price of that share the market maker is not bound to honour those prices.

Market makers' revenue comes from three different sources:
1 Dealing spreads. Market makers quote two prices; the difference between the two – it used to be known as the 'jobbers turn' is used to cover costs and profit. The more uncertain the market is, the wider the spread will be.
2 Position taking. Market makers become specialists in and very knowledgeable about certain markets. For example, oils, retailing, banking or manufacturing – there are many others. They may believe that certain shares within the sector are under-valued and that the price will rise. In anticipation of this price rise they may build up a stock of shares. Alternatively, if they believe certain stock prices will fall they will leave themselves short of stock in the expectation of being able to buy more cheaply later.
3 Agency commissions, through dealing directly with the investors.

Factors affecting the price of shares

The prices at which shares are traded are published each day by the Stock Exchange, extracts of which will be reproduced in the daily papers. Each day you will find that the prices of many shares quoted will have moved. Normally the movement is marginal – perhaps 1 or 2p, but sometimes the variation is more dramatic. Underlying these changes in price is investor confidence which will be based on the factors listed below.

Primary Those relating to the firm or industry. Investors follow with great interest the fortunes of each company – after all their money is at stake! The publishing of the interim and annual financial results provides shareholders with periodic information on which to evaluate their investment. But in reality the flow of information on which investors make their judgments is continuous, for example:

- news of an important contract;
- the development of a new product;
- the possibility of a take-over bid;
- increased competition for the firm or the industry;
- the closing of factories or depots;
- the resignation of senior personnel or directors;
- poor labour relations;

may all affect share prices.

Secondary The economic and political environment of business. Business does not exist in a vacuum, and the investor should not ignore the environment within which the firm operates. It is impossible though, to identify all sources of information which may affect the investor's judgment – the following illustrate the diversity of information available:

- indices on inflation, unemployment, economic activity, balance of payments, consumer spending (especially where trends are discernible);
- surveys by the CBI, stockbrokers, universities or other government institutions;
- the value of sterling;
- the United States economy;
- legislation affecting business, e.g. consumer protection or industrial safety;
- international relations;
- political instability in other countries;
- statements by government officials or other heads of state;
- press comment.

Share Ownership

For nearly 20 years direct ownership of shares by individuals has declined. In 1963 fifty-four per cent of shares were owned by the general public compared with 28 per cent in 1981. Put another way, only one in 14 of the adult population invested on the Stock Exchange in 1981.

In contrast America, during the same period, has seen very little change in individual share ownership with approximately 60 per cent of equity (ordinary and preference shares) held by the public.

The Government is anxious to encourage wider share ownership because:

- institutions are less willing to take investment risks than individuals which makes it difficult for the small adventurous business to raise capital

- institutions may not be willing to deal in small parcels of shares, making it difficult for small firms to raise finance.

- encouraging individuals to invest provides more funds for industry

- investment by individuals reduces consumption and thereby inflationary pressure on prices

- personal shareholders tend to be more loyal than institutional investors

- it encourages an understanding of how business works and the need for profitable companies if our standard of living is to be increased.

However, in 1988, approximately one-fifth of the adult population held shares. This had been achieved by:

- privatisation of State-owned businesses

- favourable tax treatment for employees who invested in a company share scheme

- introduction of personal equity plans.

Examination questions

1 What are the major sources of finance available to a multinational company? *(PSC)*

2 Critically examine the sources of finance available to a medium-sized company. *(PSC)*

3 A small private limited company wishes to extend its operations. How may it raise the necessary finance? What difficulties could it face?

4 (a) Distinguish between the terms: (i) ordinary share; (ii) preference share; (iii) debenture.
  (b) Your business wishes to acquire a computer and has a choice of:
    (i) immediate payment; (ii) hire-purchase; (iii) leasing. Which would you choose, and why?

5 Comlon a large manufacturing company wishes to extend its business. What sources of finance should it consider and what factors should be taken into account in deciding which sources to use?

6 Explain the work of the Stock Exchange indicating its importance to industry and government.

7 Your employer, a manufacturing company, is undertaking two extra projects:

(a) to develop a new factory in a depressed area;
(b) a special order which will be completed in two years.
Both will involve an extra investment in machines, material, and labour. What sources of finance could you recommend for each of these projects? *(PSC)*

8   In what ways may:
(a) a shareholder of Comlon International plc
(b) an employee of Comlon International plc
(c) a consumer of Comlon International plc's products
be affected by the increased capital investment decisions of that company? *(PSC)*

9   Your business wishes to acquire a number of word processors. It has the choice of:
    (i)   immediate payment
    (ii) hire purchase
    (iii) leasing
Prepare a report for the chief accountant outlining the benefits and drawbacks of each method, explaining which one you recommend. *(PSC)*

10 A family-owned private limited company is contemplating the issue of further shares, as a public limited company. Consider the factors which might influence this decision. *(AEB)*

11 Indicate the major advantages and disadvantages of leasing as opposed to the purchase of an item of capital equipment, and comment on the factors to be considered in deciding whether or not an asset should be acquired by lease or purchase. *(AEB)*

12 (a) What do you understand by the term 'gearing', and how might it be measured?
    (b) how might a finance house use gearing ratios when considering an application from a medium-sized manufacturing company for a loan of £5,000,000 for expansion purposes?
    (c) What alternative source of funds might the firm examine?
    (CAMB 1987)

13 How would you suggest that a well-established computer manufacturer with (i) turnover of £25 m, (ii) low capital value fixed assets accurately represented in the balance sheet and (iii) a high debt/equity ratio, might find £5 m to manufacture and launch micro-computers?
(CAMB 1984)

Chapter 23

Consultancy, non-profit-making, and export services

Consultancy

Management consultants

As business and its environment become more complex, an ever-increasing burden is placed upon the management of the organisation. Add to this the extent to which many companies in recent years have pruned their workforce (at all levels) and it can be seen that the existing management is ill-placed to deal with any problem or project which diverts them from the task of carrying out their routine duties.

Management consultants are independent organisations or individuals who, in return for a fee, will give advice on any problem – or set of problems – which are of concern to the client firm's management. In investigating any problem consultants will draw upon their wide experience of industry. Consultants are likely to be graduates, probably with professional qualifications as well, and will have had line responsibility and experience in several companies. But the greatest strength of consultants is their accumulated experience as advisers to companies. While each situation encountered is unique in terms of environment, organisation structure, and personnel, the basic problem is often one which a consultant has met before. They are therefore able to draw upon this reservoir of knowledge in advising their clients.

Management consultants will be used when:
1. The business does not have sufficient managerial time or talent to deal with the problem.
2. Where there is not a permanent need within the firm for the particular skill and expertise required.
3. Where the firm is unable to take a sufficiently detached and analytical view of the problem.

The use of management consultants is now widely accepted in the UK – and indeed most other advanced economies. They are used not only by industry and commerce but also by central and local government and other state agencies. The range of services offered by consultants has grown considerably over the years and now includes:

1. *Policy and planning.* Establishing corporate objectives, medium- and long-term planning, organisation structure and communications problems, control procedures. Advice on expansion – mergers and take-overs.

2. *Marketing function.* Product evaluation, promotional policy, channels of distribution, marketing research.

3. *Financial function.* Advice on financial structure and the raising of capital, profitability, control of working capital, asset utilisation, costing and budgetary control, investment analysis.

4. *Personnel function.* Selection, training, and development schemes, welfare, health, and safety policies; management succession; motivation and wage-payment schemes; industrial relations.

5. *Production function.* Factory location and layout, production planning and control, materials control, quality control, organisation and methods studies.

6. *Management techniques.* Operational research, network analysis, value analysis, simulation techniques, computer applications, systems development.

Advertising agencies

The modern advertising agency has its origins in the work of the nineteenth-century space brokers. These brokers acted as intermediaries between the advertisers and the newspaper and periodical owners. They would purchase large blocks of space in a newspaper or magazine and break it down into smaller lots which would then be sold to the individual advertiser.

For their service to the media owner they received a commission. Thus, should a broker purchase £1,000 worth of advertising space in a newspaper they would be invoiced for £850 (the common rate of commission being 15 per cent), but would sell that space to their clients for £1,000.

Media owners found the service of the space broker was very much to their advantage. Administratively, it was easier for media owners to deal with and obtain their money from a limited number of brokers, rather than the very large numbers of individuals who advertised in their publications. Moreover, the risk of not filling advertising space was borne by the space broker not the media owner.

Indeed, it was this last factor which caused space brokers to break from their traditional activities, and move towards the work of the advertising agency as we know it today. Very simply, space brokers saw that it would be much simpler to sell their advertising space if they could show how it should be used. Artists and writers were employed to create advertisements for their clients.

Today's advertising agency still buys space for its clients' advertisements, receiving a commission from the media owner concerned, and still employs artists and writers to produce advertisements. But many agencies offer a far broader range of services. The typical full service agency will undertake all work involved with a large advertising campaign – the planning and buying of media space, together with the creation, production, and testing of the advertisement, as well as marketing research, public relations, sales promotion and new product development. Many of these full service agencies are well-known names such as J Walter Thompson or Saatchi and Saatchi.

In advertising parlance a clients' business is called an account. Each account held by the advertising agency will be supervised by an account executive. This person is the linchpin in the relationship between advertiser and agency, acting as liaison between the two – representing the agency to the client, and translating the client's requirements into action. The account executive must be very much an all-rounder, having experience in all aspects of advertising. They must also be an able co-ordinator and motivator – capable of drawing together those disparate skills needed to service the account, and motivating all those working for them to produce their best work.

In broad terms there will be three groups of people working with the account executive (see Fig. 24.1). The creative team, consisting of copy-writers, artists, typographers, script-writers and film producers, are responsible for developing and producing advertisements. The marketing and market research team are responsible for any research which may be undertaken to identify the target population and their attitudes towards the client's products. As a result of these investigations the client may be advised to alter the product or package in some way, undertake some form of sales promotion other than advertising, or modify their approach to public relations. The team may also carry out advertisement testing.

The aim of the media planning and research team is to identify the appropriate media for the advertisement, and advise on items

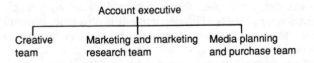

23.1 Co-ordination function of the account executive

such as size, length, or timing of advertisements. Having obtained agreement from the advertiser, space or time will then be negotiated with the media owners.

In recent years the traditional agency structure described above has been undermined by a large number of businesses also describing themselves as advertising agencies, but offering a limited specialist service. These agencies have developed through being able to offer a specific service or range of services more expertly and cheaper than the full service agency. Services offered in this way include:

1. Creative agencies – sometimes known as 'hot shops' they specialise in creativity – for example, promoting new products or inventing new product names.

2. Product development agencies – dealing with the whole process of new product development up to and including the commercial launch.

3. Media agencies – specialising in the purchase of time or space from the media owners.

4. Industrial agencies – specialising in the advertisement of industrial rather than consumer products. Their work often involves the production of sales catalogues and literature. They will also negotiate space in specialist magazines and journals.

5. Sales promotion agencies – willing to create and administer competitions, gift coupons, free samples, special offers for other products (e.g. £25 off your holiday), or any of the many other schemes devised to promote sales.

Market research companies

The roots of the independent market research organisation are to be found in the work of the early advertising agencies. Within these agencies market research was used as a tool for establishing the effectiveness of an advertising campaign. Even today many advertising agencies include a market research service as part of their range of activities.

Many large organisations find it possible to carry out their own market research work by creating a specialist department. This has the advantage that the department's workers are not only experts in their own field, but also develop considerable knowledge of the organisation's products. The department is also able to monitor continuously the organisation's markets and the performance of their products.

But large organisations are only able to afford the luxury of their own market research department because its high cost is spread over many products and units of sales. The option of a market research department is not available to medium-sized or small firms. Specialist market research organisations have therefore developed to provide this service.

The function of the commercial market research organisation is to provide its client with information on:

1. The structure of the market – its size, location, organisation, consumers, etc.
2. The acceptability of products – consumer requirements, the popularity of specific products (including competitors), the effect of advertising on acceptability, etc.
3. Channels of distribution – information on the effectiveness of various distribution systems with the aim of:
(a) reducing the risks to which the client is exposed; and
(b) identifying and highlighting new market opportunities.

These functions are achieved by planning, implementing, and interpreting market research investigations on behalf of the client. In carrying out these investigations a wide range of statistical and psychological techniques may be used. The procedure for such an investigation is described in Chapter 11 (p. 179).

Many market research organisations provide a complete service and are willing to undertake any kind of market research investigation. There are others, though, who specialise in one aspect of market research work, for example concentrating on consumer as opposed to, say, industrial market research. Alternatively, the organisation may specialise in market research investigations into certain industries (the Nielson Company, for example, provides specialist information on the food and drug industries), or certain research techniques, for example audience surveys or opinion polls.

Non-profit-making services

Chambers of commerce

Chambers of commerce, or chambers of commerce and industry as some (e.g. London, Birmingham) are called, exist in most important commercial centres throughout the U.K. They are voluntary associations of people prominent in local business – industry, commerce, and the professions.

The first chamber of commerce in this country is that of Glasgow which dates back to 1783, while the most important – the London Chamber of Commerce and Industry (LCCI) was established in 1881. Although chambers of commerce operate individually their activities are linked through membership of the Association of British Chambers of Commerce. This organisation acts as spokesman for the interests of chambers throughout the country, making representations to the Government, and representing chambers on various government bodies.

The work of the chambers of commerce is twofold. In the first place they make representations to central and local government or other bodies on matters of interest to their members. For example during its centenary year the LCCI took up the following issues on behalf of its members (there were many more):

- economic policy, public finance, and taxation policy
- the structure of local government finance and the level of rates
- the adequacy of roads, airports, and public transport in London and the south-east of England
- aid and incentives for small firms
- further and higher education fees for overseas students
- unitary tax system in the USA
- the £1 coin.

Other chambers throughout the country will be making representations on a similarly diverse range of issues.

The second broad area of work chambers of commerce are involved in is the provision of services to the business community. One important aspect of this work is aid and advice on exporting. Information can be provided on openings for trade in overseas countries, the appointment of foreign agents and distributors, international trade procedures and requirements, customs regulations, and legal restrictions. British chambers of commerce arrange overseas trade missions and exhibitions, and will also provide help and advice to overseas trade missions visiting this country. Through British chambers abroad and links with overseas chambers they are also able to provide up-to-date information on conditions in many overseas markets.

The larger chambers of commerce also aid exporters by the issue of 'export of commercial samples' carnets. These allow samples of goods to be imported temporarily into overseas countries without paying duties or going through normal customs formalities. These chambers will also issue certificates of origin, analysis, or quality in respect of goods for export.

At home, chambers of commerce, through their libraries and research facilities, can provide members with information on current legislation, be it employee rights, health and safety, consumer, restrictive practices, food and drug regulations, or many others. Chambers may provide business training courses for executives, many of which are concerned with aspects of exporting, though courses in modern business skills are also run. Many chambers will provide translator and secretarial services. Commercial disputes may also be settled through their arbitration services.

Finally, mention must be made of two chamber of commerce services available nationally. First, through the LCCI's Commercial Education Scheme, examinations are conducted in all commercial subjects, also for the Private Secretary's Diploma and Certificate and the Junior Secretary's Certificate. Secondly, in conjunction with chambers of commerce in Birmingham, Cardiff, and Merseyside, the LCCI has established a registry of business names *The LCCI Business Registry* which is intended to supersede the *Registry of Business Names* previously controlled by the Department of Trade. Registration is intended to show proprietorship of the business name, reduce the risk of confusion caused by companies having similar names, and 'warn off' a new business which searches the *Register* before setting up in business with a similar name.

Chambers of trade

Chambers of commerce tend to be found in our larger towns and cities, but most towns boast a chamber of trade. Its members are drawn from shopkeepers and traders in the locality. The services of chambers of commerce and trade overlap to some extent. Both seek to establish agreement among their members on matters of common interest and to act as spokesmen on these matters. The distinguishing feature of chambers of trade is that they concentrate almost exclusively on matters of local interest and lack the national and international dimensions of chambers of commerce. Chambers of trade would be concerned with matters such as parking facilities, shop hours, delivery regulations, or the impact of a new road on business in the town.

Trade associations

Although firms in the same industry, trade, or service are often in fierce competition with one another there are many matters in which they have a common interest and where co-operation and joint action are mutually beneficial. Trade associations, such as the Society of Motor Manufacturers and Traders, the Machine Tool Traders Association, or the Advertising Association, are the organisations created by these firms to protect and promote their common interests. Some, like the National Federation of Building Trades Employers, began as employers' associations. These, although initially established to negotiate wages and conditions of work on behalf of an firms in the industry, now offer a far broader service to their members.

Trade associations exist in most sectors of industry and commerce. Their principal functions are to decide, through meetings and conferences, policy on the many issues which affect their members' interests, and to represent that policy in discussions with the Government and other bodies.

Many trade associations provide a significant range of ancillary activities. Research is often undertaken on new materials or processes. This, and other information on the trade or industry will be made available through journals or magazines published by the trade association. Information on new and better materials, processes, and management practice may also be made available through information exchange bureaux financed and staffed by the association.

On the marketing side trade directories may be published while advertising, export production, and publicity campaigns designed to promote industry's products or image may be undertaken. Many trade associations will give advice to their members on export opportunities or procedures and have available confidential information on potential export or overseas agents.

Many trade associations are themselves members of the Confederation of British Industry (CBI). Its primary function is to represent the views of all industrialists (rather than the sectional interests of the individual trade association) to the Government and thereby influence government policy. It is very much part of the tripartite system of consultation established in British politics between the TUC representing the trade unions, the CBI representing business, and the Government. The CBI representatives sit on government bodies, submit evidence to many government enquiries or commissions, and are regularly consulted by government departments on matters affecting industry and commerce.

The CBI provides an advisory service for its members, providing information and advice on a wide range of topics such as legislation, trade statistics, export markets, methods of exporting, and finding overseas agents. It has also established a number of permanent offices abroad.

Export services

For many companies exporting is a step into the unknown. There are so many differences between home and overseas trading. In the first place language, culture, and tastes are often very different. The exporter may very well have to adapt his product to satisfy these tastes. Alternatively, product changes may be necessary to conform with local regulations relating to the sale of the product (e.g. product safety).

Quite apart from these differences in the market, many problems are caused by export documentation and procedure. Although several attempts have been made to reduce and simplify export documentation the would-be exporter is still required to fill in numerous forms. The importing country will require various forms to be completed in order to satisfy import regulations, exchange controls, and import duties. Inevitably the number and content of these forms varies between countries. Documentation relating to transport (e.g. shipping) and insurance also tends to be more complex.

Finally, the exporter may encounter financial difficulties. Banks may be less willing to finance export than home trade because of the greater risk of loss. Developing countries may be less stable politically or economically. It is more difficult to pursue a claim (and more expensive) against an importer through foreign courts. Moreover, an unforeseen fluctuation in the exchange rates may turn the exporter's profit into a loss.

Large firms are able to cope with many of these difficulties. The volume of overseas trade undertaken is often sufficient to justify a specialist function within the firm. Small firms though, unable to afford this luxury, rely heavily on external aid and advice.

Reflecting the importance of overseas trade to the UK economy, many such sources of help exist. They fall into one of three categories, namely governmental, commercial, or non-profit-making. The role of the latter, non-profit-making, organisations such as chambers of commerce or trade associations has already been noted in this chapter.

Governmental

Valuable assistance is given to the exporter through the BOTB and the ECGD. The BOTB is able to provide advice on a large number of specific markets together with information on the prospects for particular goods and services in each of these markets. The BOTB's export intelligence service also distributes on a daily basis trade information obtained from Diplomatic Service commercial posts in approximately 200 overseas centres. Moreover, should such information be insufficient for the exporter's purposes the BOTB will give advice on, and financial assistance for, additional market research.

The BOTB also helps promote British exports by organising overseas trade fairs, exhibitions, and in-store promotions. Financial assistance is given to British firms bringing potential importers of their goods to this country. Similarly, financial help may also be given for group visits to overseas markets where the visit is sponsored by a trade association or chamber of commerce. Finally, the *Board* in conjunction with the Central Office of Information and the BBC External Services operates an export publicity service. Through radio, television and press releases it aims to publicise the success stories of British Industry. While the major purpose of the project is to publicise British industry as a whole, individual firms often benefit from the world-wide publicity.

Since 1921 ECGD has provided credit, insurance, and finance for exports. The basic credit insurance policy, the comprehensive short term guarantee, covers exporters against the risk of loss for periods of up to six months. The policy-holder is required to insure all his export turnover so that the risk of default is spread as widely as possible thereby reducing premiums. In recent years though, due to economic and political instability in developing countries, the ECGD has been forced to modify the policy in respect of some markets by imposing a surcharge or modifying the conditions of cover.

As an insurance agency the ECGD does not itself provide funds for exporters. The ECGD is, however, prepared to give the exporter's bank a guarantee. In the event of the exporter being unable to repay their bank loan (due to the failure of the overseas buyer to pay them as agreed) the ECGD will make good the bank's loss. The bank having received this assurance is willing to finance the exporter's busines at favourable rates of interest.

An exporter wishing to obtain these benefits first calculates the maximum amount of export finance that they will need at any one time and then applies to the ECGD for a guarantee to be given to their banker for this amount. Should the department agree to the application it issues a facility letter to the exporter's bank outlining the terms and conditions of the guarantee. At the same time the exporter is required to pay a premium for this service and also to sign a 'recourse agreement' with ECGD. This allows the department to claim from the exporter any sums which it has to pay out under guarantee. The exporter in turn makes a claim against the ECGD under their separate comprehensive short-term insurance policy.

An exporter also has the option of arranging 'buyer credit finance'. This has the advantage of enabling the importer to settle with the exporter on cash terms. These loans carry extremely favourable rates of interest for the importer. Buyer credit finance is often used in large capital contracts undertaken by a consortium of UK firms. Once the principle of buyer credit has been agreed by the consortium and importer a financial institution ready to finance the borrowing has to be found. Most commercial banks are willing to participate in these schemes. The exporter and prospective lender will then approach the ECGD in order to negotiate a 'buyer credit guarantee'. This guarantee will cover the whole of the loan made by the financier and ensures that he will receive payment should the importer default on payments of interest or repayments of capital.

Commercial

Goods may be exported direct or through the services of an intermediary. Where the product being sold is in one of the specialist fields of engineering, where the firm's export business is sizeable, or the exporter has considerable experience of selling overseas, selling direct to an importer may prove advantageous. However, in most cases the task of selling directly to an overseas customer is extremely difficult and can create many problems. The small or inexperienced exporter is well advised to turn to one of the many intermediaries in the export trade.

Buying houses   The origins of many buying houses are to be found in the activities of the great trading companies of the British Empire. For very many years these companies have been involved in the export of local produce and the import of those consumer and capital products not manufactured locally. Today it is cheaper and easier for local business to use the buying houses' long-established international connections to find and purchase whatever imports are required than to establish their own network of overseas contacts.

Buying houses are agents for their overseas principals, acting on their instructions and solely in their interests. Their work may be limited to confirming an order which has already been provisionally arranged through other intermediaries. For this reason buying houses are sometimes also known as 'confirming houses'. In confirming the order the buying house guarantees the exporter payment for the goods supplied, paying for them on the due date and recouping their expenditure from the importer.

Where the buying house receives an order from the importer which stipulates the business from which the goods are to be obtained it is termed a 'closed indent'. An 'open indent' specifies the goods to be obtained but leaves the choice of supplier to the buying house. In this case they will discuss contract terms and obtain quotations from several manufacturers before placing an order.

Once an order has been placed the buying house will arrange for the packing and freighting of the goods, and undertake the necessary documentation. For their services to the importer buying houses are paid a commission which is calculated on the value of goods purchased.

Export houses   In its widest sense the term 'export house' encompasses many of the intermediaries engaged in promoting international trade including buying houses, buying agents, and confirming houses. More strictly the term refers to a situation where the house acts as manager for a manufacturer's export business, or purchases on its own behalf.

An export management agency acts as a UK firm's export department. The agency is responsible for familiarising itself with the exporter's product range, conducting market research to identify suitable outlets, entering into contracts on their principal's behalf, and dealing with all aspects of export administration.

Many export management agencies will also act as export factors. In this role they pay the manufacturer for the goods as soon as they are shipped, obtaining settlement at a later date from the overseas customers. This is primarily a financial service to the exporter not a form of insurance. The export management agency is not a party to the contract and may (depending upon the terms of the contract) have recourse to the exporter should the buyer fail to make payment to the agency. However in return for an extra fee or commission the agent may guarantee the exporter against bad debts. In these circumstances he is termed a *del credere agent* and the extra payment he receives is termed the *del credere* commission.

Export merchants, unlike management agencies, operate on their own behalf. Merchants purchase goods from the exporter on their own behalf as principal, and then resell them at a profit to an overseas client. Merchants thus take the risk of not finding a customer, or not making a profit on the transaction. At the same time as purchasing the goods they may also negotiate a 'sole distributorship' agreement giving them exclusive rights to sell this product in specified markets overseas. They may then appoint distributors to act for them in different localities or alternatively undertake distribution themselves.

Overseas agents These are intermediaries who undertake, in return for a payment, to represent an exporter in an overseas market. Great care should be taken before appointing such an agent – a wrong decision may result in few export orders, a damaged reputation, and much wasted time and money. The exporter must ensure that the prospective agent:

- is not representing a competitor;

- has experience in promoting the right group of products;

- has the ability (finance staff and other resources) to take on additional commitments;

- has a good reputation within the business community;

- is able to supply satisfactory credit and trade references;

- shows an enthusiasm for the exporter's business.

Exporters looking for an overseas agent to represent their business may obtain help from various sources. The BOTB, with the help of British embassies, provides an Agency Finding Service. The large commercial banks maintain lists of suitable agents. They will also provide information on the prospective agent's financial standing and arrange introductions where required. Chambers of commerce, through their connections with overseas chambers, provide a similar service to that of the BOTB and the banks. They will also advise on the form and terms of agreement which should be entered into with an overseas agent.

It is important that the terms of the agreement are clearly understood by both exporter and agent. Once an agent is appointed their position is protected by law. Dismissal will be difficult and costly. A typical agreement will contain terms relating to the area in which they are the exporter's representative, whether they are the sole or exclusive representative in that area, the products covered by the contract, what sales promotion they are required to undertake, how they are to be paid, the date the agreement starts and ends, reasons for terminating the agreement, and provision for arbitration in the case of a dispute.

Shipping and freight agents Where manufacturers conduct their own export business, either personally or through an agent, much of the detailed work associated with overseas trade can be avoided by using shipping and freight forwarding agents. Shipping agents perform the more limited service, dealing with the transportation of goods from port to port. Freight forwarding agents, on the other hand, undertake to convey goods from the manufacturer's to the agent's or importer's premises overseas. In doing so they will:
1. Advise on the best form of transport, having regard for the nature of the goods, their destination, the time factor, the costs involved, and the buyer's wishes.
2. Advise on packing, labelling, and export documentation to conform with the requirements of the carriers and regulations of the importing country.
3. Arrange freight space, warehousing, customs clearance, and co-ordinate all transportation.
4. Offer the benefits of special (low) freight rates through the grouping of numerous exporter's products into one large consignment.
5. Provide container facilities, especially for traffic between the UK and Europe.

Shipping and freight forwarding agents advise on and arrange transportation for a very large proportion of UK exports.

Banks Almost inevitably exporting makes extra demands on a firm's financial resources. Generally both delivery of the goods and payment for them take longer. However, in accordance with Bank of England instructions, banks in the UK will give priority to providing finance for those firms engaged in exporting. This finance can be provided in a number of ways.

Many businesses will already have an overdraft facility with their bank. It is extremely easy to extend this facility to provide the extra funds required for exporting. For a small premium the ECGD will guarantee that it will reimburse the exporter's bank should the importer default on payment. Drawing on existing bank overdraft facilities provides much of the finance for 'open-account' transactions (nearly three-quarters of UK exports are paid for by this method). Under an open-account transaction goods, together with all necessary documents, are sent to the buyer. He, in return, agrees to pay the amount owing within a specified period – normally not more than six months. The method is particularly appropriate where there are regular two-way dealings between the firms with say, a UK firm exporting goods to a firm in Hong Kong and importing goods from the same business.

The use of the open-account method of payment is based upon trust in the integrity of the importer – often established over many years' trading. There are, however, many situations where the degree of trust between the two parties is insufficient to warrant using this method of payment. Historically, the most important alternative has been the bill of exchange (see Ch. 29, p. 423). Here the banking system aids the exporter in two very different ways.

First, the exporter may utilise their bank's international connections by sending a bill of exchange for the value of the exports to the importer through the banking system. The UK bank will pass the bill of exchange, plus all relevant documents, to its overseas branch (or bank which acts for it). This bank – termed the collecting bank – presents the bill to the importer for them to sign and acknowledge liability. The documents are then released to the overseas buyer. This procedure gives exporters greater control over their goods, and also means that the importer does not have to pay for the goods before delivery.

Second, banks are also willing to either purchase bills of exchange from the exporter holding them to maturity, or alternatively advance moneys against the security of the bill.

Finally, banks may also aid the exporter by means of a documentary letter of credit – a method by which the exporter receives payment. It consists of a promise by a banker that bills of exchange drawn upon the bank will be honoured, provided the exporter has complied with the terms of the credit. It has the advantage of replacing the name of the little-known importer on the bill of exchange for that of a well-known bank. The exporter is thus able to discount the bill more easily and at a finer rate of interest.

The letter of credit is established by the overseas buyer instructing a bank in their own or the exporter's country to accept a bill of exchange (alternatively the letter of credit could stipulate immediate payment for the goods) against the deposit of documents relating to the goods being exported. By selecting a reputable bank the exporter is guaranteed payment, and the importer is confident that the export documents needed for transfer of title have been completed satisfactorily and delivered to the bank.

Letters of credit are normally irrevocable. By this we mean that once the exporter has agreed or complied with the terms of the letter of credit they cannot be cancelled or altered without the exporter's agreement.

Even greater security of payment can be obtained by the exporter should the irrevocable letter of credit be 'confirmed' by the UK bank through whom the credit is advised. Provided then that the exporter has conformed to the terms of the letter of credit the exporter will receive payment from the confirming bank who in turn look to the overseas bank for payment. The exporter is not liable to reimburse the confirming bank in the case of default on payment by the overseas buyer or their bank.

Examination questions

1 Chambers of commerce, trade associations and the CBI are all concerned with the promotion of trade. Outline the work of *two* of them.

2 What are chambers of commerce? How do they differ from employer's associations? In what ways are they useful to business people?

3 A company manufacturing electrical consumer products wishes to improve its marketing. How could market research companies and advertising agencies help?

4 Outline the major functions and the relationships which exist between the business community and two of the following: advertising agencies; market research companies; management consultants. *(PSC)*

5 Selecting examples from your own country, explain how the process of exporting may be aided by both government and non-government bodies. *(PSC)*

6 What factors discourage firms from exporting? How does the Government help overcome these difficulties?

Studying for your examination

I wonder how many of you when telling friends and relatives of impending examinations have been wished 'good luck'. No doubt such wishes were genuinely meant, but you shouldn't need luck – the work you've done throughout the course should be your guarantee of success. – All too often though candidates fail to do themselves justice. The following notes are intended to help you throughout your course of study.

During the course

Compared with the time available for revision, the time available for study throughout the course is far greater. This time must be used effectively to ensure you get a complete set of notes (ask your lecturer for a copy of the syllabus, and whether you will cover all of it), to undertake supplementary reading and also any assignments. All these will be used later on as a basis for your revision. Unfortunately, many candidates come to the revision period with incomplete revision materials. It is impossible to make up this lost time at the last moment.

Revision

Some of your contemporaries may boast that they won't start revision until the week before the exams. Few will actually be able even to pass let alone do well on such limited revision. Indeed, many who make these claims will be quietly working away at home chuckling to themselves that they have lulled the opposition (that's you!) into a false state of complacency. Most students will start revising at least *six weeks* before their examinations.

The key to revising effectively is to plan your revision. Identify periods during the day when you will be able to revise. Hopefully there will be at least one session each day where you can allocate several hours to revision, but don't forget those 20 or 30 minute gaps (e.g. in the bus on the way to college) as these can add significantly to total revision time.

Your revision plan should be realistic – you must allow reasonable time for meals, socialising and sleeping! It is often a good idea to involve your family/friends in the revision plan. Let them know when you expect to revise each day so that they can encourage and support you during this period – or just keep out of your way.

In order to make most use of your limited revision time you need to have available not only your complete set of notes but also:

- the syllabus – check to see that it has all been covered

- past exam papers – these will give you information on the format of the examination – how long it is, total number of questions, number to answer, compulsory sections or questions and so on.

- model answers: these show the way recognised teachers in the subject would answer a question.

- examiners reports – these highlight past candidates' failings and indicate very generally what the Chief Examiner was looking for in a good answer.

As you can see all provide you with valuable background information.

Having drawn up a revision timetable and obtained all the necessary revision material we now need to look at *how* to revise. Much student revision time is used ineffectively by merely revising passively. Re-reading your old notes is often pretty boring and you will find that concentration is easily lost. Instead, you should try to revise actively. In practice, there are many ways of doing this – using a pen to high-light existing notes is perhaps the most obvious. Many students will try to create a new more concise set of notes. These could be put on index cards – which are easy to carry round and read at odd moments.

Another very useful method of revising is to practice answering past examination questions. It is not necessary to write out answers in full, instead try creating a skeleton plan of the type you would actually use in the examination. These skeleton answers can then be compared against model answers or examiners' reports (to see if you've fallen into any of the common traps). Alternatively, share or swap answers with a fellow student and see how they would have dealt with the same question.

There are many methods which can be used for revision – not all will suit you but try to use two or three different techniques to bring some variety into your revision. But whatever methods you adopt, you should not revise for periods of longer than an hour without a break because the brain gets tired very easily. Your best revision will be done in short sharp bursts.

471

The examination

You should start your preparations for the examination well before the event. Double check to make sure you know where the examination is to be held. Each year students will arrive hot and flustered at an examination after it has started because they thought it was on another part of the campus. As a separate point you should also give yourself plenty of time for getting to the examination, after all it is not unknown for public transport to be delayed or even cancelled.

The night before the examination should not be spent revising into the small hours. Such revision is unproductive because you will arrive at the examination tired and jaded, unable to produce your best work. If you must revise, and I suspect many will want to, it should be limited to one or two hours. The rest of the evening should be spent in gathering together the equipment necessary for the examination (e.g. pens, pencils, rubbers, calculators and spare battery, etc) and *relaxing*.

Once in the examination room, read the exam paper carefully, noting any special instructions to candidates. (e.g. answer *4* questions, or You must answer *one* question from Section A). Check the exam paper from front to back so as to make sure you've read *all* the questions. Make sure you haven't turned two pages over instead of one. This period is one of the most crucial in the examination. The decisions made here regarding the selection of questions, the order in which to take them and the outline plans developed will shape the rest of your examination period.

Before selecting an exam question to answer look at it critically. Underline what you consider to be the key words. These key words will give you three kinds of information

- the *subject-matter* which you will need to know and use in answering the question

- *verbs* which instruct you how to use this information e.g. *compare* and *contrast*

- *special requirements* for presentation e.g. write a *report* to . . .

Now consider whether you can meet the requirements of the question. This process should be repeated for each question on the paper. Then, and only then, should you select questions for answer, and begin preparing the essay plan.

Reasons for examination failure

Each year examiners are disappointed at the performance of many candidates. Regretably the causes of poor performance repeat themselves regularly each year despite being brought to candidates' attention in the examiners' report. The most important causes are dealt with below

- *Poor Preparation.* Examiners often find that candidates show a surprising lack of knowledge on the questions they attempt. Alternatively, the information they produce is out of date or no longer relevant.

- *Not answering the question.* Many candidates will misread a vital part of the question rendering part of this answer valueless. Other candidates will write down all they know about a subject without relating it to the question or provide a model answer to the question which they wish had been asked.

- *Inadequate planning.* In many cases candidates' answers suffer from a lack of structure. An ideal answer will develop all points properly and move from one to another in a logical fashion. Alternatively, candidates fail to allocate time properly. Where marks are awarded equally between questions you should spend an equal amount of time on each question. Where marks vary between questions allocate time to questions according to their proportion of total marks. Do not be tempted to over-run on any question. It is considerably more difficult to move an exam mark from $\frac{15}{20}$ to $\frac{20}{20}$ than from $\frac{0}{20}$ to $\frac{5}{20}$.

Index

Index

476